Reclaiming
the
Imagination

Philosophical Perspectives
for Writers and
Teachers of Writing

Reclaiming the Imagination

Philosophical Perspectives for Writers and Teachers of Writing

Edited by

ANN E. BERTHOFF

BOYNTON/COOK PUBLISHERS, INC.
UPPER MONTCLAIR, NEW JERSEY 07043

Acknowledgments

AMERICAN PSYCHOLOGICAL ASSOCIATION "Analogy in Science" by J. Robert Oppenheimer from *The American Psychologist*, Vol. 11, January, 1956. Copyright 1956 by the American Psychological Association. Reprinted by permission of the publisher.

BASIC BOOKS, INC. Chapter 1 from *The Interpretation of Cultures: Selected Essays* by Clifford Geertz. Copyright © 1973 by Basic Books, Inc., New York. Reprinted by permission of the publisher.

BENNINGTON COLLEGE BULLETIN "De Beginnibus," Commencement Address, 1962. Reprinted by permission of the college.

JOHN A. BRITTAIN "A Personal Experience in Interpretative Memory" from *The Long Road of Woman's Memory* by Jane Addams. Macmillan, 1916. Reprinted by permission of Mr. Brittain, Executor of the Estate of Jane Addams.

ENCYCLOPAEDIA BRITANNICA from "Thought and Language" from *The Labyrinth of Language*, originally commissioned as a *Britannica Perspective*. © 1968 by Encyclopaedia Britannica. Reprinted by permission of the publisher.

Library of Congress Cataloging in Publication Data

Main entry under title:

Reclaiming the imagination.

1. English language—Rhetoric—Study and teaching.
2. Creation (Literary, artistic, etc.)—Addresses, essays, lectures. 3. Knowledge, Theory of—Addresses, essays, lectures. I. Berthoff, Ann E. II. Title: Philosophical perspectives for writers.
PE1403.R4   1983   808'.001   83-15537
ISBN 0-86709-059-6

For information address Boynton/Cook Publishers, Inc., 52 Upper Montclair Plaza, P.O Box 860, Upper Montclair, NJ 07043

Printed in the United States of America

84   85   86   87   10   9   8   7   6   5   4   3   2   1

Acknowledgments (cont.)

EXELROD PRESS Excerpts from *Heidi's Horse* by Sylvia Fein and Heidi Scheuber. Copyright © 1976 by Exelrod Press. Reprinted by permission of the publisher.

FARRAR, STRAUS & GIROUX, INC. "Metaphor as Mistake" from *The Message in the Bottle* by Walker Percy. Copyright © 1958, 1975 by Walker Percy. Reprinted by permission of the publisher.

HARVARD UNIVERSITY PRESS Excerpts from *Mind in Society* by L. S. Vygotsky, ed. Michael Cole et al. Copyright © 1978 by the President and Fellows of Harvard College. Reprinted by permission of the publisher.

JOHNS HOPKINS UNIVERSITY PRESS "Speculations on the Origins of Speech and Its Communicative Function" from *Philosophical Sketches* by Susanne K. Langer, Copyright © 1962 by Johns Hopkins University Press. Reprinted by permission of the publisher.

SUSANNE K. LANGER from "In the Pattern of Human Culture" from *Language and Myth* by Ernst Cassirer. Translated by Susanne K. Langer. Reprinted by permission of the translator.

MACMILLAN PUBLISHING COMPANY, INC., "Expression" from *Modes of Thought* by Alfred North Whitehead. Copyright 1938 by Macmillan Publishing Company, renewed 1966 by T. North Whitehead. Reprinted by permission of the publisher.

McGRAW-HILL BOOK COMPANY, INC., Excerpt from *The Intelligent Eye* by R. L. Gregory. Copyright © 1970 by R. L. Gregory. Reprinted by permission of the publisher.

JOHN MURRAY (PUBLISHERS) LTD. "Words" from *Perseus in the Wind* by Freya Stark. Copyright © by John Murray Ltd. Reprinted by permission of the publisher.

OPEN COURT PUBLISHING COMPANY "On Cassirer's Theory of Language and Myth" by Susanne K. Langer in *The Philosophy of Ernst Cassirer*, ed. Paul Arthur Schilpp. Copyright © by Open Court Publishing Co. Reprinted by permission of the publisher.

OXFORD UNIVERSITY PRESS "The Historical Imagination" from *The Idea of History* by R. G. Collingwood (1946). Excerpt from "Poetic Diction and Legal Fiction" by Owen Barfield, from *Essays Presented to Charles Williams* (1947). Both reprinted by permission of the publisher.

N. W. PIRIE "Selecting Facts and Avoiding Assumptions" from *Rationalist Annual*, 1959. Reprinted by permission of the author.

PRAEGER PUBLISHERS Excerpt from *Barbara Hepworth: A Pictorial Autobiography* by Barbara Hepworth. Copyright © by Barbara Hepworth. Reprinted by permission of the publisher.

PRINCETON UNIVERSITY PRESS Excerpts from *The Mustard Seed Garden Manual of Painting* by Chieh Tzu Yuan Hua Chuan (1679–1701), trans. and ed. by Mai-Mai Sze, Bolligen Series. Copyright © 1956, 1963 by Princeton University Press. Reprinted by permission of the publisher.

DOROTHEA RICHARDS "Toward a Theory of Comprehending" from

Acknowledgments (cont.)

Speculative Instruments by I. A. Richards. Copyright © by I. A. Richards. Reprinted by permission of Mrs. Richards.

UNIVERSITY OF CALIFORNIA PRESS Excerpts from *Art and Visual Perception* by Rudolf Arnheim. Copyright © 1954, 1974 by The Regents of the University of California. Reprinted by permission of the publisher.

YALE UNIVERSITY PRESS from "Language" from *An Essay on Man* by Ernst Cassirer. Copyright © 1944 by Yale University Press. Reprinted by permission of the publisher.

Preface

Thinking of old batteries and broken chairs, a friend of mine asked while I was working on this book, "But *can* you 'reclaim' imagination?" I explained that my project was not to pretty up or to repair or recycle the imagination but only to help bring it back alive, from captivity. For imagination has been abducted by psychologists and transported across false borders to a suffocating locale called The Affective Domain. Coleridge labored to reclaim Imagination from the domain of Fancy, declaring that it was not only the agency whereby the genial spirit was made manifest but was, as well, "the Prime agent of all human perception." The Romantic program of liberating the imagination, reclaiming it as the "all-in-each of every mind," is an unending enterprise which this book attempts to further. What we need, I think, is to reclaim *Imagination* as a name for the active mind, the mind in action making meaning.

We can learn or teach better if we know how learning any one thing is related to learning anything else. I have found Gordon Allport's formulation invaluable: "Whatever else learning might be, it is clearly a disposition to form structures." Forming is the work of the active mind; imagination is the shaping spirit: I take writing to be a process of shaping and forming. When we write, we represent our recognitions of relationships: that is what *composing* means. By coming to see how writing thus continues the work of the active mind, we can discover that we know more about composing than we might have thought we did. We can come, as Coleridge put it, to know our knowledge.

This book is meant to guide that discovery. It brings together essays—and passages from notebooks, letters, articles, and talks—about knowing, about how we make sense of our experience of the world. Reading these selections by artists, philosophers, and scientists, we find that our questions about the nature of knowing are perennial, that what confounds us—if we learn to formulate just what that is—has troubled and fascinated others who have thought about the making of meaning. Their observations and speculations are encouraging to anyone who wants to think about thinking: that is a philosophical enterprise and my hope is that this book can demystify the practice of philosophy. For one thing, learning to write and learning to teach writing are, I think, unspeakably boring activities unless they are thought about philosophically. And for another, when we think about thinking; when we think about the nature of language, thought, perception and the relationship of each to the others, we are, willy-nilly, philosophers. What we need is guidance and vision.

By proceeding philosophically—by reclaiming the imagination—those learning to write and to teach writing will discover that language is itself the great heuristic. Language enables us to make the meanings by whose means we discover further meaning. We don't just think *about* concepts; we think *with* them. I. A. Richards put it this way: "All [studies] are *both* subject matter and language studies. . . . There is no study which is not a language study, concerned with the speculative instruments it employs."* This book is meant for all students and teachers who recognize the need for speculative instruments, for ways of thinking about *what* we are trying to do when we write so that we can discover *how* to do it. The selections offer "assisted invitations"** to get the *what* and the *how* together, to bring theory to bear on practice so that methods can be developed. The power of naming and of predication is ours by virtue of the fact that we are language animals; learning to write is, in large part, learning to take advantage of that fact, methodically.

I believe, with Richards, that the classroom should be a "philosophic laboratory" where students and teachers explore together ways to assure better understanding, ways to comprehend their comprehensions more comprehensively. Among the speculative instruments needed in our laboratories are *forming, thinking, knowing, abstracting, meaning, making, acting, creating, learning, interpreting: Imagination* names them all. Indeed, we could say with Blake: "To the Eyes of the Man of Imagination, Nature is Imagination itself."

The pieces collected here have provided points of departure for my own exploration of ways to understand the composing process and to teach it as the work of the active mind. They have served so for others, though not everyone who has practiced using the speculative instruments they provide finds them all congenial. Nor any longer do I, but when I tried to drop one or another essay, I found that it had in the meantime become a favorite of other readers. One of the book's chief functions will be served if it inspires others to gather their own commonplaces.

About half the fifty or so items come from books which are either out of print or not easily accessible. They are not meant to represent the entire range of what thinking philosophically might teach us about composing, nor are they offered primarily to represent the work of the chosen authors. Reading a five page excerpt from a single essay of Cassirer might indeed inspire a reader to search out the entire essay, the complete book, the great life work of this important philosopher, but that is not its chief function here.

Speculative Instruments (New York: Harcourt, 1955), pp. 115–16.

**This phrase of Richards—from *Design for Escape* (New York: Harcourt, 1968), p. 111—I have used to name the exercises and experiments in my textbook, *Forming/ Thinking/Writing*.

The range and complexity of Vygotsky's insights cannot be suggested even by extensive excerpts, but my hope is that, read in conjunction with passages from Susanne K. Langer, I. A. Richards, Rudolf Arnheim, et al., he can help us form the concept of forming.

All the selections are, without exception I think, well-written and they deserve the kind of careful, expectant reading we give literature, in contrast to the adversarial attitude much criticism and theory demands. Some selections are very short and are meant as foils for the arguments of the longer pieces. Each can find a place in different contexts. Any one selection can be juxtaposed with any number of others, not just those with which it has been presented. Its character will change somewhat as the setting changes. Reading this book is perhaps best modelled by the children's book in which figures of a variety of characters—ordinary, exotic, grotesque—are printed on pages cut horizontally in such a way that heads, bodies, and legs can be intermingled and matched with astonishing effect. Thus by judicious mixing, we could have Cassirer/Barbara Hepworth/Kenneth Burke . . . Jane Addams/Whitehead/ Bachelard . . . Cézanne/Walker Percy/Arnheim . . . Lu Ch'ai/Klee/Vygotsky . . . etc. And, of course, since all writers here share a belief in the powers of imagination, there will be occasions for enjoying the shock of recognition. For instance, in the final stage of assembling the pieces, I noted that the Egyptians appear as the type and emblem of a way of thinking in the selections from Cassirer, Whitehead, Arnheim, Oppenheimer, and Jane Addams—each of whom interprets them in his or her own light. Such echoes are there to be enjoyed if the selections are read philosophically—that is to say, with a tolerance for ambiguity and an interest in exploring the practical implications.

To encourage the discovery of ideas which can serve as speculative instruments, readers of this book should, I suggest, keep a dialectical notebook as a way of auditing the meanings which emerge. The dialectic is started and kept going by using the facing pages of a notebook in dialogue with the author being read: notes, phrases, texts copied on one side; queries, speculations, suggested implications, counter-texts and redactions on the other. The familiar procedure of marginal notation is thus developed as a way of formulating responses so that they are accessible, reviewable, reclaimable as speculative instruments.

All responses whould be made with an eye to practice: So what? So how? What then? As I. A. Richards noted of his own contextual theorem of meaning, "how we use a theory best tells us what it is." This is, of course, the heart of pragmatism. The most important research to be done concerns what actually happens in the classroom. Documentation of a composition class is extremely difficult: we are lucky, I think, if we can identify, describe, and characterize two or three moments—exchanges or comments or responses—which, as we recollect the class in tranquility immediately afterwards or later that day, seem significant—of what, we might not yet know. Now, one of the chief purposes of a dialectical reading notebook is to provide a theoretical sounding board which can help us catch the tune in class: we can hear, apprehend, only that which we in some way expect to hear or apprehend. A dialectical reading notebook is most productive when it is in tandem with a dialectical class log.

Practice is often considered trivial, tiresome, not worth thinking about; indeed, the perennial complaint about composition classes is the almost intolerable boredom of what is going on, to say nothing of the resultant writing. And theory is often considered elusive or "abstract." Most current research is a travesty of both theory and practice because it almost never has anything to do with method, with pedagogy, with the way we teach. But theory and practice need one another and when they are brought to bear on one another—and that nexus is method—we stand a good chance of making our classrooms real philosophic laboratories.

With the help of a Faculty Development Grant from the University of Massachusetts at Boston, an early version of this collection of essays was circulated to friends and colleagues whose response gave me some of the limits I could usefully work within. In a second state, the collection was used in my graduate seminar in the teaching of composition at UMB in the Spring of 1980. The following summer, *Reclaiming the Imagination*, in another version, served as the main text for the National Endowment for the Humanities Summer Seminar for College Teachers I directed at UMB, "Philosophy and the Composing Process." Lil Brannon, Neal Bruss, and James Slevin gave the final version a careful reading. I want to thank them and all those whose response has helped shape the selections and their presentation.

Warner Berthoff suggested Bachelard and Collingwood; Lucy Carner brought me to Jane Addams, whose colleague she was in Chicago; Richard Coe recommended R. L. Gregory; Albert Divver, Clifford Geertz; Brenda Engel, *Heidi's Horse*; Jane Oppenheimer, the essay by N. W. Pirie; Jan Watson, the passage from Hans Jonas and Cézanne's description of himself on the river bank. Pat D'Arcy, Angela Dorenkamp, Phoebe Ellsworth, Dixie Goswami, Philip Keith, and Robert Boynton have cheered me on by their energetic interest in this project of reclaiming the imagination. For them, that is a supererogatory task.

Contents

Preface

I Perception and the Apprehension of Form 3

The Intelligent Eye 5

R. L. Gregory, from *The Intelligent Eye* 6
J. J. Gibson, from "Pictures, Perspectives, and Perception" 19
Hans Jonas, from *The Phenomenon of Life* 19
Erwin Schrödinger, from *Mind and Matter* 20
Rudolf Arnheim, from *Visual Thinking* 21

Body and Soul 22

C. K. Ogden, from *Opposition* 22
E. H. Gombrich, from *Art and Illusion* 23
Kenneth Burke, from *Counterstatement* 24
Kenneth Burke, "De Beginnibus" 29

Abstraction 38

C. S. Peirce (on "medisense") 39
Owen Barfield, from *Poetic Diction* 39
Susanne K. Langer, from *Philosophy in a New Key* 40
I. A. Richards, from *The Philosophy of Rhetoric* 41
Sylvia Fein and Heidi Scheuber, from *Heidi's Horse* 42
Rudolf Arnheim, from *Art and Visual Perception* 50

II Language and the Making of Meaning 57

The Unit of Meaning 59

L. S. Vygotsky, from *Mind in Society* 61
Max Black, from *The Labyrinth of Language* 72
I. A. Richards, from "Functions and Factors of Language" 84
Alfred North Whitehead, "Expression" 84
W. H. Auden, "The True Word Twisted by Misuse and Magic" 97

Words   101

C. S. Peirce (on words)   101
Freya Stark, "Words"   102
Ernst Cassirer, from *An Essay on Man*   107
Susanne K. Langer, "Speculations on the Origins of
    Speech and Its Communicative Function"   114
Camille Norton, "Eating the Pasture"   128

The Logic of Metaphor   129

Freya Stark, from *The Journey's Echo*   130
Owen Barfield, from "Poetic Diction and Legal Fiction"   130
Walker Percy, "Metaphor as Mistake"   132
Ernst Cassirer, from *Language and Myth*   145
Susanne K. Langer, "On Cassirer's Theory of Language
    and Myth"   148

III   Interpretation and the Act of Knowing   165

Mediation   167

C. S. Peirce (on signs and diagrams)   169
I. A. Richards, "Toward a Theory of Comprehending"   172
Kenneth Burke, from *Permanence and Change*   186
Gaston Bachelard, from *The Psychoanalysis of Fire*   187

Method   188

C. S. Peirce (on method)   189
J. Robert Oppenheimer, "Analogy in Science"   189
N. W. Pirie, "Selecting Facts and Avoiding Assumptions"   203
R. G. Collingwood, from *The Idea of History*   212

Perspective and Context   225

C. S. Peirce (on interpretation)   226
Clifford Geertz, "Thick Description: Toward an
    Interpretive Theory of Culture"   226
Jane Addams, "A Personal Experience in Interpretative
    Memory"   249

IV   Artists at Work   261

Samuel Taylor Coleridge, from *Biographia Literaria*   264
Paul Klee, from *The Thinking Eye*   264
Paul Klee, from "On Modern Art"   265
Paul Cézanne, from *Letters*   265
Gerard Manley Hopkins, from *Notebooks*   267
The Mustard Seed Garden Manual of Painting (selections)   268

Ingmar Bergman (from an interview)   274
Barbara Hepworth, from *Barbara Hepworth: A Pictorial*
     Autobiography   275
Doris Humphrey, from *The Art of Making Dances*   278
Joyce Mekeel (a conversation about music notation)   279

Sources   285

Reclaiming
the
Imagination

Philosophical Perspectives
for Writers and
Teachers of Writing

Part One

Imagination is the primary talent of the human mind, the activity in whose service language was evolved.

Susanne K. Langer

The vitality and energies of the imagination do not operate at will; they are fountains, not machinery.

D. G. James

Imagination cannot be acquired once and for all, and then kept indefinitely in an ice box to be produced periodically in stated quantities. The learned and imaginative life is a way of living, and is not an article of commerce.

Alfred North Whitehead

"What," it will be Questioned, "when the Sun rises, do you not see a round disk of fire somewhat like a Guinea?" O no, no, I see an Innumerable company of the Heavenly host crying, "Holy, Holy, Holy is the Lord God Almighty." I question not my Corporeal or Vegetative Eye any more than I would question a Window concerning a Sight. I look thro' it & not with it."

William Blake

Thinking begins with perception.

C. S. Peirce

Sensory data activate a feedback process whereby a learned template, or expectancy, deforms the sensory data until a consensus is reached between what the "data" are and what we "expect" them to be. Only then do we "perceive" anything.

Stephen Grossberg

Beasts do not read symbols; that is why they do not see pictures.

Susanne K. Langer

Perception and the
Apprehension of Form

Any composition course should begin, I believe, with exercises in observation. The more "civilized" we become, the more we need to school ourselves in looking. It is a delusion to think that television has created a "visual" generation. The electronic maps of the "meteorologists" do not improve the ability to look carefully at a cloud formation or, indeed, to recognize a weather sign when we see it. Commercial and educational television spectaculars and documentaries have had no noticeable effect on students' capacity for looking at a drawing or a dance, a beetle or a bison, or at landscapes of any kind, including their own backyards.

The reason for a writer to have a lot of practice in looking is not to gain skill in amassing detail to be deployed in descriptive writing. Each new rhetoric-reader offers (almost without exception) an opening chapter which implies that particulars somehow "come first." Since, it is alleged, we see details before we get the whole picture, we therefore should begin writing with particularization. There is rarely any attempt to demonstrate the relationship of observation to interpretation or logical analysis or narrative or, indeed, to *anything* we do with language.

The real reason for beginning with observation is that looking—and looking again—engages the mind, and until that happens, no authentic composing is going to take place. Perception is of *form*, not just particular examples of one or another aspect or surface. To find in perception a model of the composing process is not difficult; one of the chief benefits of reclaiming the imagination is discovering how much we already know about perception. When Coleridge spoke of imagination, he meant both "the Prime agent of all human perception" and the shaping power, that "all-in-each" of every mind as it gives form to thought and feeling. Both visual images—percepts—and the "mental" images we call up from memory, or which we invent, are representative of the forms of understanding; thus we say, "I *see* what you *mean*."

Modern psychology is rediscovering this notion of "the intelligent eye," even though it entails conceptions of meaning-making long considered

3

"mentalistic" and therefore unworthy of scientific interest. Studies in the psychology of vision now reveal phenomena whose existence C. S. Peirce arrived at by logical analysis almost a century ago: "Thinking," he concluded, "begins with perception." And perception, we might say, begins with the body: our first apprehensions of reality are in the spatial terms provided by the body, our primordial speculative instrument. Studying perception and the apprehension of reality is a way to reclaim the imagination as the forming power of the mind.

The Intelligent Eye

Nobody has to be taught to focus his eyes or set his ear drums or develop his tactile sense; the concomitant power to interpret develops as the human infant comes into his own as part of the social fabric. Interpretation, like perception, has survival value; it is as much a part of our biological inheritance as the opposable thumb. Man, as Cassirer has it, is the *animal symbolicum*. The powers of symbolization are profoundly biological, but their development presupposes the social character of the species. The city is not a hive; man is not in any sense analogous to the insects; the human being is fully individuated, though necessarily a social creature.

Richard Gregory explains the survival value of selection and focus, suggesting how the other senses were precursors of the eye, whose evolution in turn prepared for the development of the brain. I have added very short excerpts from other scientists who have studied the biology of vision, Erwin Schrödinger, J. J. Gibson, and Hans Jonas, by way of noting the extremely ambiguous character of all terms used in discussing perception, e.g. *picture* and *image*. The difference between neurological coding and symbolization is explored thoroughly by Rudolf Arnheim in "The Intelligence of Perception," a chapter from *Visual Thinking*. The entire chapter should be carefully studied; I have quoted from the opening.

R. L. GREGORY
from *The Intelligent Eye*

We are surrounded by objects. Our lives are spent identifying, classifying, using and judging objects. Objects are tools, shelter, weapons; they are food; they are things precious, beautiful, boring, frightening, lovable . . . almost everything we know. We are so used to objects, to seeing them wherever we look, that it is quite difficult to realize that they present any problem. But objects have their existence largely unknown to the senses. We sense them as fleeting visual shapes, occasional knocks against the hand, whiffs of smell—sometimes stabs of pain leaving a bruise-record of a too-close encounter. What we experience is only a small part of what matters about objects. What matters is their "physical properties," which allow bridges to stay up, and car engines to run, though the insides are hidden. The extraordinary thing is how much we rely on properties of objects which we seldom or never test by sensory experience.

It has sometimes been thought that behavior is controlled by information immediately available to the eyes and other senses. But sensory information is so incomplete—is it adequate to guide us among surrounding objects? Does it convey all that we need to know about an object in order to behave to it appropriately? At once we see the difficulty—the continuous problem the brain has to solve. Given the slenderest clues to the nature of surrounding objects we identify them and act not so much according to what is directly sensed, *but to what is believed*. We do not lay a book on a "dark brown patch"—we lay it on a table. To belief, the table is far more than the dark brown patch sensed with the eyes; or the knock with the knuckle, on its edge. The brown patch goes when we turn away; but we accept that the table and the book remain.

Bishop Berkeley (1685–1753) questioned whether objects in fact continue to exist when not sensed—for what evidence could there be? But rather than allow objects to have, as Bertrand Russell puts it, "a jerky life," he supposed that they exist continuously because God is always observing them, which Berkeley used as an argument for the existence of God. His doubt, and later certainty, are expressed in Ronald Knox's famous limerick and reply:

There was a young man who said, "God
Must think it exceedingly odd
   If He finds that this tree
   continues to be
When there's no one about in the Quad."

Dear Sir:
   Your astonishment's odd:
I am always about in the Quad.
   And that's why the tree
   Will continue to be,
Since observed by
   Yours faithfully GOD

Berkeley's doubt raises an important question: what can we *know* beyond sensation?

The optical images in the eyes are but patterns of light: unimportant until used to read non-optical aspects of things. One cannot eat an image, or be eaten by one—in themselves images are biologically trivial. The same is not, however, true for all sensory information. The senses of touch and taste do signal directly important information: that a neighboring object is hard or hot, food or poison. These senses monitor characteristics immediately important for survival: important no matter what the object may be. Their information is useful before objects are identified. Whether the hand is burned by a match, a soldering-iron or boiling water makes little difference—it is rapidly withdrawn in any case. What matters is the burning heat, and this is directly monitored. The nature of the object may be established afterwards. Such responses are primitive—pre-perceptual reactions, not to objects but to physical conditions. Recognizing objects, and behaving appropriately to their hidden aspects, comes later.

In the evolution of life the first senses must have been those which monitor physical conditions which are immediately important for survival. Touch, taste and temperature senses must have developed before eyes: for visual patterns are only important when interpreted in terms of the world of objects. But this requires an elaborate nervous system (indeed almost a metaphysics) if behavior is controlled by belief in what the object is rather than directly by sensory input.

A curious hen-and-egg type of question arises: which came first, the eye or the brain? For what use is an eye without a brain capable of using visual information—but then why should a "visual" brain develop before there were eyes to feed it with visual information?

What may have happened is that the primitive touch nervous system was taken over to serve the first eyes, the skin being sensitive not to touch only but also to light. The visual sense probably developed from a response to moving shadows on the surface of the skin—which would have given warning of near-by danger—to recognition of patterns when eyes developed optical systems. The stages seem to have been, first a concentration of specially light-sensitive cells localized at certain regions, and then "eye pits," the light-sensitive cells forming the bottom of gradually deepening pits which served to increase the contrast of shadows at the light-sensitive regions, by shielding them from ambient light. The lens most probably started as a transparent window, protecting the eye pits from being blocked by small particles floating in the sea in which the creatures lived. The protective windows may have gradually thickened in their centers, for this would at first increase the intensity of light on the sensitive cells until—dramatically—the central thickening produced an image-forming eye: to present optical patterns to the ancient touch nervous system.

Touch can be signalled in two quite distinct ways. When an object is in contact with an area of skin, its shape is signalled from many touch receptors, down many parallel nerve fibers simultaneously to the central nervous system. But shape can also be signalled with a single moving finger, or probe, exploring shapes by tracing them in time. A moving probe can not merely signal the two-dimensional shape that happens to be in contact, but can trace shapes in three dimensions, though it will take a considerable time to do so. Also, if the object it is exploring is itself alive, it will certainly give the game away—as we know by being tickled.

Touch is not a secret sense, and it is limited to objects in physical contact. This means that when a foe is identified by touch, it is too late to devise and carry out a strategy. Immediate action is demanded, and this cannot be subtle or planned. Eyes give warning of the future, by signalling distant objects. It seems very likely that brains as we know them could not have developed without senses—particularly eyes—capable of providing advance information, by signalling the presence of distant objects. As we shall see, eyes require intelligence to identify and locate objects in space, but intelligent brains could hardly have developed without eyes. It is not too much to say that eyes freed the nervous system from the tyranny of reflexes, leading to strategic planned behavior and ultimately to abstract thinking. We are still dominated by visual concepts. Our problem now is to understand the world of objects without being limited by what we have learned through the senses.

The data that most philosophers consider are limited to sensory experience. This is not so for physics, which accepts data from instruments capable of monitoring characteristics of the world quite unknown before instruments were invented. Radio and X-rays were totally unknown to brains until less than a century ago: they have changed our intellectual view of the world, though not sensed directly. This presents something of a paradox for empiricist philosophy, for science uses "observational data" which can only be "observed" with instruments: so the senses can no longer be said to be the sole source of direct knowledge.

Since perception is a matter of reading non-sensed characteristics of objects from available sensory data, it is difficult to hold that our perceptual beliefs—our basic knowledge of objects—is free of theoretical contamination. We not only believe what we see: to some extent we see what we believe.

A central problem of visual perception is how the brain interprets the patterns of the eye in terms of external objects. In this sense "patterns" are very different from "objects." By a pattern we mean some set of inputs, in space or time, at the receptor. This is used to indicate and identify external objects giving rise to the sensory pattern. But what we perceive is far more than patterns—we perceive *objects* as existing in their space and time.

An initial problem is how objects are distinguished from their surroundings. This problem becomes clear if we look at a picture where the object is difficult to distinguish. Figure 1 is a photograph of a spotted dog

Figure 1 Retinal images are patterns in the eye—patterns made up of light and dark shapes and areas of color—but we do not see patterns, we see objects. We read from pictures in the eye the presence of external objects: how this is achieved is the problem of perception. Objects appear separate, distinct; and yet as pictures on the retina they may have no clear boundaries. In this photograph of a spotted dog, most half-tones have been lost (as in vision by moonlight) and yet we can distinguish the spots making up the dog from similar spots of the background. To make this possible there must be stored information in the brain, of dogs and thousands of other objects.

against a dappled background—it is quite difficult to see the dog. Contours and differences of texture or color help, but quite often boundaries of objects are not sharp and color differences can be misleading. There is a similar problem in hearing speech or music. Words sound distinct from each other, but physically they are not separated. Physically they run into each other, just as the images of objects do upon the retina. Objects are somehow extracted from the continuous patterns at the receptors.

There is a well-known visual effect: "figure-ground reversal." Figure 2 shows a face—or does it? Here perception fluctuates between two possibilities. This is important, for it shows at once that perception is not simply determined by the patterns of excitation at the retina. There must be subtle processes of interpretation, even at this elementary level.

The psychologist whose name is associated with figure-ground reversal is the Dane, Edgar Rubin. He used simple but cunningly contrived line drawings in which a pair of shapes, either of which taken alone would be seen as an object of some kind, share a common border-line. What happens is that, when joined, each competes with the other. Alternatively, one is relegated to mere background, and hardly seen, while the other dominates as object: then this one fades perceptually away to become for a time mere background in its turn. This spontaneous alternation of figure and ground is a curious effect. It shows something of the dynamic nature of perceptual processes.

There are many subtle effects related to figure-ground reversal. When a region becomes figure, it generally looks quite different. Of Figure 3 Rubin says:

> One can experience alternately a radially marked or concentrically marked cross. If the concentric cross is seen as figure after the radial one, it is possible to note a characteristic change in the concentric markings which depends on whether they belong to the figure or the ground. When they are part of the ground, they do not appear inter-

Figure 2

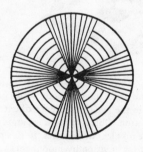

Figure 3

rupted. On the contrary, one has the impression that the concentric circles continue behind the figure. Nothing of this kind is noticed when the concentrically marked sectors compose that which is seen as figure.

Rubin was well aware of the significance of his demonstration-experiments to the problem of how we see objects, though curiously this aspect of his work was largely ignored by later writers. Rubin says in this connection:

When a reversal of figure and ground occurs, one can observe that the area affected by the shape-giving function of the contour at the same time obtains a characteristic which is similar to that which leads one to call objects "things" . . . . Even when the figure does not look like any known thing, it can still have this thing-character. By "thing-character" we mean a similarity to what is common to all experienced objects . . .

Rubin's most striking example is given in Figure 4. This is seen alternately as a pair of faces "looking at each other" and as a vase, which becomes the space between the faces when they are object. Seeing the vase perpetually fade away, to be replaced by the pair of faces emerging from sinister shadows is a queer, almost frightening experience. (The same reversal occurs whether the faces are black and the space between—the vase—is white, or whether the faces are white and the vase is black, as in Figure 5.) Rubin comments as follows:

The reader has the opportunity not only to convince himself that the ground is perceived as shapeless but also to see that a meaning read into a field when it is figure is not read in when the field is seen as ground.

Figure 4   Figure 5

Unfortunately we still do not know in detail which are the features which *prevent* figure-ground (or "object-space") reversal. These are, however, important. Small areas enclosed in larger areas are taken as figure, or object. Repeated pattern is taken as belonging either to figure or to ground but not to both. Straight lines are attributed to figure. Emotionally-toned shapes are also attributed to figure and, when present, tend to make figure dominant. In addition, the observer's perceptual "set" and his individual interests can bias the situation.

Rubin used line drawings almost exclusively for his perceptual experiments, as did almost all psychologists until recently. But as we will try to show, pictures are in some ways highly artificial inputs for the eye. Although we can learn a lot about perception from pictures, and they are certainly convenient for providing stimulus patterns, they are a very special kind of object which can give quite atypical results. Object-space reversals can take place (for example when we look at roofs of houses against an evening sky) as well as the figure-ground reversals described by Rubin for pictures. Object-space reversals merit further study, for what happens as we gradually introduce more data showing that a certain shape *is* an object? How are some patterns established as representing objects? The problem is acute, for we often see patterns without attributing "thingness" to them. We see patterns of leaves, of clouds, of fine or coarse texture on the ground. The decorative arts present formal or random patterns, which we may see as patterns not as objects. True, we may almost "see" Queen Victoria in a cloud formation, or a wicked face, fleetingly, in the flickering flames of a fire. We may see as it were *hints* of objects in patterns, and ramdom shapes, but we certainly can see patterns without accepting them as objects.

The Gestalt psychologists, in the early part of the century, made much play of "perceptual organization": that there are Principles, largely inherited, by which stimulus patterns are organized into "wholes" (*Gestalten*). This organizing into "wholes" was demonstrated with black and white figures, mainly patterns composed of dots. The point is that even an array of random dots tends to form "configurations." It is almost impossible to see three dots, with any spacing, without also seeing at the same time a triangle. In a random array we see triangles, squares, rows—all sorts of figures emerge. Patterns of dots were used to try to establish Laws of Organization. These were discussed in a classical paper by Max Wertheimer, entitled: "Principles of Perceptual Organization" (1923).

Wertheimer presented several patterns, such as Figure 6, and pointed out that they are seen as groups of dots, the closer dots forming perceptual pairs. They are seen as "belonging" to each other. In Figure 7, each sloping line forms a "unit"; they may also combine to form sloping rectangles. This shows that *proximity* is a factor in perceptual grouping.

Figure 6

Figure 6 Simple dot patterns were used by the Gestalt psychologists to investigate their "Principles of perceptual organization." We may think of these as primary stages in perception—the linking of data from retinal patterns in terms of probable objects. This may be regarded as like a detective gathering and combining available clues used for making decisions on who is the criminal—or in perception, what is the *object*? This figure illustrates how points close together are seen to "belong" to each other: the pattern is seen as *pairs* of dots.

Figure 7

Another Principle is shown in Figure 8. The circles and the squares are seen separately, each forming rows. This demonstrates that *similarity* is a factor in perceptual grouping. The Gestalt writers put a lot of weight on what they called "good figure," and "closure"; by this they meant properties such as geometrical simplicity, particularly approximations of circles, tending to "organize the parts into wholes of these shapes." Considering movement, "common fate" was regarded as important—that related movement of parts makes the parts cohere into a "whole."

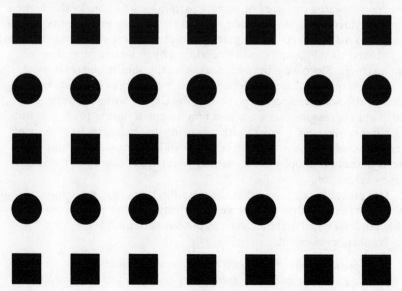

Figure 8

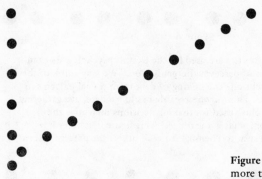

Figure 9 This shows that there is more to perceptual "grouping" than proximity. The lowest dot of the oblique row is closest to the dots in the vertical row. Evidently the tendency to organize dots into rows is stronger than the tendency of association by proximity.

To the Gestalt writers, these Organizing Principles were innate, inherited. They gave very little weight to individual past experience. Clear evidence of perceptual learning was perhaps lacking at that time and there were reasons, stemming from the contemporary German metaphysics, which made emphasis on innateness attractive. But it is perfectly possible to accept their observations as valid while denying that they are due to innate organizing principles. There is no strong argument against saying that most objects are rather simple, and closed in shape, that the parts of objects move together, that objects often have repeated structure or texture patterns—and so on. In short, there seems no evidence against supposing that the organizing principles represent attempts to make objects out of patterns—typical object characteristics being favored—and the "Principles" were developed by inductive generalization from instances. Since we all experience essentially similar objects it would not be too surprising if we developed similar, even identical, generalizations. Although this was considered by some of the Gestalt writers it was rejected, though not for reasons that we would now accept as having any force. But possibly they were right, possibly there are innate tendencies to organizing parts into wholes. This would still be accepted by some writers, though the general Gestalt philosophy is very largely rejected as being an extreme case of non-explanation.

It is probably fair to say that the Gestalt writers were more interested in how we see patterns than in how we see objects, for they generally used highly artificial visual material, such as the dot patterns.

Wertheimer claims that:

Perceptual organization occurs from above to below; the way in which parts are seen, in which the sub-wholes emerge, in which grouping occurs, is not an arbitrary, piecemeal and-summation of elements, but is a process in which characteristics of the whole play a major determining role.

But if this were true in normal perception, we might expect that the world would look like a wobbly jelly.

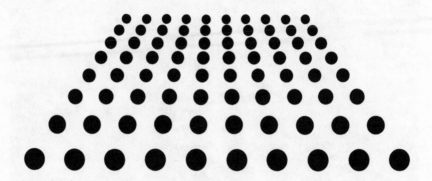

Figure 10 Lines of dots (or solid lines) which converge, are perceptually organized in three dimensions. Normal objects exist and are seen in three-dimensional space, though pictures—including retinal images—are flat. Converging features are generally taken to indicate depth by perspective shrinking of the image with increasing distance. For normal retinal images this is a good bet, but in pictures the convergence of perspective is presented to the eye on the flat plane of the picture—making pictures essentially paradoxical. Here the organization is appropriate to normal three-dimensional space and not to the converging dots which lie on the flat plane of the page. They are organized in terms of normal space rather than the picture-plane.

Granted that organizing into "wholes" is important, it is easy to find examples of where this must be due to individual past experience. For example, we find it in grouping letters in a language—which is most certainly learned. There used to be an English comedian, who called himself NOSMO KING. This was not in fact his real name. He "discovered" it one day seeing, written across a double door at the theatre: NO SMOKING. When the doors opened he saw his new name appear.

This was anticipated by Helmholtz, the great German physicist (1821–94), when he argued for individual learning as important for perception, in the following:

There are numerous illustrations of fixed and inevitable associations of ideas due to frequent repetition, and even when they have no natural connections, but are dependent merely on some conventional arrangement, as, for example, the connection between written letters in a word and its sound and meaning. . . . Facts like these show the wide-spread influence that experience, training and habit have on our perceptions.

Figure 11   This oblique camera angle of a textured surface gives a compelling impression of a slanting surface. The bricks are seen as slanting, yet the page on which the picture lies is not—and does not appear to be—slanting. This double reality is part of the paradox of pictures.

Few would disagree with him, but there remains the possibility that some perceptual organizing processes are "wired in" at birth. For reasons of economy, we might expect it. At any rate it is now clear from neurological studies that some visual feature-detectors are built into retina and brain structure. This has been established over the last ten years from direct electrical recording from individual nerve cells of the eye and the brain.

When the electrical activity of local regions of a frog's retina are recorded from electrodes placed in excised eyes, it is found that only a few features of the pattern of stimulation on the retina are represented in terms of neural activity, and so signalled to the brain. Signals are given when the stimulus light is changed in intensity—some cells signalling when it is switched on, others when it is switched off, while others signal any change. (They are known as "on," "off" and "on-off" receptors.) Receptors signalling changes of illumination are probably responsible for signalling movement, which is vital for the frog for detecting and catching flies; as indeed it is to all animals for survival, since movement is generally associated with potential food or danger. At the first stage of visual perception—the retina—we find neural mechanisms responding to specific patterns in space or time. In a delightful paper, "What the Frog's Eye Tells the Frog's Brain," by Lettvin, Maturana, McCulloch and Pitts, several specific pattern-receptive mechanisms are identified. The eye responds to movement, to changes of illumination and to what we may call "rotundity." A small black shadow is signalled strongly and serves to evoke the fly-catching reflex. This "bug-detector" gives an immediate response—the tongue shooting out for fly-catching—without loss of time by information processing by the brain. The frog's brain receives but few kinds of pattern information from its eyes. In general as brains develop up the evolutionary scale eyes signal more information and become simpler. The retina is not merely a layer of light-sensitive cells, it is also a "satellite computer" in which visual information is pre-processed for the brain. Vital information, such as movement, is extracted and signalled directly by the retina in eyes as highly developed as the rabbit and, most likely, in our own.

A really basic discovery was made by two American neurophysiologists, D. Hubel and T. N. Wiesel, some ten years ago. Placing micro-electrodes in the "visual brain" (the *area striata* of the occipital cortex) of the cat, they found that certain brain cells respond to specific patterns at the eye, other brain cells to other patterns. Some cells responded to movement in one direction but not the opposite or any very different direction; other cells responded to lines oriented at a certain angle; others to corners. Activity at the surface of this region of cortex corresponds rather crudely to the spatial position of stimulation of the retina—a rough electrical spatial map is projected on the occipital cortex from the eye—but deeper down spatial position is lost and patterns are represented by the firing of a few cells regardless of position on the eye.

More recently Hubel and Wiesel have found that pattern information of various kinds is brought together in "columns" arranged at right angles to the clearly visible layers of the striate cortex. These functional columns were discovered with subtle techniques as they are invisible to the eye. They seem to solve the problem of how the brain relates together not only three spatial dimensions but also color, movement and other object-characteristics. A simple map would be quite inadequate, for there are insufficient spatial dimensions to represent more than the three spatial dimensions of external objects—since the brain is itself an object in normal three-dimensional space.

It seems from the electrophysiological data that perceptions are built from neural mechanisms responding to certain simple shapes, movement and color. These are combined in the newly discovered cortical "columns." This is—logically—something like letters being combined to form words: the selected features are evidently basic units of the perceptual "language" of the brain. What is not at all clear is how—to continue the language analogy—the neural "words" are combined to form perceptual "sentences." It is not known at the neurological level how the outputs from the "columns" are combined to give object-perception. We may guess that there is an intimate connection with memory stores, but at the present time how memory is stored is not known. It is not even known whether single cells store units of memory, or whether memories are stored as patterns involving very many cells, possibly by a process similar to the storing of optical patterns by holography and unlike the usual point-to-point representation as in normal photography. The answers to these questions remain for the future, but meanwhile it is worth preparing the ground by considering the phenomena of perception. Neurophysiological explanation is not everything. The activity of the nervous system cannot be interpreted without knowing what functions are served. Many useful explanations are in terms of function rather than in terms of underlying structure and activity within this structure. For example, the computer engineer does not have to know much physics to understand computer circuits; and the mathematician does not have to understand much electronics to understand their logic and use them. (To say, "I understand why she went off with Bill," may be perfectly meaningful without any knowledge of what—in physical terms—went on in her brain.)

At this point we might be tempted into thinking that perception is simply a matter of combining activity from various pattern-detecting systems, to build up neural "descriptions" of surrounding objects. But perception cannot be anything like as simple, if only because of a basic problem confronting the perceptual brain—the ambiguity of sensory data. The same data can always "mean" any of several alternative objects. But we experience but one, and generally correctly. Clearly there is more to it than the putting together of neurally represented patterns to build perceptions, for decisions are required. We should look at the ambiguity of objects to see this more clearly. Establishing that a given region of pattern represents an object and not background is only a first step in the perceptual process. We are left with the vital decision: *What (kind of) object is this?*

The problem is acute because any two-dimensional image could represent an *infinity of possible three-dimensional shapes*. Often there are extra sources of information available; for example stereoscopic vision, or changing parallax as the head moves, but the fact remains that we can nearly always arrive at a reasonably reliable solution to the problem: "What object is this?" Even though the number of possibilities is infinite.

Some shapes are seen, at different times, in more ways than one. Just as the object-space reversible figures spontaneously change, so some shapes though continuously identified as object yet spontaneously change as to *what* object it is, or what position it is being viewed from.

J. J. GIBSON

from "Pictures, Perspectives, and Perception"

We can now clear up a misunderstanding which has persisted for centuries: the notion that a retinal image is like a picture. However a picture may be defined, everyone would agree that it is something to be looked at by an observer. A retinal image is not something to be looked at by an observer. It is therefore profoundly unlike a picture. There is a distribution of energy on a sensory mosaic, but it is not a replica, or a copy, or a model, or a record. It is a continuous "input," as computer theorists say. It starts impulses in the optic nerve. The retinal image is easily visualized, but one should do so only at one's peril, for it encourages the fallacy of assuming a little man in the brain who looks at the retinal image. Whenever one is tempted to think in this way, one should remember the eye of the bee. A retinal image is no more like a picture in the eye than an auditory stimulus is like a phonograph record in the ear.

HANS JONAS

from *The Phenomenon of Life*

What faculties and attitudes are involved in image-making? For our initial conviction that no mere animal would or could produce an image we may at this stage just adduce the biological uselessness of any mere representation. The artifacts of animals have a direct physical use in the promotion of vital ends, such as nutrition, reproduction, hibernation. A representation, however, changes neither the environment nor the condition of the organism itself. An image-making creature, therefore, is one that indulges in the making of useless objects or has ends in addition to the biological ones, or can serve the latter in ways remote from the direct usefulness of instrumental things. Whichever it is (and it may be all three), in the pictorial representation the object is appropriated in a new, nonpractical way, and the very fact that the interest in it can shift to its *eidos* [appearance] signifies a new object relation.

ERWIN SCHRÖDINGER
from *Mind and Matter*

We are faced with the following remarkable situation. While the stuff from which our world picture is built is yielded exclusively from the sense organs as organs of the mind, so that every man's world picture is and always remains a construct of his mind and cannot be proved to have any other existence, yet the conscious mind itself remains a stranger within that construct, it has no living space in it, you can spot it nowhere in space. We do not usually realize this fact, because we have entirely taken to thinking of the personality of a human being, or for that matter also that of an animal, as located in the interior of its body. To learn that it cannot really be found there is so amazing that it meets with doubt and hesitation, we are very loath to admit it. We have got used to localizing the conscious personality inside a person's head—I should say an inch or two behind the midpoint of the eyes. From there it gives us, as the case may be, understanding or loving or tender—or suspicious or angry looks. I wonder has it ever been noted that the eye is the only sense organ whose purely receptive character we fail to recognize in naive thought. Reversing the actual state of affairs, we are much more inclined to think of "rays of vision," issuing from the eye, rather than of the "rays of light" that hit the eyes from outside. You quite frequently find such a "ray of vision" represented in a drawing in a comic paper, or even in some older schematic sketch intended to illustrate an optic instrument or law, a dotted line emerging from the eye and pointing to the object, the direction being indicated by an arrow-head at the far end.—Dear reader, recall the bright, joyful eyes with which your child beams upon you when you bring him a new toy, and then let the physicist tell you that in reality nothing emerges from these eyes; in reality their only objectively detectable function is, continually to be hit by and to receive light quanta. In reality! A strange reality! Something seems to be missing in it.

RUDOLF ARNHEIM
from *Visual Thinking*

. . . the cognitive operations called thinking are not the privilege of mental processes above and beyond perception but the essential ingredients of perception itself. I am referring to such operations as active exploration, selection, grasping of essentials, simplification, abstraction, analysis and synthesis, completion, correction, comparison, problem solving, as well as combining, separating, putting in context. These operations are not the prerogative of any one mental function; they are the manner in which the minds of both man and animal treat cognitive material at any level. . . . As I open my eyes, I find myself surrounded by a given world: the sky with its clouds, the moving waters of the lake, the wind-swept dunes, the window, my study, my desk, my body—all this resembles the retinal projection in one respect, namely, it is given. It exists by itself without my having done anything noticeable to produce it. But is this awareness of the world all there is to perception? Is it even its essence? By no means. That given world is only the scene on which the most characteristic aspect of perception takes place. Through that world roams the glance, directed by attention, focusing the narrow range of sharpest vision now on this, now on that spot, following the flight of a distant sea gull, scanning a tree to explore its shape. This eminently active performance is what is truly meant by visual perception. . . . The world emerging from this perceptual exploration is not immediately given. . . .

Body and Soul

Loren Eiseley once remarked that our bones are calcium and not, say, copper, because we came from the sea where we got the calcium habit. There is something of the same kind of happy obviousness about the claims that the body's form determines—up to a point—psychological forms. As C. K. Ogden points out, we don't see reality the way we would if we were oriented in space the way a starfish is. In "physiognomic perception," we represent our recognitions by images which the body provides. Playing Gombrich's parlor game of ping/pong is one way to become aware of our most primitive means of apprehending. Psychoanalysis, of course, provides the best-known taxonomy of the ways we map the psyche on the soma. Kenneth Burke, in one of the most interesting of the entries in his early "Lexicon Rhetoricae," considers how it is that "the human mind is prone to feel beginnings and endings *as such*." He explores this matter, too, in what is probably one of the few entertaining Commencement Addresses ever delivered.

C. K. OGDEN
from *Opposition*

Opposites . . . may be either the two extremes of a scale or the two sides of a cut; the cut marking the point of neutrality, the absence of either of two opposed characters in the field of opposition. . . . The symbolic forms which have been developed in ordinary language for the expression of these distinctions have been crystalized not only in terms of two-dimensional projection, but also in a very special relation to the human body.

In the first place, the spatial cut has been identified with the body itself, and more specifically with its vertical axis, in the opposition of *sides*, right and left, and the opposed rectilinear directions, right and left, along the arms in a horizontal position. Secondly, the *extremes* of the scale are represented by the head and feet, the two opposite ends of a single continuum, measured primarily upward, from the base to the top, as with the minimum and maximum of the thermometer. Hence the convention whereby *In front of* and *Behind*, which also give us the opposition of Before and After, Future and Past, are diagrammatically on the horizontal line of right and left—in terms of the position of the body (facing either right or left) and of a progress along the line; while Up and Down are primarily movements from one extreme of the vertical scale to the other.

This dependence of our symbolization of opposition on the symmetry of the body is emphasized when we consider the oppositional requirements of such an actinian as the starfish. We, too, have elaborated secondary oppositions for the upper and lower *surface*, the opposite ends of a *diameter, radial* opposition, etc.; but since they are not "our" surface, "our" diameter, and "our" radius, neither our primary projections and diagrams nor our linguistic metaphors are in these terms.

E. H. GOMBRICH
from *Art and Illusion*

. . . What is called "synesthesia," the splashing over of impressions from one sense modality to another, is a fact to which all languages testify. They work both ways—from sight to sound and from sound to sight. We speak of loud colors or of bright sounds, and everyone knows what we mean. Nor are the ear and the eye the only senses that are thus converging to a common center. There is touch in such terms as "velvety voice" and "a cold light," taste with "sweet harmonies" of colors or sounds, and so on through countless permutations. . . . Synesthesia concerns relationships. I have tried out this suggestion in a party game. It consists of creating the simplest imaginable medium in which relationships can still be expressed, a language of two words only—let us call them "ping" and "pong." If these were all we had and we had to name an elephant and a cat, which would be ping and which pong? I think the answer is clear. Or hot soup and ice cream. To me, at least, ice cream is ping and soup pong. Or Rembrandt and Watteau? Surely in that case Rembrandt would be pong and Watteau ping. I do not maintain that it always works, that two blocks are sufficient to categorize all relationships. We find people differing about day and night and male and female, but perhaps these different answers would be reduced to unanimity if the question were differently framed: pretty girls are ping and matrons pong; it may depend on which aspect of womanhood the person has in mind, just as the motherly, enveloping aspect of night is pong, but its sharp, cold, and menacing physiognomy may be ping to some.

KENNETH BURKE
from *Counterstatement*

The Individuation of Forms

11. *Appeal of Forms.* Form, having to do with the creation and gratification of needs, is "correct" in so far as it gratifies the needs which it creates. The appeal of the form in this sense is obvious: form *is* the appeal. The appeal of progressive and repetitive forms as they figure in the major organization of a work, needs no further explanation. Conventional form is a shiftier topic, particularly since the conventional forms demanded by one age are as resolutely shunned by another. Often they owe their presence in art to a survival from a different situation (as the invocation to the Muses is the conventionalization of a prayer based upon an earlier belief in the divine inspiration of poetry; and the chorus in the religious rites of Dionysus survives in the secular drama that grew out of these rites). At other times a conventional form may arise from a definite functional purpose, as the ebb, flow, and close of a sonnet became a conventional form through repeated usage. Thereafter a reader will be disturbed at a sonnet of fifteen lines, even though it attain precisely the ebb, flow, and close that distinguishes the sonnet. The reader has certain categorical expectations which the poet must meet. As for the formality of beginnings and endings—such procedures as the greeting of the New Year, the ceremony at laying a cornerstone, the "house-warming," the funeral, all indicate that the human mind is prone to feel beginnings and endings *as such*.

When we turn to minor form and carry examination down to the individual sentence, or the individual figure of speech, the relation between form and the gratification of desire becomes admittedly more tenuous. The formal appeal of the single sentence need not, it is true, be sought in the sentence alone—the sentence can also "gratify" us by its place in a context (it contributes to progressive form in so far as it contains a statement that advances the plot; and it contributes to repetitive form if, for instance, it corroborates our expectations with respect to a certain character). But, since the single sentence has form, we are forced by our thesis to consider the element of gratification in the sentence apart from its context. There are certain rudimentary kinds of balance in which the factor of desire is perceptible, as when a succession of monosyllables arouses the "need" of a polysyllabic word to break their monotony. And the same factor exists clearly enough in the periodic sentence, where the withholding of some important detail until the last drives us forward to the close. But is not every sentence a "periodic" sentence? If one, for instance, enters a room and says simply, "The man . . ." unless the auditor knows enough about the man to finish the sentence in his own thoughts, his spontaneous rejoinder will be, "The man what?" A naming must be completed by a doing, either explicit or implicit. The subject demands a predicate as resolutely as the antecedent of a musical phrase in Mozart calls for its consequent. Admittedly, when we carry the discussion to so small a particle (almost like discussing one brush stroke as a test of a definition of form in painting) the element of "gratification" will not usually be prominent. The formal satisfaction of completion will be clear only in cases where the process of completing is stressed, as in the periodic sentence. Otherwise it can be better revealed by our dissatisfaction with an uncompleted thought than by our satisfaction with a completed one.

The appeal of form as exemplified in rhythm enjoys a special advantage in that rhythm is more closely allied with "bodily" processes. Systole and diastole, alternation of the feet in walking, inhalation and exhalation, up and down, in and out, back and forth, such are the types of distinctly motor experiences "tapped" by rhythm. Rhythm is so natural to the organism that even a succession of uniform beats will be interpreted as a succession of accented and unaccented beats. The rhythm of a page, in setting up a corresponding rhythm in the body, creates marked degrees of expectancy, or acquiescence. A rhythm is a promise which the poet makes to the reader— and in proportion as the reader comes to rely upon this promise, he falls into a state of general surrender which makes him more likely to accept without resistance the rest of the poet's material. In becoming receptive to so much, he becomes receptive to still more. The varied rhythms of prose also have their "motor" analogies. A reader sensitive to prose rhythms is like a man hurrying through a crowd; at one time he must halt, at another time he can leap forward; he darts perilously between saunterers; he guards himself in turning sharp corners. We mean that in all rhythmic experiences one's "muscular imagination" is touched. Similarly with sounds, there is some analogy to actual movement, since sounds may rise and fall, and in a remote way one rises and falls with them.

12. *"Priority" of forms.* There are formal patterns which distinguish our experience. They apply in art, since they apply outside of art. The accelerated motion of a falling body, the cycle of a storm, the gradations of a sunrise, the stages of a cholera epidemic, the ripening of crops—in all such instances we find the material of progressive form. Repetitive form applies

to all manner of orientation, for we can continue to discuss a subject only by taking up in turn various aspects of it. (Recalling the schoolmen's subdivisions of a topic: *quis, quid, ubi, quibus, auxiliis, cur, quo modo, quando*. One talks about a thing by talking about something else.) We establish a direction by co-ordinates; we establish a curve by three points, and thereupon can so place other points that they will be intercepted by this curve. Thus, though forms need not be prior to experience, they are certainly prior to the work of art exemplifying them. Psychology and philosophy may decide whether they are innate or resultant; so far as the work of art is concerned they simply *are*: when one turns to the production or enjoyment of a work of art, a formal equipment is already present, and the effects of art are involved in its utilization. Such ultimate minor forms as contrast, comparison, metaphor, series, bathos, chiasmus, are based upon our modes of understanding anything; they are implicit in the process of abstraction and generalization by which we think. (When analyzed so closely, they manifest the principles of repetitive and progressive form so fraily that we might better speak of co-existent unity and diversity—"something" in relation to "something else"—which is probably the basic distinction of our earliest perceptions. The most rudimentary manifestation of such coexistent unity and diversity in art is perhaps observable in two rhyming monosyllables, room—doom, where diversity of sound in the initial consonants coexists with unity of sound in the vowels and final consonants, a relation describable either as repetitive or as progressive.)

Such basic forms may, for all that concerns us, be wholly conventional. The subject–predicate form of sentence, for instance, has sanction enough if we have learned to expect it. It may be "natural" only as a path worn across a field is natural. But if experience has worn a path, the path is there—and in using the path we are obeying the authority of a prior form.

An ability to function in a certain way implies gratification in so functioning. A capacity is not something which lies dormant until used—a capacity is a command to act in a certain way. Thus a pinioned bird, though it has learned that flight is impossible, must yet spread out its wings and go through the motions of flying: its muscles, being equipped for flight, require the process. Similarly, if a dog lacks a bone, he will gnaw at a block of wood; not that he is hungry—for he may have his fill of meat—but his teeth, in their fitness to endure the strain of gnawing, feel the need of enduring that strain. So the formal aspects of art appeal in that they exercise formal potentialities of the reader. They enable the mind to follow processes amenable to it. Mother Goose is little more than an exerciser of simple mental functions. It is almost wholly formal, with processes of comparing, contrasting, and arranging. Though the jingles may, in some instance, have originated as political lampoons, etc., the ideas as adapted in the nursery serve purely as gymnastics in the fundamental processes of form.

The forms of art, to summarize, are not exclusively "aesthetic." They can be said to have a prior existence in the experiences of the person hearing or reading the work of art. They parallel processes which characterize his experiences outside of art.

13. *Individuation of forms.* Since there are no forms of art which are not forms of experience outside of art, we may—so far as form is concerned—discuss the single poem or drama as an individuation of formal principles. Each work re-embodies the formal principles in different subject-matter. A "metaphor" is a concept, an abstraction—but a specific metaphor, exemplified by specific images, is an "individuation." Its appeal as form resides in the fact that its particular subject-matter enables the mind to follow a metaphor-process. In this sense we would restore the Platonic relationship between form and matter. A form is a way of experiencing; and such a form is made available in art when, by the use of specific subject-matter, it enables us to experience in this way. The images of art change greatly with changes in the environment and the ethical systems out of which they arise; but the principles of art, as individuated in these changing images, will be found to recur in all art, where they are individuated in one subject-matter or another. Accordingly, the concept of the individuation of forms constitutes the bridge by which we move from a consideration of form to a consideration of subject-matter.

14. *Form and information.* The necessity of embodying form in subject-matter gives rise to certain "diseases" of form. The subject-matter tends to take on an intrinsic interest, to appeal independently of its functional uses. Thus, whereas realism originated to meet formal requirements (the introduction of life-like details to make outlandish plots plausible), it became an end in itself; whereas it arose in the attempt to make the unreal realistic, it ended by becoming a purpose in itself and making the real realistic. Similarly, description grows in assertiveness until novelists write descriptions, not for their use in the arousing and fulfilling of expectation, but because the novelists have something to describe which they consider interesting in itself (a volcano, a remarkable savage tribe, an unusual thicket). This tendency becomes frankly "scientific" in the thesis drama and the psychological novel, where the matter is offered for its value as the "exposure" of a burning issue. In the psychological novel, the reader may often follow the hero's mental processes as noteworthy facts, just as he would follow them in a scientific treatise on the human mind, except that in the novel the facts are less schematically arranged from the standpoint of scientific presentation. In so far as the details in a work are offered, not for their bearing upon the business of molding and meeting the reader's expectations, but because these details are interesting in themselves, the appeal of form retreats behind the appeal of information. Atrophy of form follows hypertrophy of information.

There is, obviously, no "right" proportion of the two. A novelist, for instance, must give enough description for us to feel the conviction of his story's background. Description, to this extent, is necessary in the interests of form—and there is no clearly distinguishable point at which description for the purpose of the plot goes over into description for its own sake. Similarly, a certain amount of psychological data concerning the characters of a fiction helps the author to make the characters of moment to the reader, and thus has a formal function in the affecting of the reader's desires: yet the psychology can begin to make claims of its own, and at times the writer will analyze his hero not because analysis is formally needed at this point, but because the writer has some disclosures which he considers interesting in themselves.

The hypertrophy of information likewise tends to interfere with our enjoyment in the repetition of a work. For the presence of information as a factor in literature has enabled writers to rely greatly upon ignorance as a factor in appeal. Thus, they will relieve the reader's ignorance about a certain mountain of Tibet, but when they have done so they will have less to "tell" him at a second reading. Surprise and suspense are the major devices for the utilization of ignorance (the psychology of information), for when they are depended upon, the reader's interest in the work is based primarily upon his ignorance of its outcome. In the classic drama, where the psychology of form is emphasized, we have not surprise but disclosure (the surprise being a surprise not to the audience, but to the characters); and likewise suspense here is not based upon our ignorance of the forthcoming scenes. There is, perhaps, more formal suspense at a second reading than at a first in a scene such as Hamlet's giving of the pipes to Guildenstern. It is the suspense of certain forces gathering to produce a certain result. It is the suspense of a rubber band which we see being tautened. We know that it will be snapped—there is thus no ignorance of the outcome; our satisfaction arises from our participation in the process, from the fact that the beginnings of the dialogue lead us to feel the logic of its close.

Painting, architecture, music are probably more amenable to repetition without loss because the formal aspects are not so obscured by the subject-matter in which they are embodied. One can repeat with pleasure a jingle from Mother Goose, where the formality is obvious, yet one may have no interest whatsoever in memorizing a psychological analysis in a fiction. He may wish to remember the observations themselves, but his own words are as serviceable as the author's. And if he does choose to memorize the particular wording of the author, and recites it with pleasure, the passage will be found to have a formal, as well as an informational, validity.

KENNETH BURKE
"De Beginnibus"

[Burke begins his Commencement Address at Bennington College (1962) with a laconic, rambling discourse on the difficulties of deciding what to talk about and then, rather suddenly, he shifts gears.]

. . . Now we're over the rough parts. But I have other bad news for you. This talk hasn't begun yet. For in trying to decide what I should talk about, after discarding many possibilities I arrived at my subject by sheer deduction. My trouble had been simply that the solution was too obvious to be seen. Obviously, a *Commencement* Address should be on the subject of *Beginnings*. And there we now are.

When I got to that point in my preparations, a bit of diabolic shrewdness occurred to me. The old rhetoric books taught that audiences are most attentive at the beginning of a talk. Their attention lags during the middle section, which we've only now arrived at. Then audiences pick up and take heart towards the end, when the speaker gives some encouraging indications that the talk is nearly over. (That's why I hold up all the pages now and then, and let you see the lot slowly but surely being diminished.)

The diabolic thought I had in mind was this: What if my Commencement Address were not merely about the *subject* of Beginnings? What if I so planned the talk that it itself was nothing but a Series of Beginnings?

You now see what an invention I may have hit upon. For if an audience pays closest attention to a speaker at the beginning of his talk, and if my talk were made up of nothing but beginnings, would I not have hit upon a rhetorical gadget designed to rob the audience of its natural relaxation period?

So I proceeded to build my talk along those lines. And not until too late in my preparations, did I suddenly think to ask myself: But why should a speaker want an audience to be so damned attentive? An audience's inattention is a protection to us all. After the opening words, we should *all* be allowed to relax until a minute ot two before the end.

So please think of my subsequent paragraphs, not as a series of beginnings, but merely as a continuum made up of parts somewhat disconnected with one another.

PRESIDENT FELS, FRIENDS AND FELLOW-STUDENTS,

With your permission, I should like to present a Commencement Address on the subject of Beginnings. Possible title: A Whole Batch of Beginnings.

Of course, we start with a problem. There's always a problem. And could any educator respect himself unless he can make two problems grow where but one had grown before? The problem now is that I've been around here, on and off, for quite a while. Hence, some of my best friends have heard me Beginning, and Beginning, and Re-Beginning.

Nevertheless:

Suppose, by way of beginning, we were to ask: Just what is going on in the world? And what's to be done about it? What basic rules of thumb should one live by? What is the over-all situation? What should we expect of life? (One point seems fairly certain, for instance: As regards many of the things we think we very much want, there won't be much satisfaction in getting them, though there might be a lot of dissatisfaction in not getting them.) What rudimentary purposes, hopes, fears, should we live by? What might one reasonably expect of—say—religion, politics, art, science, social life, work, leisure, floor wax, hair-sprays, detergents and deodorants?

Frankly, I don't know. And I'm afraid I wouldn't say, even if I did know. For on such a gala occasion, I don't want to be a spoil-sport.

Perhaps the handiest way to begin this lecture on Beginnings is with reference to Goethe's *Faust*. For sometimes I wonder whether it might be the most beginningest work in all history. First, there is the Title; then a Dedication; then a "Prelude on the Stage"; then a "Prologue in Heaven"; then, in the course of his meditations, Faust summons the Earth-Spirit; soon after this episode there are songs celebrating the beginning of Easter, itself the celebration of a rebeginning; after an interlude Faust sees a black poodle (the incipient manifestation of a figure whose fatal identity is still to be disclosed); next, in his study, with the poodle growing more ominous, Faust reads, "In the beginning was the Word"; he modifies this version of a beginning three times, "In the beginning was the Thought *(Sinn)*," "In the beginning was the Power *(Kraft)*," "In the beginning was the Deed, or Act *(Tat)*" —whereupon are released the developments whereby the poodle becomes transformed into Mephistopheles, and now at last the drama is under way.

This whole first part, in turn, is but a beginning, the Introduction to Part II, concerned with the successive, explicit disclosure of motives that were but implicit in Part I. It begins with Faust awaking at dawn (symbolically a birth scene); he turns from sunlight to rainbow; there will be an enigmatic scene in which he journeys back to the beginning of beginnings, the dark realm of The Mothers; out of this episode will grow his inquiries into our cultural beginnings in Greece and the North; eventually, becoming blind, he will begin to see in a profounder sense—and after some celestial revelations (themselves a kind of beginning, as all revelations necessarily are), the play ends on the subject of the motive that Goethe treats as the source of all man's striving, the "eternal feminine" *(das Ewigweibliche)*.

(Thinking freely along such lines, in case there really does happen to be a personal principle at the roots of the universe, one might in fancy ask whether all might be ultimately reducible to a beginning in the principle of woman, and deviations from the principle of woman, and deviations from those deviations. But perhaps that would be more of a conceit than a conception.)

In any case, hurrying back to sheerly terministic matters, we might note that Goethe's entire life-work was done in the sign of the ingenious German syllable that serves to designate the primal (that is, the realm of the beginning). I refer to the prefix *Ur-*, without which the spirit of German idealistic metaphysics would probably have been impossible. *Ur-* is the morpheme that, when placed in front of any word, however workaday, promptly removes that word to the realm of the pre-historic or transcendent (the universally prior). Thus, a man or *Mensch* is here and now; but an *Ur-Mensch* is of the primal past, God only knows how far back in the beginnings of things. *Geschichte* is history, but *Urgeschichte* is prehistory. And *Ursache* is the word for "cause" (the *Sache* part, usually translated "thing," really being tied in with our word "sake," as in our expression, "for the sake of").

Thus, in the spirit of *Ur-*, when Goethe studied botany he sought for what he called the Ur-plant, the *Urpflantze*. When he studied optics, he discussed not just "polarity," but *Urpolarität*. He would talk not just of "form," but of *Urform*; not just of "stone," but of *Urgestein*. Not just of "ground" but of *Urgrund*. Not just of a "beginning," even; but sometimes of an *Urbeginn*.

Meanwhile, mention of him here is good to start with, as regards the subject of "Beginnings," since we can so clearly see how the word shifts between ideas of temporal priority and ideas of logical priority.

Once you start thinking this way about beginnings, you discover that they are to be found everywhere you turn. Think how many things must have begun since I began this sentence. But first of all, I'd ask you to note how this whole question of "beginnings," as so conceived, merges into the question of "principles," or "basic assumptions," and so finally into the matter of conclusions. This is the point at which purely temporal and purely logical categories somehow merge. It's the point where we can suddenly surprise ourselves by discovering that we are not far from the realm of eschatology, thoughts on the nature of first and last things, thoughts that thus attain their most thorough-going form, perhaps, in theology, inasmuch as theology comes to a focus in the idea of God, and God may be thought of as both prime origin and ultimate end, both efficient cause and final cause. We'll settle for considerably less, though having that thought in the remote background. And you'll see how it's always likely to turn up, when I turn to my next paragraph on Beginnings.

Key terms are beginnings. Implicit in any nomenclature there are conclusions, which investigators gradually disclose. For instance, when Martin Buber starts from what he calls the "I-Thou Relation," that quick he automatically introduces a principle of personality into his view of the universe. Since, insofar as the use of a vocabulary is consistent, you can never get out of a vocabulary anything other than what you put into it, any principle you derive from it must be there *from the start*. The Bible is a perfect example of this terministic fact. It gets God into the system by putting Him into the very first sentence. The New Testament even ends on a kind of beginning, though a somewhat grim one. I refer to the book of Revelations.

Often, of course, the problem is solved coyly by introducing a term which *furtively* performs this function. For instance, since, in the strict sense of the word, only God can "create," the key term "creativity" can serve to support modes of thought that require the equivalent of theological backing. Thus, insofar as human "creativity" is viewed simply as a virtue, it functions like a word for the divine, since God is by definition wholly good. Otherwise, "creativity" must be viewed as an ambivalent term; and I think we should so consider it, in its nature as a sheerly human attribute. Sometimes we cannot be sure which is worse: lack of creativity, or over-creativity. One thing at least is certain: If the physical sciences destroy us with the new chemical, thermo-nuclear, and bacteriological weapons, it won't be from *lack* of "creativity" in their fields, though one might say that such disaster would be due to lack of corresponding "creativity" in the realm of social and political thinking. Seeing the ingenious powers that the physical sciences (guided by their key terms) have been able to build up, one sometimes hopes that they have started some things that can't or won't finish, though it's hard not to go on in that same direction, tracking down the implications of terms to their ultimate conclusions, however rough those conclusions might be.

Definitions are beginnings, though it is a somewhat ironic fact of history that often a writer does not clearly work out such "beginnings" until quite late in his speculations or investigations. That paradox has to do with the ambiguous, shifting relation between beginnings in the "temporal" sense of the term and "beginnings" in the sense of the logically prior. (This ambiguity we find exemplified most perfectly in the opening chapters of Genesis, where certain basic *principles* of human governance are stated in narrative terms, in a story about the "first" man, and his relations to authority, order, and law.) Often beginnings that are "logically prior" to a given theory involve assumptions which the propounder of the theory was not himself explicitly aware of, but which are disclosed by some other thinker, who may himself even be unsympathetic to such a mode of thought. Similarly, a theorist may finally present as his "starting point" some basic propositions that he was quite late in formulating.

Closely allied to "beginnings" in this sense are the "equations" which can often be shown to underlie many kinds of works (novels, lyrics, dramas, and the like, as well as political or metaphysical theories and such—in fact, I'm sure you'll find them embedded in all works, if you look long and hard enough). Thus, Berkeley's basic equation, "to be is to be perceived" (*esse* is *percipi*) starts things off in a scientistic direction (with a primary stress upon matters of *knowledge*), whereas the realist notion that "to be" is an "act" points at the start in the direction of *drama*. Or Spinoza's basic equating of God and Nature automatically sets things up for a pantheistic philosophy. One can also discern in his definition of God as "self-caused" (*causa sui*) implications notably different from an earlier definition of God as the "uncaused cause."

Surprisingly enough, two very clear examples of such formulations are to be found in the writings of William Carlos Williams, for all his professed distrust of such inquiries. I refer to his slogan, in connection with his *Paterson* poems, that "a city is a person," and to his manifesto-like pronouncement: "no ideas but in things," where "things" might be taken as a synonym for "images." Here the ultimate implied equation is: "good poetry equals imagism," whereas poets or critics of other schools might simply allow that imagism is one kind of poetry.

Advice is as easy to give as it is hard to take. But I do believe I can reasonably ask you to keep on the look-out for such equations, implicit or explicit, in all forms of expression. For they are by no means merely intellectualistic. For instance, one man may equate with "patriotism" precisely what his political opponent equates with "treason"—and obviously such equations dig deep, particularly when they are but implicit in a theory. For they are most effective when they are taken for granted (thus having what Bentham might have called "the force, but not the form, of an argument").

Only insofar as you inquire into such equational structures do you have a chance to escape the automatisms of terminology (as we seek to find our way between the dangers of automatism and the ingenuities of automation). It's for you to decide which equations you should accept or reject—but I do feel justified, for my part of the deal, in saying that you should always be on the look-out for such equations, particularly when they are implicit in our thinking, there merely as unexpressed assumptions. Such unobserved equations in our thinking set up the kind of "beginnings," or motivating principles, that can transform us into automata. Demagogues, headlines, the advertising in the mass media, and the like, line you up by the use of associative linkages that are ultimately reducible to such equations. The same observation applies to the best works, too. The point is: Don't expect to avoid it—but *watch* it.

Such equations, which in poetry take the form of metaphors, may also underlie our philosophies of life, our world-views, or perspectives, thereby embodying a metaphorical function that a notable member of your faculty has been brilliantly at work on recently. So I began wondering what metaphor, or equation, might most directly suit our situation. And tentatively, I'd suggest this notion as feasible:

On and off through the centuries, life has been viewed as a pilgrimage. It's a good metaphor, especially if you add the notion of journeymanship in the sense of a stage midway between apprenticeship and mastery. But as we watch the traffic, perennially unable to make up its mind, yet all the while keeping on going and adding up to a vast complexity of interlocking purposes that get variously fitted into one another somehow, might we not be justified in hopping up the metaphor accordingly? Hence, for now, not life as a pilgrimage, but life as an endless flow of traffic in a big city. With chances now and then to park at the end of a remote unpaved country road, to get out and walk for a while (all the time playing your transistor radio that keeps you hooked up with things at the center of the traffic jam).

But the more I thought about beginnings, be they beginnings in the sense of logical priority (principles, definitions, and the like) or beginnings in the sheerly narrative sense, as outright temporal firsts, the more I began to realize that I had been collecting material for this talk since I first began to think systematically about literary matters at all (roughly, half a century ago).

So these things all come to a focus in a concern with beginnings in the purely formal sense, as the classical symphony (and I do hope that the Music Department will bear me up in this) begins by saying in effect, "Now we are beginning. This is a beginning, intended to be experienced as just that, as most definitely, unmistakably, and formally a beginning." I shall be talking from now on, of beginnings in that sense, beginnings *qua* beginnings.

An appealing thing about much old poetry is that, in its way, it was so conscious of beginnings as such. For instance, the opening invocation in *The Iliad* is such an announcement. Or Milton's *Lycidas* (and, of course, *Paradise Lost*)—or Dante's opening line, *Nel mezzo del cammin di nostra vita* (it has the beginnings of the traffic metaphor: "in the middle of the roadway of our life"). The opening of Shakespeare's *Twelfth Night* seems to me so beautiful, as sheer beginning, I have tried to analyze it purely in itself, trying to figure out just what all goes on, in the enigmatic relation between our thoughts and our bodies, as Shakespeare contrives those astounding modulations from the Duke's opening apostrophe, "If music be the food of love, play on; / Give me excess of it, that, surfeiting, / The appetite may sicken, and so die," to the concluding puns on hart:

CURIO: Will you go hunt, my lord?
DUKE: What, Curio?
CURIO: The hart.
DUKE: Why, so I do, the noblest that I have.
        O! When mine eyes did see Olivia first . . . etc.

The beginning words of *The Aeneid* have been made platitudinous through no fault of their own, but simply through unthinking repetition: "Arms and the man I sing" *(arma virumque cano)*—the true marvels of which, as a beginning, we can best realize if we go back in turn to *its* beginnings, etymologically noting how the word for "arms" comes from a root that also gives us "art" and the *Greek* word for "virtue," while the word for "man" gives us the *Latin* word for "virtue." Nor should we forget that the epic is of the man who "first" from the realm of Troy, etc.

Here's one of the efforts I made, in the search to begin a story with a beginning that would be formally a beginning (beginning on an artificially impressionistic version of evolution):

Logos Verbum the Word—universal brew bubbling and collapsing—then this wad of runny iron and rock settles into a steady elliptic jog—cools, crusts, that objects wriggle in the slime, and boxlike things bump against the trees—heroic march of that one tender seed through groanings and agues of the earth, through steaming fevers, through chills slid down from the poles, hunger, fire, pestilence, war, despair, anguish of the conscience, lo! this clean-blooded man, this unscrofulous unsyphilitic neat-skinned gentleman, this ingenious isolated item, Prince Llan.

But where was Gudruff? . . .

(and so on, the question having been intended to lead into the story proper).

Or I tried another, beginning on the subject of emergence from a watery cave—an impressionistic replica of birth, though I didn't think of that at the time.

And I once started making a list of beginnings, as a way of sizing up movie plots. One, for instance: The police whistle in the darkness, the sound of running feet, the siren of the prowl car; finally, the shape hiding in the shadows.

Or another: View of office building; camera climbs up side of building, pauses at one window on high floor; next we advance through outer offices, past clerks variously busy; door opens to inner office, where there is a troubled consultation of executives sitting around a big table.

Or another: Camera approaching bridge over small stream; assorted sounds of domestic fowls; from other direction, herd of sheep being driven slowly towards bridge.

Another: Bus pulls up at out-of-the-way bus stop; out steps girl noticeably incongruous with the surroundings; perhaps goes to pay-phone, while being eyed by local loafers dully curious.

Or: Last-minute packing in preparation for a trip.

Or: Students pouring out of building; apparently bell has just rung; camera finally settles on our hero, either exceptionally popular or exceptionally unpopular, depending upon the plot.

Or the types of beginnings that seem to have to fight their way through a conglomeration of fragmentary vistas, blaring music, credit lines on cast and staff, everything so urgently cluttered that one gets the feel of being rushed, crowded, and trampled into admiration even before one knows what the admiration is to be about.

And so on.

Once, for a class in prose composition, I offered this Beginning:

Dreary dusk, in late fall. Train arrives at a deserted station in the country. One passenger gets off, and is left standing alone on the platform as the train rumbles on down the tracks. He is apparently a stranger to the town. Looking about, he finds a taxicab, operated by an old man who looks as though, some decades back, he had been a not very prosperous farmer. The stranger asks, "Could you take me to the Hargraves place?"

The taximan is startled, but agrees. As they drive off, the stranger tells him that he first wants to stop at a general store. The taximan says there is one nearby—and he waits in the cab while the stranger enters the store, where he quickly makes a couple of purchases, then returns to the cab.

It is now near dark; a cold wind is blowing across the parched, weedy fields. The two men make a few desultory attempts at conversation, then lapse into silence, broken only by the stranger's occasional irrelevant references to death.

About two miles out of town, the taxi nears an old house, with high dark windows, visible behind trees, and surrounded by an unkempt lawn.

The stranger tells the taximan, "There'll be no need to wait," as he pays and sets out along the weedy lane towards the house. The cab returns to town.

On the porch, over the door, there is a hornets' nest. The stranger now opens the package he had bought at the general store: a spray-gun and a can of insecticide. After filling the gun with the chemical, he thoroughly sprays the hornets' nest until there are no signs of life. Then reaching under the nest, he removes a key, unlocks the door, and enters the dark hall.

You can go on from there.

Beginnings! Beginnings! Beginnings! For Commencement. Hurry now, and pack in the few remaining exhibits, by way of ending.

And what of endings? Endings?

For endings, *euthanasia*. And what's euthanasia? To die suddenly, or in one's sleep, or at the height of pleasure, but in a way that causes inconvenience to no one but one's enemies.

Forget endings. Hurry, we are to end on beginnings.

Our country has the highest standard of living in the world. Evidence? The number of tranquillizers we consume.

(No, that's not it. Try again. Hurry, end on beginnings.)

Resurgam! resurgam! I shall rise again! resurgam.

(That's better—but not quite what we want.) Hurry—pack in the beginnings.

"teach disappearing me also the keen
illimitable secret of begin."

(Cummings addressing the new moon. That's better.)

Den de lam' ram sheep horns begin to blow,
Trumpets begin to soun',
Joshua commanded de chillen to start shoutin'—an'
De walls come tumblin' down, dat mornin'

(That's better, even the conclusion, "come tumblin' down," is a kind of beginning.)

In the beginning was the pre-beginning, already enigmatically containing within itself the principle of the count-down:

                6 5 4 3 2 1 — BLAST-OFF
                Roger — go go go-go ga-ga
                OVER — and over

(whereas we used to count *up*, now when we're getting ready to insert into orbit the new peace-loving weapons, we count *down*. Students of symbolism should note this enigmatic fact. It might turn out to be quite neat).

Whitman:

> "Afoot and light-hearted, I take to the open road,
> Healthy, free, the world before me,
> The long brown path before me leading wherever I choose."

Medley from Browning:

> "Marching along, fifty-score strong . . .
> Do I glide unespied
> As I ride, as I ride . . .
> Boot, saddle, to horse, and away . . .
>
> Morning's at seven;
> The hill-side's dew-pearl'd; . . .
> God's in his Heaven—
> All's right with the world!"

Beginnings   beginnings   beginnings
"When the pink sun edges flatly above the skyline, comes up as bright
and clean as a brand new dollar, as rash as a blast of unexpected
music . . ."
"when I fall on my knees, with my face to the risin' sun . . ."

So MUCH, THEN, as regards some samples of Beginnings, in connection with
Commencement.

Till tomorrow morning, then.

That, too, will be a series of beginnings. First the preparations leading
into the processional. Then the processional itself. And damn it, Bennington
students are at their most disastrously loveliest in their graduation robes.
Positively ethereal (it says here). Then the intermediate stages, each (in its
way) a kind of beginning. Then the recessional—and then, dear class, the
Commencement is over—and you are all set to begin.

Good luck to you, For the Next Phase—and for all thereafter, to the
extent that Life permits and the Law allows.

Abstraction

It is crucially important to understand that abstraction is not synonymous with generalization, that it is not the antithesis of "concrete." Abstraction is the apprehension of form and is accomplished in two different modes, by means of successive generalizations and by means of what Susanne K. Langer calls "indirect, intensive insight." The selections gathered here and in Part II make the point again and again: we abstract by deliberately generalizing, by sorting and gathering in the process of classifying; we also abstract as we dream and perceive and imagine, by forming images.

To suggest the relationship of forming and abstraction I have included brief passages from Owen Barfield, Susanne K. Langer, and I. A. Richards. And since studying children's drawings is one of the best ways to see how abstraction works in the apprehension of form, I have included a few pages from a fascinating book called *Heidi's Horse*, a selection by Sylvia Fein from the thousands of drawings her daughter made over a period of fifteen years. The full record of development is instructive, but even from the few drawings printed here one can see how constructing and construing work together. Sylvia Fein's commentary is supplemented by a few pages from Rudolf Arnheim's discussion of the conceptual character of the images in children's drawings, from *Art and Visual Perception*.

C. S. PEIRCE
(on "medisense")

7.544* All consciousness of a process belongs to this medisense. It has several varieties. In the first place there is a separative process, the centrifugal tendency of thought, by which any idea by following out its own development becomes separated from those with which it is connected. We see this in attention. When we see the little bottle with green crystals, the green idea detaches itself from the remaining ideas, the spicular form, the being bunched together in a little tube, etc. and leads to a thought (which is accurately expressed by the sentence "These crystals are green.") where the green stands off from the remaining ideas which remain confused together. It is the liveliness of the green idea which brings this about.** And in all cases it is the idea which has vigor which spontaneously detaches itself from the rest. We may call this variety of *medisense* by the name *Abstraction*.

OWEN BARFIELD
from *Poetic Diction*

A little reflection shows that all *meaning*—even of the most primitive kind—is dependent on the possession of some measure of this power [the capacity to recognize significant resemblances and analogies] . Where it was wholly absent, the entire phenomenal cosmos must be extinguished. All sounds would fuse into one meaningless roar, all sights into one chaotic panorama, amid which no individual objects—not even color itself—would be distinguishable. Let the reader imagine for a moment that he is standing in the midst of a normal and familiar environment—houses, trees, grass, sky, etc.—when, suddenly, he is deprived by some supernatural stroke of every

---

*All passages from Peirce are quoted from *The Collected Papers of Charles Sanders Peirce*, six volumes, edited by Charles Hartshorne and Paul Weiss (Cambridge: Harvard University Press, 1931–35). The first number indicates the volume; additional numbers, the particular item in the sequence arranged by the editors.

**Maintained even in furious sleep. (AB)

vestige of memory—and not only of memory, but also of all those assimilated, forgotten experiences which comprise his power of *recognition*. He is
asked to assume that, in spite of this, he still retains the full measure of his
cognitive faculty as an adult. It will appear, I think, that for the first few
moments his consciousness—if it can bear that name—will be deprived not
merely of all thought, but even of all perception—unless we choose to suppose a certain unimaginable minimum, a kind of panorama of various light,
which he will confront with a vacant and uncomprehending stare. It is not
merely that he will be unable to realize that that square, red and white object is a "house," and to form concepts of an inside with walls and ceilings—
he will not even be able to see it *as* a square, red and white object. For the
most elementary distinctions of form and color are only apprehended by us
with the help of the concepts which we have come to unite with the pure
sense-datum. And these concepts we acquire and fix, as we grow up, with the
help of words—such as *square, red,* etc. On the basis of past perceptions,
using language as a kind of storehouse, we gradually build up our ideas, and
it is only these which enable us to become "conscious," as human beings, of
the world around us.

SUSANNE K. LANGER
from *Philosophy in a New Key*

Our merest sense-experience is a process of formulation. The world that
actually meets our senses is not a world of "things," about which we are in-
vited to discover facts as soon as we have codified the necessary logical language to do so; the world of pure sensation is so complex, so fluid and full,
that sheer sensitivity to stimuli would only encounter what William James
has called (in characteristic phrase) "a blooming, buzzing confusion." Out of
this bedlam our sense organs must select certain predominant forms, if they
are to make report of *things* and not of mere dissolving sensa. The eye and
ear must have their logic—their "categories of understanding," if you like the
Kantian idiom, or their "primary imagination," in Coleridge's version of the
same concept. An object is not a datum, but a form construed by the sensitive and intelligent organ, a form which is at once an experienced individual
thing and a symbol for the concept of it, for this *sort of thing.*

. . . Mental life begins with our mere physiological constitution. A little
reflection shows us that, since no experience occurs more than once, so-
called "repeated" experiences are really *analogous* occurrences, all fitting a

form that was abstracted on the first occasion. *Familiarity* is nothing but the quality of fitting very neatly into the form of a previous experience. I believe our ingrained habit of hypostatizing impressions, of seeing *things* and not sense-data, rests on the fact that we promptly and unconsciously abstract a form from each sensory experience, and use this form to *conceive* the experience as a whole, as a "thing."

I. A. RICHARDS
from *The Philosophy of Rhetoric*

A particular impression is already a product of concrescence. Behind or in it, there has been a coming together of *sortings*. When we take a number of particular impressions—of a number of different white things, say—and abstract from them an idea of whiteness, we are explicitly reversing a process which has already been implicitly at work in our perception of them as all white. Our risk is to confuse the abstractness we thus arrive at intellectually with the primordial abstractness out of which these impressions have already grown—before ever any conscious explicit reflection took place.

Things, in brief, are instances of laws. As Bradley said, association marries only universals, and out of these laws, these recurrent likenesses of behavior, in our minds and in the world—not out of revived duplicates of individual past impressions—the fabric of our meanings, which is the world, is composed.

SYLVIA FEIN and HEIDI SCHEUBER
from *Heidi's Horse*

The artistic structures now available to Heidi consist of circles, parts of circles and radiating lines of varying length, diagonal or parallel to each other, sometimes intersecting. With these simple line and circle relationships, which characterize all prehistoric and naive art and which all children discover in this sequence, Heidi is equipped to draw her first horse.

4 years/3 months

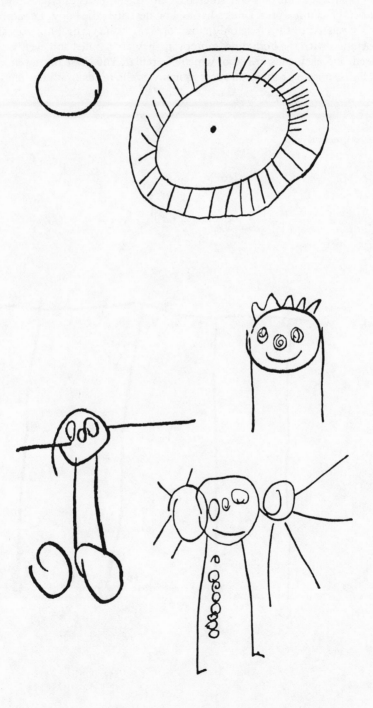

Heidi's first horse is constructed of circles and parts of circles for the head and facial features. One radiating line describes the body. Legs, previously related to the circle only, now form the same vertical-horizontal association with the body line; moreover, they are parallel and evenly spaced, and each ends in a hoof which is circular. The horse has seven legs. Heidi doesn't count them; she uses as many as she needs to fill her line.

4 years/3 months

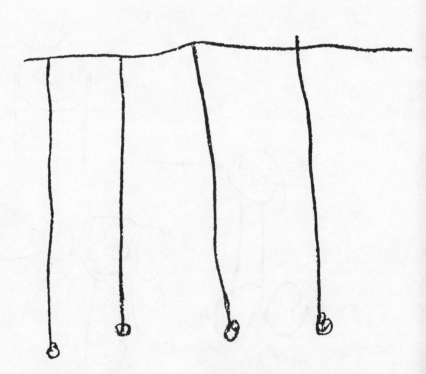

During the next five months Heidi draws many horses with body line uncontrolled and variable in length. She draws as many legs as may be required by the unequal lengths: long-bodied horses have more legs than short-bodied horses. Artistic necessity takes precedence over her knowledge that horses have four legs. Base lines, to stabilize the locus of some horses in close proximity, make their first appearance.

Some horses contain babies.

4 years/3 months to 4 years/8 months

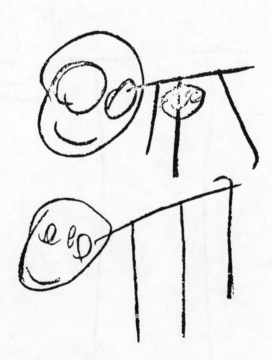

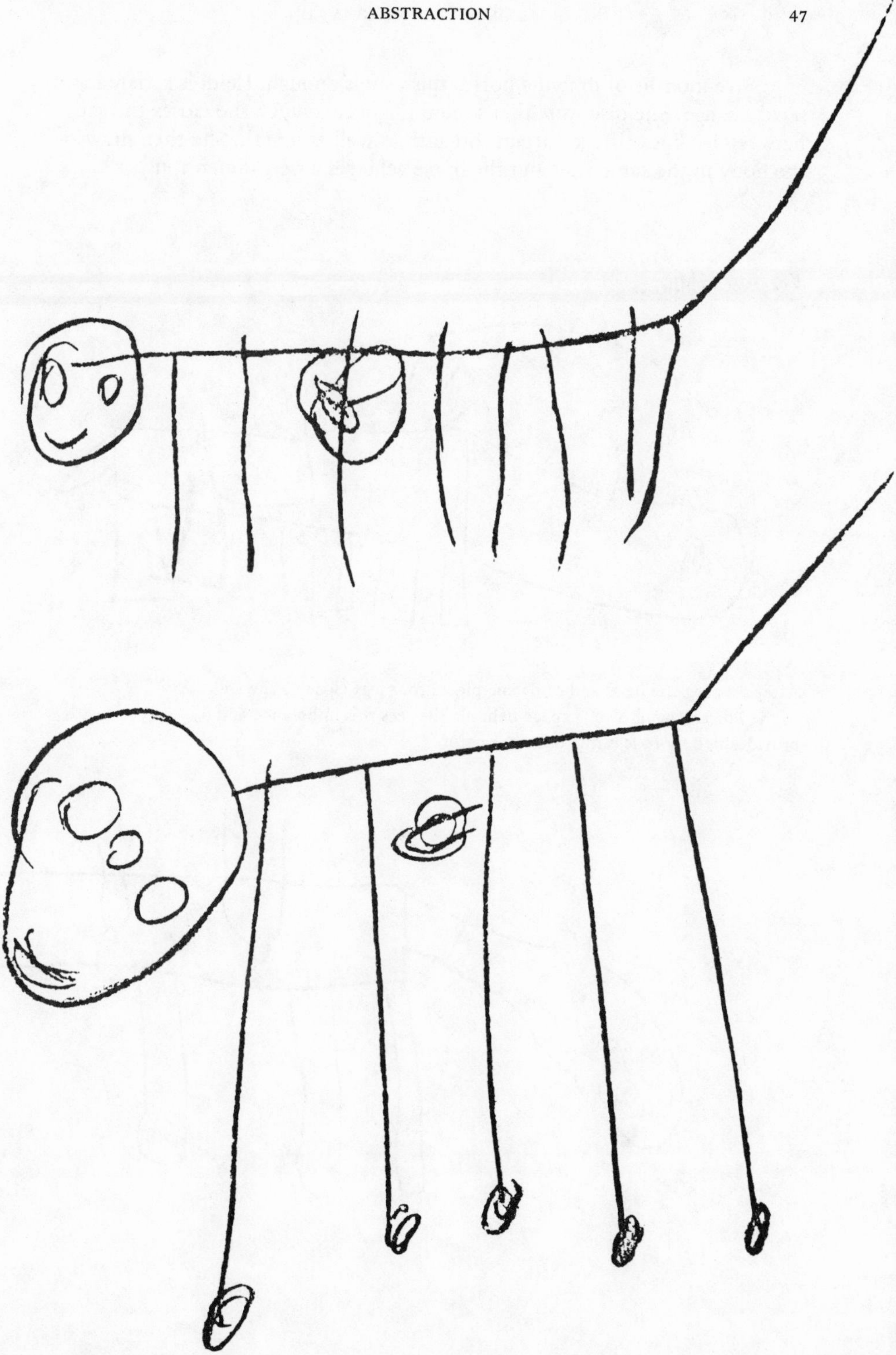

Five months of drawing horses this way is enough. Heidi is satiated and seeks change. She discovers that something occurs when she closes the gap between leg lines: the leg attains breadth as well as length. She then draws the body in the same way and the horse achieves a new dimension.

4 years/9 months

After drawing the head and body she places four legs close to the front of the horse, leaving a long space behind. She sees this imbalance and provides two more legs in a different color.

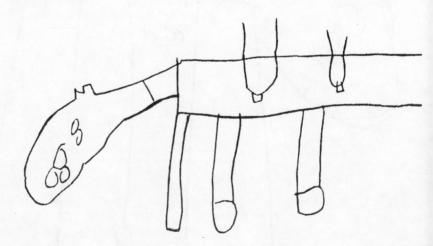

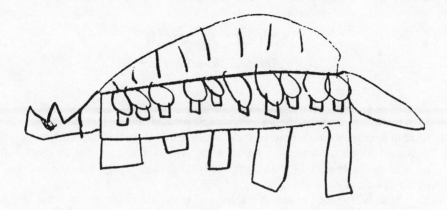

The number of legs is still determined by the length of the body and Heidi finds it necessary to draw five legs (with ten saddles!) for this horse, but with the next two drawings she attempts to plan four legs per horse.

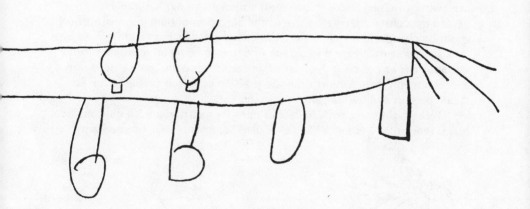

This time she centers the four hoofed legs with accompanying saddles above, but the spaces remaining on both sides of these legs still disturb the relationship between body and legs, and Heidi must again add legs. They are compromises: she treats them indifferently by omitting their hoofs.

RUDOLF ARNHEIM
from *Art and Visual Perception*

If, in a child's drawing, a face is to accommodate explicit eyes, a mouth with teeth, and a nose with nostrils, it must be made large—just as Marc Chagall enlarges a cow's head to make room inside it for another cow and a milkmaid. If, on the other hand, size is not yet differentiated, the various parts of the body—head, trunk, and limbs—are given roughly the same order of magnitude (Figure 1).

What is true for the size of objects holds also for the intervals between them. The need for clear presentation makes the child leave sufficient empty space between objects—a sort of standard distance which, from the realistic point of view, looks sometimes too large and sometimes too small, depending on the subject matter. An overlong arm may be required to connect a human figure with an apple on a tree, from which the figure is kept at suitable distance. Realistic closeness between items remains visually uncomfortable for some time.

Realistic size is only marginally relevant to the size of things in pictures because perceptual identity does not rely much on size. The shape and the spatial orientation of an object remain unimpaired by a change in size, just as in music a moderate augmentation or diminution of temporal size through a change of speed does not interfere with the recognition of a theme. The basic irrelevance of visual size is shown most strikingly by our habitual obliviousness to the constant change in size of the objects in our environment brought about by changes in distance. As far as images are concerned, nobody protests against an inch-high photograph of a human being or against a gigantic statue. A television screen looks small in the living room, but we need only concentrate on it for a short time and it becomes an acceptable frame for "real" persons and buildings.

Perhaps the most striking case of misinterpretation due to illusionistic bias is that of the "tadpole" figures, called *hommes têtards* by the French

Figure 1   **Figure 2**

and *Kopffüssler* by the Germans. The popular view is that in these very common drawings the child leaves out the trunk entirely, and that he erroneously attaches the arms to the head or the legs. Figures 2 and 3, drawn by four-year olds, show some of these mysterious creatures. Various theories have been offered. The child was believed to overlook or forget the body or even to "repress" it for reasons of modesty. If we look at the developmental process, we discover that no such explanation is pertinent, since in these drawings the trunk actually is not left out.

At the earliest stage the circle stands for the total human figure, just as it stands for so many other complete objects. Later, its shape is differentiated through the addition of appendages. For example, in Figure 4, an eight-year-old boy's drawing of a church, the original circle is gradually limited by the additions. These are essentially two types. In Figure 2 the circle functions as an undifferentiated representation of head and trunk. Therefore the child is entirely consistent in attaching legs and arms to it. Only to adults does the picture look as though something is left out. The circle is often extended to an egg-shaped oblong, which may contain the features of a face in its upper part or indications of clothing in the lower.

Figure 3 illustrates the other type. In the center is a house with two fish in it, at the right a cowboy, and at the left a cow. The cowboy has one stomach in his body, and the cow has two. These stomachs are useful for our purpose, because they show that here the two parallel vertical lines are an undifferentiated representation of trunk and legs, whereas the circle is now limited to being a head. The arms are attached where they belong—to the verticals. The double function of the line as self-contained unit and as contour is not yet clearly differentiated; the two verticals are contours (trunk) and object lines (legs) at the same time. It may be added that a similar lack

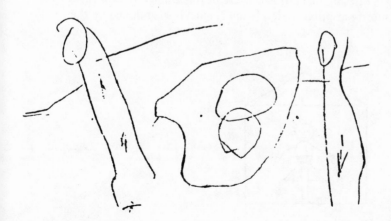

Figure 3   Figure 4

of differentiation is often evident in the way other parts of the body are represented. The features of the face may be drawn as a single circle, contained in the larger circle of the head, before they split up into eyes, nose, and mouth; and in Figure 1 the limbs are not yet articulated, so that to the adult observer the fingers may seem to be attached to the arms, and the toes to the legs.

The same point is made in the schematic diagram of Figure 5. The drawing of the house is neither a transparent front view nor a section. It is the two-dimensional equivalent of a house. The rectangle stands for cubic space, and its outline for the six boundary surfaces. The figure stands inside, completely surrounded by walls. Only a gap in the contour could provide an opening. The child's invention lingers on through the ages, so that even in the highly realistic art of a Dürer or Altdorfer the Holy Family is housed in a building without front wall, camouflaged unconvincingly as a broken-down ruin. And of course in our modern theater, the stage is accepted without hesitation by the same people who accuse the child of "X-ray pictures."

As indicated in Figure 5, pictures of this kind present hair as a single row of lines, all touching the contour of the head. This is quite correct in that the circular head line stands for the complete surface of the head, which is thus shown as being covered with hair all over. Yet there is in this method an ambiguity deriving from the fact that inevitably the child is using it for two different and incompatible purposes at the same time. Obviously the face is not meant to lie inside the head, but on its outer surface; and the two oblique lines represent arms, and not an open cape hanging down from the shoulders and surrounding the entire body. That is, the two-dimensional units of the drawings are equivalents of solids, of two-dimensional aspects of the outside of solids, or both, depending on what is needed. The relation between flatness and depth is undifferentiated, so that by purely visual means there is no way of telling whether a circular line stands for a ring, a disk, or a ball. It is because of this ambiguity that the method is used mostly at primitive levels and is quickly abandoned by the Western child.

Figure 5

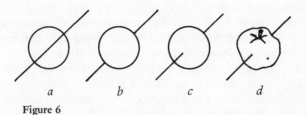

a   *b*   *c*   *d*

Figure 6

The process was well documented in an experiment by Arthur B. Clark, in which children of different ages were asked to draw an apple with a hatpin stuck horizontally through it and turned at an angle to the observer. Figure 6*d* illustrates the position in which the children saw the model. Figure 6*a* shows the earliest solution of the problem. It is logical in that the pin goes uninterruptedly through the inside of the circle, which stands for the inside of the apple. But it is ambiguous in that the straight line inevitably depicts a one-dimensional object (pin) and not a surface. At the next stage, *b*, the child makes a first concession to projective representation by showing the center part of the pin hidden inside the apple. (To the younger child this would look like a picture of two pins touching the apple at the outside.) But the contour of the circle still stands for the entire surface of the apple, as shown by the way the pin stops at the contour. At *c* the contour has become the horizon line, and the area of the circle represents the front face of the apple. With some refinement of shape, this leads to the realistic solution, *d*. This final picture is spatially consistent, but it sacrifices the striking visual clarity with which the essentials of the three-dimensional conception were rendered in the two-dimensional medium at stage *a*. The differentiation between two-dimensional and three-dimensional form has been achieved, but only through the suspect trick of making the picture plane appear as an image of three-dimensional space.

As long as the two-dimensional view is not differentiated from the projective view, the flat pictorial plane serves to represent them both. This can be done in two ways. The child can use the vertical dimension of his picture plane to distinguish between top and bottom and the horizontal for right and left and thus obtain "vertical space" (elevation). Or he can use his two dimensions to show the directions of the compass in a ground plan, which produces "horizontal space" (Figure 7). Upright objects, such as human beings, trees,

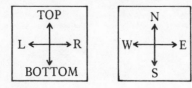

Figure 7

walls, table legs, appear clearly and characteristically in vertical space, whereas gardens, streets, table tops, dishes, or carpets ask for horizontal space. To further complicate matters, in vertical space only one among the innumerable vertical planes can be represented directly, so that the picture can take care of the front face of a house but not, at the same time, of the side faces without recourse to some trick of indirect representation. Similarly, horizontal space can show the dishes on the table top but not, in the same picture, the dog lying under the table.

In dealing with the "Egyptian method" we showed how at an early level of spatial representation the artist chooses for each object, or part of an object, the aspect presenting it most characteristically. It may be mentioned here that the highly sophisticated and realistic technique of the motion picture has recaptured some of the striking effects of elementary representation. By decomposing the visual world into a succession of partial views, the film has been able, for example, to return to the principle that the units of a visual statement are basically of equal size. If a person is shown watching a butterfly, a close-up may make the insect as large as the person. Similarly, a change in camera angle will make the screen picture switch from vertical to horizontal space, so that the spectator may see a side view of people sitting at the dinner table and, a second later, a top view of the food. This procedure is "justified" realistically through the succession of the shots in time, which sanctions a change in distance or angle. In the actual experience of the spectator, however, these changes in observation point are not clearly perceived as such. Essentially, he accepts things as being presented at a size and angle that fits them best without worrying whether or not such visual correctness is "true-to-life." In much modern art, of course, all realistic pretense has been frankly dropped: objects are clearly given whatever size and angle accords with the visual purpose.

Part Two

Language is the vocal actualization of the tendency to see reality symbolically.

Edward Sapir

A language is more than a set of associations and the learning of language is therefore more than learning by association. A language is more than a code because it permits predications as well as labellings.

J. J. Gibson

The formal or logical analogy does not prove a material or ontological similarity in the subject matter of linguistics and biology. The linguist lives in a world of his own. His is a symbolic universe, a universe of meaning. We cannot analyze meaning in the same way and according to the same methods that we use in a chemical laboratory for analyzing a chemical compound.

Ernst Cassirer

The notion of giving something a name is the vastest generative idea that ever was conceived.

Susanne K. Langer

Language and the Making of Meaning

The most important effect of reclaiming the imagination would be the development of fresh, philosophically sound conceptions of language as our chief means of making meaning. Language enables us to apprehend reality as it is given to us in our perceptions; it stabilizes and represents so that we can recognize. And language, in its tendency towards syntax, provides the means of articulation; as it goes its discursive way, it brings thought along with it. Unless we can account for both the hypostatic and the discursive functions of language, we will be unable to give an account of the composing process.*

---

*I have briefly considered these matters in "Thinking about Language," *The Making of Meaning*, pp. 107–121.

The Unit of Meaning

That writing is different from speech should not obscure the crucially important fact that, like all uses of language, it is a process of making meaning. Seeing language in the perspective of a theory of imagination encourages the recognition that meaning comes first; that complexity is there from the start; that the articulation of thought is contingent on the mind's activity in a human world. Current rhetorical theory has embraced one or another version of a "developmental" model, but they are all dangerous insofar as they tend to sanction the genetic fallacy—that what comes first is simple, not complex, and that what comes after is a bigger version of a little beginning. Thus we have the idea that there is first one word and then another, another, another, until there is enough to fill out the awaiting syntactic structures. But this isn't the way it happens. The hypostatic word, the single uttered syllable, is a proto-sentence; syntax is deeply implicated, we might say, in every human cry. Children let a single word do the work of the sentence until the discursive power of language can draw out and articulate the meaning. The conception of a semantic component added to a syntactic structure is a mechanistic conception which is pedagogically worthless.

Lev Vygotsky, who began as a philosopher and a literary critic, was a psychologist who studied the role of language in the child's intellectual development. As he explains in the first chapter of *Thought and Language*, we must begin not with "thought" or with "language" but with "the unit of meaning." Words are not sounds to which meaning is added; they are not true words unless or until there is meaning. We therefore should not begin with isolated words but with activities in which language plays a central part. His ingenious experiments show how language empowers the process of concept formation, which is "a *movement* of thought . . . , constantly alternating between two directions, from the particular to the general and from the general to the particular." He understood more profoundly than Piaget that language is dialogic: we are born with the capacity of speech but it is realized only in social settings. Language begins as a dialogue with the self, but the human self is defined from the first in social terms. *Thought and Language* should be read in its entirety; it provides an extremely important analysis of concept formation in relation to reading and writing, as well as an indispensable critique of Piaget's structuralism.

The several lengthy passages included here, all of which came originally from a study entitled *Tool and Symbol in Child Development*, have been published in *Mind and Society.* Anyone familiar with the ill-conceived experiments of modern-day psycholinguists will perhaps be surprised to see how elegantly Vygotsky proceeds, guided always by a philosophy of language as a symbolic form, a means of making meaning.

Max Black, in a chapter called "Thought and Language" from his excellent book *The Labyrinth of Language*, sets forth two views which he calls "the model of the garment" and "the model of the melody." The first is familiar from Renaissance rhetoric, but the same presuppositions can be discerned in the spatial metaphors of Chomsky's grammar in which something —never mind what—bubbles up from "deep structures" to become "surface features." Black also glances briefly at the so-called Whorf Hypothesis, a notion of linguistic determinism with which he, I think wrongly, identifies Ernst Cassirer. (Cassirer is concerned with the constitutive role of symbols, not the deterministic character of grammar. That is to say, language considered as a symbolic form is not reducible to one or another grammar.)

The brief passage from an essay by I. A. Richards reminds us of the confusions which result when the separation of language and thought is modeled in terms derived from Information Theory, providing another fashionable update of the model of the garment. Richards patiently dismantled the wiring diagram of the communication situation more than once. (See pp. 172–86.)

Not without misgivings, I have chosen "Expression," the second in a series of lectures Alfred North Whitehead delivered at Wellesley and published in 1938 as *Modes of Thought*. The essay is full of interest, but it jumps a groove every now and then; in places, it has something of the opacity of his *Symbolism: Its Meaning and Effect.* (I have silently emended some transitions and a few sentences; my guess is that Whitehead lectured the Wellesley women from notes which he then wrote up rather carelessly.) Nevertheless, "Expression" has been found by readers of the preliminary version of this book to be the most suggestive of all the essays because of the way Whitehead reclaims *expression* as one of the chief functions of language. Whitehead explains the interdependence of language and thought better than anyone I've read; he offers a brilliant analysis of the positivist trick of building a clean machine and then sneaking back in all that has been dismissed as metaphysical (mentalist) junk; his comments on the biology of language are of the sort Langer develops so ingeniously in "Speculations" and elsewhere; the arguments against Computer Assisted Instruction will never be made with greater succinctness than we find in Whitehead's remarks on "the connexity of existence"; he makes the case for the special benefits of writing so substantially that we are saved the labor of reading Jacques Derrida. With explanations of the survival value of human perception fresh in mind, it is startling to read Whitehead on how "the life-aim at survival is modified into the human aim of survival."

Ten years after Whitehead published *Modes of Thought*, B. F. Skinner delivered the Norton Lectures at Harvard University. They are, in a sense, the positivist response to Whitehead's notion of "the creative impulse." Skinner tells us that he took his title from a remark of Whitehead who had responded to Skinner's account of his concept of behavior. "Ah," said Whitehead, "but you can't speak of *verbal behavior*!" The hazards of modelling language on motor activity or other "behaviors" remain unexamined by rhetoricians.

As I planned this book, W. H. Auden's oration, "The True Word Twisted by Misuse and Magic," migrated continuously from one section and one subsection to another. It could find a place anywhere in the discussion of artists at work, of perception and the apprehension of form, of language and interpretation: Auden reclaimed the imagination in everything he wrote. He had a philosophical understanding of the powers of language and he knew what it means to say that man is a social being with an immortal soul. He offers here as much insight into the codes and conventions of language as we are likely to gain from linguists writing at somewhat greater length. He had as strong and cunning a grasp of the psychological and moral significance of art as any critic of his time, though in declaring that nobody can consume a poem he may have spoken too soon. Many will want to challenge Auden's calm judgment that art is impotent, but surely there is no stronger argument for trying to keep literature accessible to our students than Auden's reminder that the art of the past offers communion with the dead, a communion without which "a fully human life is impossible."

L. S. VYGOTSKY
from *Mind in Society*

. . . These observations lead me to the conclusion that *children solve practical tasks with the help of their speech, as well as their eyes and hands.* This unity of perception, speech, and action, which ultimately produces internalization of the visual field, constitutes the central subject matter for any analysis of the origin of uniquely human forms of behavior.

To develop the first of these two points, we must ask: What is it that really distinguishes the actions of the speaking child from the actions of an ape when solving practical problems?

The first thing that strikes the experimenter is the incomparably greater *freedom* of children's operations, their greater independence from the structure of the concrete, visual situation. Children, with the aid of speech, create greater possibilities than apes can accomplish through action. One important manifestation of this greater flexibility is that the child is able to ignore the direct line between actor and goal. Instead, he engages in a number of preliminary acts, using what we speak of as instrumental, or mediated (indirect), methods. In the process of solving a task the child is able to include stimuli that do not lie within the immediate visual field. Using words (one class of such stimuli) to create a specific plan, the child achieves a much broader range of activity, applying as *tools* not only those objects that lie near at hand, *but searching for and preparing such stimuli as can be useful in the solution of the task, and planning future actions.*

Second, the practical operations of a child who can speak become much less impulsive and spontaneous than those of the ape. The ape typically makes a series of uncontrolled attempts to solve the given problem. In contrast, the child who uses speech divides the activity into two consecutive parts. She plans how to solve the problem through speech and then carries out the prepared solution through overt activity. Direct manipulation is replaced by a complex psychological process through which inner motivation and intentions, postponed in time, stimulate their own development and realization. This new kind of psychological structure is absent in apes, even in rudimentary forms.

Finally, it is decisively important that speech not only facilitates the child's effective manipulation of objects but also controls *the child's own behavior.* Thus with the help of speech, children, unlike apes, acquire the capacity to be both the subjects and objects of their own behavior.

Experimental investigation of the egocentric speech of children engaged in various activities such as that illustrated by Levina produced the second fact of great importance demonstrated by our experiments: *the relative amount of egocentric speech,* as measured by Piaget's methods, increases in relation to the difficulty of the child's task. On the basis of these experiments my collaborators and I developed the hypothesis that children's egocentric speech should be regarded as the transitional form between external and internal speech. Functionally, egocentric speech is the basis for inner speech, while in its external form it is embedded in communicative speech.

One way to increase the production of egocentric speech is to complicate a task in such a way that the child cannot make direct use of tools for its solution. When faced with such a challenge, the children's emotional use of language increases as well as their efforts to achieve a less automatic, more intelligent solution. They search verbally for a new plan, and their utterances reveal the close connection between egocentric and socialized speech. This is best seen when the experimenter leaves the room or fails to answer the children's appeal for help. Upon being deprived of the opportunity to engage in social speech, children immediately switch over to egocentric speech.

While the interrelationship of these two functions of language is apparent in this setting, it is important to remember that egocentric speech is linked to children's social speech by many transitional forms. The first significant illustration of the link between these two language functions occurs when children find that they are unable to solve a problem by themselves. They then turn to an adult, and verbally describe the method that they cannot carry out by themselves. The greatest change in children's capacity to use language as a problem-solving tool takes place somewhat later in their development, when socialized speech (which has previously been used to address an adult) *is turned inward.* Instead of appealing to the adult, children appeal to themselves; language thus takes on an *intrapersonal function* in addition to its *interpersonal use.* When children develop a method of behavior for guiding themselves that had previously been used in relation to another person, when they organize their own activities according to a social form of behavior, they succeed in applying a social attitude to themselves. The history of the process of *the internalization of social speech* is also the history of the socialization of children's practical intellect.

The relation between speech and action is a dynamic one in the course of children's development. The structural relation can shift even during an experiment. The crucial change occurs as follows: At an early stage speech *accompanies* the child's actions and reflects the vicissitudes of problem solving in a disrupted and chaotic form. At a later stage speech moves more and more toward the starting point of the process, so that it comes to *precede* action. It functions then as an aid to a plan that has been conceived but not yet realized in behavior. An interesting analogy can be found in children's speech while drawing. Young children name their drawings only after they have completed them; they need to see them before they can decide what they are. As children get older they can decide in advance what they are going to draw. This displacement of the naming process signifies a change in the function of speech. Initially speech follows actions, is provoked by and dominated by activity. At a later stage, however, when speech is moved to the starting point of an activity, a new relation between word and action emerges. Now speech guides, determines, and dominates the course of action; *the planning function of speech* comes into being in addition to the already existing function of language to reflect the external world.

Just as a mold gives shape to a substance, words can shape an activity into a structure. However, that structure may be changed or reshaped when children learn to use language in ways that allow them to go beyond previous experiences when planning future action. In contrast to the notion of sudden discovery popularized by Stern, we envisage verbal, intellectual activity as a series of stages in which the emotional and communicative functions of speech are expanded by the addition of the planning function. As a result the child acquires the ability to engage in complex operations extending over time.

Unlike the ape, which Köhler tells us is "the slave of its own visual field," children acquire an independence with respect to their concrete surroundings; they cease to act in the immediately given and evident *space*. Once children learn how to use the planning function of their language effectively, their psychological field changes radically. A view of the future is now an integral part of their approaches to their surroundings. . . .

The specifically human capacity for language enables children to provide for auxiliary tools in the solution of difficult tasks, to overcome impulsive action, to plan a solution to a problem prior to its execution, and to master their own behavior. Signs and words serve children first and foremost as a means of social contact with other people. The cognitive and communicative functions of language then become the basis of a new and superior form of activity in children, distinguishing them from animals.

The changes I have described do not occur in a one-dimensional, even fashion. Our research has shown that very small children solve problems using unique mixtures of processes. In contrast with adults, who react differently to objects and to people, young children are likely to fuse action and speech when responding to both objects and social beings. This fusion of activity is analogous to syncretism in perception, which has been described by many developmental psychologists.

The unevenness I am speaking of is seen quite clearly in a situation where small children, when unable to solve the task before them easily, combine direct attempts to obtain the desired end with a reliance upon emotional speech. At times speech expresses the children's desires, while at other times it serves as a substitute for actually achieving the goal. The child may attempt to solve the task through verbal formulations *and* by appeals to the experimenter for help. This mixture of diverse forms of activity was at first bewildering; but further observations drew our attention to a sequence of actions that clarify the meaning of the children's behavior in such circumstances. For example, after completing a number of intelligent and interrelated actions that should help him solve a particular problem successfully, the child suddenly, upon meeting a difficulty, ceases all attempts and turns for help to the experimenter. Any obstacle to the child's efforts at solving the problem may interrupt his activity. The child's verbal appeal to another person is an effort to fill the hiatus his activity has revealed. By asking a question, the child indicates that he has, in fact, formulated a plan to solve the task before him, but is unable to perform all the necessary operations.

Through repeated experiences of this type, children learn covertly (mentally) to plan their activities. At the same time they enlist the assistance of another person in accordance with the requirements of the problem posed for them. The child's ability to control another person's behavior becomes a necessary part of the child's practical activity.

Initially this problem solving in conjunction with another person is not differentiated with respect to the roles played by the child and his helper; it is a general, syncretic whole. We have more than once observed that in the course of solving a task, children get confused because they begin to merge the logic of what they are doing with the logic of the same problem as it has to be solved with the cooperation of another person. Sometimes syncretic action manifests itself when children realize the hopelessness of their direct efforts to solve a problem. As in the example from Levina's work, children address the objects of their attention equally with words and sticks, demonstrating the fundamental and inseparable tie between speech and action in the child's activity; this unity becomes particularly clear when compared with the separation of these processes in adults.

In summary, children confronted with a problem that is slightly too complicated for them exhibit a complex variety of responses including direct attempts at attaining the goal, the use of tools, speech directed toward the person conducting the experiment or speech that simply accompanies the action, and direct, verbal appeals to the object of attention itself.

If analyzed dynamically, this alloy of speech and action has a very specific function in the history of the child's development; it also demonstrates the logic of its own genesis. From the very first days of the child's development his activities acquire a meaning of their own in a system of social behavior and, being directed towards a definite purpose, are refracted through the prism of the child's environment. The path from object to child and from child to object passes through another person. This complex human structure is the product of a developmental process deeply rooted in the links between individual and social history.

* * *

The linkage between tool use and speech affects several psychological functions, in particular perception, sensory-motor operations, and attention, each of which is part of a dynamic system of behavior. Experimental-developmental research indicates that the connections and relations among functions constitute systems that change as radically in the course of a child's development as do the individual functions themselves. Considering each function in turn, I will examine how speech introduces qualitative changes in both its form and its relation to other functions.

Köhler's work emphasized the importance of the structure of the visual field in organizing the ape's practical behavior. The entire process of problem solving is essentially determined by perception. In this respect Köhler had ample grounds for believing that these animals are bound by their sensory field by means of voluntary effort. Indeed, it would probably be useful to view as a general law the dependence of all natural forms of perception on the structure of the sensory field.

However, a child's perception, because it is *human*, does not develop as a direct continuation and further perfection of the forms of animal perception, not even of those animals that stand nearest to humankind. Experiments conducted to clarify this problem led us to discover some basic laws that characterize the higher human forms of perception.

The first set of experiments concerned developmental stages of picture perception in children. . . . A two-year-old usually limits his description to separate objects within the picture. Older children describe actions and indicate the complex relations among the separate objects within the picture. Stern inferred from these observations that a stage when children perceive separate objects precedes the stage when they perceive actions and relations in addition to objects, that is, when they perceive the picture as a whole. However, many psychological observations suggest that the child's perceptual processes are initially fused and only later become more differentiated.

We resolved the contradiction between these two positions through an experiment replicating Stern's study of children's descriptions of pictures, in which we asked children to communicate the contents of a picture without using speech. We suggested that the description be made *in pantomime.* The two-year-old child, who according to Stern's schema is still at the separate "object" stage of development, perceived the dynamic features of the picture and reproduced them with ease through pantomime. What Stern regarded as a characteristic of the child's perceptual skills proved to be a product of the limitations of her *language development* or, in other words, a feature of her *verbalized perception.*

A series of related observations revealed that labeling is the primary function of speech used by young children. Labeling enables the child to choose a specific object, to single it out from the entire situation he is perceiving. Simultaneously, however, the child embellishes his first words with very expressive gestures, which compensate for his difficulties in communicating meaningfully through language. By means of words children single out separate elements, thereby overcoming the natural structure of the sensory field and forming new (artificially introduced and dynamic) structural centers. The child begins to perceive the world not only through his eyes but also through his speech. As a result, the immediacy of "natural" perception is supplanted by a complex mediated process; as such, speech becomes an essential part of the child's cognitive development.

Later, the intellectual mechanisms related to speech acquire a new function; verbalized perception in the child is no longer limited to labeling. At this next stage of development, speech acquires a synthesizing function, which in turn is instrumental in achieving more complex forms of cognitive perception. These changes give human perception an entirely new character, quite distinct from the analogous processes in higher animals.

The role of language in perception is striking because of the opposing tendencies implicit in the nature of visual perception and language. The independent elements in a visual field are simultaneously perceived; in this sense, *visual perception is integral.* Speech, on the other hand, requires sequential processing. Each element is separately labeled and then connected in a sentence structure, *making speech essentially analytical.*

Our research has shown that even at very early stages of development, language and perception are linked. In the solution of nonverbal tasks, even if a problem is solved without a sound being uttered, language plays a role in the outcome. These findings substantiate the thesis of psychological linguistics as formulated many years ago by A. Potebnya, who argued for the inevitable interdependence between human thought and language.

A special feature of human perception—which arises at a very young age—is the *perception of real objects.* This is something for which there is no analogy in animal perception. By this term I mean that I see the world not simply in color and shape but as a world with sense and meaning. I do not merely see something round and black with two hands; I see a clock and I can distinguish one hand from the other. Some brain-injured patients say, when they see a clock, that they are seeing something round and white with two thin steel strips, but they do not know it is a clock; such people have lost their real relationship with objects. These observations suggest that all human perception consists of categorized rather than isolated perceptions.

The developmental transition to qualitatively new forms of behavior is not confined to changes in perception alone. Perception is part of a dynamic system of behavior; hence, the relation between transformations of perceptual processes and transformations in other intellectual activities is of primary importance. This point is illustrated by our studies on choice behavior, which shows the changing relation between perception and motor action in young children.

We requested four- and five-year-old children to press one of five keys on a keyboard as they identified each one of a series of picture stimuli assigned to each key. Because this task exceeds the capabilities of the children, it causes serious difficulties and more intensive efforts to solve the problem. Perhaps the most remarkable result is that the entire process of selection by the child is *external*, and concentrated in the motor sphere, thus allowing the experimenter to observe the very nature of the choice process itself in the child's movements. The child does her selecting while carrying out whatever movements the choice requires.

The structure of the child's decision does not in the least resemble the adult process. Adults make a preliminary decision internally and subsequently carry out the choice in the form of a single movement that executes the plan. The child's choice resembles a somewhat delayed *selection among his own movements.* Vacillations in perception are directly reflected in the structure of movement. The child's movements are replete with diffuse gropings that interrupt and succeed one another. A mere glance at the chart tracing the child's movements is sufficient to convince one of the basic motor nature of the process.

The main difference between the choice processes in the child and in the adult is that for the child the series of tentative movements constitute the selection process. The child does not choose the *stimulus* (the necessary key) as the starting point for the consequent movement but rather selects the *movement*, using the instruction as a guide to check the results. Thus, the child resolves her choice not through a direct process of visual perception but through movement, hesitating between two stimuli, her fingers hovering above and moving from one key to another, going half-way and then coming back. When the child transfers her attention to a new location, thereby creating a new focus in the dynamic structure of perception, her hand obediently moves toward this new center, in unison with the eye. In short, movement is not separated from perception: the processes coincide almost exactly.

In the behavior of the higher animals, visual perception forms part of a more complex whole in a similar way. The ape does not perceive the visual situation passively; a complex behavioral structure consisting of reflexive, affective, motor, and intellectual factors is directed toward acquiring the object that attracts it. The ape's movements constitute an immediate dynamic continuation of its perception. In human children, this early, diffusely structured response undergoes a fundamental change as soon as a more complex psychological function is utilized in the choice process. The natural process present in animals is then transformed into a higher psychological operation.

Subsequent to the experiment described above we attempted to simplify the task of selection by marking each key with a corresponding sign to serve as an additional stimulus that could direct and organize the choice process. The child was asked, upon the appearance of a target stimulus, to press the key marked with the corresponding sign. As early as age five or six the child is able to fulfill this task easily. The addition of this new ingredient radically changes the structure of the choice process. The elementary, "natural" operation is replaced by a new and more complicated one. The simpler task evokes a more complexly structured response. When the child attends to the auxiliary sign in order to find the key corresponding to the given stimulus, he no longer exhibits those motor impulses that arise directly from perception. There are no uncertain groping movements in the air such as we observed in the earlier choice reaction when auxiliary aids were not used.

The use of auxiliary signs breaks up the fusion of the sensory field and the motor system and thus makes new kinds of behavior possible. A "functional barrier" is created between the initial and final moments of the choice response; the direct impulse to move is shunted by preliminary circuits. The child who formerly solved the problem impulsively now solves it through an internally established connection between the stimulus and the corresponding auxiliary sign. The movement that previously had been the choice now serves only to fulfill the prepared operation. *The system of signs restructures the whole psychological process and enables the child to master her movement.*

It reconstructs the choice process on a totally new basis. Movement detaches itself from direct perception and comes under the control of sign functions included in the choice response. This development represents a fundamental break with the natural history of behavior and initiates the transition from the primitive behavior of animals to the higher intellectual activities of humans.

Attention should be given first place among the major functions in the psychological structure underlying the use of tools. Beginning with Köhler, scholars have noted that the ability or inability to direct one's attention is an essential determinant of the success or failure of any practical operation. However, the difference between the practical intelligence of children and animals is that children are capable of reconstructing their perception and thus freeing themselves from the given structure of the field. With the help of the indicative function of words, the child begins to master his attention, creating new structural centers in the perceived situation. As K. Koffka so aptly put it, the child is able to determine for herself the "center of gravity" of her perceptual field; her behavior is not regulated solely by the salience of individual elements within it. The child evaluates the relative importance of these elements, singling out new "figures" from the background and thus widening the possibilities for controlling her activities.

In addition to reorganizing the visual-spatial field, the child, with the help of speech, creates a time field that is just as perceptible and real to him as the visual one. The speaking child has the ability to direct his attention in a dynamic way. He can view changes in his immediate situation from the point of view of past activities, and he can act in the present from the view-point of the future.

For the ape, the task is unsolvable unless the goal and the object needed to reach it are both simultaneously in view. For the child, this gap is easily overcome by verbally controlling her attention and thereby reorganizing her perceptual field. The ape will perceive a stick one moment, but cease to pay attention to it after its visual field has changed and the goal comes into view. The ape must see his stick in order to pay attention to it; the child may pay attention in order to see.

Thus, the child's field of attention embraces not one but a whole series of potential perceptual fields that form successive, dynamic structures over time. The transition from the simultaneous structure of the visual field to the successive structure of the dynamic field of attention is achieved through the reconstruction of the separate activities that are a part of the required operations. When this occurs, we can say that the field of attention has de-tached itself from the perceptual field and unfolded itself in time, as one component of a dynamic series of psychological activities. The possibility of combining elements of the past and present visual fields (for instance, tool and goal) in one field of attention leads in turn to a basic reconstruction of another vital function, *memory*. Through verbal formulations of past situations and activities, the child frees himself from the limitations of direct recall; he succeeds in synthesizing the past and present to suit his purposes. The changes that occur in memory are similar to those that occur in the child's perceptual field where centers of gravity are shifted and figure and ground relationship are altered. The child's memory not only makes fragments of the past more available, but also results in a *new method of uniting the elements of past experience with the present.*

Created with the help of speech, the time field for action extends both forward and backward. Future activity that can be included in an ongoing activity is represented by signs. As in the case of memory and attention, the inclusion of signs in temporal perception does not lead to a simple lengthening of the operation in time; rather, it creates the conditions for the development of a single system that includes effective elements of the past, present, and future. This emerging psychological system in the child now encompasses two new functions: *intentions and symbolic representations of purposeful action.*

This change in the structure of the child's behavior is related to basic alterations in the child's needs and motivations. When Lindner compared the methods by which deaf children solved tasks to the methods used by Köhler's ape, he noted that the motives guiding the ape and those guiding the child to achieve mastery of a goal were not the same. The "instinctive" urges predominating in the animal become secondary in the child. New motives, socially rooted and intense, provide the child with direction. K. Lewin described these motives as *Quasi-Beduerfnisse* (quasi-needs) and argued that their inclusion in any given task leads to the reorganization of the child's whole affective and voluntary system. He believed that with the development of these quasi-needs, the child's emotional thrust is shifted *from a preoccupation with the outcome* to *the nature of the solution.* In essence, the "task" (*Aufgabe*) in experiments with apes exists only in the eyes of the experimenter; as far as the animal is concerned there exists only the bait and the obstacles standing in his way. The child, however, strives to solve the given problem and thus has an entirely different purpose. Because he is able to form quasi-needs, the child is capable of breaking the operation into its separate parts, each of which becomes an independent problem that he formulates for himself with the help of speech.

In his excellent analysis of the psychology of purposeful activity, Lewin gives a clear-cut definition of voluntary activity as a product of the historical-cultural development of behavior and as a unique feature of human psychology. The fact that man displays extraordinary freedom with respect to even the most senseless intention is astounding in itself, he asserts. This freedom is incomparably less characteristic of children and probably of nonliterate humans, too. There is reason to believe that voluntary activity, more than highly developed intellect, distinguishes humans from the animals which stand closest to them.

* * *

A comparative investigation of human memory reveals that, even at the earliest stages of social development, there are two, principally different, types of memory. One, dominating in the behavior of nonliterate peoples, is characterized by the nonmediated impression of materials, by the retention of actual experiences as the basis of mnemonic (memory) traces. We call this *natural memory*, and it is clearly illustrated in E. R. Jaensch's studies of eidetic imagery. This kind of memory is very close to perception, because it arises out of the direct influence of external stimuli upon human beings. From the point of view of structure, the entire process is characterized by a quality of immediacy.

Natural memory is not the only kind, however, even in the case of nonliterate men and women. On the contrary, other types of memory belonging to a completely different developmental line coexist with natural memory. The use of notched sticks and knots, the beginnings of writing and simple memory aids all demonstrate that even at early stages of historical development humans went beyond the limits of the psychological functions given to them by nature and proceeded to a new culturally-elaborated organization of their behavior. Comparative analysis shows that such activity is absent in even the highest species of animals; we believe that these sign operations are the product of specific conditions of *social* development.

Even such comparatively simple operations as tying a knot or marking a stick as a reminder change the psychological structure of the memory process. They extend the operation of memory beyond the biological dimensions of the human nervous system and permit it to incorporate artificial, or self-generated, stimuli, which we call *signs*. This merger, unique to human beings, signifies an entirely new form of behavior. The essential difference between it and the elementary functions is to be found in the structure of the stimulus-response relations of each. The central characteristic of elementary functions is that they are totally and directly determined by stimulation from the environment. For higher functions, the central feature is self-generated stimulation, that is, the creation and use of artificial stimuli which become the immediate causes of behavior.

Every elementary form of behavior presupposes a *direct* reaction to the task set before the organism (which can be expressed by the simple S⟶R formula). But the structure of sign operations requires an intermediate link between the stimulus and the response. This intermediate link is a second order stimulus (sign) that is drawn into the operation where it fulfills a special function; it creates a new relation between S and R. The term "drawn into" indicates that an individual must be actively engaged in establishing such a link. This sign also possesses the important characteristic of reverse action (that is, it operates on the individual, not the environment).

Consequently, the simple stimulus-response process is replaced by a complex, mediated act, which we picture as:

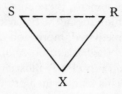

Figure 1

In this new process the direct impulse to react is inhibited, and an auxiliary stimulus that facilitates the completion of the operation by indirect means is incorporated.

Careful studies demonstrate that this type of organization is basic to all higher psychological processes, although in much more sophisticated forms than that shown above. The intermediate link in this formula is not simply a method of improving the previously existing operation, nor is it a mere additional link in an S—R chain. Because this auxiliary stimulus possesses the specific function of reverse action, it transfers the psychological operation to higher and qualitatively new forms and permits humans, by the aid of extrinsic stimuli, *to control their behavior from the outside.* The use of signs leads humans to a specific structure of behavior that breaks away from biological development and creates new forms of a culturally-based psychological process.

MAX BLACK
from *The Labyrinth of Language*

. . . The words a speaker uses in an utterance are one thing; the thought "behind the words" is another. The words may be adequate or inadequate to the thought; the speaker may wish to conceal at least part of his thought; and so on. It is natural, therefore, to ask about the relations between the two. Are they to be regarded as mutually independent, so that any thought might in theory be matched with any utterance? Or is the relation between the two closer and more intimate?

Before trying to offer even the crudest answers, it will be as well to raise some preliminary questions about the meaning of these large and imprecise questions. One way of understanding a question about the relation between one thing and another is in terms of their *causal* interactions. Taken in this way, the issue about the relations between thinking and speaking resembles a question about the relations between poverty and crime. We are then asking how far "thought" gives rise to speech and, still more interestingly, how far speech, in its turn, can causally influence thought. Some questions of this form will be considered in the next division of this chapter.

Another and more functional way of understanding the traffic between thinking and speaking concerns the *logical* relations between the two. Thus understood, our question resembles a question concerning the relations between a map and the terrain mapped. Indeed, it might plausibly be taken to be a special case of that question. A typical sub-question might then concern the possibility of "pure thought"—thought unexpressed in language or in any other symbolism. Again, we might wonder whether *thought* and *language,* however distinct, might not be "polar concepts" such as *husband* and *wife,* to take a much simpler analogue, providing complementary views of one and the same complex phenomenon. Such questions are quite distinct from those concerning causal influence, previously instanced.

So understood, the questions we have raised may seem somewhat remote from any practical interest. Yet our conception of the nature of language will be profoundly affected by any explicit or implicit stand we take on this matter of logical relationship. And so, less directly, will be our attitudes to such specific issues as the proper place of language teaching in education, the relative importance of textual studies in literature, the justification of propaganda, and much else.

Before embarking upon these troubled waters, we must linger a while longer to consider some duplicities of the key terms "thinking" and "thought." We can distinguish the following three, distinct but related, uses:

1. To refer to some ill-defined and vaguely delineated *process,* contrasted, for instance, with "hoping," "wishing," "day-dreaming," and other "mental processes." The word is used in this sense when we say, "I am thinking about what to do," or, perhaps, "I am still thinking about what you said." In such cases, there is, typically, no ready answer to the supplementary question, *What* are you thinking? We are dealing with what might be called a *non-specifying* use of "thinking."

2. Sometimes, however, we do use "thought" or its cognate, "thinking," to refer to a definite mental episode, occurring at some particular time. We say: "The thought flashed across my mind—'he's dead!' " or, "I was thinking to myself, 'That's a strange thing to say,' but of course I didn't say so." In such examples, "thought" and "thinking" may be said to be used in an *episodic* sense, the reference being to some definite mental episode or event in a particular speaker's biography. Such "episodic" thoughts, as here understood, will be true or false—will have "truth-value." (I am ignoring, at least for the time being, more amorphous mental episodes.)

3. Finally, we shall need to recognize a use of "thought" to pick out what might be called the *cognitive kernel* of certain remarks. We say "I think *that he will come*" or "I thought *that I saw a bear* (but I was mistaken)" or "We both agree *that he should be given another chance.*" In each of these cases, the "thought" in question is identified by a clause commencing with the word "that" (a "that-clause"). Here we have, in what might be called a *propositional* sense of "thought," something more abstract than thinking as a process or as an episode. A propositional thought, expressed by a that-clause (or in the form of a complete sentence) can be shared by more than one person. And a thought, in this sense, is internal to its expression: to ask a man who has said "It's four o'clock" whether he thought it was four o'clock when he said so, could only mean that we took him to have been mistaken; it is clearly not a substantive question as to whether his utterance was backed by an episode of thinking: his saying what he did counts, by convention, as his having the propositional thought in question.

Of the three senses now at our disposal, the second and third are the more clearly relevant, though in different ways, to our initial question about the logical relations between thought and speech. And any answer we give will obviously depend upon which of the senses we choose to emphasize. It is one thing to ask the question about a thought (propositional sense) already identified by its adequate verbal expression in the form of a that-clause. It is another when we are considering less precise, possibly confused or inchoate, thought-episodes. But in either case, we are dealing, for present purposes, with "thoughts" (in either sense) that *can be put into words.* If it makes sense to talk about "thoughts too deep for words" we must here regretfully decide to ignore them. (Which is not to deny that thoughts might be suitably expressed in some non-linguistic medium. But if they are, they are potentially expressible in language also.)

Two extreme positions, both much alive, in spite of their paradoxical flavor, will define the range of our own choice. The first is, approximately, an assertion of the complete separability of thought and its linguistic expression. A potential speaker can have a thought, it is claimed, before there is any question of how it is to be expressed: the relation between a thought and its outward manifestation is, in this respect, like the relation between a human body and its clothes. A body is what it is, quite independently of any suit that may cover it; and a thought is what it is, quite independently of its verbal dress. We may call this *the model of the garment.*

The second view flatly rejects this conception: to think of a "thought" as separable from its linguistic manifestation is as absurd as to imagine a human being without his body. Talk about a thought is just talk, from another perspective, about a certain kind of verbal complex. The relation between a thought and its verbal expression is like that between a melody and its embodiment in actual sounds: the same melody, transposed into different keys or played on different instruments, still retains its identity, but the idea of a melody separate from any acoustic representation is an absurdity. This might be called *the model of the melody.*

Thought is to speech as body is to garment; thought is to speech as melody to sound: which of these conceptions is the better? This is like asking whether it is better to think of men as animals or as spirits: they are both and neither, as we please. Here there is no question of some objectively certifiable allegation of fact, but rather of a more or less fruitful comparison. (And that is why I have spoken of the rival conceptions as "models.") The decision to be made is whether it conduces better to understanding and illumination, on the whole, to emphasize the analogy between language and a separable garment—or whether more insight is to be expected from stressing thought's likeness to something intrinsic to its expression, like a melody. We might hope, in the long run, for perspectives more adequate than either of these (and the reader may be reminded here of the variety of approaches outlined in the first chapter); but if we must choose now, the model of the melody is preferable to that of the garment. My reasons for saying so I shall now try to explain.

An examination of the vast literature concerning the nature of language will show that discussion of this subject has been dominated for at least 2,000 years by what I have been calling the model of the garment.

The picture of the function of speech that emerges is both simple and plausible. A speaker's thoughts, as I have said, are taken to be logically quite separate from the words in which he clothes them. Hence, in speaking, his task is to express those thoughts—or, as some writers would prefer to say now, to "encode" them—in adequate words. And the hearer's task is the reverse one of passing from the words he hears to thoughts corresponding as closely as possible to those of the original speaker (to "decode" the message). Successful communication involves this double transformation of thoughts into words, and words back again into thoughts.

If speech is regarded in this way, it is natural, though not essential, to regard the speaker's original thought as the *meaning* of his verbal message. Taking this further step, innumerable writers have adhered to a conception of "meanings in the mind"—meanings that have to be transformed into audible or visible substitutes for transmission to the mind of another.

Thus we find Aristotle saying:

> Spoken words are the *symbols of mental experience* and written words are the symbols of spoken words.

Locke says:

> ... words, in their primary or immediate signification, stand for nothing but *the ideas in the mind of him that uses them,* how imperfectly soever or carelessly those ideas are collected from the things which they are supposed to represent.

Similar ideas constantly recur in modern times. Collingwood says:

Understanding what some one says to you is thus attributing to him the idea which his words arouse in yourself . . .

And another modern philosopher of a different persuasion says:

Meanings are commonly conveyed by language; by series of ink-marks or of sounds. But it would at best be doubtful that meaning arises through communication or that verbal formulation is essential. Presumably the meanings to be expressed must *come before* the linguistic expression of them, however much the development of language may operate retroactively to modify the meanings entertained.

So it goes, in one text after another.

Thoughts "come before" the words in which they are clothed; words mean the speaker's thoughts that gave rise to them. A thorough examination of these important contentions would be impracticable here. I must confine myself to a few remarks that may help to explain why this dominant conception, so powerful for 2,000 years, is gradually losing its appeal.

Obviously, there must be some approximation to adequacy in a conception that has appealed for so long to so many diverse thinkers of the first rank. The common admonition to "Think before you speak!" implicitly testifies to the possibility of thinking *before* one speaks, and to the difference between speaking "thoughtlessly" or "realizing and meaning everything one says."

Nor need we suppose that the thought that sometimes precedes speech itself takes the form of silent speech, as if every speaker had to rehearse to himself what he then proceeded to expose in public. Even when we do soliloquize in this way, it is rare for complete grammatical sentences to be used; everybody has his own argot of truncated words, sketched phrases, kinesthetic and visual images.[1] Silent speech is idiosyncratic—a kind of mental shorthand barely intelligible to another. (Compare the indecipherability of the scrawled notes and symbols that a thinker will record for his own benefit.) We must also recognize the existence and importance of still less articulate mental episodes in which the thinker gropes for expression and is swayed by dimly perceived intimations of significance, or promising roads to solution.

To deny all this, or its relevance to formal expression, would be closing one's eyes to an entire range of fascinating experience. But it would be a serious conceptual error to suppose that such varied mental activity must precede or accompany speech; or to suppose that in the absence of such

---

[1] So far as I can trust my own introspection, thinking about the next move in a game of chess can take the form of a series of schematic images of possible positions, with the possible movements of the pieces appearing as imagined shifts in position. Verbal images appear to play almost no part. Yet it would be easy to *translate* this sequence of images into full sentences. A psychologist, himself a strong player, claims that "chess-thinking is typically non-verbal." But he does not deny that such thinking is in symbols. (Adrianus D. de Groot, *Thought and Choice in Chess,* Mouton, The Hague, 1965, p. 335.)

mental accompaniment, words lose their "life" and become meaningless; or that the meaning of words is to be sought in the "inner drama" played in the privacy of the speaker's mind.

It is, in the first place, preposterous to imagine that rapid speech is *always* accompanied by a parallel flow of mental images or "thoughts." A lecturer thoroughly familiar with his subject, an advocate skillfully developing an argument extempore, are prime examples of speakers who "mean what they say." Yet it would be altogether unplausible, as such speakers will confirm from their own introspection, to suppose that the flow of rapid speech is invariably accompanied by a parallel stream of "mental" events. Speech needs no mental correlate in order to be meaningful.

What is there to show, it may be asked, that the spoken words *are* meaningful, in a case where they are unaccompanied by the "mental drama"? Well, for one thing, there are the subsequent uses that the speaker can make of his utterance. When he can comment upon what he said, elaborate it, defend it against objections, cite illustrations, and so on, that is excellent evidence that he meant and understood what he said. It is also excellent evidence of *what* his meaning was. (Where such a process of defense, elaboration, application fails, there is sufficient evidence of the thoughtless or meaningless use of words.) The "life" of the words, we might say, is not in some supposed mental afflatus, but rather in the capacity of the particular utterance to interact with, and to provide a point of departure for, further symbolic activity.

Finally, a dogmatic attempt to locate meaning in some supposed feature of mental acts is practically useless and theoretically pernicious. To seek the meaning of words in something supposedly occurring in the privacy of the speaker's mind is pointless. For if, by some miracle of technology, we could have access to the verbal and other images in the speaker's mind, we should still have to *interpret* those images before we could grasp the meaning: a "private," mental language is still a *language*.[2] And if we succeeded in translating the private language into, say English, we should still be faced with the problem of understanding *that*. Renewed recourse to mental scrutiny would get us no further. (Which is of course not to deny the value of an author's commentary upon his own writing. But such commentary will be ineffective unless expressed in words that are intelligible to another.) Focusing upon fleeting images and thoughts in the mind will not reveal meaning, whether to ourselves or to our hearers. It may, however, serve the purpose of emphasizing the inadequacy of the words we have used and lead to a search for better expression.

[2] This point was clearly understood by medieval writers on language. "For medieval logicians this 'meaning' was a content of an individual mind, an inner utterance in an immaterial language: Ockham took this idea of mental language and its structure so seriously and so naively that he tries to determine which parts of speech, and which grammatical attributes like voice, case, and number, are to be found in the mental language." (P. T. Geach, *Reference and Generality*, Cornell University Press, Itahca, N. Y., 1962, p. 54.)

What is "theoretically pernicious" about this model is the support it gives to inclinations, always strong, to evade the difficult search for the meanings in words, in favor of an exploration of the never-never land of "mental life." Thus, instead of renewed attempts at a rich and imaginative understanding of the text before us, whether it be a casual utterance or a poem, we get speculative theories, usually impossible to verify, about "what is really going on" in the speaker's mind, or about the motives that led him to say what he did. And thus attention is diverted from what in the end really matters, the articulated expression of thought. Of course, I do not wish to deny the value, if tactfully used, of knowledge about the author's life, the provenance of his literary work, the circumstances of composition, and all the other information that is the staple of those who write about the background of literature. Nor do I underestimate the technical and other difficulties of the policy of staying close to the text and constantly returning to it after explorations of the "background."

I have been recommending here a conception of thought as *immanent* or indwelling in its adequate symbolic expression. (The model of the melody.) Whether it is as illuminating as I think, the reader must decide for himself, bearing in mind always the platitude that a model is only a model; and that no model can be a substitute for the hard work of delineating and responding to the meaning of actual "texts."

All thought, I have been arguing, strives toward symbolic and, ultimately, linguistic expression. Indeed, in the end, it is hardly possible to distinguish between thought and its verbal manifestation. A man is free to speak or not, as he pleases, free also to choose the words that satisfy him; yet the linguistic medium that he must use is "out there" and given, beyond his power to modify at will. However much the speaker may wish to express *his own* thought, he must make do with a social instrument, fashioned for other purposes than individual expression and often recalcitrant to personal desire. Hence the repeated revolts of great writers against the constraints and limitations of the language of their day. Those who write in the style of their fathers find it hard to avoid repeating their fathers' mistakes. Language, one might say, has a kind of inertia that limits the speaker's freedom to project a distinctive meaning; words, for all their flexibility, mean at any given time what they have come to mean through repeated use and the writer or speaker must do the best he can with these worn counters.[3]

Language constrains thought most plainly by the scope of what might be called the available vocabulary, the stock of words and phrases that will be

---

[3] How galling this will be must depend upon the speaker's interest in spontaneity: in highly conventional situations, like the initial salutation of a letter, conventional formulas are a convenience. Yet I have known a man who could not bring himself to write "Sincerely yours" and ended his letter with "Am I sincere? Of course!" (But this device could easily become an affectation.)

readily understood by the intended hearer or reader. Obsolescent or unfamiliar words like *conspue, subfusc,* or *irenic,* however vivid or appropriate, can only be used for special effects: a writer who indulges in too many of them will lose his audience. This working vocabulary, amounting to no more than a few thousand words in all, is, however, based upon a crude analysis and classification of experience. It registers, as it were, a lowest common denominator of response.

While the eye can distinguish millions of different shades (and specialists have an elegant scheme for analyzing the "color-solid" along the three dimensions of "hue," "intensity," and "saturation"), the simple color words of ordinary discourse are only a handful, in somewhat haphazard logical relations. Of course, a skilled writer can convey a vivid characterization of a particular shade, but he has to take special pains to do so, relying upon simile or other figures of speech. But to "work hard" much of the time defeats the purpose of communication. Even more obvious defects of the "available vocabulary" can be seen in the realm of feelings and sentiments, where we must make do, for the most part, with such crude labels as "jealousy," "hatred," or "love" to indicate an incomparably more varied and more complex set of resemblances, oppositions, and relationships.[4]

More insidious is the extent to which the use of familiar words or expressions commits speaker and hearer alike to the acceptance of dubious presuppositions. For the items in the "available vocabulary" of a given group at a given epoch typically embody far-reaching theories *about* the phenomena represented. For instance, to talk in the popular pseudo-Freudian jargon about "complexes," "repressions," and "unconscious motivations" is to accept, without examination, much dubious and unexamined psychological doctrine.

Behind such efforts as these, we can dimly discern and guess at more general influences exercised upon thought by the overall pattern of a given language. Here we approach a theme that has received much attention in this century.

Does the overall structure of a language channel the thoughts of its users in some far-reaching way? A number of distinguished thinkers have thought so. Some have gone so far as to claim that an entire metaphysics is embodied in a given language. Georg Christoph Lichtenberg said, "Our false philosophy is incorporated in the whole of language; we cannot reason without, so to speak, reasoning wrongly. We don't realize that to speak, no matter about what, is to philosophize." Similar views have been expressed by thinkers as powerful, though diverse in their views, as von Humboldt, Cassirer, and

---

[4] Can anything be done to improve the situation? Probably not much. The reductive pressures of daily intercourse are too strong to offer much hope for the introduction of more adequate language. The best that can be expected, on the whole, is a more general awareness of the crude simplifications of the common vocabulary—and a greater familiarity with the works in which the great poets and scientists, in their different ways, highlight the complexities of human experience.

Wittgenstein. The last was fond of saying that a given language is a "form of life."

Languages can differ very strikingly in their vocabularies and grammars. Hence, if a distinctive "philosophy" or world-view is associated with a given language, we should expect the corresponding "world-view" to vary widely from one culture to another. Many anthropologists, impressed by the great diversity of the ways in which various societies solve their problems, find this corollary congenial. It seems to confirm the widely held view that human societies somehow "construct" the world of social experience out of a relatively undifferentiated and unstructured continuum. The following remarks are typical:

> Any language is more than an instrument for the conveying of ideas, more even than an instrument for working upon the feelings of others and for self-expression. Every language is also a means of categorizing experience. What people think and feel, and how they report what they think and feel, is determined, to be sure, by their individual physiological state, by their personal history, and by what actually happens in the outside world. But it is *also determined by a factor which is often overlooked; namely, the pattern of linguistic habits which people have acquired as members of a particular society.* The events of the "real" world are never felt or reported as a machine would do it. There is a selection process and an interpretation in the very act of response. Some features of the external situation are highlighted; others are ignored or not fully discriminated.[5]

Even skeptical critics find this initially plausible. And there is an appealing romantic charm about the idea of freedom to respond to "reality" in a variety of styles, reflecting different, but perhaps equally valid, modes of thoughts and feelings. We are all "relativists" nowadays and belief in "universal laws of Reason" or absolutes of any sort is likely to be regarded as dogmatic.

For one thing, even a slight acquaintance with different languages confirms the suspicion that a language is more than a neutral reflection of some independently given "external world"—more like a distorting mirror than a sheet of unflawed glass. For instance, an English reader has the feeling, confirmed by experts, that the "world" somehow looks and feels different if one thinks and writes about it in Russian. (A shift of view that eludes even the best translators and makes foreign fiction sound neither authentically English —nor authentically anything else.) We are not surprised to be told that the Malay language is "poetical, metaphorical, happier with proverbs than with abstract constatations" in a way that is "entirely fitted to the needs of a people concerned with the concrete processes of everyday living—fishing,

[5] Clyde Kluckhohn and Dorothea Leighton, *The Navaho*, Harvard University Press, Cambridge, Mass., 1946, p.197. Italics added.

gathering fruit and coconuts, begetting children, lying in the sun."[6] Again, it seems altogether natural to learn that a classical language, such as Hebrew, offers a distinct resistance to its adaptation for the purposes of a modern society.[7]

But how are these vague, if stimulating, ideas about the "genius of a language" (to use an old-fashioned expression) to be rendered precise enough for verification? Is the "influence" of a language upon the thoughts and attitudes of its users to be ascribed to the distinctive nature of its vocabulary,[8] its commonplace expressions, the associations of "unconscious use," the tang and rhythm of ordinary speech, to syntactical structure? And how are we to tell? For provoking and controversial answers, I turn to the views of Benjamin Lee Whorf.

> . . . the background linguistic system (in other words, the grammar) of each language is not merely a reproducing instrument for voicing ideas but rather is itself the shaper of ideas, the program and guide for the individual's mental activity, for his analysis of impressions, for his synthesis of his mental stock in trade. Formulation of ideas is not an independent process, strictly rational in the old sense, but is part of a particular grammar, and differs, from slightly to greatly, between different grammars. We dissect nature along lines laid down by our native languages. The categories and types that we isolate from the world of phenomena we do not find there because they stare every observer in the face; on the contrary, the world is presented in a kaleidoscopic flux of impressions which has to be organized in our minds—and this means largely by the linguistic systems in our minds. We cut nature up,

[6] Anthony Burgess, *Language Made Plain,* English Universities Press, London, 1964, p. 167. But Burgess goes on to mention "A new world of words, bewildering to the peasant," based largely upon borrowings from Arabic, Portuguese, and English, introduced for commercial and administrative purposes. "Cultures" are rarely as uniform as the outsider is inclined to think, and imputed correlations between language and "world-view" are correspondingly precarious.

[7] See, for instance, the charming article, "Reflections on Two Languages" (*Midstream,* New York, vol. xii, no. 8, October, 1966), by Aharon Megged, a distinguished writer and native speaker of Hebrew. Comparing Hebrew with Yiddish, Megged ascribes the "resistance" of Hebrew to its powerful "aristocratic" associations with ritual and holiness. If the Israelis had chosen to speak Yiddish, their "modes of thought and behavior would be different." For "the structure of a Yiddish sentence, the manner of its pronunciation, the linguistic associations, the flavor of each individual word are so remote from Hebrew" (p. 36). Similarly, one might speculate about how different life would be in the United States if everyone spoke Spanish.

[8] Each language contains words especially hard to translate, that seem to embody some distinctive and central concept of the culture. Cf., for instance, *on* in Japanese (very roughly: an obligation, burdensome to receive, demanding a reciprocal and balancing moral transfer); or *philotimo* in Greek (very roughly, again: self-esteem).

organize it into concepts, and ascribe significances as we do, largely because we are parties to an agreement to organize it in this way—an agreement that holds throughout our speech community and is codified in
the patterns of our language. The agreement is, of course, an implicit and
unstated one, BUT ITS TERMS ARE ABSOLUTELY OBLIGATORY; we cannot talk at
all except by subscribing to the organization and classification of data
which the agreement decrees.[9]

The program formulated here would have little interest but for the attempts that Whorf made to apply it to specific American Indian languages,
and notably to Hopi.[10] Let us see how the Hopi think about the universe,
according to Whorf. They do not emphasize temporal relations, as Europeans
do; nor do they make our familiar distinctions between time and space; instead they think in terms of two grand categories (which Whorf labels MANI-
FESTING and MANIFESTED), that may be roughly conceived as "subjective" and
"objective." The subjective realm, that embraces the as yet unrealized future,
is conceived as a spiritual domain of "burgeoning" and "fermenting" activity,
embracing natural and animal phenomena as well as human behavior; the
"objective" realm consists, as it were, of the unchanging deposit, in the past
and present, of this universal psychic activity. (Perhaps the relation between
life and history is conceived on the model of a potter's design-in-the-head
and the unchanging artifact that he ultimately produces? If all this seems
unsatisfyingly vague to the reader, he must be referred to Whorf's own
writings for further detail.) The Hopi, we are told, think of reality mainly
as composed of *events*, eschewing the emphasis upon subject and predicate
built into Indo-European language and thought. Objectively, events are identified by such features as outlines, colors, and types of movement; subjec-
tively as "the expression of invisible intensity factors, on which depend their
stability and persistence, or their fugitiveness and proclivities."[11]

Even in so crude a summary of the more detailed and more suggestive
accounts supplied by Whorf and other anthropologists, a sympathetic reader
may darkly discern unfamiliar ways of patterning the universe, remote from
our own familiar distinctions between past, present, and future, between
"mental" and "physical"—and the like. But it is hard for even the most sympathetic reader to know how deeply such sophisticated renderings of a "world-

[9] John B. Carroll, ed., *Language, Thought and Reality: Selected Writings of Benjamin
Lee Whorf,* The M. I. T. Press, Cambridge, Mass., 1956, pp. 212–214. Capitals in original.

[10] Benjamin Lee Whorf (1897-1941) was a greatly gifted amateur linguist, described
by those who knew him as a "near-genius," by profession an engineer specializing in fire
prevention, by avocation a linguist, anthropologist, and philosopher of language. His theories about the Hopi world-view were almost exclusively based upon information supplied
by a single speaker of Hopi living in New York. (He paid a short visit to the Arizona Hopi
reservation later.) Whorf undoubtedly achieved an extraordinary *tour de force* in reconstructing, on so narrow a basis, an interpretation of Hopi thought and culture that competent experts have praised for its faithfulness and insight.

[11] In Carroll, *Whorf,* p. 147.

view" really influence the thought ways of philosophically unsophisticated users of the language. (How many English speakers recognize the shards of Aristotelian metaphysics preserved in such words as "essence," "specific," "substance," "entity," and the like?) And when we come to the supposed linguistic "reflections" of the delineated "world-view," the course of the argument becomes dubious indeed. Writers who share Whorf's general views about the relations between grammar and culture are apt to draw inferences from selected grammatical features, emphasizing some as significant while neglecting others as irrelevant. But no firm criterion has ever been offered for such discrimination. One anthropologist, for instance, will discover the notion of the "given as undifferentiated content"[12] built into certain general features of the nouns of a given language. The Wintu use the same word for *red, redness,* and *red-mess;* "the care which we bestow on the distinction of number is lavished by the Wintu on the distinction between particular and generic,"[13] and this distinction, in turn, is regarded by them as "subjective." Well, this interesting way of handling ultimate categories may indeed be characteristic of Wintu thought, for all that any outsider can tell; but it may be doubted whether it would ever have been discovered as a "reflection" in their grammar if the theorist had not already known what he expected to find. So long as communication between members of radically different cultures remains as crude as it is apt to be at best,[14] the perception of patterns of thought embodied in the formal structure of a language will remain a controversial and speculative exercise. And even if some reliable procedures for conducting this kind of investigation were to be evolved, it would be a further and a very difficult step to argue from such formal features to the existence of causal influence upon the thought habits of the language users. (The existence of diverse philosophical systems, all expressed with equal facility in such a language as English or German, must cast doubt upon the possibility of any *simple* causal relation between grammar and thought.)

On the whole, the verdict of competent anthropologists and linguists upon Whorf's suggestive ideas is that until some other "near-genius," with a talent for exact thought, succeeds in deriving some reasonably precise hypotheses, there is little scope for profitable argument.

[12] Dorothy Lee, "Linguistic Reflection of Wintu Thought," in her *Freedom and Culture,* Prentice-Hall, Inc., Englewood Cliffs, N.J., 1959, p. 122.

[13] Lee, p. 122.

[14] "If the Wintu offers me an English word in translation for a Wintu one, I rarely have any way of knowing exactly what the word means to him. When he says that *watca* is to *weep,* for example, is he, like me, thinking of the whole kinesthetic activity with all its emotional implications, or is he merely concerned with the sound of keening, as I think he is?" (Lee, p. 126) (And here one may wonder what Miss Lee means by "keening"!) Yet this frank recognition of limitation is immediately followed by a sentence which runs: "Whenever I find a group of words derived from the same root, *I can clearly see* that they point to a preoccupation with form alone" (italics added). What is thus "clearly seen" by some will seem murky enough to others.

I. A. RICHARDS
from "Functions and Factors of Language"

Messages are generated by contexts; they are conveyed by signals. Messages are living. They are animated instances of meaning, determinations from the context field; the signals which convey them are dead. My thinking, doubting, wondering at this moment is living activity; so is the nerve-muscle-joint process guiding my pen as I compose my message. But the motions of the pen itself are inanimate, as are the configurations its point is tracing on the paper, the signals. The typist, the printer, the library, etc. put the page before you. As you read the inanimate lines of print, a living activity of thinking, doubting, wondering—despairing perhaps—arises in you. That is the Message coming into being again. It was not in the pen or on the page. So too with a speaker: his gestures, postures facial expressions, actions and the rest, together with what his voice does in the sound wave channel—anything that videotape can take down: all that is signal, merely. Not until it is interpreted by some living recipient does anything that should be called the Message appear. It is essential to a Message that what forms in the Addressee or other recipient should be of the same order of being with what has formed in the Addresser. He may get it all wrong (and often does) but there is an IT. The two apparitions are both meanings. But a sound track and a system of meanings are not things of a sort, able to agree or disagree.

ALFRED NORTH WHITEHEAD
"Expression"

This lecture is concerned with various ideas involved in the notion of Expression. The more general notion of Importance is presupposed by Expression. Something is to be diffused throughout the environment which will make a difference. But there is a distinction between the two notions. Importance is primarily monistic in its reference to the Universe. Importance, limited to a finite individual occasion, ceases to be important. In some sense or other, Importance is derived from the immanence of infinitude in the finite.

But Expression is founded on the finite occasion. It is the activity of finititude impressing itself on its environment. Thus it has its origin in the finite; and it represents the immanence of the finite in the multitude of its fellows beyond itself. The two together, namely Importance and Expression, are witnesses both to the monistic aspect of the universe and to its pluralistic character. Importance passes from the World as one to the World as many; whereas, Expression is the gift from the World as many to the World as one.

Selection belongs to expression. A mood of the finite thing conditions the environment. There is an active entity which fashions its own perspective, implanted on the world around. The laws of nature are large average effects which reign impersonally. Whereas, there is nothing average about expression. It is essentially individual. In so far as an average dominates, expression fades.

Expression is the diffusion, in the environment, of something initially entertained in the experience of the expressor. No conscious determination is necessarily involved; only the impulse to diffuse. This urge is one of the simplest characteristics of animal nature. It is the most fundamental evidence of our presupposition of the world without.

In fact, the world beyond is so intimately entwined in our own natures that unconsciously we identify our more vivid perspectives of it with ourselves. For example, our bodies lie beyond our own individual existence. And yet they are part of it. We think of ourselves as so intimately entwined in bodily life that a man is a complex unity—body and mind. But the body is part of the external world, continuous with it. In fact, it is just as much part of nature as anything else there—a river, or a mountain, or a cloud. Also, if we are fussily exact we cannot define where a body begins and where external nature ends.

Consider one definite molecule. It is part of nature. It has moved about for millions of years. Perhaps it started from a distant nebula. It enters the body; it may be as a factor in some edible vegetable; or it passes into the lungs as part of the air. At what exact point as it enters the mouth, or as it is absorbed through the skin, is it part of the body? At what exact moment, later on, does it cease to be part of the body? Exactness is out of the question. It can only be obtained by some trivial convention.

Thus we arrive at this definition of our bodies: The Human Body is that region of the world which is the primary field of human expression.

For example, anger issues into bodily excitements, which are then publicized in the form of appropriate language, or in other modes of violent action. We can leave it to the physiologists, in the various departments of that science, to analyze the special sorts of bodily functioning thus elicited. Philosophy should refrain from trespassing upon specialist investigations. Its business is to point out fields for research. Some fields remain untilled for centuries. The fruitful initiation is absent, or perhaps interest has never concentrated upon them.

In the present instance, we have defined an animal body—for the higher grade of animals— and have indicated the sort of researches required. Of course, mankind has been engaged on this job for some thousands of years, with some lack of comprehension of its full import. It is the business of philosophy to elicit this consciousness; and then, to coordinate the results of all such specialist enquiries.

So far, we have been considering the bodies of animals with dominant centers of feeling and of expression. We can now enlarge the definition so as to include all living bodies, animal and vegetable:

Wherever there is a region of nature which is itself the primary field of the expressions issuing from each of its parts, that region is alive.

In this second definition, the phrase "expressions issuing from each of its parts" has been substituted for the phrase "human expression," as used previously. The new definition is wider than the former by extending beyond human beings, and beyond the higher animals. Also it will be noticed that these definitions involve the direct negation of any extreme form of Behaviorism. In such behavioristic doctrines, "importance" and "expression" must be banished and can never be intelligently employed. A consistent behaviorist cannot feel it important to refute my statements. He can only behave.

There are two sides to an animal body of the higher type, and so far we have only developed one of them. The second, and wider definition enables us to find the distinction between vegetation and animal life. This distinction, like others, refuses to be pushed to meticulous exactness. In the animal, there is the one experience expressing itself throughout the animal body. But this is only half the tale.

The other half of the tale is that the body is composed of various centers of experience imposing the expression of themselves on each other. Feeling (in the sense here used), or prehension, is the reception of expressions. Thus the animal body is composed of entities, which are mutually expressing and feeling. Expressions are the data for feeling diffused in the environment; and a living body is a peculiarly close adjustment of these two sides of experience, namely, expression and feeling. By reason of this organization, an adjusted variety of feelings is produced in that supreme entity which is one animal considered as one experiencing subject.

Thus the one animal, and the various parts of its body considered as themselves centers of experience, are in one sense on a level. Namely, they are centers of experience expressing themselves vividly to each other, and obtaining their own feelings mainly by reason of such mutual expressions.

In another sense, the animal as one center of experience is on a higher level than its other bodily centers. For these subordinate centers are specialists. They only receive restricted types of emotional feeling, and are impervious beyond such types. Throughout the body there is a complex coordination of a vast variety of emotional types. The bodily organization is such that the unity of feeling, which is the one animal as a sentient being, receives its complex variety of experience from these bodily activities. Thus the combined data for feeling in the animal center are on a higher level than are the corresponding data for its other bodily centers.

In the case of vegetables we find bodily organizations which decisively lack any one center of experience with a higher complexity either of expressions received or of inborn data. A vegetable is a democracy; an animal is dominated by one, or more, centers of experience. But such domination is limited, very strictly limited. The expressions of the central leader are relevant to that leader's reception of data from the body.

Thus an animal body exhibits the limited domination of at least one of its component activities of expression. If the dominant activity be severed from the rest of the body, the whole coordination collapses, and the animal dies. Whereas in the case of the vegetable, the democracy can be subdivided into minor democracies which easily survive without much apparent loss of functional expression.

It is evident that our statement is oversimplified. In the first place, the distinction between animals and vegetables is not sharp cut. Some traces of dominance can be observed in vegetables, and some traces of democratic independence can be found in animals. For example, portions of an animal body preserve their living activities when severed from the main body. But there is failure in variety of energy and in survival power. Yet allowing for such failure, the vegetable characteristics of equality and independence do manifest themselves. Thus ordinary vegetation and the higher animals represent extremes in the bewildering variety of bodily formations which we term "living things."

Then we have neglected the differentiation of functions which are to be found alike in vegetables and animals. In the case of the flora, there are the roots, and the branches, and the leaves, and the flowers, and the seeds—all obvious to common inspection. And the detailed observations of botanists supplement these blatant examples of differentiation by a hundred other functional activities which constitute the physiology of plant life.

When we turn to the animal body, the notion of the sole domination of the directing experience requires limitation. There are subordinate agencies which have essential control of the bodily functioning. The heart is one example among many others. The activities of the heart are necessary to the bodily survival, in a way that contrasts with the feet. A foot can be severed with slight damage to the internal functioning; the heart is essential. Thus an animal body in its highest examples is more analogous to a feudal society, with its one overlord.

This final unity of animal intelligence is also the organ of reaction to novel situations, and is the organ introducing the requisite novelty of reaction. Finally, the overlord tends to relapse into the conventionality of routine imposed upon the subordinate governors, such as the heart. Animal life can face conventional novelties with conventional devices. But the governing principle lacks large power for the sudden introduction of any major novelty.

The bodies of the higher animals have some resemblance to a complex society of insects, such as ants. But the individual insects seem to have more power of adaptation to their problems than does the community as a whole.

The opposite holds in the case of animals. For example, an intelligent dog has more power of adaptation to new modes of life than has its heart, as it functions in the animal body. The dog can be trained, but its heart must go its own way within very close limits.

When we come to mankind, nature seems to have burst through another of its boundaries. The central activity of enjoyment and expression has assumed a reversal in the importance of its diverse functionings. The conceptual entertainment of unrealized possibility becomes a major factor in human mentality. In this way outrageous novelty is introduced, sometimes beatified, sometimes damned, and sometimes literally patented or protected by copyright. The definition of mankind is that in this genus of animals the central activity has been developed on the side of its relationship to novelty. This relationship is two-fold. There is the novelty received from the aggregate diversities of bodily expressions. Such novelty requires decision as to its reduction to coherence of expression.

Again there is the introduction of novelty of feeling by the entertainment of unexpressed possibilities. This second side is the enlargement of the conceptual experience of mankind. The characterization of this conceptual feeling is the sense of what might be and of what might have been. It is the entertainment of the alternative. In its highest development, this becomes the entertainment of the Ideal. It emphasizes the sense of Importance. . . . And this sense exhibits itself in various species, such as, the sense of morality, the mystic sense of religion, the sense of that delicacy of adjustment which is beauty, the sense of necessity for mutual connection which is understanding, and the sense of discrimination of each factor which is consciousness.

Also it is the nature of feeling to pass into expression. Thus the expression of these various feelings produces the history of mankind as distinct from the narrative of animal behaviors. History is the record of the expressions of feelings peculiar to humanity.

There is, however, every gradation of transition between animals and men. In animals we can see emotional feeling, dominantly derived from bodily functions, and yet tinged with purposes, hopes, and expression derived from conceptual functioning. In mankind, the dominant dependence on bodily functioning seems still there. And yet the life of a human being receives its worth, its importance, from the way in which unrealized ideals shape its purposes and tinge its actions. The distinction between men and animals is in one sense only a difference in degree. But the extent of the degree makes all the difference. The Rubicon has been crossed.

Thus in nature we find four types of aggregations of actualities: the lowest is the non-living aggregation, in which mutual influence is predominantly of a formal character expressible in formal sciences, such as mathematics. The inorganic is dominated by the average. It lacks individual expression in its parts. Their flashes of selection (if any) are sporadic and ineffective. Its parts merely transmit average expressions; and thus the structure survives. For the average is always there, stifling individuality.

The vegetable grade exhibits a democracy of purposeful influences issuing from its parts. The predominant aim within the organism is survival for its own coordinated individual expressiveness. This expressiveness has a large average character. But the nature of this average is dominated by the intricacies of its own bodily formation. It has added coordinated, organic individuality to the impersonal average formality of inorganic nature. What is merely latent potentiality in lifeless matter has awakened into some realization in the vegetable. But in each instance of vegetation, the total bodily organism strictly limits the individuality of expression in the parts.

The animal grade includes at least one central actuality, supported by the intricacy of bodily functioning. Purposes transcending (however faintly) the mere aim at survival are exhibited. For animal life the concept of importance, in some of its many differentiations, has a real relevance. The human grade of animal life immensely extends this concept, and thereby introduces novelty of functioning as essential for varieties of importance. Thus morals and religion arise as aspects of this human impetus towards the best in each occasion. Morals can be discerned in the higher animals; but not religion. Morality emphasizes the detailed occasion; while religion emphasizes the unity of ideal inherent in the universe.

In every grade of social aggregation, from a nonliving material society up to a human body, there is the necessity for expression. It is by reason of average expression, and of average reception, that the average activities of merely material bodies are restrained into conformity with the reigning laws of nature. It is by reason of individual expression and reception that the human body exhibits activities expressive of the intimate feelings, emotional and purposeful, of the one human person.

These bodily activities are very various and intensely selective. An angry man, except when emotion has swamped other feelings, does not usually shake his fist at the universe in general. He makes a selection and knocks his neighbor down. Whereas a piece of rock impartially attracts the universe according to the law of gravitation.

The impartiality of physical science is the reason for its failure as the sole interpreter of animal behavior. It is true that the rock falls on one special patch of earth. This happens, because the universe in that neighborhood is exemplifying one particular solution of a differential equation. The fist of the man is directed by emotion seeking a novel feature in the universe, namely, the collapse of his opponent. In the case of the rock, the formalities predominate. In the case of the man, explanation must seek the individual satisfactions. These enjoyments are constrained by formalities, but in proportion to their intensities they pass beyond them, and introduce individual expression.

Consciousness is the first example of the selectiveness of enjoyment in the higher animals. It arises from expression coordinating the activities of physiological functionings. There is a baseless notion that we consciously observe those activities of nature which are dominant in our neighborhood.

The exact opposite is the case. The animal consciousness does not easily discriminate its dependence on detailed bodily functioning. Such discrimination is usually a sign of illness. When we observe the functionings of our viscera, something has gone wrong. We take the infinite complexity of our bodies for granted.

The first principle of epistemology should be that the changeable, shifting aspects of our relations to nature are the primary topics for conscious observation. This is only common sense; for something can be done about them. The organic permanences survive by their own momentum: our hearts beat, our lungs absorb air, our blood circulates, our stomachs digest. It requires advanced thought to fix attention on such fundamental operations.

The higher animals have developed superficial relationships to nature, such as eyesight, hearing, smell, and taste. Also such connections are alterable in proportion to their high-grade character. For example, we have only got to shut our eyes, and visual experience has vanished. We can block our ears, and there is no hearing.

The experiences on which accurate science bases itself are completely superficial. The blind and the deaf are capable of the ultimate greatness of human life. They are deprived of its walking-sticks. The traffic-lights on the highways are useful for the accomplishment of modern purposes. And yet there have been great civilizations without motor-cars, and without traffic-lights.

But though any one of these sense-experiences is non-essential to the existence of the organism, the whole group is quite essential for the development of the higher forms of animal life. Mankind and the animals with analogous abilities are distinguished by their capacity for the introduction of novelty. This requires a conceptual power which can imagine, and a practical power which can effect. The role of sense-experiences consists in the fact that they are manageable.

The animals evolved and emphasized the superficial aspects of their connexity with nature, and thus obtained a manageable grip upon the world. The central organism which is the soul of a man is mainly concerned with the trivialities of human existence. It does not easily meditate upon the activities of fundamental bodily functions. Instead of fixing attention on the bodily digestion of vegetable food, it catches the gleam of sunlight as it falls on the foliage. It nurtures poetry. Men are the children of the Universe, with foolish enterprises and irrational hopes. A tree sticks to its business of mere survival; and so does an oyster with some minor divergencies. In this way, the life-aim at survival is modified into the human aim at survival for diversified worthwhile experience.

The pitfall of philosophy is exclusive concentration on these manageable relationships, to the neglect of the underlying necessities of nature. Thus thinkers repudiate our intimate vague experiences in favor of a mere play of distinct sensations, coupled with a fable about underlying reality. I am now pleading that our whole experience is composed out of our relationships to the rest of things, and of the formation of new relationships constitutive of things to come. The present receives the past and builds the future. But there are grades of permanence and of compulsive stability.

During many generations there has been an attempt to explain our ultimate insights as merely interpretive of sense-impressions. Indeed this school of thought can trace itself back to Epicurus. It can appeal to some phrases of Plato. I suggest to you that this basis for philosophic understanding is analogous to an endeavor to elucidate the sociology of modern civilization as wholly derivative from the traffic-signals on the main roads. The motions of the cars are conditioned by these signals. But the signals are not the reasons for the traffic. Common sense supplies this conclusion, so overwhelmingly that illustration is unnecessary.

It is this direct insight, vague as to detail and yet the basis of all rationality, that has been denied by the prevalent epistemology of the preceding century. Interest and importance are the primary reasons for the effort after exact discrimination of sense-data. The traffic-signals are the outcome of the traffic.

Importance generates interest. Interest leads to discrimination. In this way, interest is increased; and the two factors, interest and discrimination, stimulate each other. Finally consciousness develops, gradually and fitfully; and it becomes another agent of stimulation.

In this lecture, the dominant topic is Expression. Accordingly, we now pass to the outstanding example of the way in which mankind has fabricated its manageable connections with the world into a means of expression. Language is the triumph of human ingenuity, surpassing even the intricacies of modern technology. It tells of widespread intelligence, sustained throughout scores of thousands of years. It is interesting that from the alternatives, sight and sound, sound was the medium first developed. There might have been a language of gesticulation. Indeed, there is a trace of it. But the weak point of gesticulation is that one cannot do much else while indulging in it. The advantage of sound is that the limbs are left free while we produce it.

But there is a deeper reason for the unconscious recourse to sound-production. Hands and arms constitute the more unnecessary parts of the body. We can do without them. They do not excite the intimacies of bodily existence. Whereas in the production of sound, the lungs and throat are brought into play. So that in speech, while a superficial, manageable expression is diffused, yet the sense of the vague intimacies of organic existence is also excited. Thus voice-produced sound is a natural symbol for the deep experiences of organic existence.

This sense of reality is of great importance for the effectiveness of symbolism. Personal interviews carry more weight than gramophone records. What an economy could be achieved if the Faculties of Colleges could be replaced by fifty gramophones and a few thousand records! Indeed, we might have expected that in the sixteenth century printed books would have replaced universities. On the contrary, the sixteenth and seventeenth centuries were an active period in the development of educational foundations. The sense of reality can never be adequately sustained amidst mere sensa, either of sound or sight. The connexity of existence is of the essence of understanding.

Language has two functions. It is converse with another, and it is converse with oneself. The latter function is too often overlooked, so we will consider it first. Language is expression from one's past into one's present. It is the reproduction in the present of sensa which have intimate association with the realities of the past. Thus the experience of the past is rendered distinct in the present, with a distinctness borrowed from the well-defined sensa. In this way, an articulated memory is the gift of language, considered as an expression from oneself in the past to oneself in the present.

Again by the aid of a common language, the fragmentary past experiences of the auditor, as enshrined in words, can be recombined into a novel imaginative experience by the reception of the coherent sentences of the speaker. Thus in both functions of language the immediate imaginative experience is enormously increased, and is stamped with a sense of realization, or of possible realization.

When we examine the content of language, that is to say, the experiences which it symbolizes, it is remarkable how largely it points away from the abstractions of high grade sensa. Its meaning presupposes the concrete relations of real events happening and issuing from each other. What Descartes, in his *Meditations,* terms a "Realitas Objectiva" clings to most sentences, especially to those recording the simpler experiences.

Consider, for example, the homely illustration, used earlier in this lecture, of the angry man who knocks his neighbor down. We each of us frame a pictorial imagination of such a scene. But the flux of imagined sensa is not of the essence of our thought. The event may have generated sensory schemes in a thousand ways. It may have happened by day, or by night. It may have happened in the street, or in a room. Every variety of attitudes for victor and for vanquished is indifferent. Yet amid all this ambiguity of sensa, the stubborn flux of events is asserted, that the fist of the angry man completely upset the stable functioning of his victim's body. It is not a flux of sensa which is asserted, but a bodily collapse as the result of the expressiveness of the angry man.

Also the anger of the man undoubtedly affected the functioning of his own body. A careful physiological examination with a microscope could have yielded many visual sensa to an observer! Again, consider the variety of sensory pictures which are aroused by the notion of one man knocking another down. What is it that binds them together? In themselves, they are merely different compositions of visual sensa. Their unity consists in the type of connected process in the world that they suggest.

Deserting this special example, different sensory experiences derived from the same action have a unity, namely, in the identity of the action. The accounts may be in different languages and may fasten upon different transitions of visual or auditory sensa; and yet they refer to the same action. Also the action may not be purely physical. Heroism, and courage, and love, and hatred are possible characteristics of things that happen.

The essence of language is that it utilizes those elements in experience most easily abstracted for conscious entertainment, and most easily reproduced in experience. By the long usage of humanity, these elements are associated with their meanings which embrace a large variety of human experiences. Each language embalms a historic tradition. Each language is the civilization of expression in the social systems which use it. Language is the systemization of expression.

Of all the ways of expressing thought, beyond question language is the most important. It has been held even that language is thought, and that thought is language. Thus a sentence is the thought. There are many learned works in which this doctrine is tacitly presupposed; and in not a few it is explicitly stated.

If this extreme doctrine of language be adopted, it is difficult to understand how translation from language to language, or within the same language between alternative sentences, is possible. If the sentence is the thought, then another sentence is another thought. It is true that no translation is perfect. But how can the success of imperfection be achieved when not a word, or a syllable, or an order of succession is the same. If you appeal to grammar, you are appealing to a meaning which lies behind words, syllables, and orders of succession. Some of us struggle to find words to express our ideas. If the words and their order together constitute the ideas, how does the struggle arise? We should then be struggling to obtain ideas; whereas we are conscious of ideas verbally unexpressed.

Let it be admitted then that language is not the essence of thought. But this conclusion must be carefully limited. Apart from language, the retention of thought, the easy recall of thought, the interweaving of thought into higher complexity, the communication of thought, are all gravely limited. Human civilization is an outgrowth of language, and language is the product of advancing civilization. Freedom of thought is made possible by language: we are thereby released from complete bondage to the immediacies of mood and circumstance. It is no accident that the Athenians from whom we derive our Western notions of freedom enjoyed the use of a language supreme for its delicate variety.

The denial that language is of the essence of thought is not the assertion that thought is possible apart from the other activities coordinated with it. Such activities may be termed the expression of thought. When these activities satisfy certain conditions, they are termed a language. The whole topic of these lectures is the discussion of the interdependence of thought and its expressive activities.

Such activities, emotional and physical, are older than thought. They existed in our ancestors when thought slumbered in embryo. Thought is the outcome of its own concurrent activities; and having thus arrived upon the scene, it modifies and adapts them. The notion of pure thought in abstraction from all expression is a figment of the learned world. A thought is a tremendous mode of excitement. Like a stone thrown into a pond it disturbs the whole surface of our being But this image is inadequate. For we should conceive the ripples as effective in the creation of the plunge of the stone into the water. The ripples release the thought, and the thought augments and distorts the ripples. In order to understand the essence of thought we must study its relation to the ripples amid which it emerges.

Nevertheless, putting aside these refinements as to the origins and effects of thought, language, as commonly understood in the most simple-minded way, stands out as the habitual effect of thought, and the habitual revelation of thought. In order to understand the modes of thought we must endeavor to recall the psychology which has produced the civilization of language—or, if you prefer to invert the expression, the language of civilization.

The first point to notice is that we now employ two distinct types of language, namely, the language of sound and the language of sight. There is speech, and there is writing. The language of writing is very modern. Its history extends for less than ten thousand years, even if we allow for the faint anticipations of writing in the primitive pictures. But writing as an effective instrument of thought, with widespread influence, may be given about five or six thousand years at the most.

Writing as a factor in human experience is comparable to the steam-engine. It is important, modern, and artificial. Speech is as old as human nature itself. It is one of the primary factors constituting human nature. We must not exaggerate. It is now possible to elicit the full stretch of human experience by other devices when speech in exceptional instances is denied. But speech, developing as a general social acquirement, was one leading creative factor in the uprise of humanity. Speech is human nature itself, with none of the artificiality of written language.

Finally, we now so habitually intermingle writing and speech in our daily experience that, when we discuss language, we hardly know whether we refer to speech, or to writing, or to the mixture of both. But this final mixture is very modern. About five hundred years ago, only a small minority could read —at least among the European races. That is one great reason for the symbolism of religion, and for the pictorial signs of inns and of shops. The armorial bearings of great nobles were a substitute for writing. The effect of writing on the psychology of language is a neglected chapter in the history of civilization.

Speech, in its embryonic stage as exemplified in animal and human behavior, varies between emotional expression and signalling. In the course of such variation it rapidly becomes a mixture of both. Throughout its most elaborate developments, speech retains these three characterizations, namely, emotional expression, signalling, and interfusion of the two. And yet somehow in the intellectualized language of advanced civilization, these characteristics seem to fade into the background. They suggest something which has lost its dominating position. We cannot understand modes of thought in the recent civilizations of the last thirty centuries unless we attend to this subtle change in the function of language. The presuppositions of language are various.

Language arose with a dominating reference to an immediate situation. Whether it was signal or expression, above all things it was *this* reaction to *that* situation in *this* environment. In the origin of language the particularity of the immediate present was an outstanding element in the meaning conveyed. The genus "bird" remained in the background of undiscerned meaning; even these particular birds on some other occasion were but dimly sensed. What language primarily conveyed was the direction of attention to these birds, here, now, amid these surroundings.

Language has gradually achieved the abstraction of its meanings from the presupposition of any particular environment. The fact that the French dictionary is published in Paris, at a definite date, is irrelevant to the meanings of the words as explained in the dictionary. The French equivalent to the English word "green," means just "green," whatever be the state of Europe, or of the planetary system. "Green" is "green," and there is the end of it. There is nothing more to be said, when you once understand the word in reference to its meaning.

Of course, we are much more civilized than our ancestors who could merely think of green in reference to some particular spring morning. There can be no doubt about our increased powers of thought, of analysis, of recollection, and of conjecture. We cannot congratulate ourselves too warmly on the fact that we are born among people who can talk about green in abstraction from springtime. But at this point we must remember the warning— Nothing too much.

So long as language is predominantly speech, the reference to some particularity of environment is overwhelming. Consider the simple phrase "a warm day." In a book, as interpreted by a standard dictionary, the words have a generalized meaning which refers to the rotation of the earth, the existence of the sun, and the scientific doctrine of temperature. Now put aside the dictionary, and forget all scraps of science. Then with this abstraction from learning, the experience indicated by the ejaculation "a warm day" is very different for speakers in Texas, or on the coast of England bordering on the North Sea. And yet there is an identity of meaning. Nothing too much.

We have to understand language as conveying the identities on which knowledge is based, and as presupposing the particularity of reference to the environment which is the essence of existence. Spoken language is immersed in the immediacy of social intercourse. Written language lies hidden in a volume, to be opened and read at diverse times and in diverse places, in abstraction from insistent surroundings. But a book can be read aloud. Here we find an instance of the fusion of writing and speech. Reading aloud is an art, and the reader makes a great difference. The immediacy of the environment then enters into the abstraction of writing.

The abstraction, inherent in the development of language, has its dangers. It leads away from the realities of the immediate world. Apart from a balanced emphasis, it ends in the triviality of quick-witted people. And yet, for all its dangers, this abstraction is responsible for the final uprise of civilization. It gives expression to the conceptual experiences, latent throughout nature, although kept under by vast conformity to average matter-of-fact. In mankind, these conceptual experiences are coordinated, and express themselves throughout their environment. This coordination has two aspects, aesthetic and logical. . . .

In conclusion, it is time to sum up what I have been saying this afternoon. This lecture is nothing else than a modern rendering of the oldest of civilized reflections on the development of the Universe as seen from the perspective of life on this earth. In comparing modern thought with ancient records, we must remember the difficulties of translation, and the difficulties of any thinker battling with the verbal expression of thought which penetrates below the ordinary usages of the market place. For instance, how differently would Aristotle's metaphysical reflections read if we persisted in translating one of his metaphysical key-words by the English term "wood," and also insisted on giving the most literal meaning to that word.[1] There is evidence that three thousand years ago there were deep thinkers, enmeshed as to their imaginations in the trivial modes of presentation belonging to their own days.

But we can discern in the records, which have been edited and re-edited by unimaginative scribes, the notion of the evolution of the universe as viewed from the perspective of life on this earth. We can discern the classification, involving the large physical grades, the grades of vegetation and of animal life, the final rise to human life.

We can also discern the notion of the interweaving of language with the rise of human experience, in the naive, childish account of the naming of things. In fact, the whole ancient account is simple-minded in the extreme. And yet the pretentious generalities of the modern rendering do not attain much more than an endeavor to avoid the over-sharp divisions between the various stages, and the excessive simplification of the agencies involved.

This lecture has been written in terms of immanence, and in terms of action and re-action. Its final conclusion respecting human nature is that the mentality of mankind and the language of mankind created each other. If we like to assume the rise of language as a given fact, then it is not going too far to say that the souls of men are the gift from language to mankind.

The account of the sixth day should be written, He gave them speech, and they became souls.

---

[1] The Greek word *hylē* means wood, forest, firewood, literally; by extension, it means stuff, matter, material.

W. H. AUDEN
"The True Word Twisted by Misuse and Magic"

Our principal enemies of the True Word are two: the Idle Word and the Black Magician.

He who tells a deliberate lie is aware of what he is doing; lying may corrupt his heart but not his intellect or the language in which he lies. But we corrupt our hearts, our intellects and our language when we use words for purposes to which the judgment true/or/false is irrelevant. We can, for instance, speak, not because we have anything we believe it important to say, but because we are afraid of silence or of not being noticed. And we can listen to or read the words of others, not in order to learn something, but because we are bored and need to fill up time. Cocktail-party chatter and journalism in the pejorative sense are two aspects of the same disease, what the Bible calls Idle Words for which at Judgment Day God will hold us accountable. Since the chatterer has nothing he really wishes to say, and the journalist nothing he really wishes to write, it is of no consequence to either what words they actually use. In consequence, it is not long before they forget the exact meanings of words and their precise grammatical relations and, presently, without knowing it, are talking and writing nonsense.

This kind of corruption of language has been enormously encouraged by mass education and the mass media. Until quite recently, most people spoke the language of the social class into which they were born. Their vocabulary might be limited, but they had learned it at firsthand from their parents and neighbors, so that they knew the correct meanings of such words as they did know, and made no attempt to use any others. Today, I would guess that nine-tenths of the population do not know what thirty percent of the words they use actually mean. Thus, it is possible to hear someone who is feeling sick say *I am nauseous,* for a reviewer of a spy-thriller to describe it as *enervating,* and for a television star to say of an investment agency which was sponsoring his program *They are integrity-ridden.*

To make polite conversation is, of course, essential to a civilized society, and if idleness of speech has become such a problem in our time, one of the reasons is that polite conversation is no longer regarded as an art which has to be learned. When we are children, the only society we know is a society of intimates, parents, brothers and sisters, uncles, aunts, etc. It is only as we grow older that we encounter strangers, some of whom may in the future become intimate friends, others casual acquaintances, while others we shall never see again, and we have to learn that we cannot speak to strangers, or, for that matter, to the public, in the same way that we speak to intimates. One of the worst characteristics of present society is its childish indiscretion which ignores this difference. Both in conversation and in books people to-day are only too ready to take their clothes off in front of total strangers.

Again, while it is a great blessing that a man no longer has to be rich in order to enjoy the masterpieces of the past, for paperbooks, first-rate color reproductions and stereo-phonograph records have made them available to all but the very poor, this ease of access, if misused—and we do misuse it—can become a curse. We are all of us tempted to read more books, look at more pictures, listen to more music, than we can possibly absorb; and the result of such gluttony is not a cultured mind but a consuming one; what it reads, looks at, listens to, is immediately forgotten, leaving no more traces behind it than yesterday's newspaper.

More deadly than the Idle Word is the use of words as Black Magic. Like the White Magic of poetry, Black Magic is concerned with enchantment. But, while the poet is himself enchanted by the subjects he writes about and only wishes to share his enchantment with others, the Black Magician is perfectly cold. He has no enchantment to share with others, but uses enchantment as a means of securing domination over others and compelling them to do his will. He does not ask for a free response to his spell; he demands a tautological echo.

In all the ages, the technique of the Black Magician has been essentially the same. In his spells the words are deprived of their meanings and reduced to syllables or verbal noises. This may be done literally, as when magicians used to recite the Lord's Prayer backwards, or by reiterating a word over and over again as loudly as possible until it has become a mere sound. For millions of people today, words like Communism, Capitalism, Imperialism, Peace, Freedom, Democracy, have ceased to be words the meanings of which can be inquired into and discussed, and have become right or wrong noises to which the response is as involuntary as a knee-reflex. It makes no difference if the magic is being employed simply for the aggrandizement of the magician him-self, or if, as is more usual, he claims to be serving some good cause. Indeed, the better the cause he claims to be serving, the more evil he does. Most com-mercial advertising, revoltingly vulgar though it is, is comparatively harmless. If advertising conditions me to buy a brand of toilet soap, provided that the Law prevents the sale of a substance which poisons my skin or leaves me dirtier than I was before, no harm is done me, for it can make no difference to my body or soul which brand I use. Political and religious propaganda are another matter, for politics and religion are spheres where personal choice is essential.

As a practitioner of the art, I could wish, for worldly reasons, that Poetry were more popular. I am, however, glad and proud that it is not. Poetry cannot be employed by the Black Magician: if one responds to a poem at all, the response is conscious and voluntary. And poetry cannot, it would seem, be reduced to an idle word. Novels, even good ones, can be read simply to pass the time; music, even the greatest, can be used as background noise; but nobody has yet learned to consume a poem; either one cannot read it at all, or one must listen to it as its author intended it to be listened to.

Language, as such, is the concern of every human being at all times, but artists, whose medium is language, that is to say, poets and novelists, have special problems of their own, and these vary with times and places. In cultures, polytheistic societies, for example, in certain historical epochs, like the Romantic age, literary artists have been accorded a public status which tempted them to think of themselves more highly than they ought to think. Today, they are in danger of not taking their art seriously enough. Their reaction to their diminished status may take two forms.

They may in a futile attempt to recover social importance, attempt to become propagandists for some good cause, to be, as current jargon has it, *engagé*. The world about us is, as it always has been, full of gross evils and appalling misery, but it is a fatal delusion and a shocking overestimation of the importance of the artist in the world, to suppose that, by making works of art, we can do anything to eradicate the one or alleviate the other. The political and social history of Europe would be what it has been if Dante, Shakespeare, Goethe, Titian, Mozart, Beethoven, *et al.,* had never existed. Where social evils are concerned, the only effective weapons are two: political action and straight reportage of the facts, journalism in the good sense. Art is impotent. The utmost an artist can hope to do for his contemporary readers is, as Dr. Johnson said, to enable them a little better to enjoy life or a little better to endure it. Further, let us remember that, though the great artists of the past could not change the course of history, it is only through their work that we are able to break bread with the dead, and without communion with the dead a fully human life is impossible.

The opposite reaction is to imagine that, if it is true, and I think it is, that art cannot be effective as serious action, then let it be frivolous action; instead of making political speeches, let us invent happenings. But the Pop artist, like his *engagé* brother, forgets that the artist is not a man of action but a maker, a fabricator of objects. To believe in the value of art is to believe that it is possible to make an object, be it an epic or a two-line epigram, which will remain permanently on hand in the world. The probabilities of success are against him, but an artist must not attempt anything less. Until quite recently, this seemed self-evident, for all fabrication was carried on in the same way. Houses, furniture, tools, linen, table-ware, wedding dresses, etc., were made to last and be handed on from one generation to the next. This is no longer the case: such things are now deliberately designed to become obsolescent in a few years. This, however deplorable, is possible because such craft objects are to some extent necessary: men must have dwelling-places, chairs and so on. But the so-called "fine" arts which are purely gratuitous—nobody has to write or read a poem or a novel—cannot follow this path without becoming extinct.

In defending us against losing our nerve, let us take comfort from the masterpieces of the past, for one thing they have to teach us is that social and technological change are not as fatal to a genuine work of art as we are inclined to fear. Our world is already utterly different from the worlds in which they were created; yet we can still comprehend and enjoy them.

The future looks gloomy enough, but there is one change in our ways of thought which seems to me encouraging. Since the end of the 18th century until quite recently, the scientists believed and succeeded in convincing most people that they were right, that science could arrive at an objective knowledge of things-in-themselves. To this assertion artists reacted in two ways: some tried to become as much like scientists as possible and banded together under the slogan of naturalism: others averted their eyes from the phenomenal world altogether as the abode of Satan, and tried to create purely aesthetic worlds out of their subjective feelings.

If today, it seems to me, the word "real" can be used at all, the only world which is real for us, as the world in which all of us, including scientists, are born, work, love, hate and die, is the primary phenomenal world as it is and always has been presented to us through our senses, a world in which the sun moves across the sky from east to west, the stars are hung in the vault of heaven, the measure of magnitude is the human body, and objects are either in motion or at rest. If this be accepted, it is possible that artists may become both more modest and more self-assured. None will produce the kind of work which demands that a reader spend his whole life reading it and nothing else. The claim to be a genius will become as strange a notion as it would have seemed to the Middle Ages. There might even be a return to a belief in the phenomenal world as a realm of sacred analogies.

But this is guessing. In the meantime, and whatever is going to happen, we must try to live as Mr. E. M. Forster recommends that we should:

> "The people I respect must behave as if they were immortal and as if Society were eternal. Both assumptions are false. Both must be accepted as true if we are to go on working and eating and loving, and are able to keep open a few breathing-holes for the human spirit."

Words

To illustrate the range of the philosophical contemplation of words, I have juxtaposed Peirce and Freya Stark, a rare essayist who combines speculation and highly personal insights without preciosity.

Cassirer, student of mythic thought and the growth and development of the scientific imagination, saw more deeply than any modern semioticist into the nature of language as a means of making meaning—our chief and readiest means. I have included a passage from the long chapter on language in *Essay on Man*, his popular presentation of the ideas explored so thoroughly in his massive *Philosophy of Symbolic Form.* Susanne K. Langer turns the old philosophical game of speculating on the origins of speech to new uses. The essay included here brings to bear on the philosophy of mind (for which *Philosophical Sketches* serves as an introduction) certain ideas about the relationship of feeling and form which she had developed in her theory of art, in a book with that title. Camille Norton, a student in my course, "Language and Literature," at the University of Massachusetts at Boston, read Freya Stark and Susanne K. Langer in conjunction with a semester's speculations about mythic ideation and poetic form. "Eating the Pasture" is one of the results.

C. S. PEIRCE
(on words)

2.298, 2.299, 2.302 Any ordinary word, as "give," "bird," "marriage," is an example of a symbol. It is *applicable to whatever may be found to realize the idea connected with the word*; it does not, in itself, identify those things. It does not show us a bird, nor enact before our eyes a giving or a marriage, but supposes that we are able to imagine those things, and have associated the word with them. . . . The symbol is connected with its object by virtue of the idea of the symbol-using mind, without which no such connection would exist. . . . Symbols grow. They come into being by development out of other signs. . . . We think only in signs. . . . If a man makes a new symbol, it is by thoughts involving concepts. So it is only out of symbols that a new symbol can grow. *Omne symbolum de symbolo.* A symbol, once in being, spreads among the peoples. In use and in experience, its meaning grows. Such words as *force, law, wealth, marriage,* bear for us very different meanings from those they bore to our barbarous ancestors. The symbol may, with Emerson's sphynx, say to man,

Of thine eye I am eyebeam.

FREYA STARK

"Words"

. . . for we have discovered that names have by nature a truth, and that not every man knows how to give a thing a name.

Plato, Cratylus

O my good lord! the world is but a word.

Shakespeare, Timon of Athens

Look you, the worm is not to be trusted but in the keeping of wise people; for, indeed, there is no goodness in the worm.

Shakespeare, Antony and Cleopatra

Yea, words which are our subtlest and delicatest outward creatures, being composed of thoughts and breath, are so muddy and thick, that our thoughts themselves are so, because (except at the first rising) they are leavened with passions and affections.

Donne

La conversation de Charles était plate comme un trottoir de rue et les idées de tout le monde y défilaient, dans leur costume ordinaire.

Flaubert, Madame Bovary

Thamus replied . . . this discovery of yours will create forgetfulness in the learners' souls, because they will not use their memories: they will trust to the external written characters and not remember of themselves. The specific which you have discovered is an aid not to memory, but to

reminiscence, and you give your disciples not truth, but only the sem-
blance of truth; they will be hearers of many things and will have learned
nothing; they will be tiresome company, having the show of wisdom
without the reality.

Plato, Phaedrus

Where are now the warring kings,
Word be-mockers?

Yeats, The Song of the Happy Shepherd

The country about Asolo produces silk in quantity, and long straight avenues of mulberry trees, pollarded to a monotonous cabbage roundness, inter-
sect the plain and feed the silk grubs in their season. These are hatched from
small eggs like the heads of white and yellow pins, and are kept on shallow
trays in a moist warm atmosphere, eating continually; until they grow to the
size of a baby's finger, grey and flabby as dead flesh, with soft twigs of legs
and horns. The worms eat day and night. Nothing but the mulberry leaf will
content them; and in a year when late seasons or other disasters overtake their
trees, they, like the poor people of Bengal, die rather than change their diet.
Ordinarily, however, they munch busily for several weeks, until a collective
idea drives them to climb from their pastures into faggots of sticks which the
peasants keep ready, where they spin their cocoons and sleep. I have often
seen them in all these stages, and later also, when the cocoon dances in
boiling water and the thin spun thread is unwound from its packed maze, and
eventually lies in coils of hard yellow silk—moth wings which will never fly;
for the grub has been boiled to death, and the heaps of carnage become the
best of all manures for roses, and are sold for a good price.

The peasants have little to do with the later stages, for they pull the
cocoons out of their faggots and put them in sacks and sell them; but, while
the grubs are still growing, they have required sleepless attention and have
been supplied constantly with sacks of the heart-shaped leaves. These they
instantly submerge in their crawling numbers, and devour. In a great farm,
I have seen a row of long rooms, opening one from the other, filled with the
restless shallow trays, so that all the air seemed to shimmer with a blind movement, as if molecules of formless matter had become visible. There is something obscene in almost any promiscuous heap: one's instinct thinks of it as
dead rather than alive: and it causes uneasiness to see it moving, blind, anar-
chic, inspired by greed pure and simple, without a touch of any nobler
pleasure.

Sometimes, out of a pile of these feeders, a little grey body lifts itself
and waves blunt head and needy helpless arms in air: it is only asking more
mulberry leaf of the invisible gods and is soon prone again and glued to the
business of mastication. And if one listens, a terrifying noise like a smooth
tide over shingle becomes audible—the grinding of the small innumerable jaws.

I sometimes think that words are like those feeders, biting their way
into the substance of our lives. We shuffle them, obscure and neutral in

themselves, and throw to them not only the thoughts of our mind and the feelings of our heart—their proper diet—but any refuse of imitation that comes to hand; for, unlike the silkworm, the word-grub will accept promiscuous garbage for his food. Yet he can produce the fine and shining thread which makes our kingly garments; and he, too, waking from sleep, can grow wings, like that creature in whose brightness the Greek poets recognized the soul. And at any moment, if we listen, we can hear the sound of the minute teeth of the sleepless words lisping or hissing, soothing or menacing, biting into the lives of men.

Nothing today is more ominous than our disregard of these small dangerous slaves. They are being used as it were to corrupt themselves. And we are coming to forget that they, who in themselves are nothing but emptiness and air, must embody other, more solid things—justice, for instance— whose very existence depends on an awareness of exactitude in words.

"This would be a very quiet world if those who had nothing to say—said it." The notice was put up, pathetically, in an American business man's office.

One of the pleasant things among the Arabs is their recognition of silence as a part of human intercourse: they sit round in a large gathering and, when the formal greetings and enquiries after health or absent friends are over, they let the minutes pass, two, four, ten minutes, in meditation, until someone takes an idea and throws it like a stone into the middle of a pond, where all have time to watch its ripples spread. Perhaps one must have country memories to fall easily into this way. I can recall days with my father or my godfather—both lovers of walking and hills. We would step side by side or—on narrow paths—one behind the other for many hours, and talk would come to the surface and die, easily, with long gaps, like those underground rivers whose course is shown by occasional stretches that vanish again among the stones. The landscape would seem to take a part in this conversation, washing into its pauses with changing views and the shadows of traveling clouds and westering light; so that the things one said or heard came to be like small jewels set in their twist of hours, made permanent by the frame into which they fell. Ever since these days I have thought that the luxury of conversation is to hold it in such surroundings as may enrich its pauses, and have wondered whether the British taciturnity is not responsible in some measure for the care we take of our homes by comparison with more talkative races, making them pleasant places for words to drift into silence.

"As all suns pass before the face of darkness, and hide it awhile with their splendor, so on many-colored wings thought flies through the silence, but the silence endures."*

Built up into the pauses of Time, words sparkle more brightly, like necklaces set on black velvet. And with so advantageous a background it becomes a matter of importance that the gems should be real.

*George Santayana, *Dialogues in Limbo*.

But we seem to have forgotten the dignity of the only instruments, among all our inventions, that can carry and make articulate the thoughts, the soul of man. Even when used without so high an intention, words may yet be innocent and make a pleasant noise in the world, like brooks on moss and stones, or the wind in the trees. But their *misuse* perverts the divine. And we have now come to a pass where truthlessness is tolerated, and even expected, in politics, diplomacy, advertisement, the education of children and the privacy of marriage. The depth of our degradation of words may be measured by the surprise any newspaper editor would feel if his news were criticized merely for being untrue.

A good deal of this comes, I believe, from dullness and the notion that truth is indivisible and single. We are apt to think of virtue as monotony and to allow all the graces of variety to the other side. As a matter of fact nothing is more capricious than accuracy, nor more elusive, nor more difficult to hold when caught; for every word is blurred to begin with by being molded twice over in different molds—first in the mind of the speaker and then in that of the listener—so that even with every precaution it can never do more than be approximate to the object of which it speaks.

Anyone who tries to write knows that there is not the simplest, most tangible thing in existence that can be described entire. The roots of all go down uncharted, like sea rocks whose wizened surface the smallest waves lick over—though great mountains and submarine valleys may underlie them, with monsters or mermaids in their depths. All this and more, to the very center of earth and extremity of time, is part of their truth; and the task of every statement or description is to decide how much of it all is to be included.

As a rule, we are satisfied with a surface verity and say of these rocks that they are bleached or dry or sharp or rounded, ignoring and even contradicting the foundations on which they stand: but those who possess the secret of words are able as it were to pack the meaning, and fill it with greater space and wider time, so that a more capacious quality of truth is implicit in the things they say. Shakespeare does this constantly with the use of images and comparisons which he compresses until they fuse, so that only the surface point of a noun or verb or adjective is left to show what range of country lies submerged below.

Any number of such single, revealing words can be collected in any one of the plays.

In *Timon of Athens*:

> . . . all kind of natures
> That labor on the *bosom* of this sphere.

> Bowing his head against the steepy mount
> To *climb* his *happiness.*

> My uses *cry* to me.

> Our vaults have *wept*
> With drunken spilth of wine.

> If I would *broach* the *vessels* of my love.

Lucius' Servant: What do you think the hour?
Philotus: *Laboring* for nine.

> Convert, o' the instant, green *virginity.*

Like Juliet's "Bloody Tybalt, yet but *green* in earth."

Every one of these words is a compression of two images, and could be a detailed simile or metaphor such as:

> Thou art a slave, whom Fortune's tender arm
> With favor never clasp'd; but bred a dog.

Which might easily have been: "Thou art Fortune's dog," if Shakespeare, hurrying on as usual, had left us to reconstruct the rest. I think that the delight which moves across his pages is very largely due to these signposts, which he scatters with careless prodigality to be deciphered and followed by readers as they can. Each of them owes its value to the accuracy of the resemblance which first inspired the image of which the one intrusive word remains; the word itself is solitary and swift as a fork of lightning, but it lifts out of darkness a landscape which the reader may recognize.

Yet neither Shakespeare nor any other magician can ever utter the whole truth, or even express what he really means to say. This penalty was laid on human speech when or before the tower of Babel stood: perhaps it produced the germ of discontent in Eden. Every later revolution in history is the record of human efforts to keep words and their meaning as nearly together as they can, for the quality of civilization depends on the calling of things by their proper names as far as we can know them. It is the endless quest, and the nations that turn from it totter and fall. Therefore with no idle misgiving we now watch governments build with useless words, and meet and part again with their fallacious hope that the nature of things has been altered when they find different epithets to call them by. I once heard of a little Arab boy whose parents familiarly referred to him as "Puncture," so that by the lowly disguise—the most depressing they could think of—the celestial envy might be disarmed. Our official spokesmen have less humility, but the process is often the same.

To cherish words is, it seems to me, the only safety. The love of them is natural to children, so that they can be fostered and by many arts be made allies of truth though imperfect, until they come to be chosen as carefully as one would choose a walking stick, smooth and strong and free of knots, to bear without breaking the weight of the deeds that lean upon them.

ERNST CASSIRER
from *An Essay on Man*

In order to find a clue of Ariadne to guide us through the complicated and baffling labyrinth of human speech we may proceed in a twofold manner. We may attempt to find a logical and systematic or a chronological and genetic order. In the second case we try to trace the individual idioms and the various linguistic types back to a former comparatively simple and amorphous stage. Attempts of this sort were often made by linguists of the nineteenth century when the opinion became current that human speech, before it could attain its present form, had had to pass through a state in which there were no definite syntactical or morphological forms. Languages at first consisted of simple elements, of monosyllabic roots. Romanticism favored this view. A. W. Schlegel propounded a theory according to which language developed from a former unorganized amorphous state. From this state it passed in a fixed order to other, more advanced stages—to an isolating, an agglutinating, a flexional stage. The flexional languages are according to Schlegel the last step in this evolution; they are the really organic languages. A thorough descriptive analysis has in most cases destroyed the evidence on which these theories were based. In the case of Chinese, which was usually cited as an example of a language consisting of monosyllabic roots, it could be made to appear probable that its present isolating stage was preceded by a former flexional stage. We know of no language devoid of formal or structural elements, although the expression of formal relations, such as the difference between subject and object, between attribute and predicate, varies widely from language to language. Without form language has the appearance of being not merely a highly questionable historical construct but a contradiction in terms. The languages of the most uncivilized nations are by no means formless; on the contrary they exhibit in most cases a very complicated structure. A. Meillet, a modern linguist who possessed a most comprehensive knowledge of the languages of the world, declared that no known idiom gives us the slightest idea of what primitive language may have been. All forms of human speech are perfect in so far as they succeed in expressing human feelings and thoughts in a clear and appropriate manner. The so-called primitive languages are as much in congruity with the conditions of primitive civilization and with the general tendency of the primitive mind as our own languages are with the ends of our refined and sophisticated culture. In the languages of the Bantu family, for instance, every substantive belongs to a definite class, and every such class is characterized by its special prefix. These prefixes do not appear only in the nouns themselves but have to be repeated, in accordance with a very complicated system of concords and congruences, in all other parts of the sentence which refer to the noun.

The variety of individual idioms and the heterogeneity of linguistic types appear in a quite different light depending on whether they are looked at from a philosophical or from a scientific viewpoint. The linguist rejoices in this variety; he plunges into the ocean of human speech without hoping to sound its real depth. In all ages philosophy has moved in the opposite direction. Leibniz insisted that without a *Characteristica generalis* we shall never find a *Scientia generalis.* Modern symbolic logic follows the same tendency. But even if this task were accomplished, a philosophy of human culture would still have to face the same problem. In an analysis of human culture we must accept the facts in their concrete shape, in all their diversity and divergence. The philosophy of language is here confronted with the same dilemma as appears in the study of every symbolic form. The highest, indeed the only, task of all these forms is to unite men. But none of them can bring about this unity without at the same time dividing and separating men. Thus what was intended to secure the harmony of culture becomes the source of the deepest discords and dissensions. This is the great antinomy, the dialectic of the religious life. The same dialectic appears in human speech. Without speech there would be no community of men. Yet there is no more serious obstacle to such community than the diversity of speech. Myth and religion refuse to regard this diversity as a necessary and unavoidable fact. They attribute it rather to a fault or guilt of man than to his original constitution and the nature of things. In many mythologies we find striking analogies to the Biblical tale of the Tower of Babel. Even in modern times, man has always retained a deep longing for that Golden Age in which mankind was still in possession of a uniform language. He looks back at his primeval state as at a lost paradise. Nor did the old dream of a *lingua Adamica*—of the "real" language of the first ancestors of man, a language which did not consist merely of conventional signs but which expressed rather the very nature and essence of things—vanish completely even in the realm of philosophy. The problem of this *lingua Adamica* continued to be seriously discussed by the philosophical thinkers and mystics of the seventeenth century.

Yet the true unity of language, if there is such a unity, cannot be a substantial one; it must rather be defined as a functional unity. Such a unity does not presuppose a material or formal identity. Two different languages may represent opposite extremes both with respect to their phonetic systems and to their parts-of-speech systems. This does not prevent them from accomplishing the same task in the life of the speaking community. The important thing here is not the variety of means but their fitness for and congruity with the end. We may think that this common end is attained more perfectly in one linguistic type than in another. Even Humboldt, who, generally speaking, was loath to pass judgment on the value of particular idioms, still regarded the flexional languages as a sort of paragon and model of excellence. To him the flexional form was *die einzig gesetzmässige Form,* the only form which is entirely consistent and follows strict rules. Modern linguists have warned us against such judgments. They tell us that we have no common and unique standard for estimating the value of linguistic types. In comparing types it may appear that the one has definite advantages over the other, but a closer analysis usually convinces us that what we term the defects of a certain type may be compensated and counterbalanced by other merits. If we wish to understand language, declares Sapir, we must disabuse our minds of preferred values and accustom ourselves to look upon English and Hottentot with the same cool yet interested detachment.

If it were the task of human speech to copy or imitate the given or ready-made order of things we could scarcely maintain any such detachment. We could not avoid the conclusion that, after all, one of two different copies must be the better; that the one must be nearer to, the other farther from, the original. Yet if we ascribe to speech a productive and constructive rather than a merely reproductive function, we shall judge quite differently. In this case it is not the "work" of language but its "energy" which is of paramount importance. In order to measure this energy one must study the linguistic process itself instead of simply analyzing its outcome, its product, and final results.

Psychologists are unanimous in emphasizing that without insight into the true nature of human speech our knowledge of the development of the human mind would remain perfunctory and inadequate. There is, however, still considerable uncertainty as to the methods of a psychology of speech. Whether we study the phenomena in a psychological or phonetic laboratory or rely on merely introspective methods we invariably derive the same impression that these phenomena are so evanescent and fluctuating that they defy all efforts at stabilization. In what, then, consists that fundamental difference between the mental attitude which we may ascribe to a speechless creature—a human being before the acquisition of speech or an animal—and that other frame of mind which characterizes an adult who has fully mastered his mother tongue?

Curiously enough it is easier to answer this question on the basis of abnormal instances of speech development. Our consideration of the cases of Helen Keller and Laura Bridgman illustrated the fact that with the first understanding of the symbolism of speech a real revolution takes place in the life of the child. From this point on his whole personal and intellectual life assumes an entirely new shape. Roughly speaking, this change may be described by saying that the child passes from a more subjective state to an objective state, from a merely emotional attitude to a theoretical attitude. The same change may be noted in the life of every normal child, though in a much less spectacular way. The child himself has a clear sense of the significance of the new instrument for his mental development. He is not satisfied with being taught in a purely receptive manner but takes an active share in the process of speech which is at the same time a process of progressive objectification. The teachers of Helen Keller and Laura Bridgman have told us with what eagerness and impatience both children, once they had understood the use of names, continued to ask for the particular names of all the objects in their environment. This, too, is a general feature in the normal development of speech. . . . The name, in the mental growth of the child, has a function of the first importance to perform. If a child when learning to talk had simply to learn a certain vocabulary, if he only had to impress on his mind and memory a great mass of artificial and arbitrary sounds, this would be a purely mechanical process. It would be very laborious and tiresome, and would require too great conscious effort for the child to make without a certain reluctance since what he is expected to do would be entirely disconnected from actual biological needs. The "hunger for names" which at a certain age appears in every normal child and which has been described by all students of child psychology proves the contrary. It reminds us that we are here confronted with a quite different problem. By learning to name things a child does not simply add a list of artificial signs to his previous knowledge of ready-made empirical objects. He learns rather to form the concepts of those objects, to come to terms with the objective world. Henceforth the child stands on firmer ground. His vague, uncertain, fluctuating perceptions and his dim feelings begin to assume a new shape. They may be said to crystallize around the name as a fixed center, a focus of thought. Without the help of the name every new advance made in the process of objectification would always run the risk of being lost again in the next moment. The first names of which a child makes conscious use may be compared to a stick by the aid of which a blind man gropes his way. And language, taken as a whole, becomes the gateway to a new world. All progress here opens a new perspective and widens and enriches our concrete experience. Eagerness and enthusiasm to talk do not originate in a mere desire for learning or using names; they mark the desire for the detection and conquest of an objective world.

We can still when learning a foreign language subject ourselves to an experience similar to that of the child. Here it is not sufficient to acquire a new vocabulary or to acquaint ourselves with a system of abstract grammatical rules. All this is necessary but it is only the first and less important step. If we do not learn to think in the new language all our efforts remain fruitless. In most cases we find it extremely difficult to fulfil this requirement. Linguists and psychologists have often raised the question as to how it is possible for a child by his own efforts to accomplish a task that no adult can ever perform in the same way or as well. We can perhaps answer this puzzling question by looking back at our former analysis. In a later and more advanced state of our conscious life we can never repeat the process which led to our first entrance into the world of human speech. In the freshness, in the agility and elasticity of early childhood this process had a quite different meaning. Paradoxically enough the real difficulty consists much less in the learning of the new language than in the forgetting of a former one. We are no longer in the mental condition of the child who for the first time approaches a conception of the objective world. To the adult the objective world already has a definite shape as a result of speech activity, which has in a sense molded all our other activities. Our perceptions, intuitions, and concepts have coalesced with the terms and speech forms of our mother tongue. Great efforts are required to release the bond between words and things. And yet, when we set about to learn a new language, we have to make such efforts and to separate the two elements. Overcoming this difficulty always marks a new and important step in the learning of a language. When penetrating into the "spirit" of a foreign tongue we invariably have the impression of approaching a new world, a world which has an intellectual structure of its own. It is like a voyage of discovery in an alien land, and the greatest gain from such a voyage lies in our having learned to look upon our mother tongue in a new light. "Wer fremde Sprachen nicht kennt, weiss nichts von seiner eigenen," said Goethe. So long as we know no foreign languages we are in a sense ignorant of our own, for we fail to see its specific structure and its distinctive features. A comparison of different languages shows us that there are no exact synonyms. Corresponding terms from two languages seldom refer to the same objects or actions. They cover different fields which interpenetrate and give us many-colored views and varied perspectives of our experience.

This becomes especially clear if we consider the methods of classification employed in different languages, particularly in those of divergent linguistic types. Classification is one of the fundamental features of human speech. The very act of denomination depends on a process of classification. To give a name to an object or action is to subsume it under a certain class concept. If this subsumption were once and for all prescribed by the nature of things, it would be unique and uniform. Yet the names which occur in human speech cannot be interpreted in any such invariable manner. They are not designed to refer to substantial things, independent entities which exist by themselves. They are determined rather by human interests and human purposes. But these interests are not fixed and invariable. Nor are the classifications to be found in human speech made at random; they are based on certain constant and recurring elements in our sense experience. Without such recurrences there would be no foothold, no point of support, for our linguistic concepts. But the combination or separation of perceptual data depends upon the free choice of a frame of reference. There is no rigid and pre-established scheme according to which our divisions and subdivisions might once for all be made. Even in languages closely akin and agreeing in their general structure we do not find identical names. As Humboldt pointed out, the Greek and Latin terms for the moon, although they refer to the same object, do not express the same intention or concept. The Greek term (*mēn*) denotes the function of the moon "to measure" time; the Latin term (*luna, luc-na*) denotes the moon's lucidity or brightness. Thus we have obviously isolated and focused attention on two very different features of the object. But the act itself, the process of concentration and condensation, is the same. The name of an object lays no claim upon its nature; it is not intended . . . to give us the truth of a thing. The function of a name is always limited to emphasizing a particular aspect of a thing, and it is precisely this restriction and limitation upon which the value of the name depends. It is not the function of a name to refer exhaustively to a concrete situation, but merely to single out and dwell upon a certain aspect. The isolation of this aspect is not a negative but a positive act. For in the act of denomination we select, out of the multiplicity and diffusion of our sense data, certain fixed centers of perception. These centers are not the same as in logical or scientific thought. The terms of ordinary speech are not to be measured by the same standards as those in which we express scientific concepts. As compared with scientific terminology the words of common speech always exhibit a certain vagueness; almost without exception they are so indistinct and ill-defined as not to stand the test of logical analysis. But notwithstanding this unavoidable and inherent defect our everyday terms and names are the milestones on the road which leads to scientific concepts; it is in these terms that we receive our first objective or theoretical view of the world. Such a view is not simply "given"; it is the result of a constructive intellectual effort which without the constant assistance of language could not attain its end.

This end is not, however, to be reached at any one time. The ascent to higher levels of abstraction, to more general and comprehensive names and ideas, is a difficult and laborious task. The analysis of language provides us with a wealth of materials for studying the character of the mental processes which finally lead to the accomplishment of this task. Human speech evolves from a first comparatively concrete state to a more abstract state. Our first names are concrete ones. They attach themselves to the apprehension of particular facts or actions. All the shades or nuances that we find in our concrete experience are described minutely and circumstantially, but they are not subsumed under a common genus. Hammer-Purgstall has written a paper in which he enumerates the various names for the camel in Arabic. There are no less than five to six thousand terms used in describing a camel; yet none of these gives us a general biological concept. All express concrete details concerning the shape, the size, the color, the age, and the gait of the animal. These divisions are still very far from any scientific or systematic classification, but serve quite different purposes. In many languages of aboriginal American tribes we find an astounding variety of terms for a particular action, for instance for walking or striking. Such terms bear to each other rather a relation of juxtaposition than of subordination. A blow with the fist cannot be described with the same term as a blow with the palm, and a blow with a weapon requires another name than one with a whip or rod. In his description of the Bakairi language—an idiom spoken by an Indian tribe in Central Brazil— Karl von den Steinen relates that each species of parrot and palm tree has its individual name, whereas there exists no name to express the genus "parrot" or "palm." "The Bakairi," he asserts, "attach themselves so much to the numerous particular notions that they take no interest in the common characteristics. They are choked in the abundance of the material and cannot manage it economically. They have only small coin but in that they must be said to be excessively rich rather than poor." As a matter of fact there exists

no uniform measure for the wealth or poverty of a given idiom. Every classification is directed and dictated by special needs, and it is clear that these
needs vary according to the different conditions of man's social and cultural
life In primitive civilization the interest in the concrete and particular aspects
of things necessarily prevails. Human speech always conforms to and is com-
mensurate with certain forms of human life. An interest in mere "universals"
is neither possible nor necessary in an Indian tribe. It is enough, and it is more
important, to distinguish objects by certain visible and palpable characteristics.
In many languages a round thing cannot be treated in the same way as a
square or oblong thing, for they belong to different genders which are distinguished by special linguistic means, such as the use of prefixes. In languages
of the Bantu family we find no less than twenty gender classes of nouns. In
languages of aboriginal American tribes, as for instance in Algonquian, some
objects belong to an animate gender, others to an inanimate gender. Even
here it is easy to understand that and why this distinction, from the viewpoint
of the primitive mind, must appear to be of particular interest and of vital importance. It is indeed a much more characteristic and striking difference than
that which is expressed in our abstract logical class names. The same slow passage from concrete to abstract names can also be studied in the denomination
of the qualities of things. In many languages we find an abundance of color
names. Each individual shade of a given color has its special name, whereas
our general terms—blue, green, red, and so on—are missing. Color names vary
according to the nature of the objects: one word for gray may, for example,
be used in speaking of wool or geese, another of horses, another of cattle, and
still another when speaking of the hair of men and certain other animals. The
same holds good for the category of number: different numerals are required
for referring to different classes of objects. The ascent to universal concepts
and categories appears, therefore, to be very slow in the development of
human speech; but each new advance in this direction leads to a more comprehensive survey, to a better orientation and organization of our perceptual
world.

SUSANNE K. LANGER
"Speculations on the Origins of Speech
and Its Communicative Function"

Ever since the Darwinian theory of human evolution—tracing the descent
of man from animal ancestors—has become generally accepted, the origin of
speech has become more and more mystifying. Language is so much the mark
of man that it was classically supposed to have been bestowed on him at his
creation. But if he·has not been created separately from the animals, but has
arisen, as most of us now believe, just as they arose, from a more primitive
animal ancestry, then surely at some time his own precursors did not speak.
When, why, and how did man begin to speak? What generations invented that
great social instrument, language? What development of animal communication has eventuated in human communication? What pre-Adamite thought of
assigning a particular little squeak to a particular object as the name of that
object, by which you could refer to it, demand it, make other people think
of it? How did the other pre-Adamites all agree to assign the same squeaks to
the same things? What has led to the concatenation of those primitive words
in syntactically structured sentences of interrelated meanings? As far as
anthropologists know, there is no human language that is not discursive—
propositional—in form. Its propositions may be very different from ours, but
their semantic structure is always equivalent to what we call a statement.
Language always expresses relations among acts or things, or their aspects. It
always makes reference to reality—that is, makes assertions or denials—either
explicitly or implicitly. Some nouns imply relations, and where they do,
verbs may not be needed. In classical Latin the verb is often understood
through the inflections of nouns and adjectives. Verbs, in some languages,
may imply their subject or object or even both, and make nouns all but unnecessary, as Whorf found in Hopi. But no language consists of signs that only
call attention to things without saying anything about them—that is, without
asserting or denying something. All languages we know have a fairly stabile
vocabulary and a grammatical structure. No language is essentially exclamatory (like ah! and oh!), or emotional (like whining and yodeling), or even
imperative. The normal mode of communicative speech, in every human society, is the indicative; and there is no empirical evidence, such as a correlation

of increasing discursiveness with increasing culture, to support the belief that it was ever otherwise.

Language may be used to announce one's presence, to greet people, to warn, to threaten, to express pain or joy, or even for directing action. Whenever people speak of "animal language" they refer to such uses of observable signs among animals. Leaving aside, for the moment, the alleged "language" of social insects, we may use the term *vocal signs* among animals.

Now, it is an obvious common-sense assumption that human language has grown from some such lower form of vocal communication. But common sense is a very tricky instrument; it is as deceptive as it is indispensable. Because we use it, and have to use it, all the time, we tend to trust it beyond its real credentials, and to feel disconcerted if its simple interpretations of experience fail. Yet common-sense conceptions of the nature and origin of human speech have always led into dilemmas, until the problem of its beginning and development has been generally given up.

Even methodology develops its common-sense principles. One of these is that, if you would find the important relationships between two phenomena, you should begin by checking what the phenomena have in common. So, in comparing the vocal communications of animals and men, respectively, we find that all the things animals communicate by sound may also be communicated by human language; and it seems reasonable enough that those things which human language can do and animal vocalization cannot have been added to the primitive animal language, to make the greatly elaborated system of verbal intercourse. But the finding of these common elements leads no further. Common-sense methodology, like the common-sense assumptions, produces nothing more than what we already knew—by common sense.

So it may be in order to question our obvious premises, and even depart from the method of seeking common factors in animal and human communication. Instead of noting points of similarity, let us consider the cardinal difference between human and animal language. That difference is in the *uses* to which utterances are put. All those functions that animal and human utterances share—calling, warning, threatening, expressing emotion—are essential uses of animal sounds, and incidental uses of human speech. The functions of animal vocalization are self-expression and sometimes, perhaps, indication of environmental conditions (like the bark of a dog who wants to be let in). The chief function of speech is denotation.

Animal language is not language at all, and, what is more important, *it never leads to language.* Dogs that live with men learn to understand many verbal signals, but only as signals, in relation to their own actions. Apes that live in droves and seem to communicate fairly well never *converse*.[1] But a

---

[1] See R. M. Yerkes and H. W. Nissen, "Prelinguistic Sign Behavior in the Chimpanzee," *Science,* LXXXIX, n.s. (1939), 585–87. The upshot of the reported experiments is "that delayed response, in the absence of spatial cues or with misleading cues, is either extremely

baby that has only half a dozen words begins to converse: "Daddy gone."
"Daddy come? Daddy come." Question and answer, assertion and denial,
denotation and description—these are the basic uses of language.

The line between animal and human estate is, I think, the language line;
and the gap it marks between those two kinds of life is almost as profound
as the gap between plants and animals. This makes it plausible that we are
not dealing with just a higher form of some general animal function, but with
a new function developed in the hominid brain—a function of such complexity that probably not one, but many, subhuman mental activities underlie it.

The complexity of living forms and functions is something that we are
apt to underestimate in speculating on the origins of psychological phenomena. In textbook accounts the facts have to be generalized and simplified to
make them comprehensible to beginners; but as soon as you tackle the mono-
graphic literature presenting actual cases of growth, maturation, and the conduct of life, and follow actual analyses of function and structure, especially
in neurology, the complexity and variability of vital processes are brought
home to you with great force. Consider only the chemical activities, that
differ enough from any one organism to another to produce the so-called
"individuality factor." Or think of the structural organization of the brain;
in the small brain center known as the "lateral geniculate body" where the
optic nerve ceases to be one bundle of fibers and fans out toward the cortex
of the occipital lobe, anatomists have found scores of so-called "boutons,"
points of reception or emission of electrical impulses, directly on nerve cells,
besides the synaptic connections of the branching axons and dendrites of
those same cells. The potentialities of such a brain for different courses of
activity run into billions and trillions, so that even if inhibiting mechanisms
eliminate a hundred thousand connections at a time, the range of possible
responses, especially in the crowded circuits of the forebrain, is as good as
infinite.

difficult or impossible for most chimpanzees. . . . There is abundant evidence that various
other types of sign process than the symbolic are of frequent occurrence and function effectively in the chimpanzee" (p.587). Perhaps the title "*Non*linguistic Sign Behavior . . . "
would have been more accurate.

Despite such observations, the authors of *Animal Language* do not hesitate to attribute conversation to monkeys, and even to animals below the primates, or to refer to
their repertoire of sounds as a vocabulary having direct affinities with human speech.
"The gregarious baboons," writes Sir Julian, who composed the text, "are very conversa-
tional animals. Most of its communications, both in the pack and in its component family
groups, are effected by voice" (Huxley and Koch, *op. cit.*, p. 55). And more remarkable
still: "The sea-lions . . . as befits their social and intelligent nature, are noisy animals, and
possess a considerable vocabulary, although the different sounds are all variations on one
theme—the familiar, rather raucous bark. Mr. Koch believes that sea-lions also express
different meanings (as do the Chinese) by merely changing the pitch of their note"
(*ibid.*, p 49).

It is very wholesome for a philosopher who tries to conceive of what we call "mind" to take a long look at neurological exhibits, because in psychological studies we usually see and consider only the integrated products—actions and intentions and thoughts—and with regard to speech, words and their uses. Words seem to be the elements of speech; they are the units that keep their essential identity in different relational patterns, and can be separately moved around. They keep their "roots" despite grammatical variations, despite prefixes and suffixes and other modifications. A word is the ultimate semantic element of speech. A large class of our words—most of the nouns, or names—denote objects, and objects are units that can enter into many different situations while keeping their identity, much as words can occur in different statements. This relation gives great support to the conception of words as the units of speech.

And so, I think, they are. But this does not mean that they are original elements of speech, primitive units that were progressively combined into propositions. Communication, among people who inherit language, begins with the word—the baby's or foreigner's unelaborated key word, that stands proxy for a true sentence. But that word has a phylogenetic history, the rise of language, in which probably neither it nor any archaic version of it was an element.

I think it likely that words have actually emerged through progressive simplification of a much more elaborate earlier kind of utterance, which stemmed, in its turn, from several quite diverse sources, and that none of its major sources were forms of animal communication, though some of them were communal.

These are odd-sounding propositions, and I am quite aware of their oddness, but perhaps they are not so fantastic as they sound. They merely depart rather abruptly from our usual background assumptions. For instance, the idea that a relatively simple part of a complex phenomenon might not be one of its primitive factors, but might be a product of progressive simplification, goes against our methodological canons. Ever since Thomas Hobbes set up the so-called genetic method of understanding, we have believed that the simplest concepts into which we could break down our ideas of a complex phenomenon denoted the actual elements of that phenomenon, the factors out of which it was historically compounded. Locke's construction of human experience from pure and simple sense data, Condillac's fancied statue endowed with one form of perception after another, and in our own time Bertrand Russell's "logical atomism," all rest on this belief.[2] But close empirical study of vital processes in nature does not bear it out. A great many advanced behavior patterns *are* elaborations of simpler responses, but some are simplifications of very complicated earlier forms of action. The same holds

---

[2] A belief which has, indeed, been challenged a good many times, but it seems to be ingrained.

true of the structures that implement them. When the reflex arc was discovered, physiologists felt themselves in possession of a key to all animal response, for here was a simple unit that could be supposed to engender all higher forms by progressive elaboration. But Herrick and Coghill, through careful studies of salamanders in their larval stages, found that the reflex arc is not a primitive structure ontogenetically at all, but is preceded by much more elaborate arrangements in the embryo that undergo simplifications until a unified afferent-efferent circuit results. This finding was corroborated by Lorente de Nó.

A principle that is operative in the development of an individual is at least possible in the larger development of a stock. There is nothing absurd about the hypothesis that the simple units in a very advanced function, such as human speech, may be simplifications within an earlier more intricate vocal pattern.

Most theories of the origin of language presuppose that man was already man, with social intentions, when he began to speak.[3] But in fact, man must have been an animal—a high primate, with a tendency to live in droves like most of the great apes—when he began to speak. And it must have been rather different from the ancient progenitors of our apes, which evidently lacked, or at least never possessed in combination, those traits that have eventuated in speech.

What were those traits? Speech is such a complex function that it has probably not arisen from any single source. Yet if it developed naturally in the hominid stock, every one of its constituents must have started from some spontaneous animal activity, not been invented for a purpose; for only human beings invent instruments for a purpose preconceived. Before speech there is no conception; there are only perceptions, and a characteristic repertoire of actions, and a readiness to act according to the enticements of the perceived world. In speech as we know it, however, there seems to be one flowing, articulate symbolic act in which conventional signs are strung together in conventional ways without much trouble, and similar processes evoked in other persons, all as nicely timed as a rally of ping-pong. Nothing seems more integral and self-contained than the outpouring of language in conversation. How is one ever to break it down into primitive acts?

It was from the psychiatric literature on language—on aphasia, paraphasia, agrammatism, alexia, and kindred subjects—that something like a guiding principle emerged. The most baffling thing about the cerebral disturbances of

---

[3] J. B. S. Haldane ("Animal Communication and the Origin of Human Language," *Science Progress*, CLXXI [1955], 385–401) says, "A *Pithecanthropus* child which gave the danger call or the food discovery call without due cause was probably punished" (p. 398). But animals do not punish their young for mischief done; the "cuffing" a cub may receive from its mother is always interference with its momentary annoying act, to stop it. The concept of a *deed,* and hence praise and punishment, belong to human life.

speech is, what strange losses people can sustain, loss of grammatical form without any loss or confusion of words, so that the patient can speak only in "telegraph style"; or contrariwise, loss or confusion of words without loss of sentence structure, so that speech flows in easy sentencelike utterances, but only the prepositions, connectives, and vocal punctuations are recognizable; the informative words all garbled or senseless. Lewis Carroll's

> 'Twas brillig, and the slithy toves
> Did gyre and gimble in the wabe

illustrates this separation of sentence form and verbal content. There may be inability to understand spoken language, yet without any defect of hearing, or the other way about—without any ocular trouble. There are cases of alexia for words but not for letters, and the recognition, naming, and using of numbers are often intact where neither letters nor words can be recognized. Furthermore, some brain injuries leave the victim able to repeat words spoken for him, but not to speak spontaneously, and others make him unable to repeat words just heard, but not unable to utter them in spontaneous speech. There are even several cases on record of persons in whom a cerebral lesion caused inability to name any inanimate object, but not inability to name living things, or call people by their proper names, and, conversely, cases of inability to name persons, animals, or any parts of them, but not to find the words for inanimate objects like watches and slippers.

In the face of these peculiar, sometimes really bizarre exhibits, it occurred to me that what can be separately lost from the integral phenomenon of speech may have been separately developed in the prehistoric, prehuman brain. Here is at least a working notion of a new way to break down the verbal process that might yield a new conception of what has gone into it.

In singling out such elements, and trying to trace them back to some plausible—though of course hypothetical—prehuman proclivities, one meets with the surprising fact that some of these habits, that may be supposed to have prepared speech, actually exist in the animal kingdom, and are even quite highly developed, sometimes in relatively low animals. But they are far from any kind of speech. They are raw, unassembled materials, that would be needed in conjunction, as a foundation, if speech were to arise. In the prehuman primate they must have coincided at some time to provide that foundation.

This principle of analysis takes us much further back into preparatory phases of mental development than the usual anthropological approach to the problem of speech, which reaches back only to the supposed archaic forms of genuine language. Not only mental activities, but some grosser somatic conditions that made them possible, must have met in the animal stock that produced the human race. For instance, the continuity of language requires a bodily mechanism that can sustain a long process of vocalization. Not all animals can do that; it is interesting that the chimpanzee, which is nearest to man in mental capacity, cannot sustain a vowel sound; also it rarely produces a pure and simple sound. Its larynx is too complicated, and it has more than one source of air supply for it, and no fine control of a single set of bellows to mete out its vocal power. The gibbon has a simpler larynx, more like ours, and also the requisite propensity to utter long, chant-like ululations in chorus: that is, it has the physical powers of vocalization, and the habit of using them in a gathered company—two prerequisites for speech. But its brain is too inferior to endow its joyful noise with anything but self-expression and mutual stimulation to keep it up.

Another condition of speech is the epicritical ear, that distinguishes one sound from another, beyond the usual distinction of noises according to their sources—that is, beyond distinguishing them as calls of other creatures, as footsteps, perhaps as the splash of water, and for the rest either as meaningless rumbles and creaks, or not at all. The epicritical power of hearing requires a highly specialized cochlea and a distribution of the auditory nerve in the brain that is not found in all the higher animals, but occurs in several birds—an anomalous development in a relatively low type of brain. Those birds that imitate the whistles of other birds and the sounds of human speech, whereby we know they have a highly analytic hearing (which anatomical findings bear out), have something more that is relevant to our own powers: the control of the vocal apparatus by the ear, which seems to be rudimentary in most animals, although the mechanisms of hearing and sound-making are always associated—even in the cricket, which has its peripheral organs of hearing in the thighs. The kind of feedback that molds an utterance according to sounds heard, and makes formal imitation possible, is another specialization beyond the epicritical receptor organ. Dogs have the fine receptor, the ear that discriminates articulate sounds within a general category, for they can respond selectively to quite a gamut of verbal signals, and Pavlov found their discrimination of tonal pitch superior to man's; but dogs never show the slightest impulse or ability to imitate foreign sounds.

So we find several prerequisites for speech—sustained and variable vocalization, the tendency to responsive utterance, the epicritical hearing and fine control of vocalization by the ear that implement imitation—prefigured in the behavior patterns of widely different animals. Yet none of those animals use language. These traits are only some of its conditions, and even they do not coincide in any one species. In the protohuman primate they must have coincided—not only with each other, but with some further ones as well, that may or may not occur in other creatures.

The decisive function in the making of language comes, I think, from quite another quarter than the vocal-auditory complexes that serve its normal expression. That other quarter is the visual system, in which the visual image —the paradigm of what, therefore, we call "imagination"—almost certainly is produced.

How a visual image is engendered and what nervous mechanisms participate in its creation no one has yet described; I have gathered a few ideas on the subject, but they need not detain us here. The important thing is that images are the things that naturally take on the character of symbols. Images are "such stuff as dreams are made on"; dreams have the tendency to assume symbolic value, apparently very early in our lives, and the peculiar involutions of meaning in their imagery, the vagueness of connections, the spontaneity of their presentations, and the emotional excitement of any very vivid dream may well reflect the nature of primitive symbolic experience.

The old problem, how words became attached to objects as their distinctive names, and how they became generalized so that they denoted kinds of things rather than individuals, may find its solution if we can give up the notion that primitive man *invented* speech, and agreed on names for things and other basic conventions. I do not believe names were originally assigned to things at all; *naming* is a process that presupposes speech. Now that we have language, we can give names to new comets, new gadgets, and constantly to new babies. But in the making of speech, I think it more likely that definite phonetic structures were already at hand, developed in another context, and that meanings accrued to them—vaguely and variably at first, but by natural processes that tended to specify and fix them. Such meanings were not pragmatic signal values of specific sounds for specific things; several eminent psychiatrists to the contrary notwithstanding,[4] primitive denotation was not like using a proper name. When words took shape, they were general in intent, from the beginning; their connotations inhered in them, and their denotations were whatever fitted this inherent sense.

Now that I have thus pontificated on what happened, let me explain why I think something like this must have happened, and how it would account for the greatest of all mysteries of language—the fact that language is symbolic, when no animal utterance shows any tendency that way. The biological factors that caused this great shift in the vocal function were, I believe, the development of visual imagery in the humanoid brain, and the part it came to play in a highly exciting, elating experience, the festal dance. (How prehuman beings advanced from animal behavior to formalized tribal dance is another relevant subject I cannot broach here.) The mental image was, I

---

[4] Sylvano Arieti, "The Possibility of Psychosomatic Involvement of the Central Nervous System in Schizophrenia," *J. Nervous & Mental Disease*, CXXIII (1956), 324-33, esp. 332; where he (with whose views of symbol formation I agree in some respects, as will shortly be apparent), for instance, holds that in a primordial family a baby might babble "ma-ma" and associate the utterance "with the mother or with the image of the mother," and that "if a second sibling understands that the sound ma-ma refers to mother, language is originated. . . . But at this level the sound ma-ma denotes, but does not possess much connotation power."

See also J. S. Kasanin, "The Disturbance of Conceptual Thinking in Schizophrenia," in *Language and Thought in Schizophrenia*, ed. by J. S. Kasanin and N. D. C. Lewis (Berkeley, Calif. 1944): " . . . when the child says 'table' or 'chair' he does not mean tables or chairs in general, but the table or chair which is in his house or which belongs to him."

think, the catalyst that precipitated the conceptual import of speech.

As I remarked before, images are more prone than anything else we know to become symbols; they have several attributes that work together to make them symbolic. So it was another of the evolutionary coincidences that the Calibans who preceded us suffered a peculiar specialization in their visual systems, so that we produce mental images without even trying—most successfully, in fact, while we sleep.

There is a reason, of course, why this should be a hominid specialty, and we can at least guess what caused our odd and rather impractical habit of *visualizing*, with and without stimulation from the end organs, the eyes. The human brain presumably developed, like any animal brain we know, as a mediating organ between afferent impulses and their efferent completion, that is, their spending themselves in action. In animals, typically, every stimulation that takes effect at all is spent in some overt act, which may be anything from a reflex twitch of the skin to a directed act of the whole aroused creature. But the messages which come into our brains are so many and various that it would be impossible and exhausting to spend each afferent impulse in overt action. So a great many, especially the countless visual impressions we take in, have to be finished within the brain; the cerebral response is the formation of an image. This automatic process may occur in animals, too, but sporadically and at a lower intensity, and therefore without further consequences. If animals have images, I don't think they are bothered by them or use them; such passing visions may be like our after images, automatic products of sensory stimulation.

In human beings, however, image making has become a normal conclusion for acts of focused gazing. Since, in the waking state, it is easier to look at things than not to, image production is generally effortless and unintentional, and in the normal course of development soon becomes so rich that there is a constant play of imagery. Every impression is apt to produce an image, however briefly and incompletely, and out of this welter a few more definite visualizations emerge at intervals.

The several characteristics that make the mental image prone to become symbolic are, in the first place, this spontaneous, quasi-automatic production; secondly, a tendency of image-making processes to mesh, and pool their results; then, their origin in actual perception which gives images an obvious relation to the sources of perception—things perceived—a relation we call "representation"; furthermore, the very important fact that an image, once formed, can be reactivated in many ways, by all sorts of external and internal stimulations; and finally, its involvement with emotion. Let us consider what each of these traits has to do with the making of the primitive symbol, and with the enlistment of the vocal organs for its projection.

A biological mechanism that is about to assume a new function is usually developed at least somewhat beyond the needs of its original function—that is, its activity has a certain amount of play, sometimes called "excess energy," which allows unpredictable developments. A new departure is not likely to be based on rare occurrences, for to become established it has to survive many miscarriages, and that means that it has to begin over and over again—that is, the conditions for it have to be generous. So, in a brain where imagination was to take on a new and momentous function—symbolization— the production of images had to be a vigorous business, generating images all the time, so that most of them could be wasted, and the symbolic activity could still begin again and again, and proceed to various degrees, without interfering with the normal functions of the brain in the whole organic econ- omy. So the normality and ease of image producing met one of the first re- quisites for the rise of a higher function.

The second important feature of mental images for symbol making is the fact that the processes of imagination seem particularly prone to affect each other, to mingle and mesh and share their paths of activity, inhibiting or reinforcing nervous impulses in progress, and especially inducing all sorts of neighboring reactions. Consequently, their products tend to fuse: images that share some features fuse into one image with emphasis on those features, which thereby are stressed, and dominate the welter of other characters that, for their part, are weakened by fusion. Images, therefore, modify each other; some dominate others, and all tend to become simplified. Emphasis is what gives contours and gradients and other structural elements to images. Empha- sis is the natural process of abstraction, whereby our visual representations are made to differ from the direct perceptions that started them. Rudolph Arnheim in his book, *Art and Visual Perception,* has gone quite deeply into the distinctions between the laws of perception and those of representation. The point of interest here is that the power of abstract symbolic thinking, which plays such a great part in later human mentality, rests on a relatively primitive talent of abstractive seeing that comes with the nature of the visual image.[5]

The third major condition is simply the fact that images stem from per- cepts, and the process of their derivation is an original continuity of a peri- pheral event, the effect of a visible object on the eye, with the further nervous events that terminate in the formation of an image in the brain. The eye is the end organ of the visual apparatus; what goes on behind the retina, and espe- cially, perhaps, beyond the chiasma, is the rest of our seeing, with all its reverberations and complications and their astounding effects. The recognition

---

[5] Some interesting comments on abstractive seeing may also be found in Leo Steinberg's paper, "The Eye Is a Part of the Mind," *Partisan Rev.,* XX (1953), 194–212; reprinted in *Re- flections on Art* (Baltimore, 1958). There are also various studies of the neural processes involved in such sensory abstraction, e.g., D. M. Purdy, "The Structure of the Visual World," *Psychol. Rev.,* XLIII (1936), 59–82, esp. Pt. III; Fred Attneave's technological essay, "Some Informational Aspects of Visual Perception," *Psychol. Rev.,* LXI (1954), 183–93; Norbert Wiener's *Cybernetics* (New York, 1948); and especially in a study by W. H. Marshall and S. A. Talbot, "Recent Evidence for Neural Mechanisms in Vision Leading to a General Theory of Sensory Acuity," in H. Klüver, *Visual Mechanisms* (1942), pp. 117–64.

of an image as something connected with the external world is intuitive, as the response to external things in direct visual perception, which all seeing animals exhibit, is instinctive. This recognition of images as representations of visible things is the basis on which the whole public importance of symbols is built—their use for reference. But there must have been another coincidence to make that happen.

This crucial fourth factor is really part of that lability of imagination, and openness to influence, that we have already remarked; but more precisely, it is the fact that the occurrence of an image may be induced by a great many different kinds of stimulation, either from outside the organism or from within. Often one cannot tell what evokes a mental image; sometimes a whole situation that often recurs will always do it; for instance, whenever you step out on a pier and smell salt water you may have an image of your first sailboat. Even the salt smell alone may invoke it. So may the mention of the boat's name. Those are more specific stimuli, but there can be all kinds. This readiness to occur in a total context, but also to be touched off by small fragments of that context encountered in other settings, is the trait that frees the mental image from its original connection with peripheral vision, that is, from the thing it first represented. Add to this the tendency of images with traits in common to fuse and make a simplified image—that is, to become schematic—and you see how much of our image making would become casual acts of ideation, without any specific memory bonds to perceptual experiences. Not only the images themselves that share a schematic character, but also their representational functions fuse; any one of them can represent the original percept of any other; that is, as representations whole families of them can stand proxy one for another. Any image of a grasshopper can represent any grasshopper we have actually seen that was not so distinctive that it created an image too different to fit the schema. If such an oddity appears we form an image of a *special kind* of grasshopper. With its liberation from perception the image becomes general; and as soon as it can represent something else than its own original stimulus, it becomes a symbol. Schematic similarities in otherwise distinct images make it possible to recall one object through the image of another. Thus, for instance, the outline of the new moon as a canoe, or a canoe as a moon. Either assimilation reinforces the perception of shape. This is the natural process of abstraction. We speak of the sickle, the bowl, the disk of the moon in its various phases. In developed thinking we know whether we are talking about the moon or about a boat— that is, we know which image is standing proxy for the other. But studies in the symbolic functions occurring in dream and myth and some psychoses give support to the belief that this is a sober insight which was probably not very early. At the level of prehuman image mongering, the question is rather how one image, even without sensory support, becomes dominant over others, so that they are its symbolic representatives in imagination.

Here, the mechanism seems to be the connection of imagery with emotion. In the complex of images, the one most charged with emotion becomes the dominant image which all the others repeat, reinforce, and represent within the brain itself, even below the level of awareness—in the limbo of what Freud called "the dream work," whereby the significant images, the symbols for conception, are made.

These are, I think, the main physical and behavioral factors that must have existed conjointly in the one animal species that has developed speech: the power of elaborate vocalization, the discriminative ear that heard patterns of sounds, the nervous mechanisms that controlled utterance by hearing inner and outer sounds, and the tendency to utter long passages of sound in gatherings of many individuals—that is, the habit of joint ululation—with considerable articulation that recurred at about the same point within every such occasion, and, in these same beings, the high mental activity that issued in visual image making. The gatherings were probably communal rituals, or rather, awesome aesthetic precursors of genuine ritual, the ululations the vocal elements in primitive dance. This idea was propounded long ago by J. Donovan,[6] but no one seems to have paid much attention to it. I adopted it in an early book, *Philosophy in a New Key,* and the more I reflect on it the more I think it is sound. It was Donovan's idea that words were not primitive elements in human utterance when it became symbolic, but that meaning first accrued to longer passages, which were gradually broken or condensed into separate bits, each with its own fixed sense. But what he did not say—and I did not see, twenty years ago—was how conceptual meaning accrued to any vocal products at all. I certainly never realized what part the private mental image played in preparing the way for symbolic language—that the whole mechanism of symbolization was probably worked out in the visual system before its power could be transferred to the vocal-auditory realm. Now, with that helpful surmise, let us see how the transfer would be possible, and not too improbable.

In the elaborate development of tribal dance all individuals of the primitive horde became familiar with the vocal sounds that belonged to various sequences of steps and gestures, some perhaps mimetic, others simply athletic, but working up to climaxes of excitement. The "song," or vocal part of the dance, became more and more differentiated with the evolution of the gestic patterns. At high points there were undoubtedly special shouts and elaborate halloos. In the overstimulated brains of the celebrants, images must have been evoked at these points of action and special vocalization—images that tended to recur in that context, until for each individual his own symbolic images were built into the familiar patterns of tribal rituals. A dance passage takes time and energy and usually several persons to produce, but the vocal ingredient can be produced with little effort and a minimum of time by any

[6] "The Festal Origin of Human Speech," *Mind,* XVI, o.s. (1891), 498–506, and XVII (1892), 325–39.

individual. To remember the dance would bring the vocal element to his throat; as the memory of playing "London Bridge" will usually cause a child to hum the tune,

"Lon-don Bridge is fal-ling down,"

with no thought of a bridge or a fair lady, but of the game. So people could reactivate their emotional symbolic images by a snatch of the festal songs. If the dance action is, say, swinging a club, or even feels like that familiar and expansive act, the various images evoked will be of a club, or clubs, or raising or swinging clubs, or cracking them against each other. It is the image that symbolizes the activity and the objects involved in it. The image is the magical effect of the sound pattern when it is intoned apart from the dance.

The image is a pure conception; it does not signalize or demand its object, but it denotes it. Of course, this denotative symbol, the image, begets no communication, for it is purely private. But the things imaged are public, and the sounds that activate images are public; they affect everybody by evoking images at roughly the same moments of dance action. Within a fairly wide range it does not matter how different the private images are. They are equivalent symbols for the act or the objects that mark those stations in the ritual where the vocal bits belong, which may be uttered out of context by some individual; and suddenly meaning accrues to the phrase, other beings *understand*, especially if a connoted object is physically at hand, apart from its ritual context.

I suspect that the first meanings of such secularized vocalization were very vague; swing a club, hit a man with a club, kill man and beast, whirl and hit, get hit, wave a club at the moon—may all have belonged by turns to one long utterance, in which the separate articulate parts need not have had any separable meanings.[7] But once such passages were used to evoke ideas, their vocalization would quickly become modified, especially by reduction to the *speaking voice*, which can utter its sounds with more speed and less effort than any singing voice. This everyday utterance would tend to emphasize vowels and consonants—that is, mouth articulations—to replace distinctions of pitch. Some languages today use tonal distinctions, without precise pitch, as semantic devices. But in most human speech, tones serve only for punctuation and emotional coloring.

The great step from anthropoid to anthropos, animal to man, was taken when the vocal organs were moved to register the occurrence of an image, and stirred an equivalent occurrence in another brain, and the two creatures referred to the same thing. At that point, the vocal habit that had long served for communion assumed the function of communication. To evoke ideas in each other's minds, not in the course of action, but of emotion and memory

---

[7] In the *Encyclopaedia Britannica* (1957 ed., *s.v.* "Language"), Otto Jespersen voices the same opinion.

—that is, in reflection—is to communicate *about* something, and that is what no animals do.

From then on, speech probably advanced with headlong speed; the vaguely articulated phrases of the gathered horde contracted around their cores of meaning and made long, rich, omnibus words, and broke up into more specifically denotative words, until practically the whole phonetic repertoire was formalized into separable bits, and language entered the synthetic stage of making sentences out of words—the reverse of its pristine articulative process. The new motive of communication must have driven it like wildfire. At this stage if not before, the actual evocation of images became dispensable. We do not need vision to learn speech. The symbolic function has passed to the act of speech itself, and from there finally to the word itself, so that even hearing may be prosthetically replaced. For when verbalization is complete, people have not only speech, but language.

I think there were other uses of speechlike utterance, too—the principle of tracking down the elements of language that may be separately lost by cerebral impairment even today leads in many directions. Proper names may not have had the same origin as genuine nouns, and numerals are something different again; onomatopoetic words, too, seem to have had their own genesis, apart from the main source of language. But under the influence of language all utterances tended to become words. This is still the case. For instance, our expletives, that have no real verbal meaning in present-day language, always fall under its influence. Only a German says "ach"—most Americans cannot even pronounce it—he says "au" where an American says "ouch"; and who but a Frenchwoman would ever say "ou-la-la"?

Once communication got started, the rise of human mentality may have been cataclysmic, a matter of a few generations wherever it began at all. It must have been an exciting and disconcerting phase of our history. We have traces of it even to this day in the holy fear in which many people hold divine names, blessings, curses, magic formulas—all verbal fragments, imbued with the mystic power of thought that came with speech.

In looking back over all these processes that must have come together to beget language, I am struck by a few outstanding facts: in the first place, the depth to which the foundations go, on which this highest of all creature attainments is built; secondly, the complexity of all living functions, for every one of those preparatory traits was itself a highly integrated complex of many nervous processes; in the third place, the fact that not one of the constituents in the new and fateful talent was a mode of animal communication. It seems most likely that the office of communication was taken over by speech, from entirely different activities, when speech was well started; but undoubtedly communication was what henceforth made its history. Finally, it is a notable fact that the two senses which hold the greatest places in the human cortex, sight and hearing, were both needed to produce language; neither a sightless nor a deaf race could have evolved it. If man could either hear no evil or see no evil, he could speak no evil—nor yet any good.

CAMILLE NORTON
"Eating the Pasture"

Before there was a name for it,
a surprise of bitterness under the tongue.
It stung saliva into the mouth's sweet well,
a quickness awakening taste.
Then came a dissolving.

I took it where it was abundant,
where its spindling bodies
covered the ground in pasture.
I took it by its scalp, I uncovered
an underside of roots so white,
so come-alive and dangling
I was frightened, the fear of it
trembled inside my feeling hand.

Too late, I had already taken
the pulpy roots inside me,
their strange milkiness vanishing,
and after I swallowed
I ate what I encountered—
the flat stone, the fat slug,
a greening in my hands,
the tufts of bitter grasses.

Before the mind had words,
I tasted each of these, one by one,
each tang sharper than the one before,
the shocked tongue naming
the things of the world into meaning.

The Logic of Metaphor

Metaphor has been, for modern criticism, an important focus in which to study poetic language. I. A. Richards proposed (*Philosophy of Rhetoric,* 1936) that we study "how words work" (his definition of rhetoric) by looking carefully at metaphor. He contributed the terms "vehicle" and "tenor" to name the "what is said" and the "what is meant," but since the relationship there is only an intensified instance of that of language and thought, it can readily be seen that these terms are inadequate for the task of analysis. Richards came to see the usefulness of metaphor as a speculative instrument which can help us recognize the fact that in naming we identify and differentiate simultaneously; that in seeing anything, we are necessarily seeing with respect to something else; that all learning depends on relating the novel to the familiar. In short, metaphor illuminates the relationship of imagination and language.

Freya Stark writes lyrically of the often-remarked power of archetypal imagery in commonly used figures of speech. In "Poetic Diction and Legal Fiction," Owen Barfield returns to the question of how metaphor makes meaning which he first discussed in *Poetic Diction* (1927). His term *tarning* may be no more successful than *vehicle* and *tenor*, but Barfield's attempt to use it is instructive.

Walker Percy's essays on semiotics are unusual because he understands the implications of Peirce's insistence on the triadic character of the meaning relationship. "Metaphor as Mistake," besides being amusing and full of interesting speculation, provides a gloss on Cassirer's argument that it is in poetry, especially in metaphor, that the mythic force of language is reclaimed.

Three passages from two books of Ernst Cassirer are followed by Susanne K. Langer's essay, "On Cassirer's Theory of Language and Myth." Mrs. Langer translated *Language and Myth* before the three volumes of *Philosophie der symbolischen Formen* were available in English, because the short book provided, as she put it, "a look into the mental laboratory where new ideas are generated and developed." "On Cassirer's Theory of Language and Myth" appeared shortly after as a contribution to the Library of Living Philosophers volume on Cassirer. It is invaluable as an introduction to Cassirer's philosophy of symbolic form, but it is clearly more than that, for she has extended those ideas and has brought them to points which Cassirer himself had only begun to develop at the time of his death. This essay should be read in conjunction with "Speculations on the Origins of Speech . . ." (pp. 114–27), which lays the ground work for Mrs. Langer's own theory of symbolic expression developed in *Mind: An Essay on Human Feeling.*

FREYA STARK
from *The Journey's Echo*

A lot of observation lies under common figures of speech. One's heart stands still, or sinks, or leaps; one sees red, or is frozen with horror: no more accurate words could be found to describe what actually those feelings are. And it is ever our figurative thinking that is accurate, gives, that is to say, the unmistakable picture of what we intend. When they carry a picture, the simplest words can hold an extraordinary weight of meaning. Who, for instance, but one accustomed to the desert horizon could say like the Psalmist that the Lord has removed our sins from us "as far as the East from the West"? When we think of the words, we use what the Psalmist saw, and it is the fact of his having seen it that makes it live—not a deliberate skill with words which can never take the place of real vision.

OWEN BARFIELD
from "Poetic Diction and Legal Fiction"

. . . The language of poetry has always been in a high degree *figurative*; it is always illustrating or expressing what it wishes to put before us by comparing that with something else. Sometimes the comparison is open and avowed, as when Shelley compares the skylark to a poet, to a high-born maiden, and to a rose embowered in its own green leaves; when Keats tells us that a summer's day is:

like the passage of an angel's tear
That falls through the clear ether silently.

or when Burns writes simply: "My love is like a red red rose." And then we
call it a "simile." Sometimes it is concealed in the form of a bare statement,
as when Shelley says of the west wind, not that it is *like*, but that it *is* "the
breath of Autumn's being," calls upon it to "make him its lyre" and says of
himself that *his* leaves are falling. This is known as "metaphor." Sometimes
the element of comparison drops still farther out of sight. Instead of saying
that A is like B or that A is B, the poet simply talks about B, without making
any overt reference to A at all. You know, however, that he intends A all the
time, or, better say that you know he intends *an* A; for you may not have a
very clear idea of what A is and even if you have got an idea, somebody else
may have a different one. This is generally called "symbolism." . . . When we
start from the simile and move towards the symbol, the criterion or yardstick
by which we measure our progress is the element of *comparison*—paramount
in the simile and very nearly vanished out of sight in the symbol. When, on
the other hand, we move backwards, starting from the symbol, we find ourselves with another yardstick, viz. the fact of saying one thing and meaning
another. The poet says B but he means A. He hides A in B. B is the normal
everyday meaning which the words so to speak "ought" to have on the face
of them, and A is what the poet *really* has to say to us, and which he can only
say through or alongside of, or by modifying, these normal everyday meanings. A is his own new, original, or poetic meaning. If I were writing this article in Greek or German, my public would no doubt be severely restricted,
but there would be this advantage to me—that I could run the six words "say-
one-thing-and-mean-another" together and use the resulting conglomerate as
a noun throughout the rest of it. I cannot do this, but I will make bold to
borrow another German word instead. The word *Tarnung* was, I believe,
extensively used under the heel of the Nazi tyranny in Germany for the pre-
cautionary practice of hiding one meaning in another, the allusion being to
the *Tarnhelm* of the Nibelungs. I shall give it an English form and call it
"Tarning"—[by which is meant] the concept of saying one thing and meaning another.

WALKER PERCY
"Metaphor as Mistake"

In Mississippi, the coin record players, which are manufactured by Seeburg, are commonly known to Negroes as seabirds.

During the Korean war, one way of saying that someone had been killed was to say that he had bought the farm.

I remember hunting as a boy in South Alabama with my father and brother and a Negro guide. At the edge of some woods we saw a wonderful bird. He flew as swift and straight as an arrow, then all of a sudden folded his wings and dropped like a stone into the woods. I asked what the bird was. The guide said it was a Blue Dollar Hawk. Later my father told me the Negroes had got it wrong: it was really a Blue Darter Hawk. I can still remember my disappointment at the correction. What was so impressive about the bird was its dazzling speed and the effect of alternation of its wings, as if it were flying by a kind of oaring motion.

> As a small boy of six or seven walking the streets of Cambridge I used often to pass little dead-end streets, each with its signpost which at its top read, say, Trowbridge Place or Irving Terrace, and underneath in letters of a different color and on a separate board, the following mysterious legend: Private Way Dangerous Passing. The legend meant of course merely that the City of Cambridge, since it neither built nor maintained the roadbed of this place or this terrace, would not be responsible for injury to life or property sustained through its use. But to me it meant something else. It meant that there was in passing across its mouth a clear and present danger which might, and especially at dusk, suddenly leap out and overcome me. Thus, to say the least of it, I had the regular experience of that heightened, that excited sense of being which we find in poetry, whenever I passed one of those signs.
>
> R. P. Blackmur, in *Language as Gesture*

Misreadings of poetry, as every reader must have found, often give examples of this plausibility of the opposite term. I had at one time a great admiration for that line of Rupert Brooke's about

> The keen
> Impassioned beauty of a great machine,

a daring but successful image, it seemed to me, for that contrast between the appearance of effort and the appearance of certainty, between forces greater than human and control divine in its foreknowledge, which is what excites one about engines; they have the calm of *beauty* without

its complacence, the strength of *passion* without its disorder. So it was
a shock to me when I looked at one of the quotations of the line one is
always seeing about, and found that the beauty was *unpassioned*, because machines, as all good nature poets know, have no hearts. I still
think that a prosaic and intellectually shoddy adjective, but it is no
doubt more intelligible than my emendation, and sketches the same
group of feelings.

William Empson, in *Seven Types of Ambiguity*

Four of the five examples given above are mistakes: misnamings, misunderstandings, or misrememberings. But they are mistakes which, in each
case, have resulted in an authentic poetic experience—what Blackmur calls
"that heightened, that excited sense of being"—an experience, moreover,
which was notably absent before the mistake was made. I have included the
fifth, the Korean war expression "he bought the farm," not because it is a
mistake but because I had made a mistake in including it. The expression had
struck me as a most mysterious one, peculiarly potent in its laconic treatment
of death as a business transaction. But then a kind Korean veteran told me
that it may be laconic all right, but he didn't see anything mysterious about
it: the farm the G. I. was talking about was six feet of ground. This is probably obvious enough, but I have preserved this example of my own density as
instructive in what follows.

It might be useful to look into the workings of these accidental stum-
blings into poetic meaning, because they exhibit in a striking fashion that
particular feature of metaphor which has most troubled philosophers: that
it is "wrong"—it asserts of one thing that it is something else—and further,
that its beauty often seems proportionate to its wrongness or outlandishness.
Not that the single linguistic metaphor represents the highest moment of the
poetic imagination; it probably does not. Dante, as Allen Tate reminds us, uses
very few linguistic metaphors. The "greatest thing by far" which Aristotle had
in mind when he spoke of the mastery of the metaphor as a sign of genius
may very well have been the sort of prolonged analogy which Dante did use,
in which the action takes place among the common things of concrete experience and yet yields an analogy—by nothing so crude as an allegorization
wherein one thing is designated as standing for another but by the very density and thingness of the action. As Mr. Tate puts it: "Nature offers the symbolic poet clearly denotable objects in depth and in the round, which yield
the analogies to the higher syntheses." Yet the fact remains that the linguistic
metaphor is, for better or worse, more peculiarly accessible to the modern
mind—it may indeed be a distinctive expression of modern sensibility. And
it has the added advantage from my point of view of offering a concentrated
field for investigation—here something very big happens in a very small place.

Metaphor has scandalized philosophers, including both scholastics and
semioticists, because it seems to be wrong: it asserts an identity between two
different things. And it is wrongest when it is most beautiful. It is those very
figures of Shakespeare which 18th century critics undertook to "correct"

because they had so obviously gotten off the track logically and were sometimes even contradictory—it is just these figures which we now treasure most.

This element of outlandishness has resulted in philosophers' washing
their hands of beauty and literary men being glad that they have, in other
words, in a divorce of beauty and ontology, with unhappy consequences to
both. The difficulty has been that inquiries into the nature of metaphor have
tended to be either literary or philosophical with neither side having much
use for the other. The subject is divided into its formal and material aspects,
with philosophers trying to arrive at the nature of metaphor by abstracting
from all metaphors, beautiful and commonplace; with critics paying attention to the particular devices by which a poet brings off his effects. Beauty,
the importance attached to beauty, marks the parting of the ways. The philosopher attends to the formal structure of metaphor, asking such general
questions as, what is the relation between metaphor and myth? is metaphor
an analogy of proper or improper proportionality? and in considering his
thesis is notably insensitive to its beauties. In fact, the examples he chooses
to dissect are almost invariably models of tastelessness, such as smiling
meadow, leg of a table, John is a fox, etc. One can't help wondering, incidentally, if Aristotle's famous examples of "a cup as the shield of Ares" and
"a cup as the shield of Dionysus" didn't sound like typical philosopher's
metaphors to contemporary poets. Literary men, on the other hand, once
having caught sight of the beauty of metaphor, once having experienced what
Barfield called "that old authentic thrill which binds a man to his library for
life," are constrained to deal with beauty alone, with the particular devices
which evoke the beautiful, and let the rest go. If the theorist is insensitive to
the beauty of metaphor, the critic is insensitive to its ontology. To the question, why is this beautiful? the latter will usually give a *material* answer,
pointing to this or that effect which the poet has made use of. He is unsympathetic—and understandably so—to attempts to get hold of art by some
larger schema, such as a philosophy of being—feeling in his bones that when
the cold hand of theory reaches for beauty, it will succeed in grabbing everything except the beautiful.

Being neither critic nor philosopher, I feel free to venture into the no
man's land between the two and to deal with those very metaphors which
scandalize the philosopher because they are "wrong" and scandalize the critic
because they are accidental. Philosophers don't think much of metaphor to
begin with and critics can hardly have much use for folk metaphors, those
cases where one stumbles into beauty without deserving it or working for it.
Is it possible to get a line on metaphor, to figure out by a kind of lay empiricism what is going on in those poetic metaphors and folk metaphors where
the wrongness most patently coincides with the beauty?

When the Mississippi Negro calls the Seeburg record player a *seabird*, it
is not enough to say that he is making a colorful and poetic contribution to
language. It is less than useless to say that in calling a machine a bird he is
regressing into totemism, etc. And it is not even accurate to say that he knows

what the thing is and then gives it a picturesque if far-fetched name. In some fashion or other, he conceives the machine under the symbol *seabird*, a fashion, moreover, in regard to which we must be very wary in applying the words "right" or "wrong," "poetic" or "discursive," etc. Certainly the machine is not a seabird and no one imagines that it is, whatever the semanticists may say. Yet we may make a long cast and guess that in conceiving it as a *seabird*, the namer conceives it with richer overtones of meaning, and in some sense neither literal nor figurative, even as being more truly what it is than under its barbarous title, Seeburg automatic coin record player. There is a danger at this point in my being misunderstood as trying to strike a blow for the poetic against the technical, feeling against science, and on the usual aesthetic grounds. But my intention is quite the reverse. I mean to call attention to the rather remarkable fact that in conceiving the machine under the "wrong" symbol *seabird*, we somehow know it better, conceive it in a more plenary fashion, have more immediate access to it, than under its descriptive title. The sooner we get rid of the old quarrel of artistic *vs* prosaic as constituting the grounds of our preference, the sooner we shall be able to understand what is going on. Given these old alternatives, I'll take the prosaic any day—but what is going on here is of far greater moment.

The moments and elements of this meaning-situation are more easily grasped in the example of the boy seeing the strange bird in Alabama. The first notable moment occurred when he saw the bird. What struck him at once was the extremely distinctive character of the bird's flight—its very great speed, the effect of alternation of the wings, the sudden plummeting into the woods. This so distinctive and incommunicable something—the word which occurs to one is Hopkins' "inscape"—the boy perceived perfectly. It is this very uniqueness which Hopkins specifies in inscape: "the unspeakable stress of pitch, distinctiveness, selving."

The next moment is, for our purposes, the most remarkable of all, because it can receive no explanation in the conventional sign theory of meaning. The boy, having perfectly perceived the flight of the hawk, now suffers a sort of disability, a tension, even a sense of imminence! He puts the peculiar question, *what is that bird?*, and puts it importunately. He is really anxious to know. But to know what? What sort of answer does he hope to hear? What in fact is the meaning of his extraordinary question? Why does he want an answer at all? He has already apprehended the hawk in the vividest, most plenary way—a sight he will never forget as long as he lives. What more will he know by having the bird named? (No more, say the semioticists, and he deceives himself if he imagines that he does.)

We have already come to the heart of the question, and a very large question it is. For the situation of the boy in Alabama is very much the same sort of thing as what Cassirer calls the "mythico-religious Urphenomenon." Cassirer, following Usener and Spieth, emphasized the situation in which the primitive comes face to face with something which is both entirely new to him and strikingly distinctive, so distinctive that it might be said to have a *presence*—an oddly shaped termite mound, a particular body of water, a particular abandoned road. And it is in the two ways in which this tensional encounter is resolved that the Urphenomenon is said to beget metaphor and myth. The Tro or momentary god is born of the sense of unformulated presence of the thing; the metaphor arises from the symbolic act in which the emotional cry of the beholder becomes the vehicle by which the thing is conceived, the name of the thing. "In the vocables of speech and in primitive mythic configurations, the same inner process finds its consummation: they are both resolutions of an inner tension, the representation of subjective impulses and excitations in definite object forms and figures."

One recognizes the situation in one's own experience, that is, the metaphorical part of it. Everyone has a Blue Dollar Hawk in his childhood, especially if he grew up in the South or West where place names are so prone to poetic corruption. Chaisson Falls, named properly after its discoverer, becomes Chasin' Falls. Scapegoat Mountain, named after some Indian tale, becomes Scrapegoat Mountain—mythic wheels within wheels. And wonderfully: Purgatoire River becomes Picket Wire River. A boy grows up in the shadow of a great purple range called Music Mountain after some forgotten episode— perhaps the pioneers' first hoedown after they came through the pass. But this is not how the boy conceives it. When the late afternoon sun strikes the great pile in a certain light, the ridges turn gold, the crevasses are cast into a thundering blue shadow, then it is that he imagines that the wind comes soughing down the gorges with a deep organ note. The name, mysterious to him, tends to validate some equally mysterious inscape of the mountain.

So far so good. But the question on which everything depends and which is too often assumed to be settled without ever having been asked is this: given this situation and its two characteristics upon which all agree, the peculiar presence or distinctiveness of the object beheld and the peculiar need of the beholder—is this "need" and its satisfaction instrumental or ontological? That is to say: is it the function of metaphor merely to diminish tension, or is it a discoverer of being? Does it fit into the general scheme of need-satisfactions?—and here it doesn't matter much whether we are talking about the ordinary pragmatic view or Cassirer's symbolic form: both operate in an instrumental mode, one, that of biological adaption, the other, according to the necessities of the mythic consciousness. Neither provides for a real knowing, a truth-saying about what a being is. Or is it of such a nature that at least two sorts of realities must be allowed: one, the distinctive something beheld; two, the beholder (actually *two* beholders, one who gives the symbol and one who receives the symbol as meaningful, the Namer and Hearer) whose special, if imperfect gift it is to know and affirm this something for what it actually is? The question can't be bracketed, for the two paths lead in opposite directions, and everything one says henceforth on the subject must be understood from one or the other perspective. In this primitive encounter which is at the basis of man's cognitive orientation in the world, either we are trafficking in psychological satisfactions or we are dealing with that unique joy which marks man's ordainment to being and the knowing of it.

We come back to the "right" and "wrong" of Blue Dollar Hawk and Blue Darter Hawk. Is it proper to ask if the boy's delight at the "wrong" name is a psychological or ontological delight? And if the wrong name is cognitive, how is it cognitive? At any rate, we know that the hawk is named for the boy and he has what he wants. His mind, which had really suffered a sort of hunger (an ontological hunger?), now has something to feast on. The bird is, he is told, a Blue Darter Hawk. Two conditions, it will be noticed, must be met if the naming is to succeed. There must be an authority behind it—if the boy's brother had made up the name on the spur of the moment, it wouldn't have worked. Naming is more than a matter of a semantic "rule." But apparently there must also be—and here is the scandal—an element of obscurity about the name. The boy can't help but be disappointed by the logical modifier, Blue Darter Hawk—he feels that although he has asked what the bird *is*, his father has only told him what it *does*. If we will prescind for a moment from premature judgments about the "pre-logical" or magic character of the boy's preference, and also forego the next question, why is it called a Blue Dollar Hawk? which the boy may or may not have put but probably did not because he knew there was no logical answer the guide could give[1] — the function of the answer will become clearer. It is connected with the circumstance that the mysterious name, Blue Dollar Hawk, is both the "right" name—for it has been given in good faith by a Namer who should know and carries an *ipso facto* authority—and a "wrong" name—for it is not applicable as a logical modifier as Blue Darter is immediately and univocally applicable. Blue Dollar is not applicable as a modifier at all, for it refers to a *something else* beside the bird, a something which occupies the same ontological status as the bird. Blue Darter tells us something about the bird, what it does, what its color is; Blue Dollar tells, or the boy hopes it will tell, what the bird *is*. *For this ontological pairing, or, if you prefer, "error" of identification of word and thing, is the only possible way in which the apprehended nature of the bird, its inscape, can be validated as being what it is.* This inscape is, after all, otherwise ineffable. I can describe it, make crude approximations by such words as darting, oaring, speed, dive, etc., but none of these will suffice to affirm this so distinctive something which I have seen. This is why, as Marcel has observed, when I ask what something is, I am more satisfied to be given a name even if the name means nothing to me (especially if?), than to be given a scientific classification. Shelley said that poetry pointed out the before unapprehended relations of things. Wouldn't it be closer to the case to say that poetry validates that which had already been privately apprehended but had gone unformulated for both of us?

Without getting over one's head with the larger question of truth, one might still guess that it is extraordinarily rash of the positivist to limit truth

---

[1] Or if the guide did give an answer, it would be its very farfetchedness which would satisfy: "They calls him that because of the way he balls hisself up and rolls—"

to the logical approximation—to say that we cannot know what things are but only how they hang together. The copy theory gives no account of the *what* we are saying *how* about. As to the what: since we are not angels, it is true that we cannot know what it is intuitively and as it is in itself. The modern semioticist is scandalized by the metaphor, flesh is grass; but he is also scandalized by the naming sentence, this is flesh. As Professor Veatch has pointed out, he is confusing an instrument of knowing with what is known. The word *flesh* is not this solid flesh, and this solid flesh is not grass. But unless we name it *flesh* we shall not know it at all, and unless we call flesh grass we shall not know how it is with flesh. The semioticist leaves unexplained the act of knowing. He imagines naively that I know what this is and then give it a label, whereas the truth is, as Cassirer has shown so impressively, that I cannot know anything at all unless I symbolize it. We can only *con*ceive being, sidle up to it by laying something else alongside. We approach the thing not directly but by pairing, by apposing symbol and thing. Is it not premature to say with the mythist that when the primitive calls the lightning serpentine, he conceives it as a snake and is logically wrong? Both truth and error may be served here, error in so far as the lightning is held to participate magically in snakeness, truth in so far as the conception of snake may allow the privately apprehended inscape of the lightning to be formulated. I would have a horror of finding myself allied with those who in the name of instrumentality or inner warmth or whatnot would so attenuate and corrupt truth that it meant nothing. But an analysis of the symbol-relation reveals aspects of truth which go far beyond the notion of structural similarity which the symbolic logicians speak of. Two other traits of the thing are discovered and affirmed: one, that it *is*; two, that it is *something*.

Everything depends on this distinction between the thing privately apprehended and the thing apprehended and validated for you and me by naming. But is it proper to make such a distinction? Is there any difference, no difference, or the greatest possible difference, between that which I privately apprehend and that which I apprehend and you validate by naming in such a way that I am justified in hoping that you "mean" that very ineffable thing?

For at the basis of the beautiful metaphor—which one begins to see as neither logically "right" nor "wrong" but analogous—at the basis of that heightened sensibility of the poetic experience, there is always the hope that this secret apprehension of my own, which I cannot call knowing because I do not even know that I know it, has a chance of being validated by what you have said.

There must be a space between name and thing, for otherwise the private apprehension is straitened and oppressed. What is required is that the thing be both sanctioned and yet allowed freedom to be what it is. Heidegger said that the essence of truth is freedom. The essence of metaphorical truth and the almost impossible task of the poet is, it seems to me, to name unmistakably and yet to name by such a gentle analogy that the thing beheld by both of us may be truly formulated for what it is.

Blackmur's and Empson's examples are better "mistakes" than mine. The street sign in Cambridge, *Private Way Dangerous Passing*, misunderstood, allowed the exciting possibility that it was one's own secret forebodings about the little dead-end streets that was meant. But for all of Blackmur's unsurpassed analysis of this mysterious property of language, I think it unfortunate that he has chosen to call it "gesture," in view of the semioticist's use of the word to denote a term in a stimulus-response sequence (i.e., G. H. Mead's "conversation of gesture")—because this is exactly what it is not. It is a figurational and symbolic import in that sense which is farthest removed from gestural intercourse (such as the feint and parry of Mead's two boxers). It is, in fact, only when the gesture, word, or thing, is endowed with symbolic meaning, that is, united with a significance other than itself, that it takes on the properties which Blackmur attributes to it.

In Empson's examples, the beauty of the line depends on an actual misreading of what the poet wrote or on a corruption of the spelling. In the former case the poetic instincts of the reader are better than the poet's. What is important is that the reader's "mistake" has rescued the poet's figure from the logical and univocal similarity which the poet despite his best efforts could not escape and placed it at a mysterious and efficacious distance. The remembering of Brooke's *unpassioned machine* as *impassioned machine* is a good example of this. Another is a line of Nash which may or may not have been a mistake. What matters for our purpose is that it could have been.

> Beauty is but a flower
> Which wrinkles will devour
> Brightness falls from the air.

There is a cynical theory, Empson writes, that Nash wrote or meant *hair*:

> Brightness falls from the hair.

which is appropriate to the context, adequate poetically but less beautiful. Why? I refer to Professor Empson's analysis and venture only one comment. It may be true, as he says, that the very pre-Raphaelite vagueness of the line allows the discovery of something quite definite. In the presence of the lovely but obscure metaphor, I exist in the mode of hope, hope that the poet may mean such and such, and joy at any further evidence that he does. What Nash's line may have stumbled upon (if it is a mistake) is a perfectly definite but fugitive something—an inscape familiar to one and yet an inscape in bondage because I have never formulated it and it has never been formulated for me. Could the poet be referring to that particular time and that particular phenomenon of clear summer evenings when the upper air holds the last trembling light of day: one final moment of a soft diffused brilliance, then everything *falls* into dusk?

But Empson's most entertaining mistake is

> Queenlily June with a rose in her hair
> Moves to her prime with a langorous air.

For what saves the verse from mediocrity is the misreading of queenlily as Queen Lily, where the poet had intended the rather dreary adverb of queenly! Again I defer to Professor Empson's *material* analysis of what gives the misread line its peculiar charm. The question I would raise, in regard to this and many other examples in *Seven Types of Ambiguity*, has to do with Empson's main thesis. This thesis is, of course, that beauty derives from ambiguity—in this particular case, the felt possibility and interaction of the *two* readings of *queenlily*. But I submit that in this and other examples, as I read it and apparently as Empson read it, *the intended adverbial reading is completely overlooked!* The line is read with Queenlily and is charming; it only belatedly occurs to one, if it occurs at all, that the poet meant the adverb—and I feel certain Empson is not maintaining that I was aware of the adverb all along but "unconsciously." What one wonders, in this and in many other of Empson's quotations, is whether it is the ambiguity which is the operative factor, or *whether the beauty does not derive exclusively from the obscure term of the ambiguity*, the logically "wrong" but possibly analogous symbol.

In all those cases where the poet strains at the limits of the logical and the univocal, and when as a result his figure retains a residue of the logical and so has two readings: the univocal and the analogous—is it not in the latter that he has struck gold? We must be careful not to confuse ambiguity, which means equivocity, with true analogy, simply because both are looked upon as more or less vague. It is always possible, of course, to do what Empson does so well with his obscure metaphors, that is, to cast about for all the different interpretations the line will allow. But does the beauty of the line reside in its susceptibility to two or more possible readings or in the possibility of a *single* figurational meaning, which is the less analyzable as it is the more beautiful?

I can't help thinking, incidentally, that this hunt for the striking catachrestic metaphor in a poet of another time, such as Chaucer or Shakespeare, is a very treacherous game. For both the old poet and his modern reader are at the mercy of time's trick of cancelling the poet's own hard won figures and setting up new ones of its own. A word, by the very fact of its having been lost to common usage or by its having undergone a change in meaning, is apt to acquire thereby an unmerited potency.

One is aware of skirting the abyss as soon as one begins to repose virtue in the obscure. Once we eliminate the logical approximation, the univocal figure, as unpoetic and uncreative of meaning—is it not then simply an affair of trotting out words and images more or less at random in the hope of arriving at an obscure, hence efficacious, analogy? and the more haphazard the better, since mindfulness, we seem to be saying, is of its very nature, self-defeating? Such in fact is the credo of the surrealists: "To compare two objects, as remote from one another in character as possible, or by any other method put them together in a sudden and striking fashion, this remains the highest task to which poetry can aspire."[2] There is something to this. If, as

---

[2] André Breton, quoted by Richards in *The Philosophy of Rhetoric.*

so many modern poets appear to do, one simply shuffles words together, words plucked from as diversified contexts as possible, one will get some splendid effects. Words are potent agents and the sparks are bound to fly. But it is a losing game. For there is missing that essential element of the meaning situation, the authority and intention of the Namer. Where the Namer means nothing or does not know what he means or the Hearer does not think he knows what he means, the Hearer can hardly participate in a co-intention. Intersubjectivity fails. Once the good faith of the Namer is so much called into question, the jig is up. There is no celebration or hope of celebration of a thing beheld in common. One is only trafficking in the stored-up energies of words, hard won by meaningful usage. It is a pastime, this rolling out the pretty marbles of word-things to see one catch and reflect the fire of another, a pleasant enough game but one which must eventually go stale.

It is the cognitive dimension of metaphor which is usually overlooked, because cognition is apt to be identified with conceptual and discursive knowing. Likeness and difference are canons of discursive thought, but analogy, the mode of poetic knowing, is also cognitive. Failure to recognize the discovering power of analogy can only eventuate in a noncognitive psychologistic theory of metaphor. There is no knowing, there is no Namer and Hearer, there is no world beheld in common; there is only an interior "transaction of contexts" in which psychological processes interact to the reader's titillation.

The peculiar consequences of judging poetic metaphor by discursive categories are especially evident in Professor Richards' method. Lord Kames had criticized the metaphor "steep'd" in Othello's speech

> Had it pleas'd heaven
> To try me with affliction, had he rain'd
> All kinds of sores, and shames, on my bare head,
> Steep'd me in poverty to the very lips,

by saying that "the resemblance is too faint to be agreeable—Poverty must here be conceived to be a fluid which it resembles not in any manner." Richards goes further: "It is not a case of lack of resemblances but too much sheer oppositeness. For Poverty, the Tenor, is a state of deprivation, of desiccation; but the vehicle—the sea or vat in which Othello is to be steep'd—gives an instance of superfluity . . ." True, disparity as well as resemblance works in metaphor, but Richards says of this instance of disparity: "I do not myself find any defence of the word except this, which seems indeed quite sufficient —as dramatic necessities commonly are—that Othello is himself horribly disordered, that the utterance is part of the 'storm of horror and outrage'." Thus, Professor Richards gives "steep'd" a passing mark, but only because Othello is crazy. He may be right: the figure is extravagant, in a sense "wrong," yet to me defensible even without a plea of insanity. The only point I wish to make is that there is another cognitive ground on which it can be judged besides that of logical rightness and wrongness, univocal likeness and unlikeness.

Judged accordingly, it must always be found wanting—an 18th century critic would have corrected it. But do the alternatives lie between logical sense and nonsense? Or does such a view overlook a third way, the relation of analogy and its cognitive dimension? In the mode of analogy, "steep'd" is not only acceptable, it is striking; "steep'd" may be wrong univocally but right analogically. True, poverty is, logically speaking, a deprivation; but in its figuration it is a veritable something, very much a milieu with a smell and taste all its own, in which one is all too easily steep'd. Poverty is defined as a lack but is conceived as a something. What is univocally unlike in every detail may exhibit a figurative proportionality which is more generative of meaning than the cleverest simile.

An unvarying element in the situation is a pointing at by context. There must occur a preliminary meeting of minds and a mutually intended subject before anything can be said at all. The context may vary all the way from a literal pointing-by-finger and naming in the aboriginal act, to the pointing context of the poem which specifies the area where the metaphor is to be applied. There is a reciprocal relationship between the selectivity of the pointing and the univocity of the metaphor: the clearer the context and the more unmistakable the pointing, the greater latitude allowed the analogy of the metaphor. The aboriginal naming act is, in this sense, the most obscure and the most creative of metaphors; no modern poem was ever as obscure as Miss Sullivan's naming water *water* for Helen Keller. A perfectly definite something is pointed at and given a name, a sound or a gesture to which it bears only the most tenuous analogical similarities.[3]

[3] The old debate, started in the *Cratylus,* goes on as lively as ever: what is the relation between the name and the thing, between the word *green* and the color green, between *slice* and slice, *tree* and tree? Most linguists would probably say there is no relation, that the name is purely an arbitrary convention (except in a few cases like *boom*), that any seeming resemblance is false onomatopoeia (no matter how much you might imagine that *slice* resembles and hence expresses the act of slicing, it really does not).

But here again, do likeness and unlikeness exhaust the possibilities?

Apparently not. Curtius remarks that "despite all change, a conservative instinct is discernible in language. All the peoples of our family from the Ganges to the Atlantic designate the notion of standing by the phonetic group *sta-*; in all of them the notion of flowing is linked with the group *plu*, with only slight modifications. This cannot be an accident. Assuredly the same notion has remained associated with the same sounds through all the millenia, because the peoples felt a certain *inner connection* between the two, i.e., because of an instinct to express this notion by these particular sounds. The assertion that the oldest words presuppose some relation between sounds and the representations they designate has often been ridiculed. It is difficult, however, to explain the origin of language without such assumptions." (Quoted by Cassirer, *The Philosophy of Symbolic Forms,* vol. 1, p. 191)

It is this "inner connection" which concerns us. The sounds *plu* and *sta*, which could hardly be more different from the acts of flowing and standing, must nevertheless exhibit some mysterious connection which the mind fastens upon, a connection which, since it is not a kind of univocal likeness, must be a kind of analogy.

Given the situation of Naming and Hearing, there can only be one of three issues to an act of pointing at and naming. What is said will either be old, that is, something we already know and know quite overtly; or something new, and if it is utterly new, I can only experience bafflement; or new-old, that is, something that I had privately experienced but which was not available to me because it had never been formulated and rendered inter-subjective. Metaphor is the true maker of language.

The creative relationship of *inscape,* the distinctive reality as it is apprehended, and the distanced metaphor is illustrated by Hopkins' nature metaphors. His favorite pursuit in the nature journals is the application of striking (sometimes strained) like-yet-unlike metaphors to nature inscapes. There are some pleasing effects. A bolt of lightning is

> a straight stroke, broad like a stroke with chalk and liquid, as if the blade of an oar just stripped open a ribbon scar in smooth water and it caught the light.

We are aware that the effect is achieved by applying the notions of water and scars to lightning, the most unwaterlike or unscarlike thing imaginable. But are these metaphors merely pleasing or shocking or do they discover?—discover an aspect of the thing which had gone unformulated before?

Clouds are called variously bars, rafters, prisms, mealy, scarves, curds, rocky, a river (of dull white cloud), rags, veils, tatters, bosses.

The sea is

> paved with wind . . . bushes of foam

> Chips of foam blew off and gadded about without weight in the air.

> Straps of glassy spray.

In these metaphors both the likeness and unlikeness are striking and easily discernible. One has the impression, moreover, that their discovering power has something to do with their unlikeness, the considerable space between tenor and vehicle. Hard things like rocks, bosses, chips, glass, are notably unlike clouds and water; yet one reads

> Chips of foam blew off and gadded about

with a sure sense of validation.

If we deviate in either direction, toward a more univocal or accustomed likeness or toward a more mysterious unlikeness, we feel at once the effect of what Richards calls the tension of the bow, both the slackening and tightening of it. When one reads fleecy clouds or woolly clouds, the effect is slack indeed. Vehicle and tenor are totally inter-articulated: clouds are ordinarily conceived as being fleecy; fleecy is what clouds are (just as checkered is what a career is). You have told me nothing. Fleecy cloud, leg of a table, are tautologies, a regurgitation of something long since digested. But

> A straight river of dull white cloud

is lively. One feels both knowledgeable and pleased. But

  A white shire of cloud

is both more interesting and more obscure. The string of the bow is definitely
tightened. The mind is off on its favorite project, a casting about for analogies
and connections. Trusting in the good faith of the Namer, I begin to wonder
if he means thus and so—this particular sort of cloud. The only "shire" I
know is a geographical area and what I more or less visualize is a towering
cumulus of an irregular shire-shape.

  Two levels of analogy-making can be distinguished here. There is the
level of metaphor proper, the saying about one thing that it is something
else: one casts about to see *how* a cloud can be a shire, and in hitting on an
analogy, one validates an inscape of cloud. But there is the more primitive
level of naming, of applying a sound to a thing, and of the certification of
some sounds as being analogous to the thing without being like it (as in the
mysterious analogy between *plu* and flowing, *sta* and standing). Thus *shire*
may be applicable to a certain kind of cloud *purely as a sound* and without
a symbolized meaning of its own. For as it happens, concrete nouns beginning
with *sh* often refer to objects belonging to a class of segmented or sectioned
or roughly oblong flattened objects, a "geographical" class: shape, sheath,
shard, sheet, shelf, shield, shire, shoal, shovel, shroud, etc. One speculates
that the vocable *sh*—is susceptible of this particular spatial configuration. (I
easily imagine that the sound *sh* has a flatness or parallelness about it.) This
relation is very close to the psychological phenomenon of synaesthesia, the
trans-sensory analogy in which certain sounds, for example, are characteristically related to certain sounds—*blue* to color blue (could blue ever be
called *yellow*?).

  To summarize: the examples given of an accidental blundering into
authentic poetic experience both in folk mistakes and in mistaken readings
of poetry are explored for what light they may shed on the function of metaphor in man's fundamental symbolic orientation in the world. This "wrongness" of metaphor is seen to be not a vagary of poets but a special case of
that mysterious "error" which is the very condition of our knowing anything
at all. This "error," the act of symbolization, is itself the instrument of
knowing and is an error only if we do not appreciate its intentional character.
If we do not take note of it, or if we try to exorcize it as a primitive residue,
we shall find ourselves on the horns of the same dilemma which has plagued
philosophers since the 18th century. The semanticists, on the one horn, imply
that we know as the angels know, directly and without mediation (although
saying in the next breath that we have no true knowledge of reality); all that
remains is to name what we know and this we do by a semantic "rule"; but
they do not and cannot say how we know. The behaviorists, on the other,
imply that we do not know at all but only respond and that even art is a mode
of sign-response; but they do not say how they know this. But we do know, not
as the angels know and not as dogs know but as men who must know one
thing through the mirror of another.

ERNST CASSIRER
from *Language and Myth*

. . . The mythical form of conception is not something super-added to
certain definite *elements* of empirical existence; instead, the primary "experience" itself is steeped in the imagery of myth and saturated with its atmosphere. Man lives with *objects* only in so far as he lives with these *forms*; he
reveals reality to himself, and himself to reality, in that he lets himself and
the environment enter into this plastic medium, in which the two do not
merely make contact, but fuse with each other.

Consequently all those theories which propose to find the roots of myth
by exploring the realm of experience, of *objects*, which are supposed to have
given rise to it, and from which it then allegedly grew and spread, must always
remain one-sided and inadequate. There are, as is well known, a multitude of
such explanations—a great variety of doctrines about the ultimate origin and
real kernel of mythmaking, hardly less motley than the world of objects itself.
Now it is found in certain psychical conditions and experiences, especially
the phenomenon of dreaming, now in the contemplation of natural events,
and among the latter it is further limited to the observation of natural objects
such as the sun, the moon, the stars, or else to that of great occurrences such
as storms, lightning and thunder, etc. Thus the attempt is made again and
again to make soul mythology or nature mythology, sun or moon or thunder
mythology the basis of mythology as such.

But even if one of these attempts should prove successful, this would
not solve the real problem which mythology presents to philosophy, but at
best would push it back one step. For mythical formulation as such cannot
be understood and appreciated simply by determining the *object* on which it
is immediately and originally centered. It is, and remains, the same miracle of
the spirit and the same mystery, no matter whether it covers this or that
realistic matter, whether it deals with the interpretation and articulation of
psychical processes or physical things, and in the latter case, just what particular things these may be. Even though it were possible to resolve all mythology
to a basic astral mythology—what the mythical consciousness derives from
contemplation of the stars, what it *sees* in them directly, would still be something radically different from the view they present to empirical observation
or the way they figure in theoretical speculation and scientific "explanations"
of natural phenomena. Descartes said that theoretical science remains the
same in its essence no matter what object it deals with—just as the sun's light
is the same no matter what wealth and variety of things it may illuminate.
The same may be said of any symbolic form, of language, art, or myth, in
that each of these is a particular way of seeing, and carries within itself its

particular and proper source of light. The function of envisagement, the dawn of a conceptual enlightenment can never be realistically derived from things themselves or understood through the nature of its objective contents. For it is not a question of what we see in a certain perspective, but of the perspective itself. If we conceive the problem in this way, it is certainly clear that a reduction of all myth to one subject matter brings us no nearer to the solution, in fact it removes us further than ever from any hope of a real answer. For now we see in language, art and mythology so many archetypal phenomena of human mentality which can be indicated as such, but are not capable of any further "explanation" in terms of something else. The realists always assume, as their solid basis for all such explanations, the so-called "given," which is thought to have some definite form, some inherent structure of its own. They accept this reality as an integrated whole of causes and effects, things and attributes, states and processes, of objects at rest and of motions, and the only question for them is which of these elements a particular mental product such as myth, language or art originally embodies. If, for instance, the phenomenon in question is language, their natural line of inquiry must be whether names for things preceded names for conditions or actions, or vice versa—whether, in other words, nouns or verbs were the first "roots" of speech. But this problem itself appears spurious as soon as we realize that the distinctions which here are taken for granted, the analysis of reality in terms of things and processes, permanent and transitory aspects, objects and actions, do not precede language as a substratum of given fact, but that language itself is what initiates such articulations, and develops them in its own sphere. Then it turns out that language could not begin with any phase of "noun concepts" or "verb concepts," but is the very agency that produces the distinction between these forms, that introduces the great spiritual "crisis" in which the permanent is opposed to the transient, and Being is made the contrary of Becoming. So the linguistic fundamental concepts must be realized as something prior to these distinctions, forms which lie between the sphere of noun conception and that of verb conception, between thinghood and eventuality, in a state of indifference, a peculiar balance of feeling.

A similar ambiguity seems to characterize the earliest phases to which we can trace back the development of mythical and religious thought. It seems only natural to us that the world should present itself to our inspection and observation as a pattern of definite forms, each with its own perfectly determinate spatial limits that give it its specific individuality. If we see it as a whole, this whole nevertheless consists of clearly distinguishable units, which do not melt into each other, but preserve their identity that sets them definitely apart from the identity of all the others. But for the mythmaking consciousness these separate elements are not thus separately given, but have to be originally and gradually derived from the whole; the process of culling and sorting out individual forms has yet to be gone through. For this reason the mythic state of mind has been called the "complex" state, to distinguish it from our abstract analytic attitude.

* * *

. . . Myth receives new life and wealth from language, as language does from myth. And this constant interaction and interpenetration attests the unity of the mental principle from which both are sprung, and of which they are simply different expressions, different manifestations and grades.

Yet in the advance of human mentality even this conjunction, close and essential though it seems to be, begins to disintegrate and dissolve. For language does not belong exclusively to the realm of myth; it bears within itself, from its very beginning, another power, the power of logic. How this power gradually waxes great, and breaks its way by means of language, we cannot undertake to set forth here. But in the course of that evolution, words are reduced more and more to the status of mere conceptual signs. And this process of separation and liberation is parallelled by another: art, like language, is originally bound up entirely with myth. Myth, language and art begin as a concrete, undivided unity, which is only gradually resolved into a triad of independent modes of spiritual creativity. Consequently, the same mythic animation and hypostatization which is bestowed upon the words of human speech is originally accorded to *images*, to every kind of artistic representation. Especially in the magical realm, word magic is everywhere accompanied by picture magic. The image, too, achieves its purely representative, specifically "aesthetic" function only as the magic circle with which mythical consciousness surrounds it is broken, and it is recognized not as a mythico-magical form, but as a particular sort of *formulation*.

But although language and art both become emancipated, in this fashion, from their native soil of mythical thinking, the ideal, spiritual unity of the two is reasserted upon a higher level. If language is to grow into a vehicle of thought, an expression of concepts and judgments, this evolution can be achieved only at the price of forgoing the wealth and fullness of immediate experience. In the end, what is left of the concrete sense and feeling content it once possessed is little more than a bare skeleton. But there is one intellectual realm in which the word not only preserves its original creative power, but is ever renewing it; in which it undergoes a sort of constant palingenesis, at once a sensuous and a spiritual reincarnation. This regeneration is achieved as language becomes an avenue of artistic expression. Here it recovers the fullness of life; but it is no longer a life mythically bound and fettered, but an aesthetically liberated life. Among all types and forms of poetry, the lyric is the one which most clearly mirrors this ideal development. For lyric poetry is not only rooted in mythic motives as its beginning, but keeps its connection with myth even in its highest and purest products. The greatest lyric poets, for instance Hölderlin or Keats, are men in whom the mythic power of insight breaks forth again in its full intensity and objectifying power. But this objectivity has discarded all material constraints. The spirit lives in the word of language and in the mythical image without falling under the control of either. What poetry expresses is neither the mythic word-picture of gods and daemons, nor the logical truth of abstract determinations and relations. The world of poetry stands apart from both, as a world of illusion and fantasy—

but it is just in this mode of illusion that the realm of pure feeling can find utterance, and can therewith attain its full and concrete actualization. Word and mythic image, which once confronted the human mind as hard realistic powers, have now cast off all reality and effectuality; they have become a light, bright ether in which the spirit can move without let or hindrance. This liberation is achieved not because the mind throws aside the sensuous forms of word and image, but in that it uses them both as *organs* of its own, and thereby recognizes them for what they really are: forms of its own self-revelation.

SUSANNE K. LANGER
"On Cassirer's Theory of Language and Myth"

Every philosopher has his tradition. His thought has developed amid certain problems, certain basic alternatives of opinion, that embody the key concepts which dominate his time and his environment and which will always be reflected, positively or by negation, in his own work. They are the forms of thought he has inherited, wherein he naturally thinks, or from which his maturer conceptions depart.

The continuity of culture lies in this handing down of usable forms. Any campaign to discard tradition for the sake of novelty as such, without specific reason in each case to break through a certain convention of thought, leads to dilettantism, whether it be in philosophy, in art, or in social and moral institutions. As every person has his mother tongue in terms of which he cannot help thinking his earliest thoughts, so every scholar has a philo-sophical mother tongue, which colors his natural *Weltanschauung*. He may have been nurtured in a particular school of thought, or his heritage may be the less conscious one of "common sense," the popular metaphysic of his generation; but he speaks some intellectual language that has been bestowed on him, with its whole cargo of preconceptions, distinctions, and evaluations, by his official and unofficial teachers.

A great philosopher, however, has something new and vital to present in whatever philosophical mold he may have been given. The tenor of his thought stems from the past; but his specific problems take shape in the face of a living present, and his dealing with them reflects the entire, ever-nascent activity of his own day. In all the great periods of philosophy, the leading minds of the time have carried their traditional learning lightly, and felt most deeply the challenge of things which were new in their age. It is the new that calls urgently for interpretation; and a true philosopher is a person to whom something in the weary old world always appears new and uncomprehended.

There are certain "dead periods" in the history of philosophy, when the whole subject seems to shrink into a hard, small shell, treasured only by scholars in large universities. The common man knows little about it and cares less. What marks such a purely academic phase of philosophical thought is that its substance as well as its form is furnished by a scholastic tradition; not only the categories, but the problems of debate are familiar. Precisely in the most eventful epochs, when intellectual activity in other fields is brilliant and exciting, there is quite apt to be a lapse in philosophy; the greatest minds are engaged elsewhere; reflection and interpretation are in abeyance when the tempo of life is at its highest. New ideas are too kaleidoscopic to be systematically construed or to suggest general propositions. Professional philosophers, therefore, continue to argue matters which their predecessors have brought to no conclusion, and to argue them from the same standpoints that yielded no insight before.

We have only recently passed through an "academic" phase of philosophy, a phase of stale problems and deadlocked "isms." But today we are on the threshold of a new creative period. The most telling sign of this is the tendency of great minds to see philosophical implications in facts and problems belonging to other fields of learning—mathematics, anthropology, psychology, physics, history, and the arts. Familiar things like language or dream, or the mensurability of time, appear in new universal connections which involve highly interesting abstract issues. Even the layman lends his ear to "semantics" or to new excitements about "relativity."

Cassirer had all the marks of a great thinker in a new philosophical period. His standpoint was a tradition which he inherited—the Kantian "critical" philosophy seen in the light of its later developments, which raised the doctrine of transcendental forms to the level of a transcendental theory of Being. His writings bear witness that he often reviewed and pondered the foundations of this position. There was nothing accidental or sentimental in his adherence to it; he maintained it throughout his life, because he found it fruitful, suggestive of new interpretations. In his greatest works this basic idealism is implicit rather than under direct discussion; and the turn it gives to his treatment of the most baffling questions removes it utterly from that treadmill of purely partisan reiteration and defense which is the fate of decadent metaphysical convictions. There is little of polemic or apologetic in Cassirer's writings; he was too enthusiastic about solving definite problems to spend his time vindicating his method or discussing what to him was only a starting-point.

One of the venerable puzzles which he treated with entirely new insight from his peculiarly free and yet scholarly point of view is the relation of language and myth. Here we find at the outset the surprising, unorthodox working of his mind: for what originally led him to this problem was not the contemplation of poetry, but of science. For generations the advocates of scientific thinking bemoaned the difficulties which nature seems to plant in its path—the misconceptions bred by "ignorance" and even by language itself. It took Cassirer to see that those difficulties themselves were worth investigating. Ignorance is a negative condition; why should the mere absence of correct conceptions lead to *mis*conceptions? And why should language, supposedly a practical instrument for conveying thought, serve to resist and distort scientific thought? The misconceptions interested him.

If the logical and factual type of thought which science demands is hard to maintain, there must be some other mode of thinking which constantly interferes with it. Language, the expression of thought, could not possibly be a hindrance to thought as such; if it distorts scientific conception, it must do so merely by giving preference and support to such another mode.

Now, all thinking is "realistic" in the sense that it deals with phenomena as they present themselves in immediate experience. There cannot be a way of thinking that is not true to the reports of sense. If there are two modes of thinking, there must be two different modes of perceiving things, of apprehending the very data of thought. To *observe* the wind, for instance, as a purely physical atmospheric disturbance, and *think* of it as a divine power or an angry creature would be purely capricious, playful, irresponsible. But thinking is a serious business, and probably always has been; and it is not likely that language, the physical image of thought, portrays a pattern of mere fancies and vagaries. In so far as language is incompatible with scientific reasoning, it must reflect a system of thought that is soberly true to a *mode of experiencing*, of seeing and feeling, different from our accepted mode of experiencing "facts."[1]

This idea, first suggested by the difficulties of scientific conception, opened up a new realm of epistemological research to its author; for it made the *forms of misunderstanding* take on a positive rather than a negative importance as *archaic forms of understanding.* The hypostatic and poetic tinge of language which makes it so often recalcitrant to scientific purposes is a record not only of a different way of thinking, but of seeing, feeling, conceiving experience—a way that was probably paramount in the ages when language itself came into being. The whole problem of mind and its relation to "reality" took a new turn with the hypothesis that former civilizations may actually have dealt with a "real world" differently constituted from our own world of things with their universal qualities and causal relationships. But how can that older "reality" be recaptured and demonstrated? And how can the change from one way of apprehending nature to another be accounted for?

The answer to this methodological question came to him as a suggestion from metaphysics. *"Es ist der Geist der sich den Körper baut,"* said Goethe. And the post-Kantian idealists, from Fichte to Hermann Cohen, had gone even beyond that tenet; so they might well have said, *"Es ist der Geist der sich das Weltall baut."* To a romanticist that would have been little more than a figure of speech, expressing the relative importance of mind and matter. But in

---

[1] Cf. *Language and Myth*, 10f.

Cassirer's bold and uncomplacent mind such a belief—which he held as a basic intellectual postulate, not as a value-judgment—immediately raised the question: How? By what process and what means does the human spirit *construct* its physical world?

Kant had already proposed the answer: By supplying the transcendental constituent of *form*. Kant regarded this form as a fixed pattern, the same in all human experience; the categories of thought which find their clearest expression in science, seemed to him to govern all empirical experience, and to be reflected in the structure of language. But the structure of language is just what modern scientific thought finds uncongenial. It embodies a metaphysic of substance and attribute; whereas science operates more and more with the concept of *function*, which is articulated in mathematics.[2] There is good reason why mathematicians have abandoned verbal propositions almost entirely and resorted to a symbolism which expresses different metaphysical assumptions, different categories of thought altogether.

At this point Cassirer, reflecting on the shift from substantive to functional thinking, found the key to the methodological problem: two different symbolisms revealed two radically different forms of thought; does not every form of *Anschauung* have its symbolic mode? Might not an exhaustive study of symbolic forms reveal just how the human mind, in its various stages, has variously construed the "reality" with which it dealt? To *construe* the equivocally "given" is to *construct* the phenomenon for experience. And so the Kantian principle, fructified by a wholly new problem of science, led beyond the Kantian doctrine to the Philosophy of Symbolic Forms.

The very plan of this work departs from all previous approaches to epistemology by not assuming either that the mind is concerned essentially with facts, or that its prime talent is discursive reason. A careful study of the scientific misconceptions which language begets revealed the fact that its subject-predicate structure, which reflects a "natural" ontology of substance and attribute, is not its only metaphysical trait. Language is born of the need for emotional expression. Yet it is not exclamatory. It is essentially hypostatic, seeking to distinguish, emphasize, and hold the object of feeling rather than to communicate the feeling itself. To fix the object as a permanent focus point in experience is the function of the *name*. Whatever evokes emotion may therefore receive a name; and, if this object is not a thing—if it is an act, or a phenomenon like lightning, or a sound, or some other intangible item—, the name nevertheless gives it the unity, permanence, and apparent substantiality of a "thing."

This hypostasis, entailed by the primitive office of language, really lies deeper even than nomenclature, which merely reflects it: for it is a fundamental trait of all *imagination*. The very word "imagination" denotes a process of image-making. An image is only an aspect of the actual thing it represents. It may be not even a completely or carefully abstracted aspect. Its importance

---

[2] See *Substance and Function*, Ch. I. (All books cited in footnotes are by Cassirer.)

lies in the fact that it symbolizes the whole—the thing, person, occasion, or what-not—from which it is an abstract. A thing has a history, an event passes irrevocably away, actual experience is transient and would exhaust itself in a series of unique occasions, were it not for the permanence of the symbol whereby it may be recalled and possessed. Imagination is a free and continual production of images to "mean" experience—past or present or even merely possible experience.

Imagination is the primary talent of the human mind, the activity in whose service language was evolved. The imaginative mode of ideation is not "logical" after the manner of discursive reason. It has a logic of its own, a definite pattern of identifications and concentrations which bring a very deluge of ideas, all charged with intense and often widely diverse feelings, together in one symbol.

Symbols are the indispensable instruments of conception. To undergo an experience, to react to immediate or conditional stimuli (as animals react to warning or guiding signs), is not to "have" experience in the characteristically human sense, which is to conceive it, hold it in the mind as a so-called "content of consciousness," and consequently be able to think *about* it.[3] To a human mind, every experience—a sensation of light or color, a fright, a fall, a continuous noise like the roar of breakers on the beach—exhibits, in retrospect, a unity and self-identity that make it almost as static and tangible as a solid object. By virtue of this hypostatization it may be *referred to,* much as an object may be *pointed at*; and therefore the mind can think about it without its actual recurrence. In its symbolic image the experience is *conceived,* instead of just physiologically remembered.[4]

Cassirer's greatest epistemological contribution is his approach to the problem of mind through a study of the primitive forms of conception. His reflections on science had taught him that all conception is intimately bound to expression; and the forms of expression, which determine those of conception, are symbolic forms. So he was led to his central problem, the diversity of symbolic forms and their interrelation in the edifice of human culture.

He distinguished, as so many autonomous forms, language, myth, art, and science.[5] In examining their respective patterns he made his first startling discovery: myth and language appeared as genuine twin creatures, born of the same phase of human mentality, exhibiting analogous formal traits, despite their obvious diversities of content. Language, on the one hand, seems to have articulated and established mythological concepts, whereas, on the other hand, its own meanings are essentially images functioning mythically. The two modes of thought have grown up together, as conception and expression, respectively, of the primitive human world.

[3] Cf. *Language and Myth,* 38.
[4] See *An Essay on Man,* chapters 2 and 3, *passim.*
[5] *Language and Myth,* 8.

The earliest products of mythic thinking are not permanent, self-identical, and clearly distinguished "gods;" neither are they immaterial spirits. They are like dream elements—objects endowed with daemonic import, haunted places, accidental shapes in nature resembling something ominous—all manner of shifting, fantastic images which speak of Good and Evil, of Life and Death, to the impressionable and creative mind of man. Their common trait is a quality that characterizes everything in the sphere of myth, magic, and religion, and also the earliest ethical conceptions—the quality of *holiness.*[6] Holiness may appertain to almost anything; it is the mystery that appears as magic, as taboo, as daemonic power, as miracle, and as divinity. The first dichotomy in the emotive or mythic phase of mentality is not, as for discursive reason, the opposition of "yes" and "no," of "a" and "non-a," or truth and falsity; the basic dichotomy here is between the sacred and the profane. Human beings actually apprehend *values* and expressions of values *before* they formulate and entertain *facts.*

All mythic constructions are symbols of value—of life and power, or of violence, evil, and death. They are charged with feeling, and have a way of absorbing into themselves more and more intensive meanings, sometimes even logically conflicting imports. Therefore mythic symbols do not give rise to discursive understanding; they do beget a kind of understanding, but not by sorting out concepts and relating them in a distinct pattern; they tend, on the contrary, merely to bring together great complexes of cognate ideas, in which all distinctive features are merged and swallowed. "Here we find in operation a law which might actually be called the law of the levelling and extinction of specific differences," says Cassirer, in *Language and Myth.* "Every part of a whole is the whole itself, every specimen is equivalent to the entire species."[7] The significance of mythic structures is not formally and arbitrarily assigned to them, as convention assigns one exact meaning to a recognized symbol; rather, their meaning seems to dwell in them as life dwells in a body; they are animated by it, it is of their essence, and the naive, awe-struck mind *finds* it, as the quality of "holiness." Therefore mythic symbols do not even appear to be symbols; they appear as holy objects or places or beings, and their import is felt as an inherent *power.*

This really amounts to another "law" of imaginative conception. Just as specific differences of meaning are obliterated in nondiscursive symbolization, the very distinction between form and content, between the entity (thing, image, gesture, or natural event) which is the symbol, and the idea or feeling which is its meaning, is lost, or rather: is not yet found. This is a momentous fact, for it is the basis of all superstition and strange cosmogony, as well as of

[6] See *Die Philosophie der symbolischen Formen,* II, 97ff. (Langer refers to Cassirer's study by its German title because at the time it had not been translated. The three volumes of *The Philosophy of Symbolic Forms* are now available, published by Yale University Press. AB)

[7] Pp. 91–92.

religious belief. To believe in the existence of improbable or quite fantastic things and beings would be inexplicable folly if beliefs were dictated essentially by practical experience. But the mythic interpretation of reality rests on the principle that the veneration appropriate to the meaning of a symbol is focussed on the symbol itself, which is simply identified with its import. This creates a world punctuated by pre-eminent objects, mystic centers of power and holiness, to which more and more emotive meanings accrue as "properties." An intuitive recognition of their *import* takes the form of ardent, apparently irrational belief in the physical reality and power of the significant forms. This is the hypostatic mechanism of the mind by which the world is filled with magical things—fetishes and talismans, sacred trees, rocks, caves, and the vague, protean ghosts that inhabit them—and finally the world is peopled with a pantheon of permanent, more or less anthropomorphic gods. In these presences "reality" is concentrated for the mythic imagination; this is not "make-believe," not a willful or playful distortion of a radically different "given fact," but is *the way phenomena are given* to naive apprehension.

Certainly the pattern of that world is altogether different from the pattern of the "material" world which confronts our sober common sense, follows the laws of causality, and exhibits a logical order of classes and subclasses, with their defining properties and relations, whereby each individual object either does or does not belong to any given class. Cassirer has summed up the logical contrast between the mode of mythic intuition and that of "factual" or "scientific" apprehension in very telling phrase:

> In the realm of discursive conception there reigns a sort of diffuse light
> —and the further logical analysis proceeds, the further does this even
> clarity and luminosity extend. But in the ideational realm of myth and
> language there are always, besides those locations from which the
> strongest light proceeds, others that appear wrapped in profoundest
> darkness. While certain contents of perception become verbal-mythical
> centers of force, centers of significance, there are others which remain,
> one might say, beneath the threshold of meaning.[8]

His coupling of myth and language in this passage brings us back to the intimate connection between these two great symbolic forms which he traces to a common origin. The dawn of language was the dawn of the truly human mind, which meets us first of all as a rather highly developed organ of practical response *and of imagination,* or symbolic rendering of impressions. The first "holy objects" seem to be born of momentary emotional experiences— fright centering on a place or a thing, concentrated desire that manifests itself in a dreamlike image or a repeated gesture, triumph that issues naturally in festive dance and song, directed toward a symbol of power. Somewhere in the

[8] *Language and Myth,* 91.

course of this high emotional life primitive man took to using his instinctive vocal talent as a source of such "holy objects," *sounds* with imaginative import: such vocal symbols are *names*.

In savage societies, names are treated not as conventional appellations, but as though they were physical proxies for their bearers. To call an object by an inappropriate name is to confound its very nature. In some cultures practically all language serves mystic purposes and is subject to the most impractical taboos and regulations. It is clearly of a piece with magic, religion and the whole pattern of intensive emotional symbolism which governs the pre-scientific mind. Names are the very essence of mythic symbols; nothing on earth is a more concentrated point of sheer meaning than the little, transient, invisible breath that constitutes a spoken word. Physically it is almost nothing. Yet it carries more definite and momentous import than any permanent holy object.[9] It can be invoked at will, anywhere and at any time, by a mere act of speech; merely *knowing* a word gives a person the power of using it; thus it is invisibly "had," carried about by its possessors.

It is characteristic of mythic "powers" that they are completely contained in every fragment of matter, every sound, and every gesture which partakes of them.[10] This fact betrays their real nature, which is not that of physical forces, but of meanings; a meaning is indeed completely given by every symbol to which it attaches. The greater the "power" in proportion to its bearer, the more awe-inspiring will the latter be. So, as long as meaning is felt as an indwelling potency of certain physical objects, *words* must certainly rank high in the order of holy things.

But language has more than a purely denotative function. Its symbols are so manifold, so manageable, and so economical that a considerable number of them may be held in one "specious present," though each one physically passes away before the next is given; each has left its *meaning* to be apprehended in the same span of attention that takes in the whole series. Of course, the length of the span varies greatly with different mentalities. But as soon as two or more words are thus taken together in the mind of an interpretant, language has acquired its second function: it has engendered *discursive thought*.

The discursive mode of thinking is what we usually call "reason." It is not as primitive as the imaginative mode, because it arises from the syntactical nature of language; mythic envisagement and verbal expression are its forerunners. Yet it is a natural development from the earlier symbolic mode, which is pre-discursive, and thus in a strict and narrow sense "pre-rational."

Henceforth, the history of thought consists chiefly in the gradual achievement of factual, literal, and logical conception and expression. Obviously the only means to this end is language. But this instrument, it must be

---

[9] "Often it is the *name* of the deity, rather than the god himself, that seems to be the real source of efficacy." (*Language and Myth*, 48)

[10] Cf. *Language and Myth*, 92.

remembered, has a double nature. Its syntactical tendencies bestow the laws of logic on us; yet the primacy of *names* in its make-up holds it to the hypostatic way of thinking which belongs to its twin-phenomenon, myth. Consequently it leads us beyond the sphere of mythic and emotive thought, yet always pulls us back into it again; it is both the diffuse and tempered light that shows us the external world of "fact," and the array of spiritual lamps, light-centers of intensive meaning, that throw the gleams and shadows of the dream world wherein our earliest experiences lay.

We have come so far along the difficult road of discursive thinking that the laws of logic seem to be the very frame of the mind, and rationality its essence. Kant regarded the categories of pure understanding as universal transcendental forms, imposed by the most naive untutored mind on all its perceptions, so that self-identity, the dichotomy of "*a*" and "non-*a*," the relation of part and whole, and other axiomatic general concepts inhered in phenomena as their necessary conditions. Yet, from primitive apprehension to even the simplest rational construction is probably a far cry. It is interesting to see how Cassirer, who followed Kant in his "Copernican revolution," i.e., in the transcendental analysis of phenomena which traces their form to a non-phenomenal, subjective element, broadened the Kantian concept of form to make it a variable and anthropologically valid principle, without compromising the "critical" standpoint at all. Instead of accepting one categorial scheme—that of discursive thought—as the absolute way of experiencing reality, he finds it relative to a form of symbolic presentation; and as there are alternative symbolic forms, there are also alternative phenomenal "worlds." Mythic conception is categorically different from scientific conception; therefore it meets a different world of perceptions. Its objects are not self-identical, consistent, universally related; they condense many characters in one, have conflicting attributes and intermittent existence, the whole is contained in its parts, and the parts in each other. The world they constitute is a world of values, things "holy" against a vague background of commonplaces, or "profane" events, instead of a world of neutral physical facts. By this departure, the Kantian doctrine that identified all conception with discursive reason, making reason appear as an aboriginal human gift, is saved from its most serious fallacy, an unhistorical view of mind.

Cassirer called his *Essay on Man,* which briefly summarizes the *Philosophie der symbolischen Formen,* "An Introduction to a Philosophy of Human Culture." The subtitle is appropriate indeed; for the most striking thing about this philosophy viewed as a whole is the way the actual evolution of human customs, arts, ideas, and languages is not merely fitted into an idealistic interpretation of the world (as it may be fitted into almost any metaphysical picture), but is illumined and made accessible to serious study by working principles taken from Kantian epistemology. His emphasis on the constitutive character of symbolic renderings in the making of "experience" is the masterstroke that turns the purely speculative "critical" theory into an anthropological hypothesis, a key to several linguistic problems, a source of psychological understanding, and a guidepost in the maze of *Geistesgeschichte.*

It is, as I pointed out before, characteristic of Cassirer's thought that, although its basic principles stem from a philosophical tradition, its living material and immediate inspiration come from contemporary sources, from fields of research beyond his own. For many years the metaphysic of mind has been entirely divorced from the scientific study of mental phenomena; whether mind be an eternal essence or a transient epiphenomenon, a world substance or a biological instrument, makes little difference to our understanding of observed human or animal behavior. But Cassirer breaks this isolation of speculative thought; he uses the Kantian doctrine, that mind is constitutive of the "external world," to explain the *way* this world is experienced as well as the mere fact *that* it is experienced; and in so doing, of course, he makes his metaphysic meet the test of factual findings at every turn. His most interesting exhibits are psychological phenomena revealed in the psychiatric clinic and in ethnologists' reports. The baffling incapacities of impaired brains, the language of childhood, the savage's peculiar practices, the prevalence of myth in early cultures and its persistence in religious thought—these and other widely scattered facts receive new significance in the light of his philosophy. And that is the pragmatic measure of any speculative approach. A really cogent doctrine of mind cannot be irrelevant to psychology, any more than a good cosmological system can be meaningless for physics, or a theory of ethics inapplicable to jurisprudence and law.

The psychiatric phenomena which illustrate the existence of a mythic mode of thought, and point to its ancient and primitive nature, are striking and persuasive.[11] Among these is the fact that in certain pathological conditions of the brain the power of abstraction is lost, and the patient falls back on picturesque metaphorical language. In more aggravated cases the imagination, too, is impaired; and here we have a reversion almost to animal mentality. One symptom of this state which is significant for the philosophy of symbolism is that the sufferer is unable to tell a lie, feign any action, or do anything his actual situation does not dictate, though he may still find his way with immediate realities. If he is thirsty, he can recognize and take a glass of water, and drink; but he cannot pick up an empty glass and demonstrate the act of drinking *as though* there were water in it, or even lift a full glass to his lips, if he is not thirsty. Such incapacities have been classified as "apractic" disorders; but Cassirer pointed out that they are not so much practical failures, as the loss of the basic symbolic function, *envisagement of things not given.* This is borne out by a still more serious disturbance which occurs with the destruction of certain brain areas, inability to recognize "things," such as chairs and brooms and pieces of clothing, directly and instantly as objects denoted by their names. At this point, pathology furnishes a striking testimony of the real nature of language: for here, names lose their hypostatic office, the creation of permanent and particular *items* out of the flux of

---

[11] For a full treatment of this material see *Philosophie der symbolischen Formen,* III, part 3, *passim.*

impressions. To a person thus afflicted, words have connotation, but experience does not readily correspond to the conceptual scheme of language,
which makes *names* the pre-eminent points of rest, and requires *things* as the
fundamental relata in reality. The connoted concepts are apt to be adjectival
rather than substantive. Consequently the world confronting the patient is
not composed of objects immediately "given" in experience; it is composed
of sense data, which he must "associate" to form "things," much as Hume
supposed the normal mind to do.

Most of the psychological phenomena that caught Cassirer's interest
arose from the psychiatric work of Kurt Goldstein, who has dealt chiefly
with cases of cerebral damage caused by physical accident. But the range of
psychological researches which bear out Cassirer's theory of mind is much
wider; it includes the whole field of so-called "dynamic psychology," the
somewhat chaotic store of new ideas and disconcerting facts with which
Sigmund Freud alarmed his generation. Cassirer himself never explored this
fund of corroborative evidence; he found himself in such fundamental dis-
agreement with Freud on the nature of the dynamic motive—which the psychologist regarded as not only derived from the sex impulse, but forever bound
to it, and which the philosopher saw liberated in science, art, religion, and
everything that constitutes the "self-realization of the spirit"—that there
seemed to be simply no point of contact between their respective doctrines.
Cassirer felt that to Freud all those cultural achievements were mere by-
products of the unchanging animalian "libido," symptoms of its blind activity
and continual frustration; whereas to him they were the consummation of a
spiritual process which merely took its rise from the blind excitement of the
animal "libido," but received its importance and meanings from the phenomena of awareness and creativity, the envisagement, reason, and cognition it
produced. This basic difference of *evaluations* of the life process made
Cassirer hesitate to make any part of Freud's doctrine his own; at the end of
his life he had, apparently, just begun to study the important relationship
between "dynamic psychology" and the philosophy of symbolic forms.

It is, indeed, only in regard to the *forms* of thought that a parallel
obtains between these systems; but that parallel is close and vital, none the
less. For, the "dream work" of Freud's "unconscious" mental mechanism is
almost exactly the "mythic mode" which Cassirer describes as the primitive
form of ideation, wherein an intense feeling is spontaneously expressed in a
symbol, an image seen in something or formed for the mind's eye by the
excited imagination. Such expression is effortless and therefore unexhausting;
its products are images charged with meanings, but the meanings remain implicit, so that the emotions they command seem to be centered on the image
rather than on anything it merely conveys; in the image, which may be a
vision, a gesture, a sound-form (musical image) or a word as readily as an
external object, many meanings may be concentrated, many ideas telescoped
and interfused, and incompatible emotions simultaneously expressed.

The mythic mind never perceives passively, never merely contemplates things; all its observations spring from some act of participation, some act of emotion and will. Even as mythic imagination materializes in permanent forms, and presents us with definite outlines of an 'objective' world of beings, the significance of this world becomes clear to us only if we can still detect, underneath it all, that dynamic sense of life from which it originally arose. Only where this vital feeling is stirred from within, where it expresses itself as love or hate, fear or hope, joy or sorrow, is mythic imagination roused to the pitch of excitement at which it begets a definite world of representations. (*Philosophie der symbolischen Formen*, II, 90.)

For a person whose apprehension is under the spell of this mythico-religious attitude, it is as though the whole world were simply annihilated; the immediate content, whatever it be, that commands his religious interest so completely fills his consciousness that nothing else can exist beside and apart from it. The ego is spending all its energy on this single object, lives in it, loses itself in it. Instead of a widening of intuitive experience, we find here its extreme limitation; instead of expansion . . . we have here an impulse toward concentration; instead of extensive distribution, intensive compression. This focussing of all forces on a single point is the prerequisite for all mythical thinking and mythical formulation. When, on the one hand, the entire self is given up to a single impression, is 'possessed' by it and, on the other hand, there is the utmost tension between the subject and its object, the outer world; when external reality is not merely viewed and contemplated, but overcomes a man in sheer immediacy, with emotions of fear or hope, terror or wish fulfillment: then the spark jumps somehow across, the tension finds release, as the subjective excitement becomes objectified and confronts the mind as a god or a daemon. (*Language and Myth*, 32–33.)

. . . this peculiar genesis determines the type of intellectual content that is common to language and myth . . . present reality, as mythic or linguistic conception stresses and shapes it, fills the entire subjective realm. . . . At this point, the word which denotes that thought content is not a mere conventional symbol, but is merged with its object in an indissoluble unity. . . . The potential between 'symbol' and 'meaning' is resolved; in place of a more or less adequate 'expression,' we find a relation of identity, of complete congruence between 'image' and 'object,' between the name and the thing.

. . . the same sort of hypostatization or transubstantiation occurs in other realms of mental creativity; indeed, it seems to be the typical process in all unconscious ideation. (*Ibid*., 57–58.)

Mythology presents us with a world which is not, indeed, devoid of structure and internal organization, but which, none the less, is not divided according to the categories of reality, into 'things' and 'properties.' Here all forms of Being exhibit, as yet, a peculiar 'fluidity'; they

are distinct without being really separate. Every form is capable of
changing, on the spur of the moment, even into its very opposite. . . .
One and the same entity may not only undergo constant change into
successive guises but it combines within itself, at one and the same
instant of its existence, a wealth of different and even incompatible
natures. (*Philosophie der symbolischen Formen*, III, 71–72.)

Above all, there is a complete lack of any clear division between
mere 'imagining' and 'real' perception, between wish and fulfillment,
between image and object. This is most clearly revealed by the decisive role which dream experiences play in the development of mythic
consciousness. . . . It is beyond doubt that certain mythic concepts can
be understood, in all their peculiar complexity, only in so far as one
realizes that for mythic thought and 'experience' there is but a continuous and fluid transition from the world of dream to objective 'reality.'
(*Ibid*., II, 48–49.)

The world of myth is a dramatic world—a world of actions, of
forces, of conflicting powers. In every phenomenon of nature it [mythic
consciousness] sees the collision of these powers. Mythical perception
is always impregnated with these emotional qualities. Whatever is seen
or felt is surrounded by a special atmosphere—an atmosphere of joy or
grief, of anguish, of excitement, of exultation or depression. . . . All
objects are benignant or malignant, friendly or inimical, familiar or
uncanny, alluring and fascinating or repellent and threatening.—(*An
Essay on Man*, 76–77.)

The real substratum of myth is not a substratum of thought but of
feeling. . . . Its view of life is a synthetic, not an analytical one. . . . There
is no specific difference between the various realms of life. . . . To mythical and religious feeling nature becomes one great society, the *society
of life.* Man is not endowed with outstanding rank in this society. . . .
Men and animals, animals and plants are all on the same level. (*Ibid.*,
81–83.)

To all these passages Freud could subscribe wholeheartedly; the *morphol-
ogy* of the "mythic mode" is essentially that of dream, phantasy, infantile
thinking, and "unconscious" ideation which he himself discovered and described. And 't is the recognition of this non-discursive mode of thought,
rather than his clinical hypothesis of an all-pervading disguised sexuality,
that makes Freud's psychology important for philosophy. Not the theory
of "libido," which is another theory of "animal drives," but the conception
of the unconscious mechanism through which the "libido" operates, the
dream work, the myth-making process—that is the new generative idea which
psychoanalysis contributed to psychological thinking, the notion that has
put modern psychology so completely out of gear with traditional epistemology that the science of mind and the philosophy of mind threatened to
lose contact altogether. So it is of the utmost significance for the unity of

our advancing thought that pure speculative philosophy should recognize and understand the primary forms of conception which underlie the achievement of discursive reason.

Cassirer's profound antipathy to Freud's teaching rests on another aspect of that psychological system, which springs from the fact that Freud's doctrine was determined by practical interests: that is the tendency of the psychoanalyst to range all human aims, all ideals on the same ethical level. Since he deals entirely with the evils of social maladjustment, his measure of good is simply adjustment; religion and learning and social reform, art and discovery and philosophical reflection, to him are just so many avenues of personal gratification—sublimation of passions, emotional self-expression. From his standpoint they cannot be viewed as objective values. Just as good poetry and bad poetry are of equal interest and importance to the psychoanalyst, so the various social systems are all equally good, all religions equally true (or rather, equally false, but salutary), and all abstract systems of thought, scientific or philosophical or mathematical, just self-dramatizations in disguise. To a philosopher who was also a historian of culture, such a point of view seemed simply devastating. It colored his vision of Freud's work so deeply that it really obscured for him the constructive aspect, the analysis of non-discursive ideation, which this essentially clinical psychology contains. Yet the relationship between the new psychiatry and his own new epistemology is deep and close; "*der Mythos als Denkform*"[12] is the theme that rounds out the modern philosophical picture of human mentality to embrace psychology and anthropology and linguistics,[13] which had broken the narrow limits of rationalist theory, in a more adequate conceptual frame.

The broadening of the philosophical outlook achieved by Cassirer's theory of language and myth affects not only the philosophical sciences, the *Geisteswissenschaften*, but also the most crucial present difficulty in philosophy itself—the ever increasing pendulum arc between theories of reason and theories of irrational motivation. The discovery that emotive, intuitive, "blind" forces govern human behavior more effectively than motives of pure reason naturally gave rise to an anti-rationalist movement in epistemology and ethics, typified by Nietzsche, William James, and Bergson, which finally made the truth-seeking attitude of science a pure phantasmagoria, a quixotic manifestation of the will. Ultimately the role of reason came to appear (as it does in Bergson's writings) as something entirely secondary and essentially unnatural. But at this point the existence of reason becomes an enigma: for how could instinctive life ever give rise to such a product? How can sheer imagination and volition and passion beget the "artificial" picture of the world which seems natural to scientists?

---

[12] This is the title of the first section in Vol. II of *Philosophie der symbolischen Formen*.

[13] The knowledge of linguistics on which he bases vol. I of his *Philosophie der symbolischen Formen* is almost staggering. His use of anthropological data may be found especially throughout vol. II of that work.

Cassirer found the answer in the structure of *language*; for language stems from the intuitive "drive" to symbolic expression that also produces dream and myth and ritual, but it is a pre-eminent form in that it embodies not only self-contained, complex meanings, but a *principle of concatenation* whereby the complexes are unravelled and articulated. It is the *discursive* character of language, its inner tendency to grammatical development, which gives rise to logic in the strict sense, i.e., to the procedure we call "reasoning." Language is "of imagination all compact," yet it is the cradle of abstract thought; and the achievement of *Vernunft*, as Cassirer traces it from the dawn of human mentality through the evolution of speech forms, is just as natural as the complicated patterns of instinctive behavior and emotional abreaction.

Here the most serious antinomy in the philosophical thought of our time is resolved. This is a sort of touchstone for the philosophy of symbolic forms, whereby we may judge its capacity to fulfill the great demand its author did not hesitate to make on it, when he wrote in his *Essay on Man*:

> In the boundless multiplicity and variety of mythical images, of religious dogmas, of linguistic forms, of works of art, philosophic thought reveals the unity of a general function by which all these creations are held together. Myth, religion, art, language, even science, are now looked upon as so many variations on a common theme—and it is the task of philosophy to make this theme audible and understandable.

Part Three

All knowledge is interpretation.

Susanne K. Langer

Life begins less by reaching upward than by turning back upon itself. But what a marvelously insidious, subtle image of life a coiling vital principle would be!

Gaston Bachelard

The theory of interpretation is obviously a branch of biology—a branch that has not grown very far or very healthily yet. . . . We shall do better to think of a meaning as though it were a plant that has grown—not a can that has been filled or a lump of clay that has been molded.

I. A. Richards

For philosophy, experience can only mean the total cognitive result of living, and includes interpretation as truly as it does the matter of sense. Even more truly, since this matter of sense is a hypothetical something which we never can seize as such, free from all interpretive working over.

C. S. Peirce

What we observe is not nature in itself but nature exposed to our method of questioning.

Werner Heisenberg

There is no way of arriving at any sciential End but by finding it at every step.

Samuel Taylor Coleridge

Interpretation and the Act of Knowing

Reclaiming the imagination entails understanding the role of interpretation in all learning. Interpretation is a speculative instrument of far greater power than anything rhetoric, new or old, can offer. Practicing the so-called "modes of discourse" by writing narratives and definitions and "compare-contrast" papers on assigned topics is part of the problem, not a solution. (It is foolish to consider that the categories appearing perennially in the Table of Contents of one after another rhetoric-reader constitute a psychology or an epistemology.) Struggling to match diction, tone, structure, style—whatever—to a chosen audience is an artificial enterprise for students who have not learned to form concepts, to represent their recognitions of relationships, to interpret their interpretations.

If we want to develop a pedagogy for "writing across the curriculum," interpretation will be the working concept we most need. Scientists are frequently quicker than teachers of literature to realize that writing can play several roles in the disciplines. In any case, an understanding of interpretation can help all teachers see the virtue of claiming that writing is a mode of learning and a way of knowing.

Mediation

It could be that current interest in the theory of interpretation might lead to a greater awareness of the importance of meaning in the study of composition. This is more likely to happen, I think, if interpretation is considered in the light of C. S. Peirce's semiotics. (He invented both the field and the term, which he spelled *semeiotics*.) Peirce conceived of the meaning relationship as *triadic*: the sign is constituted by a *Representamen* (or symbol), an *Object*, and an *Interpretant*, which is the mediating idea. The contrast is with the dyadic conception of a relationship between a signifier and a signified, as Saussure's system is generally thought to define. Peirce held that a sign could only be interpreted by another sign; that is to say, the Interpretant of one sign becomes the Representamen of the succeeding sign, in an infinite progression—a kind of helical version of the hermeneutic circle. A fairly easy way to grasp the point of defining meaning as a triadic relationship is to study the diagram representing "the mediated act" which accompanies the Vygotsky selection (p. 72). This curious triangle with the dotted line appears also in the opening chapter of Ogden and Richards' *The Meaning of Meaning*, which includes as an appendix several lengthy passages from Peirce.*

Peirce once wrote to William James that in explaining a point of logic he would quote himself, adding "but it is the continuous text that talks" (8.260). I've found it impossible to excerpt in a way that would show how that continuous text sounds and have, therefore, simply offered a few passages which I find full of interest. My opinion is that by reading for several hours at a stretch (especially in volumes 1, 4, and 7 of *The Collected Papers*) anyone can work out his own method of understanding this difficult but incomparably interesting philosopher. I might also add that the two selections available in paperback were edited by scholars impatient with Peirce in moods

---

The Meaning of Meaning was first published in 1923, several years before Vygotsky's papers were written. I know of no evidence that he knew the book or had read Peirce, but there is an interesting consonance. I have commented on some pedagogical implications of triadicity in "A Curious Triangle . . . ," in *The Making of Meaning.*

and modes which teachers of composition might find congenial. In any case, there is much to be learned from the attempt to read him in long stretches. His principal method is that of "ampliative inference" and with his awareness of the logical and metaphysical complexity of all statements about language (and meaning, purpose, knowing, etc.), he can easily produce twenty pages in explanation of any seemingly simple assertion. Reading Peirce reminds us of just how problematic our terms are when we come to think about thinking.

Scientists—those who do not worship the Idols of the Laboratory—recognize interpretation as crucial in scientific method. The role of analogy, the function of presuppositions and hypotheses, the principle of complementarity are all illuminated by a Peircean conception of interpretation. History and anthropology, insofar as they are informed by a sound epistemology, are the disciplines from which we have most to learn about interpretation, especially about the way perspective and context work together.

Interpretation is generally taken to mean something other than a simple decoding of conventional signs; we don't speak of "interpreting" the Morse Code. On the other hand, the power of this concept is lost to us if we take it to the other extreme and identify interpretation with idiosyncratic response. In Peirce's semiotics, interpretation is integral to signification. But to say that we "create" meaning is inaccurate; it is the idea by means of which we interpret a representation that brings meaning into being. This is why Peirce names the mediating aspect of the sign the *Interpretant*, not the *Interpreter*, though as "a sop to Cerberus" he reluctantly allowed them to be conflated. The notion of the "empty sign" is a contradiction in terms. The case is not that there is an empty sign until it is interpreted but that without an interpreter with a mediating idea, there is no sign. A text is not a symbol system which is "empty" until the intervention of the reader—a clean machine awaiting its competent operator. If the interpreter is not included in the system in the first place, there is no logical way to plug him in.

What Peirce called *Thirdness* is the mediation of an idea which is our means of relating a symbol to what it represents. He often explained mediation as a purpose or an intention and illustrated it with the act of giving. The mere transfer of an item from here to there is not a triadic relationship; only intention can make it so. Peirce contrasts *giving* with a purposeless act, often telling the story of the Persian merchant who, as he's walking along the street, throws away a date stone, tossing it without paying attention. It hits a djinn (genie) in the eye and blinds him. That is Chance, not Triadicity.

I. A. Richards, who was much influenced by Peirce throughout his long career, makes Purposing central in his theory of comprehending. In one of his first books, *Mencius on the Mind*, he developed the idea of "multiple definition," a technique which can serve the translator as he tries to identify and re-present the relationship not only between the "code" of the Chinese writer and the "code" which is the translator's language, but between the meanings which those codes make available for formulation, meanings which then guide his construing of the code. From translation theory, Richards went on to develop his notion of a "contextual theorem of meaning" (in *The*

Philosophy of Rhetoric) as being central to all interpretation. In the essay
printed here, Richards turns again to translation as a speculative instrument
for the study of interpretation seen as comprehending. Richards' Theory of
Comprehending is an advance on his contextual theorem and is through and
through triadic.*

The chief consequences of using triadicity as a speculative instrument
are that we see that no symbol can have only one interpretation and that we
must therefore be alert to possible inadequacies which we could correct, as
well as to the necessary limitations of our interpretations. Emphasizing the
interpreter and his interpretations does not license solipsism because, as
Kenneth Burke points out in *Permanence and Change,* there is a recalcitrance
which meets our formulations: that is precisely why we must interpret our
interpretations. We are able to do all this because we have language: the re-
flexiveness of linguistic form is supportive of the view of language as a mediating form. Gaston Bachelard notes some of the ramifications.

C. S. PEIRCE
(on signs and diagrams)

3.419. Diagrams and diagrammatoidal figures are intended to be applied
to the better understanding of states of things, whether experienced, or read
of, or imagined. Such a figure cannot, however, show what it is to which it is
intended to be applied; nor can any other diagram avail for that purpose. The
where and the when of the particular experience, or the occasion or other
identifying circumstance of the particular fiction to which the diagram is to
be applied, are things not capable of being diagrammatically exhibited. Describe and describe and describe, and you never can describe a date, a position,
or any homaloidal quantity. You may object that a map is a diagram showing
localities; undoubtedly, but not until the law of the projection is understood,
nor even then unless at least two points on the map are somehow previously
identified with points in nature.

Now, how is any diagram ever to perform that identification? If a diagram cannot do it, algebra cannot: for algebra is but a sort of diagram; and
if algebra cannot do it, language cannot: for language is but a kind of algebra.
It would, certainly, in one sense be extravagant to say that we can never tell
what we are talking about; yet, in another sense, it is quite true. The meanings
of words ordinarily depend upon our tendencies to weld together qualities

---

*I have discussed this essay at length in "I. A. Richards and the Audit of Meaning,"
New Literary History XIV (Fall 1982), 63-79.

and our aptitudes to see resemblances, or, to use the received phrase, upon associations by *similarity*; while experience is bound together, and only recognizable, by forces acting upon us, or, to use an even worse chosen technical term, by means of association by *contiguity*. Two men meet on a country road. One says to the other, "That house is on fire." "What house?" "Why, the house about a mile to my right." Let this speech be taken down and shown to anybody in the neighboring village, and it will appear that the language by itself does not fix the house. But the person addressed sees where the speaker is standing, recognizes his *right* hand side (a word having a most singular mode of signification) estimates a *mile* (a length having no geometrical properties different from other lengths), and looking there, sees a house. It is not the language alone, with its mere associations of similarity, but the language taken in connection with the auditor's own experiential associations of contiguity, which determines for him what house is meant. It is requisite then, in order to show what we are talking or writing about, to put the hearer's or reader's mind into real, active connection with the concatenation of experience or of fiction with which we are dealing, and, further, to draw his attention to, and identify, a certain number of particular points in such concatenation. If there be a reader who cannot understand my writings, let me tell him that no straining of his mind will help him: his whole difficulty is that he has no personal experience of the world of problems of which I am talking, and he might as well close the book until such experience comes. That the diagrammatization is one thing and the application of the diagram quite another, is recognized obscurely in the structure of such languages as I am acquainted with, which distinguishes the *subjects* and *predicates* of propositions. The subjects are the indications of the things spoken of, the predicates, words that assert, question, or command whatever is intended. Only, the shallowness of syntax is manifest in its failing to recognize the impotence of mere words and especially of common nouns, to fulfil the function of a grammatical subject. Words like *this, that, lo, hallo, hi there* have a direct, forceful action upon the nervous system, and compel the hearer to look about him; and so they, more than ordinary words, contribute towards indicating what the speech is about. But this is a point that grammar and the grammarians (who, if they are faithfully to mirror the minds of the language-makers, can hardly be scientific analysts) are so far from seeing as to call demonstratives, such as *that* and *this*, pronouns—a literally preposterous designation, for nouns may more truly be called pro-demonstratives.

2.227, 2.228, 2.229. Logic, in its general sense, is, as I believe I have shown, only another name for *semiotic*, . . . the quasi-necessary, or formal, doctrine of signs. By describing the doctrine as "quasi-necessary," or formal, I mean that we observe the characters of such signs as we know, and from such an observation, by a process which I will not object to naming Abstraction, we are led to statements, eminently fallible, and therefore in one sense by no means necessary, as to what *must be* the characters of all signs used by a "scientific" intelligence, that is to say, by an intelligence capable of learning by experience. As to that process of abstraction, it is itself a sort of observation. The faculty which I call abstractive observation is one which ordinary people perfectly recognize, but for which the theories of philosophers sometimes hardly leave room. It is a familiar experience to every human being to wish for something quite beyond his present means, and to follow that wish by the question, "Should I wish for that thing just the same, if I had ample means to gratify it?" To answer that question, he searches his heart, and in doing so makes what I term an abstractive observation. He makes in his imagination a sort of skeleton diagram, or outline sketch, of himself, considers what modifications the hypothetical state of things would require to be made in that picture, and then examines it, that is, *observes* what he has imagined, to see whether the same ardent desire is there to be discerned. By such a process, which is at bottom very much like mathematical reasoning, we can reach conclusions as to what *would be* true of signs in all cases, so long as the intelligence using them was scientific. The modes of thought of a God, who should possess an intuitive omniscience superseding reason, are put out of the question. Now the whole process of development among the community of students of those formulations by abstractive observation and reasoning of the truths which *must* hold good of all signs used by a scientific intelligence is an observational science, like any other positive science, notwithstanding its strong contrast to all the special sciences which arises from its aiming to find out what *must be* and not merely what *is* in the actual world.

A sign, or *representamen*, is something which stands to somebody for something in some respect or capacity. It addresses somebody, that is, creates in the mind of that person an equivalent sign, or perhaps a more developed sign. That sign which it creates I call the *interpretant* of the first sign. The sign stands for something, its *object.* It stands for that object, not in all respects, but in reference to a sort of idea, which I have sometimes called the *ground* of the representamen. "Idea" is here to be understood in a sort of Platonic sense, very familiar in everyday talk; I mean in that sense in which we say that one man catches another man's idea, in which we say that when a man recalls what he was thinking of at some previous time, he recalls the same idea, and in which when a man continues to think anything, say for a tenth of a second, in so far as the thought continues to agree with itself during that time, that is to have a *like* content, it is the same idea, and is not at each instant of the interval a new idea.

In consequence of every representamen being thus connected with three things, the ground, the object and the interpretant, the science of semiotic has three branches. The first is called by Duns Scotus *grammatica speculativa.* We may term it *pure grammar.* It has for its task to ascertain what must be true of the representamen used by every scientific intelligence in order that they may embody any *meaning.* The second is logic proper. It is the science of what is quasi-necessarily true of the representamina of any scientific intelligence in order that they may hold good of any *object*, that is, may be true.

Or say, logic proper is the formal science of the conditions of the truth of representations. The third, in imitation of Kant's fashion of preserving old associations of words in finding nomenclature for new conceptions, I call *pure rhetoric*. Its task is to ascertain the laws by which in every scientific intelligence one sign gives birth to another, and especially one thought brings forth another.

I. A. RICHARDS
"Toward a Theory of Comprehending"

Looking back, across more than a score of years, on the considerations with which *Mencius on the Mind* was concerned, it seems to me now that the togethernesses, the mutualities, of those considerations were omitted. There were distinctions made and differences stressed between sorts of meaning, but why they should be so made and so stressed hardly became apparent. The last chapter, "Towards a Technique for Comparative Studies," was suitably tentative in title and in treatment. It stammered away persistently, but what it was trying to say never, *as a whole*, got said. I have some doubts whether any whole was in any steady way in the mind of the sayer. The book was written hurriedly, in a whirl of lecturing on *Ulysses* and on *The Possessed*, during a first teaching visit to Harvard. It was worked up from notes made between Tsing Hua and Yenching, under the guidance of divers advisers, and written out with much of the feeling one has in trying to scribble down a dream before it fades away. The intellectual currencies of the Harvard scene, not to mention Leopold Bloom and Stavrogin, were driving out those Chinese *aperçus* all the while. Then the only manuscript was lost, stolen by Li An-che's cook by mistake. It lay on a house roof for some months, tossed there by the thief the instant he perceived how worthless it was. Then odd pages began blowing up and down the *hutung*; rumor spread and a search was made; it was found and returned to me—just in time to be compared with the proofs of a second version I had been recollecting back home again in Cambridge, where yet another local logical game had been offering yet other guide lines to be avoided. All useful experience, no doubt, in guessing about *what* makes *what* seem to mean *what—when, where,* and to *whom*—but not then and there conducive to a single comprehensive view of comprehending.

This, I now suppose, is what one should attempt to form. I suppose too that a first condition of the endeavor is a recognition of its inherent wilfulness. It is purposive; it seeks. If asked *what* it seeks, its only just answer should be: 'Itself'. It seeks to comprehend what comprehending may be. What is sought is the search.

Yet it advances. When it looks back upon its earlier phases, what it most notes are the things it took for granted *without* having put its requests into any but most indefinite form. It can bring the request and the grant nearer to terms for ever without any fear of arriving. The process of refining its assumptions must be just as endless as the endeavor itself.

Through these assumptions it divides and combines[1] —dividing in order to combine, combining in order to divide—and simultaneously. Whatever it compares is compared in a respect or in respects. These respects are the instruments of the exploration. And it is with them as with the instruments of investigation in physics but more so: the properties of the instruments enter into the account of the investigation. There is thus at the heart of any theory of meanings a principle of the instrument. The exploration of comprehension is the task of devising a system of instruments for comparing meanings. But these systems, these instruments, are themselves comparable. They belong with what they compare and are subject in the end to one another. Indeed, this mutual subjection or control seems to be the ἀρχή for a doctrine of comprehension—that upon which all else depends.[2]

There is a seeming opposition to be reconciled here. We may suppose there to be a hierarchy of instruments, each caring for those below and cared for by those above. Or we may suppose the system to be circular. I have leaned here toward a position somewhat like that of the constitutional monarchist who supports an authority which is itself under control (see Aspect 6 below). The same question seems to me to appear again as: 'How should we structure the most embracing purpose?' and this I take to be an invitation to an inquiry into Justice on Platonic lines.

This mutual control shows itself in any segment of activity (any stretch of discourse, for example) as accordance and discordance of means with ends. Ends endeavor to choose means which will choose them. The entirety of activity, if, obeying Aristotle, we may venture to attempt to conceive it, seems to consist of *choices*. Initial choices would be free; but, when choice has been made, the subsequent choices are bound thereby while the choice is held. An interpretation knows only a part, often a very small part, of the entailments of its choices. These entailments may later seem to it to be "brute fact"— something in no way and in no measure due to its choices, something upon which their success or failure depends. This is the defectiveness of the choices —made too soon or not made when choice was needed.

Enough of these preliminaries. They seemed necessary to the introduction here of the word LET as the first and all-important move in this under-

---

[1] *Phaedrus*, 265D-266B. I have written further on "these processes of division and bringing together" in *How to Read a Page* (London: Routledge & Kegan Paul, 1943), pp. 217-22.

[2] *Republic*, 511C. See *How to Read a Page*, Index: 'Dependence'.

taking. Let *let* rule every meaning for every word in every sentence which
follows. These sentences will seem for the most part to be in the indicative,
but that is for brevity and for custom's sake. Everything which seems to be
said in the indicative floats on a raft of optative invitations to mean in such
wise. Any theory of meanings which can serve as authority, as more embracing
purpose, to a theory of translation is concerned with the mutual tension of
whatever can be put together to serve as that raft.

Such are among the reflections which translation between diverse cultures can occasion. How may we compare what a sentence in English may
mean with what a sentence in Chinese may mean? The only sound traditional
answer is in terms of two scholarships—one in English, the other in Chinese.
But a sceptism which can be liberating rather than paralyzing may make us
doubtful of the sufficiency of our techniques for comparing meanings even
within one tradition. How can one compare a sentence in English poetry with
one (however like it) in English prose? Or indeed any two sentences, or the
same sentence in different settings? What is synonymy?[3] A proliferous literature of critical and interpretative theory witnesses to the difficulty. It seems
to have been felt more and more in recent decades. Is there any reason to
doubt that analogous difficulties await analogous efforts for Chinese? They
may well have been attending the conduct of that language all along.

These troubles come, perhaps, in part from insufficient attention to the
comparing activity itself. How do we compare other things? Let us see
whether what we do in comparing boxes or rooms can be helpful in suggesting
what we might do in comparing meanings. What would a sort of geometry of
comprehendings be like? With rooms, we need, in the simplest cases, three
dimensions. With length, breadth, and height ascertained, we have gone some
way toward discovering how far one room is like another. Would it be useful
to ask in how many "dimensions" meanings may agree or differ? It might be
wise to drop the geometric word and generalize at once. Let us say, then, "in
how many respects"—remembering that meanings may, if we so wish, be compared in an indefinitely great number of respects or in as few as will serve
some purpose. The purpose decides which respects are relevant. This is true
of rooms, too. So our problem is one of choice. What is the simplest system
of respects which would enable us to compare meanings in a way serviceable
to the translator's purposes? (As three dimensions serve us in comparing sizes
and shapes.)

I have just called this a *problem.* If a problem is something which has a
solution, I should not have done so. In my opening sentence I called such
things *considerations,* hoping thereby to suggest that they are fields of unlimited speculation—held within only the most unlimited framework that
even sidereal space could symbolize—and not, as problems in a branch of

---

[3] See, e.g., Willard V. O. Quine, "Two Dogmas of Empiricism," *Philosophical Re-
view,* Vol. LX (1951).

mathematics may be, formed and given their solutions by the assumptions which set them up. What this theory of meaning should be or do is not in this narrow sense a problem.

It is, on the other hand, the most searching of all considerations, for it is concerned with arranging our techniques for arranging. Since the system of respects is set up to serve our comparings, the respects in it must not be too many or too few, and they will probably vary with the comparing. But this cannot itself be described except by means of the respects which serve it, being the comparing which these respects implement and enable. (Similarly, the comparing of sizes and shapes cannot be described except by reference to the spatial dimensions.) In brief, we make an instrument and try it out. Only by trying it out can we discover what it can do for us. Likewise, only such trial can develop our comprehending of what it is with which we seek to explore comprehending. Thus what ensues will be a depiction of the whereby and the wherefore as well as the what.

We may begin by adapting the conventional diagram of the communication engineer to our wider purposes.[4] In translation we have two such diagrams to consider as a minimum. There will be (say) a Chinese communication for which we find ourselves in the role of Destination; and we assume thereupon the role of Sources for a communication in English. But since other

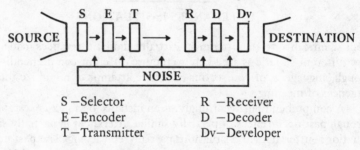

communications in Chinese and other communications in English, having *something in common* with the present communication, come in to guide the encodings and decodings, the process becomes very complex. We have here indeed what may very probably be the most complex type of event yet produced in the evolution of the cosmos.

Between two utterances[5] the operative *something in common* whereby the one influences the other may be any feature or character or respect

---

[4] Adapted with considerable changes from Claude E. Shannon and Warren Weaver, *The Mathematical Theory of Communication* (Urbana: University of Illinois Press, 1949), p. 5.

[5] I need a highly general term here, not limited to any mode of utterance, such as *overt* speech or writing. An act of comprehending may itself be regarded as an utterance, being a rebirth, after passage through the lifeless signal, of something more or less the same as the original which was transmitted.

whatever and can be itself highly complex. It may be some conjunction of respects. The comprehending of any utterance is guided by any number of partially similar situations in which partially similar utterances have occurred. More exactly, the comprehending is a function of the comparison fields from which it derives. Let the units of which these comparison fields consist be *utterances-within-situations*—the utterance and its situation being partners in the network of transactions with other utterances in other situations which

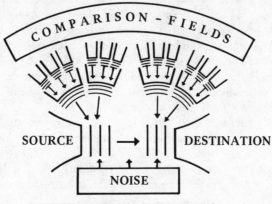

UTTERANCES-in-SITUATIONS

lends significance to the utterance. Partially similar utterances made within very different situations are likely to require different comprehendings, though language is, of course, our collective attempt to minimize these divergences of meaning.

A comprehending, accordingly, is an instance of a nexus[6] established through past occurrences of partially similar utterances in partially similar situations—utterances and situations partially co-varying. The past utterances-within-situations need not have been consciously remarked or wittingly analyzed; still less need they be explicitly remembered when the comprehending occurs. Thus the word *comparison* in the technical term "comparison-field" may mislead. It is not necessary that the members of a comparison-field— widely diverse utterances-within-situations as they may be—should ever have been taken together in explicit analytic scrutiny and examined as to their likenesses and differences. The discriminations and connections (dividings and combinings) which arise in the development of meaning are in some respects, *as though* this had been done. Sometimes they are so produced; but, for the most part, they need no such elaborate reflective procedure. Let me

---

[6] See C. K. Ogden and I. A. Richards, *The Meaning of Meaning* (London: Routledge & Kegan Paul, 1941), pp. 52–59 and Appendix B. The word 'context' there used seems to have been misleading. See my *Interpretation in Teaching* (London: Routledge & Kegan Paul, 1938), p. viii.

generalize "comparison" here to make it cover whatever putting together and setting apart (however unremarked) has been operative in the formation of the nexus. The routine of concept formation and of discriminative behavior even down to what we might call merely perceptual levels has an interesting resemblance to the highest activities of systematic conceptual classification. It is as though the nervous system had been taught Mill's Joint Method of Agreement and Difference.

What I have been sketching applies, for the translator, in the first place to the Decoding and Developing of the Chinese utterance. In the second place it applies to the Selecting and Encoding which (it is hoped) will produce an utterance in English acceptable as a translation from the Chinese. But, plainly enough, the co-varyings of utterances-within-situations for English are other than they are for Chinese. Any translator has acquired his Chinese and his English through "comparison-fields" which are different and systematically different in structure: different not only with respect to the ways in which utterances change with situations, but also with respect to those changes that are significant in utterances (e.g. phonemics) and with respect to those changes that are significant in situations (e.g. status recognition). The comparative linguist could, if he wished, illustrate this for the rest of his natural days. And it is one of the pedagogue's reasons for preferring a "direct" method to a "translation" method in beginning language learning. He finds that by keeping to one language only he can provide comparison-fields (through sequences of sentences-in-situations) which are more effective, that is, more propitious to full and deep comprehending later on. This structuring of experience will of course differ with our aim. The linguist—for his purposes—will set up one schema of respects in which comparisons will be made; the pedagogue—for his purposes—will set up another. What schema will a translator set up to serve as a theory of the sorts and interrelations of meanings to guide him in his own tasks?

Limitless in their variety, these tasks present themselves, the words, phrases, sentence forms and the situations, and the meanings, to be compared being as varied as the ways in which they may be compared. How are we to choose the respects (or dimensions) which will serve us best as headings under which to arrange those similarities and those differences of meanings which the translator must try to discern in one language and to achieve in another? In the concrete, in the minute particulars of practice, these comparison-fields are familiar enough; though we tend to forget, as scholars, what we must often, as pedagogues, recall: that these comparison-fields go back into infancy. All we have to do is to arrange, in a schema as parsimonious as adequacy will allow, a body of experience so common that if the purposing of our arrangement could be agreed on, there might be little we would then differ about.

Let us turn our communications diagram through 90 degrees now and look down it. Here is a cross-section of the activities to be found there, made at the points where what is prepared for transmission and what has been decoded and developed may be supposed—in a successful communication—to resemble one another most nearly. I have marked and numbered for labelling the seven[7] divisions in my proposed schema.

Let us label these *sorts of work* which an utterance may be doing with two or more sets of names, academic and colloquial—on the assumption that communication will be made more probable if we use here a multiplicity of largely equivalent indications. I am numbering them for convenience of reference; but I do not want to suggest that there is any fixed temporal order, that first we Select, then we Characterize, then Realize, then Value, then would Influence, then Organize and then Purpose. Nor is there any constant logical order. Let us keep these jobs as independent one of another as we can. In individual cases we will find many sorts of detailed dependence, but let us put none in by definition.

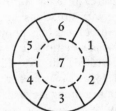

1. Points to, selects. . . .
2. Says something about, sorts. . . .
3. Comes alive to, wakes up to, presents. . . .
4. Cares about. . . .
5. Would change or keep as it is. . . .
6. Manages, directs, runs, administers itself. . . .
7. Seeks, pursues, tries, endeavors to be or to do. . . .

1. Indicating
2. Characterizing
3. Realizing
4. Valuing
5. Influencing
6. Controlling

7. Purposing

In applying this schema to translating, we can ask of two utterances in two languages:

1. How far do they pick out the same (or at least analogous) things to talk about?

2. How far do they say the same (or at least analogous) things about them?

3. How far do they present with equal vividness and/or actuality, weak or strong?

4. How far do they value in the same ways?

5. How far would they keep or change in the same ways?

---

[7] A possible eighth division might be Venting (that one of the multifarious meanings of the word *expression* which seems least well covered by my seven). Utterances from a simple 'Ouch!' or 'Ooh!' up to *The Divine Comedy* can be regarded as drive-reducing—in terms, that is, of the psychology of the utterer. But, since the purposes of a psychological investigator are not those of a translator, I would expect different schemas to be suitable. And to me, at present, this respect seems well enough taken care of—for the translator's purposes—through my seven which may *all* in their varying ways be drive-reducing. I am indebted to Dr. Irving Singer for making me see the need for this note, and to Charles Morris' *Signs, Language, and Behavior* (New York: Prentice-Hall, Inc., 1946) for suggestions contributing to my schema.

6. How far are the dependencies and interplay between 1, 2, 3, 4, 5, and 6 itself, the same in them both?

7. How widely would they serve the same purposes, playing the same parts, within the varying activities they might occur in?

Let me label this sevenfold event which my diagram depicts COMPRE-HENDING, as comprehensive a name as I can find. Any full utterance does all these things at once, and invites all of them in the comprehender. In some instances, however, one or more of these dimensions, aspects, powers, functions, jobs, variables, parameters, components, ingredients, tasks, duties (all these words are in need of the comparative study my diagram should be an instrument for) will shrink toward the null, the vanishing point. There is swearing and there is mathematics. In swearing there *may* be nothing but 4, 5, and 7; in mathematics only 1, 6, and 7 may matter. It would appear that 7 never lapses; without purposing, without the feed-forward[8] which structures all activity, no utterance and no comprehending. A full comparison between two utterances (between an original and a translation of it, for example) would require us to discern what all their dimensions, aspects, functions may be and compare them as to each and as to their relations within the entire comprehending. In comparing boxes or rooms, we need three dimensions; in comparing comprehendings, we need, I suggest, at least these seven.

Even of a single comprehending we can ask our seven sorts of questions: Under 1, we ask WHICH things are being talked (thought) of? Under 2, WHAT is being said of them? Under 3, EVEN SO? Under 4, SHOULD this be so? Under 5, WON'T YOU (WON'T I)? Under 6, HOW? Under 7, WHEREIN, WHEREBY, and WHEREFORE, TO WHAT END?

Of these, 1 and 2 may be felt to be more narrowly, more clearly, *questions* than the others; and 3 especially may seem to be rather a wondering than a questioning. Under 3, what is in question is the nearness and fulness with which something is to be present to us. *Doubting* ("is this so or not, possibly, probably, certainly?") belongs (in this schema) rather to 5 or 6 ("to be accepted or not, and how?").

Let us consider these functions in turn.

Indicating and *Characterizing* will need less comment than the others. They have been more discussed, for they correspond to the distinction logicians make under the labels "Extension-Intension" and "Denotation-Connotation." In the logician's use, the denotation of a term is whatever may be covered by the term and the connotation is the set of properties (characters) anything must have if it is to be so covered. But there is also a well-established literary use of "connotation" in which the connotation is 3, 4, and 5 in my diagram rather than 2 (which is likely then to be called the "bare, or mere meaning"). These two uses of "connotation" parallel what may be the chief difference between scientific and poetic use of language. There is some parallel, too, with what I have discussed (*Interpretation in Teaching*, p. 311)

[8]See *How to Read a Page*, Index: 'Purpose'.

as the rigid and the fluid uses of language. If we make Characterizing be *"saying something about* what is being pointed to," we have obviously to narrow down the meaning of "saying." It can open out to take in anything that an utterance can do, anything in any way said, suggested, evoked, hinted, required, and implied (the literary connotation), or it can be kept down to the logician's connotation—the 'definition' (as it is sometimes put) of a term.

The last paragraph illustrates—as must any attempt to write about the language we use or should use about language—the heavy duties we have to put on quotation marks. I have suggested (*How To Read a Page*, pp. 68–70) that we should develop sets of specialized quotes, as a technical notation by which we could better keep track of the uses we are making of our words, and I have tried out the use of a few such quotation marks in that book and elsewhere. I am now more than ever persuaded of the usefulness of this device. It can serve us to distinguish many different uses we make of quotes. For example:

$^w \ldots ^w$ to show that it is a word—that word in general, Peirce's ^{r}type^r— which is being talked of.[9] For example, ^{w}use^w is a highly ambiguous word.

$^{oc} \ldots ^{oc}$ to show that occurrences of a word—Peirce's ^{r}token^r—are being talked of. For example, I have been using ^{oc}uses^{oc} above in various ways.

$^r \ldots ^r$ to show that some special use of the word or phrase is being *referred* to. The marks may be read as *refer to* and the implication may be that only by having that particular use of the word in that passage present to us in lively attention (Realizing) can we distinguish it from other uses and avoid confusion.

$^t \ldots ^t$ to show that the word or phrase is being used as a *technical term* anchored by a definition to some state of affairs or procedure— to an operational technique perhaps or to a set of performances.

$^? \ldots ^?$ to show that how the word or phrase is to be comprehended is the question. It may be read as *query*; and we can develop this notation further by adding 1–7 after the ? to show where the focus of the question lies in my diagram. These ?'s should carry no derogatory suggestion; their work is to locate and orientate inquiry; they are servants of 6. Thus we might write $^{?2}$connotation$^{?2}$ or $^{?3,4,5}$connotation$^{?3,4,5}$ to direct attention either to the logical or to the literary questions.

$^{sw} \ldots ^{sw}$ to show that we are considering what may be *said with* a certain word or phrase without decision as yet to what that is. This enables one to bring together meanings of words and phrases, for

---

[9]*Collected Papers of Charles Sanders Peirce* (Cambridge: Harvard University Press, 1933), IV, 423.

examination, without settling anything prematurely as to how
they may be related. We need to bring these meanings together
before we pick out those we may profitably compare. I have
written elsewhere at length (*Interpretation in Teaching,* ch. xv
and xix; *How To Read a Page,* ch. x) on the troubles which the
lack of such a warning mark may lead us into.

!...! to show astonishment that people can write or talk so. Some
will want to put this whole paper within such marks.

Once we recognize to what an extent thinking is a taking care of and a keeping
account of the conduct of our words, the need for a notation with which to
study and control their resourcefulness becomes obvious.

ˢʷIndicatingˢʷ or ˢʷSelectingˢʷ —especially if we picture it to ourselves
with the image of a pointer (an arrow as of a wind vane)—may seem instable.
It can be so; but some of our selectings are the most constant things we do.
Angus Sinclair puts a further point well: "What is thus loosely describable as
the selecting and grouping which each of us carries out is not an act done once
and thereby completed, but is a continuing process which must be sustained
if our experience is to continue as it is. If for any reason it is not sustained, i.e.
if for any reason a man follows a different way of grouping in his attention,
then the experience he has will be different also. Further, this requires some
effort. . . . Knowing is not a passive contemplation, but a continuously effort-
consuming activity."[10]

Sinclair's ˢʷgroupingˢʷ seems to be my ˢʷCharacterizing, Sortingˢʷ . We
have, in English, what may seem an excess of analytic machineries to help us
in distinguishing ˈitsˈ from ˈwhatsˈ, that is, Indicating, 1, from Characterizing,
2. Such are (in most uses): for 1, ʷsubject, substance, entity, particular, thing,
being, group, classʷ ; for 2, ʷpredicate, attribute, property, quality, relation,
character, essence, universalʷ. A large methodological question which can
seem to fall near the very heart of any endeavour to translate philosophy is
this: does use of different ˀanalytic machineriesˀ entail difference of ˀviewˀ?
I put my ?'s in here to remind us that both ˢʷanalytic machineriesˢʷ and
ˢʷviewˢʷ have to do with little-explored territories though they are surrounded
by the most debatable land in ˀthe Western philosophic traditionˀ. Current use
of most of this machinery is erratic: at a popular level it cares little which of
the above words are employed; more sophisticated use varies from one philosophic school to the next.[11] There is little likelihood of increased clarity
unless some new factor enters. The exercise of choice required when thinking
which is remote from the Western philosophic tradition—thinking which
uses, perhaps, no such machinery—has to be thoroughly explored in English,

[10] Angus Sinclair, *The Conditions of Knowing* (London: Routledge & Kegan Paul,
1951), p. 35.

[11] See my *Interpretation in Teaching,* chap. xxi, "Logical Machinery and Empty
Words."

might be just such a new factor. The distinction between Indicating and Characterizing, and their queer inter-play, might, through translation studies, become again the central growing point for thought.

Realizing, 3, needs more discussion here, though what the discussion should bring out is something familiar to everyone. The two meanings we separate most easily in this cluster are exemplified by: (*a*) "She realized how he would take it" and (*b*) "He thus realized his ambition." It is with (*a*) that we are concerned, though the background influence of (*b*), ˢʷrealizingˢʷ as ˢʷthe becoming actual of the possibleˢʷ, is frequently apparent. This duality may be as relevant to Chinese modes of ?knowledge? as it is to some Aristotelian doctrines of becoming.

Within (*a*), two lines of interpretation offer themselves: (i) it may be taken as equivalent to ˢʷShe imagined vividly and livingly how he would feelˢʷ; or (ii) ˢʷShe foresaw how he would actˢʷ. (The vagueness of ᵒᶜtake itᵒᶜ reinforces the ambiguity of ᵒᶜrealizedᵒᶜ.) This exemplifies a frequent shift in ˢʷrealizeˢʷ: the shift between a lively, concrete, actualized presence and a cognizance of implications and consequences which may be (and commonly is) highly schematic. A statesman may realize what the outcome will be all the better for not realizing too vividly how *X* may feel. It thus appears that while the use of ʷrealizeʷ in (i) does entail a high degree of Realizing, 3, in my schema, ʷrealizeʷ in (ii) does not. The entirety of apprehension which is ascribed by remarks such as "He fully realized," and the contrast with "He didn't at all realize," can be handled in terms of 1, 2, 5, and 6.

What is highly realized may be distinct, explicitly structured, detailed, ?definite? in most of the senses of this strategic word.[12] But it may equally well be very indefinite. That unlocatable, indescribable, almost unidentifiable qualm which is the first emergence of nausea is something which can be Realized to the full without as yet being Characterized in any but the sketchiest fashion. Conversely, Characterizing may be most complete and minute without much Realizing having developed. In fact, fullness and detail in Characterizing frequently prevent our Realizing, though the details may be offered expressly to increase it. On the other hand, many devices—from headlines to the routines of the dispatch editor and the commentator—reduce the reality of what is presented. Much that is called ?sensationalism? has this effect. We may suspect that this is sometimes its justification. We need to be protected from the wear and tear of actuality. It would not be surprising if this wrapping-up professed to be unwrapping.

> Human kind
> Cannot bear very much reality.

None the less, increase in Realizing is in general accompanied by increased particularity in Characterizing, and by increased choosiness and discrimination in the Selecting of what shall be Characterized.

---

[12] See *Interpretation in Teaching*, ch. ix, " 'Definite'."

Realizing is very frequently brought about through metaphor, as may be illustrated by the following vivid account of a moment of Realization from Virginia Woolf: "Suddenly, as if the movement of his hand had released it, the *load* of her accumulated impressions of him *tilted up,* and *down poured in a ponderous avalanche* all she felt about him. That was one sensation. Then *up rose in a fume* the essence of his being. That was another. She felt herself *transfixed* by the intensity of her perception; it was his severity: it was his goodness."[13] (My italics.)

Metaphor, however, can serve under all my headings. It is worth remarking with regard to Chinese-English translation that the great traditional metaphors of Western thought play so large a part in shaping our conceptions that a study of any metaphors which have played a comparable part in Chinese thought suggests itself as possibly a key move. Examples in the Western tradition would be: the metaphor of conception used in the previous sentence (see *Phaedrus,* 276E); the analogy of the Self and the State from the *Republic,* and the tripartite structure of both; that other Platonic metaphor of intellectual vision, the eye of the mind; the comparison of the idea of the good with the sun; the metaphor of light as truth generally; the metaphor of inspiration; and, from Hosea, the metaphor of a marriage contract between the Lord and Israel, and indeed the use of the ideas of love (not sex) and fidelity in theology. These great originative structurings have acted in the West in innumerable minds which have had no notion of how important such metaphors can be. It would be hard to say, indeed, of the Self-State analogy whether thought about personality or about government has been the more influenced by it, for the traffic has been two-way. Where such a metaphor is absent in Chinese or where Chinese has a traditional metaphor which English lacks, the loss in translation is likely to be grave. The remedy is, perhaps, through a deeper, more systematic study of metaphor.[14] Assistance in such studies is, of course, one of the aims of the schema of comparisons offered in my diagram.

Valuing, 4, is a modern philosophic battleground, the dispute being in part whether the language of valuation, obligation, and justification is to be comprehended in some peculiar fashion or fashions (as ⌐?emotive?⌐) or in the ordinary way of description. For the purposes of comparative study of meanings, this warfare, on which so much time and talent is being spent, may not be important. It is not clear that any decision would help us to compare meanings better. It may be wise to hold that: ⌐Evaluations⌐ are a form of? empirical knowledge?,[15] which might put considerable strain on our concepts of ?empirical knowledge?; or it may be wiser still to hold that will and desire may enter into valuations in more ways than those in which they enter our

---

[13] *To the Lighthouse,* p. 41.

[14] See my *Philosophy of Rhetoric,* Lectures 5 and 6.

[15] C. I. Lewis, *An Analysis of Knowledge and Valuation* (La Salle, Ill.: Open Court Publishing Co., 1946), p. 365.

type specimens of empirical knowledge. To decide which view would be wiser, we would have to be able to make comparisons between meanings beyond our present scope. What does seem certain is that, *as an instrument for the comparison of meanings,* our diagram should avoid prejudging this issue. It should be able to represent the opposed positions more justly; they look as if they were almost equally in need of restatement. But notice here how ^{oc}should^{oc} and ^{oc}justly^{oc} and ^{oc}in need of^{oc} appear in this very remark. Any formulation of these considerations is itself valuative as well as factual; the conflict it hopes to adjudicate is alive in the bosom of the judge. The difficulties ensuing from this I shall discuss under Aspect 6, the Management, Control, or Administration of Comprehending. Meanwhile, my diagram assumes that ^{sw}Valuing^{sw} is different from Realizing, Characterizing, and Indicating; and that it $^{?}$should$^{?}$ be defined in such a way as to avoid implying any fixed relations to them—though, of course, the interplay between all three will be varied, incessant, and all-important. All study of language and thought *in action* is both an exemplification and enjoyment of this kind of interplay.

As another precaution, we may leave the full variety of Valuing unconfined. We are concerned here not only with all the attitudes which may be uttered by the aid of ^{w}good^{w} and ^{w}bad^{w}, ^{w}right^{w} and ^{w}wrong^{w}, ^{w}beautiful^{w} and ^{w}ugly^{w}, ^{w}pleasant^{w} and ^{w}unpleasant^{w}, ^{w}important^{w} and ^{w}trivial^{w}, but with the ranges of love and hate, desire and fear, hope and despair, belief and disbelief. These fields are all polar, and there is a middle zone where it may be doubtful whether any valuing is going on and whether it is positive or negative. So Valuing may often seem to lapse.

Similarly, and perhaps as a consequence, *Influencing*, 5—that part of a Comprehending which endeavors either to change or to preserve unchanged, to be changed or to remain unchanged—may be too slight to be remarked. If we ask what it is here which would change or be preserved, it may be best to reply ^{sw}the onflowing situation^{sw} and to remind ourselves that this ^{sw}onflowing situation^{sw} is at least twofold. It is (*a*) that motion of affairs within which the Comprehending is proceeding; it is also (*b*) the Selecting, Characterizing, Realizing, and Valuing, and the rest, through which the Comprehending is taking account of and dealing with (*a*). It is what is happening *and* what we take to be happening. We are lucky when these sufficiently accord. Influencing—the keeping of the stream of events so or the changing of it— concerns (*a*) as offered to us in (*b*) and, within (*a*), it includes our adjustment to the not-us as well as the adjustment of the not-us to ourselves. In general, a Comprehending is concerned to change part of the onflowing situation and keep the rest unchanged. Something has to remain unchanged; there has to be some continuant, if change is to be possible: so at least we may be wise to suppose.

Controlling or *Administering*, 6, has to do with these decisions as to what it will be wise to suppose, and with what arises through these supposals. Wisdom, we may remember, "lies in the masterful administration of the

unforeseen."[16] We may be highly surprised to discover what we are supposing. The supposals may be conscious, and arrived at through explicit
reflection and deliberation and choices wittingly made, or they may be un-
witting, picked up from the tradition or from the accidents of habit formation. And they may concern every aspect of meaning—from Selecting round
to Controlling, this would-be executive, itself. Many of our most important
supposals concern the nature of meaning and the connections of the sorts of
meaning with one another, in brief, the very topic our diagram should help us
to explore.

It is here, in this aspect of the mind as a self-ordering endeavor, as a
government hoping to maintain itself,[17] that compromise appears most
clearly as the practical art of the translator. To ask: Where in general will
compromise be most needed? is to try to divide the fields of possible discourse. There are areas of settled routine—much of trade, for example—where
the fixed and comparatively simple structuring of the things and events to be
dealt with allows of a fine practical equivalence between the languages used.
Wherever there is a clear operational check upon Comprehendings this happy
condition is likely to prevail. Mathematics, physics, the strict sciences can be
translated without loss—by the introduction of the technical term and the
use of the type-specimen, the model and the operational definition. Here
functions 1, 2, and 6 are serving a Purposing so general that it can hide behind
the ordering, 6, of what is said, 2, about what, 1. But as discourse grows less
abstract and hypothetical, more entire and actual, the probability of loss and
therefore the need for choice and compromise become greater. With narrative
and philosophy and poetry in so far as the growth and history of the language
and of other social and cultural institutions enter in, a self-denying statute is
required. If we take Ethics to be "the bringing to bear of self-control for the
purpose of realizing our desires,"[18] we have to decide which of our desires
must give way to which. The translator has first to reconcile himself to conceiving his art in terms of minimal loss and then to balance and adjudicate, as
best he can, the claims of the rival functions. His question is: Which sorts of
loss will we take in order not to lose what? And answering that is in practice
a series of decisions, 6, on behalf of a policy, 7, which may very well have to
declare itself openly, in a preface or in footnotes. The mind-state analogy is
at work all through, it will be perceived. The translator is called upon to become a statesman and serve a limitless oncoming state. His chief advantage
over his analogue is that he can, sometimes, go back and undo his mistakes.
He can cancel and choose again. But for the rest his practical sagacity must
accept the hard commonplace truths: if we try for too much, we will get less
than we might, and what we can go on to do will depend on what we have
done and are doing now.

[16] Robert Bridges, *The Testament of Beauty* (Oxford, 1939).
[17] *Republic*, 591.
[18] *Collected Papers of Charles Sanders Peirce*, I, 334.

Translation theory—over and above the aid it may afford the translator—has thus a peculiar duty toward man's self-completion, to use a concept which seems to be suggestively common to the Chinese and the Western traditions. We are not weather vanes, 1; we are not filing systems, 2; we are not even agonies or delights only, 3; we are not litmus paper, 4, or servo-mechanisms, 5. We are guardians, 6, and subject therefore to the paradox of government: that we must derive our powers, in one way or another, from the very forces which we have to do our best to control. Translation theory has not only to work for better mutual comprehension between users of diverse tongues; more central still in its purposing is a more complete viewing of itself and of the Comprehending which it should serve.

KENNETH BURKE
from *Permanence and Change*

All living organisms interpret many of the signs about them. A trout, having snatched at a hook but having had the good luck to escape with a rip in his jaw, may even show by his wiliness thereafter that he can revise his critical appraisals. His experience has led him to form a new judgment, which we should verbalize as a nicer discrimination between food and bait. A different kind of bait may outwit him, if it lacks the appearances by which he happens to distinguish "jaw-ripping food." And perhaps he passes up many a morsel of genuine food simply because it happens to have the characters which he, as the result of his informing experience, has learned to take as the sign of bait. I do not mean to imply that the sullen fish has thought all this out. I mean simply that in his altered response, for a greater or lesser period following the hook episode, he manifests the changed behavior that goes with a new meaning, he has a more educated way of reading the signs. It does not matter how conscious or unconscious one chooses to imagine this critical step; we need only note here the outward manifestation of a revised judgment.

Our great advantage over this sophisticated trout would seem to be that we can greatly extend the scope of the critical process. Man can be methodical in his attempts to decide what the difference between bait and food might be. Unfortunately, as Thorstein Veblen has pointed out, invention is the mother of necessity: the very power of criticism has enabled man to build up cultural structures so complex that still greater powers of criticism are needed before he can distinguish between the food-processes and bait-processes concealed beneath his cultural tangles. His greater critical capacity has increased not only the range of his solutions, but also the range of his problems. . . . Though all organisms are critics in the sense that they interpret the signs about them, the experimental speculative technique made available by speech would seem to single out the human species as the only one possessing an equipment for going beyond the criticism of experience to a criticism of criticism. We not only interpret the characters of events (manifesting in our responses all the gradations of fear, apprehension, expectation, assurance, for which there are rough behavioristic counterparts in animals)—we may also interpret our interpretations.

GASTON BACHELARD
from *The Psychoanalysis of Fire*

We have only to speak of an object to think that we are being objective. But, because we chose it in the first place, the object reveals more about us than we do about it. What we consider to be our fundamental ideas concerning the world are often indications of the immaturity of our minds. Sometimes we stand in wonder before a chosen object; we build up hypotheses and reveries; in this way we form convictions which have all the appearance of true knowledge. But the initial source is impure: the first impression is not a fundamental truth. In point of fact, scientific objectivity is possible only if one has broken first with the immediate object, if one has refused to yield to the seduction of the initial choice, if one has checked and contradicted the thoughts which arise from one's first observation. Any objective examination, when duly verified, refutes the results of the first contact with the object. To start with, everything must be called into question: sensation, common sense, usage however constant, even etymology, for words, which are made for singing and enchanting, rarely make contact with thought. Far from marvelling at the object, objective thought must treat it ironically. Without this malign vigilance we would never adopt a truly objective attitude. When we are dealing with men, our equals and our brothers, our method should be based on sympathy. But when confronted with this inert world whose life is not ours, which suffers none of our sorrows nor is exalted by any of our joys, we must restrain all our enthusiasms, we must repress our personal feelings. The axes of poetry and of science are opposed to one another from the outset. All that philosophy can hope to accomplish is to make poetry and science complementary, to unite them as two well-defined opposites. We must oppose, then, to the enthusiastic, poetic mind the taciturn, scientific mind, and for the scientific mind an attitude of preliminary antipathy is a healthy precaution.

Method

Working with a triadic conception of the meaning relationship means recognizing that truth belongs not to "reality" but to statements by whose means we re-present our views of reality. Triadicity entails the renunciation of the idea of perfect certainty; the recognition of mediation requires that we cultivate the attitude Peirce calls "contrite fallibilism." (This enterprise will have no appeal to positivists.) In order to tolerate the necessary ambiguities, as well as to attempt to differentiate, say, variant readings from misreadings, we need method to guide critical inquiry.

Scientific method is poorly understood by social scientists, and since current rhetorical theory borrows so heavily from psychology, misconceptions of what scientists do abound. As antidotes, I have selected two essays by scientists who explain the role of analogy and the dialectic of hypothesis and experimentation. J. Robert Oppenheimer's "Analogy in Science" was originally an address delivered to the American Psychological Association; in the tradition of Huxley, N. W. Pirie is writing for a popular audience.

This distinguished biologist's explanation of how the scientist selects facts in order to interpret is followed by R. G. Collingwood arguing that the idea of the historian's judging facts by the criterion of *how it really was* is illusory, that it is the mediating "idea of history," our conception of the past, that provides the means of selecting facts and developing evidence. It is the historical imagination which constructs the web, the form the past assumes.

C. S. PEIRCE
(on method)

5.41. . . . [That] artist's observational power is what is most wanted in the study of phenomenology. The second faculty we must strive to arm ourselves with is a resolute discrimination which fastens itself like a bulldog upon the particular feature that we are studying, follows it wherever it may lurk, and detects it beneath all its disguises. The third . . . is the generalizing power of the mathematician.

5.363. . . . Each chief step in science has been a lesson in logic . . . The old chemist's maxim had been "Lege, lege, lege, labora, ora, et relege." Lavoisier's method was not to read and pray, but to dream that some long and complicated chemical process would have a certain effect, to put it into practice with dull patience, after its inevitable failure, to dream that with some modification it would have another result, and to end by publishing the last dream as a fact: his way was to carry his mind into his laboratory, and literally to make of his alembics and cucurbits instruments of thought, giving a new conception of reasoning as something which was to be done with one's eyes open, by manipulating real things instead of words and fancies.

J. ROBERT OPPENHEIMER
"Analogy in Science"

. . . The school of Mathematics and the School of Historical Studies [Institute for Advanced Study, Princeton] have both, of course, the problem of filtering the immense, fascinating, inchoate, unmanageable complexity of our experience. But they filter in quite different ways. The School of Mathematics is concerned with relations, with forms, with logical structure, and the application of these patterns and their discovery to the empirical sciences. And so it happens that psychologists are members of the School of Mathematics.

The School of Historical Studies uses a different kind of filtration. When I was in England not long ago I talked to Namier, who has undertaken the compilation of the parliamentary biographies of all Members of Parliament, from the origin to now. In the first Parliaments almost nothing is available in the record about most of the members, so it is hard to write about this. And at present it is hard to write the biographies because there are such volumes available about everybody; only in the 16th and 17th and 18th centuries is the amount of material fit for human compass. The filtration of history is, of course, a very special one. It not only reduces the volume of available evidence and experience; it does so through the eyes of once living people who, by their actions, their evaluation, their tradition, have selected the things which are to remain meaningful over the years.

It is very often in history that just the unique point, the point that has no satisfactory, exhaustive, formal relation to more general patterns, is what is interesting. In the School of Mathematics it can only be things general enough so that structure can be recognized. I need to add that one mathematician, who has made such great contributions to logic, Gödel, has said of mathematics that it is purely an historical accident that it developed along quantitative lines. This, which is one of the themes which I take as text for today, may moderate somewhat the austerity of the two schools of learning. Yet taking it all-in-all I can only describe the relations of the Institute to psychology by a story.

About twenty years ago for the first time I visited the great laboratory in New York where Professor Rabi and his colleagues were beginning to do the most exciting experiments on molecular beams: and I had a fine time. But, as I left, I noticed that over the door it said in somewhat dusty letters, "Cosmic Ray Laboratory," and I asked Rabi, "What the heck?" "Well," he said, "you see, we don't keep them out."

I have thus given up talking about the Institute; and my second thought is rather simpler. It is to say a few things about physics which are, I think, interesting and which, I hope, may be helpful if not taken too literally and too seriously, also in the various fields of psychology. I know that it is a terrible bear trap to talk of the philosophy of science; only in a very, very limited sense am I going to do that.

One would think that the two sciences could hardly be further apart. In all hierarchical schemes they are put far apart. Psychology, to everyone who works in the field, is felt to be a new subject in which real progress and real objectives are recent. Physics is, perhaps, as old as the sciences come; physics is reputed to have a large, coherent, connected corpus of certitudes. This does not exist in psychology, and only the beginnings of it, the beginnings of things that are later going to be tied together, are now before us.

But I have always had a feeling that there were ways in which the two sciences had a community; in some sense, of course, all sciences do. One very simple one is that each is responsive to a primitive, permanent, pervasive, human curiosity: what material bodies are and how they behave, on the one hand, and how people and the people-like animals behave and feel and think and learn. These are the curiosities of common life and they will never be abated. Both, for this reason, can hardly make important pronouncements of a technical sort which do not appear to have some bearing on our views of reality, on metaphysics. Both manifestly have, and continue to have, a fresh and inspiriting effect on the theory of knowledge, on epistemology.

There are other ways in which we are brothers. In the last ten years the physicists have been extraordinarily noisy about the immense powers which, largely through their efforts, but through other efforts as well, have come into the possession of man, powers notably and strikingly for very large-scale and dreadful destruction. We have spoken of our responsibilities and of our obligations to society in terms that sound to me very provincial, because the psychologist can hardly do anything without realizing that for him the acquisition of knowledge opens up the most terrifying prospects of controlling what people do and how they think and how they behave and how they feel. This is true for all of you who are engaged in practice, and as the corpus of psychology gains in certitude and subtlety and skill, I can see that the physicist's pleas that what he discovers be used with humanity and be used wisely will seem rather trivial compared to those pleas which you will have to make and for which you will have to be responsible.

The point, of course, is that as the relevance of what we find to human welfare and human destiny becomes sharper and more manifest, our responsibilities for explication, for explanation, for communication, for teaching grow. These are rather our responsibilities for being sure that we are understood than responsibilities for making decisions; they are our responsibilities for laying the basis in understanding for those decisions.

There are other ways in which we are alike. The practical usefulness of our professions gives us often the impression that we are right for the wrong reasons, and that our true nature is very different from our public presence. We are both faced with the problem of the need to keep intact the purity of academic and abstract research and, at the same time, to nourish and be nourished by practice. In physics, of course, our debt to technology and engineering is unlimited. I think it would be so in psychology as well.

Both sciences, all sciences, arise as refinements, corrections, and adaptations of common sense. There are no unique, simple scientific methods that one can prescribe; but there are certainly traits that any science must have before it pretends to be one. One is the quest for objectivity. I mean that not in a metaphysical sense; but in a very practical sense, as the quest to be sure that we understand one another, and that all qualified practitioners mean essentially the same thing. Common-sense language is inherently ambiguous; when the poet uses it, or the rhetorician, he exploits the ambiguity, and even when we talk in ordinary life we almost need ambiguity in order to get by. But in science we try to get rid of that, we try to talk in such simple terms, and match our talk with deeds in such a way that we may differ as to facts, but we can resolve the differences. This is, of course, the first step in the quest for certitude. But certitude is not the whole story. When we move from common sense into scientific things, we also move toward generality, using analysis, using observation and, in the end, using experiment. And we also do something which is even more characteristic; we look for novelty, we look for transcendence, we look for features of experience that are not available in ordinary life. Characteristic in physics are the instruments that enable us to transcend elementary, daily experience: the telescope that lets us look deep into the sky, the enormous accelerators which are, today, the logical extension of the microscope, enabling us to look on a finer and finer scale into the structure of matter.

I need to be cautious in citing parallels in psychology; but certainly the use of hypnosis, the use of drugs, are typical extensions into unfamiliar realms of human experience which just bring out characteristics of psychological phenomena that are largely lost in day-to-day experience. There is an example which may be only a physicist's idea of a perfect experiment. It is the work that was done at McGill in the last years on the effects of reducing sensory stimuli, with very simple arrangements to change the level of stimulation; these produce most striking and almost frighteningly great, though essentially temporary, changes in memory, in the intellectual and cognitive life of the subjects. This is again an example of carrying to an extreme something which is indeed encountered in ordinary experience but which only the patience and the abstractness of experimental enquiry is likely to make manifest.

We come from common sense; we work for a long time; then we give back to common sense refined, original, and strange notions, and enrich what men know and how they live. And here, I suppose, the real hero is the teacher.

I chose as my theme, "Analogy in Science." What I am going to talk about is analogy as an instrument in science and, to a much lesser extent, some traits of analogies between the sciences; mostly the second theme has led to misunderstanding and limitation; as for the first theme, analogy is indeed an indispensable and inevitable tool for scientific progress. Perhaps I had better say what I mean by that. I do not mean metaphor; I do not mean allegory; I do not even mean similarity; but I mean a special kind of similarity which is the similarity of structure, the similarity of form, a similarity of constellation between two sets of structures, two sets of particulars, that are manifestly very different but have structural parallels. It has to do with relation and interconnection. I would like to quote you a scholastic comment on analogy. It is a translation of Penido, "In a very general sense every analogy presupposes two ontological conditions; one, a plurality of real beings and thus among them an essential diversity. Monism is the born enemy of analogy. And, two, at the very heart of this multiplicity, of this inequality, a certain unity."

It is a matter about which we could argue whether these structural elements are invented by us, or whether they are discovered in the world. I find it very artificial to say that they are invented, in the sense that they are more of an artifact than the particulars which they unite and describe. I may tell one incident in the long history of astronomy and physics, which makes this very vivid for me. For practical purposes, for prophecy and ritual, the Babylonians worked out a method of predicting what days the moon would first be visible, of predicting lunar eclipses and certain rarer astronomical events. They did this by purely mathematical methods. They observed when things happened, and they got the pattern of it. They were very good. They got so good that their methods were in use in the last century in India to predict eclipses within some thirty minutes, using these two thousand year old methods. The Babylonians not only became very good, but they enjoyed it very much and they did it for fun; long after the practical reasons had gone away they published these tables, apparently as we publish articles on the internal constitution of the stars, because it is interesting. They did all of this without any celestial mechanics, without any geometry; nothing moved; there were no objects circulating around in orbits; there were no laws of motion; there was no dynamics; this was just in the field of numbers.

You know how today we predict eclipses and first risings. It would seem to me equally wrong not to recognize in celestial mechanics as we now know it, a far deeper and more comprehensive description of regularities in the physical world. I think that not only because it is a little more useful, I think that not only because it unites more subjects, but because it reveals an aspect of the regularities of the world which was wholly unseen by the Babylonians.

Perhaps I need now to quote from Charles Peirce, and get on: "However, as metaphysics is a subject much more curious than useful, the knowledge of which, like that of a sunken reef, serves chiefly to enable us to keep clear of it, I will not trouble the reader with any more Ontology at this moment."

Whether or not we talk of discovery or of invention, analogy is inevitable in human thought, because we come to new things in science with what equipment we have, which is how we have learned to think, and above all how we have learned to think about the relatedness of things. We cannot, coming into something new, deal with it except on the basis of the familiar and the old-fashioned. The conservatism of scientific enquiry is not an arbitrary thing; it is the freight with which we operate: it is the only equipment we have. We cannot learn to be surprised or astonished at something unless we have a view of how it ought to be; and that view is almost certainly an analogy. We cannot learn that we have made a mistake unless we can make a mistake; and our mistake is almost always in the form of an analogy to some other piece of experience.

This is not to say that analogy is the criterion of truth. One can never establish that a theory is right by saying that it is like some other theory that is right. The criterion of truth must come from analysis, it must come from experience, and from that very special kind of objectivity which characterizes science, namely that we are quite sure we understand one another and that we can check up on one another. But truth is not the whole thing; certitude is not the whole of science. Science is an immensely creative and enriching experience; and it is full of novelty and exploration; and it is in order to get to these that analogy is an indispensable instrument. Even analysis, even the ability to plan experiments, even the ability to sort things out and pick them apart presupposes a good deal of structure, and that structure is characteristically an analogical one.

Let me read you now a few relevant and eloquent words of William
James. He wrote them in one of his later accounts of pragmatism, at a time
when his own good sense and shrewd observation and wisdom and humanity
made him aware of the fact that to say only that an idea was true because it
worked was a rather poor description of what went on in science, that something was missing from that account. This is what he wrote:

> The point I now urge you to observe particularly is the part played by
> the older truths. Failure to take account of it is the source of much of
> the unjust criticism levelled against pragmatism. Their influence is
> absolutely controlling. Loyalty to them is the first principle—in most
> cases it is the only principle; for by far the most usual way of handling
> phenomena so novel that they would make for a serious rearrangement
> of our preconception is to ignore them altogether, or to abuse those
> who bear witness for them.

What I want to do next is to give you five examples of the use of analogy
in atomic physics. They will not all be equally familiar; perhaps that is an
understatement, for some are very new, even to such a point new that I do
not know how good the analogies are and we have not yet found the decisive
point at which they are mistaken.

The analogies in physics may very well be misleading for biologists and
psychologists, because of the enormous part that rather rigid formal structure
plays in physics. This structure is not perhaps necessarily quantitative, though
in fact much of it is quantitative. Our ability to write down synoptic relations
in symbolic form, our use of formulae, enables us to talk of vast amounts of
experience, very varied experience, very detailed experience, in a shorthand
way; and to point sharply to mistakes, to correct error on occasion by altering
only one letter, that changes everything. These examples are thus not meant
as paradigms, but rather an illustration of the fact that, in what is regarded
as one of the most rigorous and certain of the sciences, we use an instrument
which has been in great disrepute, because uncritically used it can confuse
invention with confirmation and truth.

Let me give a first example which is not from atomic physics, which is
almost from pre-physics, because it deals with very familiar things and yet
illustrates the nature of the role of form in the use of analogy in physics. This
has to do with Jean Buridan and the Paris school of the 14th century and the
theory of impetus. What was their classic view? Physics has a special meaning
for the word "classic"; classic means wrong, it means a wrong view that was
held to be right a little while ago. The classic view was that the natural state
of matter was rest, and that where you found bodies in motion you needed
to look for a cause. This was the Schoolman's view; it was Aristotle's view. It
is, in fact, supported by a lot of observation. It is not well supported by observation on projectiles; the notion that air pushes the bullet becomes less
plausible the more you watch. Buridan and his colleagues took a step, making
an analogy, probably the greatest step in the history of Western science. They

said, it is true that matter has a natural state, but it is not rest. It is true that when it departs from this natural state this must be ascribed to the intervention of a cause. But the natural state is one of constant impetus, one of constant momentum, one of uniform velocity. And with that the beginnings of rational mechanics and rational physical science were made. This seems a small change, to replace the coordinate by the velocity; it is a small change; and yet it is a change in the whole way of thinking about the physical world.

Let me list the five illustrations from atomic physics: they are what has happened to the idea of waves; what has happened to the ideas of classical physics in the atomic domain, the so-called correspondence principle; the analogy between radioactive decay and emission of light which we owe to Fermi; the analogy between electromagnetic forces and nuclear forces, between electrodynamics and mesodynamics; and a final subject which I will only call strangeness because that is about all I know about it.

Take the wave theory. It originated in the observation of regular, rhythmic changes in matter, waves on water, and was developed by an easily conducted physical exploration of sound waves, where there is a periodic change, a regular change in the density of air or other media. Both of these phenomena exhibit a characteristic. If two waves collide they can cancel each other out, or they can reinforce each other. They show interference. They have another abstract property: if waves pass through an orifice or around an obstacle that is small compared with the wave length, then the obstacle or the orifice does not cast a sharp image or shadow, but there are characteristic blurring effects which are called diffraction. Waves superpose; the sum of the two waves is just what you get by adding algebraically and not arithmetically; you may get zero if you add equal positive and negative waves; this again is interference.

This abstract set of properties is persistent; light is also a wave motion, but there is no matter in motion; there is no substrate. It was a great mark of progress for physics to recognize this disanalogy. There is still motion; and what moves are physically measurable things, rather more abstract things, electric fields and magnetic fields. Again we find interference, diffraction, and superposition, the same abstract characteristics, and again in principle, the infinitely regular, infinitely repeated pattern as a special case of a wave.

More extremely abstract examples are the waves of atomic mechanics, of wave mechanics, because these waves in the first place are in multidimensional space, then they are represented by complex numbers so that they are not directly measurable; they are indeed quite unobservable. There is nothing to measure in the physical world that corresponds to these waves. They are indirectly connected with observation; but they have again these same abstract properties—interference, linearity, superposition, diffraction; and when one talks about them, one uses much the same mathematics as for sound and light waves, although it is not the fact that one can use the mathematics but the fact that the structure and the relations are the same that is the decisive discovery. These waves represent, if one wants to say what they are, not matter, not forces, not electric fields, but essentially the state of information about an atomic system.

At each point the first scientists have tried to make a theory like the earlier theories, light, like sound, as a material wave: matter waves like light waves, like a real, physical wave: and in each case it has been found one had to widen the framework a little, and find the disanalogy which enabled one to preserve what was right about the analogy.

The second example of analogy is a massive one: it is, I think, the greatest experience in this century for the physicist, even greater than relativity: it is the discovery of atomic mechanics. Here again, in a way very characteristic of scientific theory, great conservatism presided over and guided the development. What is all this about? When one gets to the atomic domain, and this is a domain of small actions, of limited distances and limited impulses, of things such as one encounters in atoms and nuclei, then the coarseness of the whole physical world, its granular atomic structure, for the first time begins to manifest itself. This is not yet the granulation of the fundamental particles, but the granulation of atomic physics itself, of the quantum of action. What this turns out to mean is that when one tries to study such a system there are aspects of it which are accessible to experiment but are not compatibly or simultaneously accessible to experiment. A famous example is in the uncertainty relations, that one can determine the location of something in time and space, but if one does that, he uses an experimental setup which makes it impossible to know exactly what the impulse or velocity or energy of the system is. One may do the opposite; one can study the impulse and then lose all account of where the object is. And one can, of course, compromise with limited knowledge of both; but one cannot combine; and we call these the complementary aspects of an atomic system, and the complementary character of the fundamental observations. That means that we cannot talk about an atom as we can about a classical mechanical system. We cannot say the objects in it are here and they are moving in certain orbits and so on: in fact, in ordinary atoms there are no orbits. In atoms as they are ordinarily encountered there is something entirely different; there are stationary states which have a stability, a uniqueness, a reproduceability, which has no counterpart in classical physics at all, which could not exist if it were not for a revolutionary feature.

One can talk about these stationary states in a consistent way; one can describe them accurately, and predict them: but one has a vast change from the familiar experience of bodies in motion, of matter in motion. Sometimes people say that this atomic theory is characterized by the fact that we cannot observe a system without disturbing it. But that is not quite right. It is not the disturbance which makes the trouble; it is the fact that the means of observation would be frustrated as means of observation if we tried to take account of the disturbance which we are making. This is thus a slightly more subtle matter. Sometimes people say that the electron has a position and momentum but we cannot measure them simultaneously. But this is not right either, because only the act of observation, the coupling of the atom with the physical measuring equipment, makes it logically permissible to attribute a position to an electron. We cannot get the right answer by saying that the electron has a position, and since we do not know what it is, let us average. If we do that we get a wrong answer. We have to admit that unless the situation is one which is created by our physical operation on the atomic system to realize, to manifest, to objectify the localization of the electron, then it will not be localized; it will in fact have no properties at all apart from what we do to it.

All of this is extraordinarily radical and extraordinarily unlike Newtonian mechanics. But what does the physicist say? Even before the full answer was found it was said there was something going on here which limits classical ideas; they do not quite apply; but in any situation in which they do apply we know that they are right; and, therefore, whatever laws hold in the atomic domain, they must merge into the laws of classical mechanics. There must be a one-to-one correspondence, an analogy; otherwise, in capturing some insight into this new domain we will throw out all we ever knew, and throw out things that are true. This affirmation is called the correspondence principle. Let me give an example of how extremely compact is this correction of the analogy which has revolutionized everything, of how one deals with analogy in a highly formalized science.

Each law of classical mechanics may be written so that it is true in atomic mechanics: that the velocity is proportional to the momentum; that the change in time of the momentum is proportional to the force; that the energy is conserved. All of these things hold provided we make one formal change, provided we say that the momentum and the coordinate are not numbers, but are objects such that when we multiply the momentum by the coordinate and when we multiply the coordinate by the momentum we do not get the same answer, and that the difference between these two answers is an imaginary, universal, atomic constant. If we just write that one formula, then everything we had before is formally identical with what we have now. This is not only a powerful illustration of the use of analogy and disanalogy in a formal science; it played a decisive part in the exploration and discovery of the atomic world. We shall have to come back to other aspects of this great development. Let me run rather more briefly over the three other examples.

Radioactive nuclei, almost all of those that are made artificially, and many natural ones, disintegrate by sending out electrons. We puzzled and puzzled over this, since it was quite clear that there were no electrons in nuclei. Then Fermi made the suggestion that one might describe this as one describes the emission of light or light quanta from atoms. Nobody would say there was a light quantum in an atom; but still we observe light coming out; and he made a theory along these lines. It was not exactly right; the analogy was not quite perfect; but with a very little adjustment which took some fifteen years of comparison with the details of experiment, we have a description and a theory that work fine.

The Japanese physicist Yukawa proposed a somewhat braver analogy, whose fortunes are still not entirely clear. He proposed a similarity between electrical and nuclear forces. The way in which one describes the forces between electrically charged bodies is, of course, that one charged body makes electric fields; and these electric fields are propagated to other bodies, and give them some momentum to push them around. Nuclear forces, which are not electromagnetic, but are very strong and spectacular, Yukawa said, would probably be due to a field of a new kind; replacing the electric field there would be this new field; and replacing the light quanta, there would be new kinds of particles. Using general arguments of relativity and complementarity, or quantum theory, he concluded that because the forces between nucleons are of short range these new particles would have a mass some hundreds of times that of the electron; and from other particularities of nuclear forces, he drew conclusions about the nature of these particles. These particles were found in cosmic rays; they are called mesons. The analogy which Yukawa started with has been refined; one has discovered that there are many differences between mesodynamics and electrodynamics. One is at the present time not quite sure what all of the key points of difference, of disanalogy, are. Some of them have been discovered, but they appear to be rather the more trivial ones; yet the theory, as it stands now, has some predictive value; it has brought order and clarity to a part, at least, of nuclear physics; it has kept people at work, busy for twenty years of rather odd and arduous and rarified boondoggling. It has been a very major event in physics and I do not know at the moment how to describe what limits this analogy, why it is not a perfect one. If we were having a seminar on physics I would talk about it for an hour, but I still would not know.

The troubles, though, are probably connected with my fifth example. It is true that these mesons of Yukawa's were discovered; but not very long after that, in the last five years, one has found a whole lot of other objects—about six manifestly different objects and maybe more to come, which are also quite stable and last quite a while, and which are not simple mesons of the kind Yukawa envisaged. Almost certainly their intervention in the picture, which is not something that is provided for in the analogy we started from, will provide a clue to the new point. But, their existence raises a different problem. Whenever in physics one encounters a situation in which something does not happen, or happens very slowly, one finds it interesting; and the great point was why do these new particles not decay quickly. They do decay; but it takes them an inordinately long time, and they come apart into products which one would expect to emerge right away.

We have a great deal of experience with reactions that occur slowly or not at all; and the characteristic reason for that is that something does not tend to change, like the energy of a system, or the total charge: something is conserved. Whenever that turns up, it also turns out that the fact that something is invariant and unchanging is mathematically identical with the statement that something makes no difference to the behavior of the system.

Examples of what may make no difference to the behavior of a system may be its position in space, or its orientation in space, or some more abstract circumstance. Thus the first thing that we all did was to try to find the characteristic of these new particles that did not tend to change. That has not been hard to do; and a quite successful theory has been developed which accounts for some of the great peculiarities in this field. We do not have a good name for what does not tend to change, and the inventor of it calls it the "strangeness."

These five examples are not meant to exhaust, but merely to illustrate, the powerful use, the inevitable use of analogy in a well developed, in a highly organized, highly formalized, highly coherent science. I need to point out that in every case an immense amount of experience, of measurement, of observation, and of analysis has gone both to the correction of the analogies and to their confirmation.

When I turn to the question of analogies between sciences I talk of something very different. There is first of all the fact that there are often situations that are not analogies at all. There are congruences when, in two different sciences, by different techniques, different language, different concepts, it turns out that the same subject has been explored from two sides. And when it turns out that there is a mapping of one description on the other, usually one description contains more elements than the other, is richer; the other may then be more economical and more convenient. Examples: the chemical theory of valence and atomic physics, which are identical except that atomic physics does give an account of some phenomena, such as resonance, which were hard to cope with within the framework of the classical chemical theory. Another example, newer and perhaps not yet as well explored or understood, lies in classical genetics on the one hand, and the discovery of the genetic substances DNA, RNA, and so on, which are, at the moment, very close to being in a one-to-one correspondence, but in which the biochemical description will turn out richer, more relevant to dynamics, and more subtle.

These are great events of science; when they happen there is rejoicing, and when they do not happen there is hope. These are the great events which bring coherence and order and large structure to the unfolding of scientific life. But probably between sciences of very different character, the direct formal analogies in their structure are not too likely to be helpful. Certainly what the pseudo-Newtonians did with sociology was a laughable affair; and similar things have been done with mechanical notions of how psychological phenomena are to be explained. I know that when physicists enter biology their first ideas of how things work are indescribably naive and mechanical; they are how things would work if the physicists were making them work, but not how they work in life. I know that when I hear the word "field" used in physics and in psychology I have a nervousness that I cannot entirely account for. I think that, especially when we compare subjects in which ideas of coding, of the transfer of information, or ideas of purpose, are inherent and natural, with subjects in which these are not inherent and natural, that formal analogies have to be taken with very great caution.

But for all of that I would like to say something about what physics has to give back to common sense that it seemed to have lost from it, not because I am clear that these ideas are important tools in psychological research, but because it seems to me that the worst of all possible misunderstandings would be that psychology be influenced to model itself after a physics which is not there any more, which has been quite outdated.

We inherited, say at the beginning of this century, a notion of the physical world as a causal one, in which every event could be accounted for if we were ingenious, a world characterized by number, where everything interesting could be measured and quantified, a determinist world, a world in which there was no use or room for individuality, in which the object of study was simply there and how you studied it did not affect the object, it did not affect the kind of description you gave of it, a world in which objectifiability went far beyond merely our own agreement on what we meant by words and what we are talking about, in which objectification was meaningful, irrespective of any attempt to study the system under consideration. It was just the given real object; there it was, and there was nothing for you to worry about of an epistemological character. This extremely rigid picture left out a great deal of common sense. I do not know whether these missing elements will prove helpful; but at least their return may widen the resources that one can bring to any science.

What are these ideas? In our natural, unschooled talk, and above all in unschooled talk about psychological problems, we have five or six things which we have got back into physics with complete rigor, with complete objectivity, in the sense that we understand one another, with a complete lack of ambiguity and with a perfectly phenomenal technical success. One of them is just this notion that the physical world is not completely determinate. There are predictions you can make about it but they are statistical; and any event has in it the nature of the surprise, of the miracle, of something that you could not figure out. Physics is predictive, but within limits; its world is ordered, but not completely causal.

Another of these ideas is the discovery of the limits on how much we can objectify without reference to what we are really talking about in an operational, practical sense. We can say the electron has a certain charge and we do not have to argue as to whether we are looking at it to say that; it always does. We cannot say it has a place or a motion. If we say that, we imply something about what we ourselves—I do not mean as people but as physicists—are doing about it.

A third point is very closely related to this; it is the inseparability of what we are studying and the means that are used to study it, the organic connection of the object with the observer. Again, the observer is not in this case a human; but in psychology the observer sometimes is a human.

And then, as logical consequences of this, there is the idea of totality, or wholeness. Newtonian physics, classical science, was differential; anything that went on could be broken up into finer and finer elements and analyzed so. If one looks at an atomic phenomenon between the beginning and the end, the end will not be there; it will be a different phenomenon. Every pair of observations taking the form "we know this, we then predict that" is a global thing; it cannot be broken down.

Finally, every atomic event is individual. It is not, in its essentials, reproducible.

This is quite a pack of ideas that we always use: individuality, wholeness, the subtle relations of what is seen with how it is seen, the indeterminacy and the acausality of experience. And I would only say that if physics could take all these away for three centuries and then give them back in ten years, we may well say that all ideas that occur in common sense are fair as starting points, not guaranteed to work but perfectly valid as the material of the analogies with which we start.

The whole business of science does not lie in getting into realms which are unfamiliar in normal experience. There is an enormous work of analyzing, of recognizing similarities and analogies, of getting the feel of the landscape, an enormous qualitative sense of family relations, of taxonomy. It is not always tactful to try to quantify; it is not always clear that by measuring one has found something very much worth measuring. It is true for the Babylonians it was worth measuring—noting—the first appearances of the moon because it had a practical value. Their predictions, their prophecies, and their magic would not work without it; and I know that many psychologists have the same kind of reason for wanting to measure. It is a real property of the real world that you are measuring, but it is not necessarily the best way to advance true understanding of what is going on; and I would make this very strong plea for pluralism with regard to methods that, in the necessarily early stages of sorting out an immensely vast experience, may be fruitful and may be helpful. They may be helpful not so much for attaining objectivity, nor for a quest for certitude which will never be quite completely attained. But there is a place for the use of naturalistic methods, the use of descriptive methods. I have been immensely impressed by the work of one man who visited us last year at the Institute, Jean Piaget. When you look at his work, his statistics really consist of one or two cases. It is just a start; and yet I think he has added greatly to our understanding. It is not that I am sure he is right, but he has given us something worthy of which to enquire whether it is right: and I make this plea not to treat too harshly those who tell you a story, having observed carefully without having established that they are sure that the story is the whole story and the general story.

It is of course in that light that I look at the immense discipline of practice, that with all its pitfalls, with all the danger that it leads to premature and incorrect solutions, does give an incredible amount of experience. Physics would not be where it is, psychology would not be where it is if there were not a great many people willing to pay us for thinking and working on their problems.

If any of this is true there is another thing that physicists and psychologists have in common: we are going to have quite a complicated life. The plea for a plural approach to exploration, the plea for a minimal definition of objectivity that I have made, means that we are going to learn a terrible lot; there are going to be many different ways of talking about things; the range from almost un-understood practice to recondite and abstract thought is going to be enormous. It means there are going to have to be a lot of psychologists, as there are getting to be a lot of physicists. When we work alone trying to get something straight it is right that we be lonely; and I think in the really decisive thoughts that advance a science loneliness is an essential part. When we are trying to do something practical it is nice to have an excess of talent, to have more sailors than are needed to sail the ship and more cooks than are needed to cook the meal; the reason is that in this way a certain elegance, a certain proper weighing of alternatives, guides the execution of the practical task.

We are, for all kinds of reasons, worrying about how our scientific community is to be nourished and enough people who are good enough are to come and work with us. And then on the other side we are worried about how we are to continue to understand one another, and not get totally frustrated by the complexity and immensity of our enterprises.

I think there are good reasons of an inherent kind, beside the competitive compulsion of the communist world, why we would do well to have more and better scientists. I know that exhortation, money, patronage, will do something about this; but I do not think that is all that will be needed. I think that if we are to have some success it must be because, as a part of our culture, the understanding, the life of the mind, the life of science, in itself, as an end as well as a means, is appreciated, is enjoyed, and is cherished. I think that has to be a very much wider thing in the community as a whole, if we are to enjoy with the community as a whole the healthy relations without which the developing powers of scientific understanding, prediction, and control are really monstrous things.

It may not be so simple, to have in the community at large some genuine experience of the pleasures of understanding and discovery. It may not be simple because what this requires is not merely that this experience be agreeable, but that it have a touch of virtue; that not only the consideration of ends, of products, of accomplishments and status, but the texture of life itself, its momentary beauty and its nobility, be worth some attention; and that among the things that contribute to these be the life of the mind and the life of science. Let us try to make it so.

N. W. PIRIE
"Selecting Facts and Avoiding Assumptions"

Facts and assumptions are often regarded as opposites, and empirics agree that we should strive to have as many of the one and as few of the other as possible. But science is dull when it is all facts; that would give us vast tables of constants, such as melting points and gravitational intensities. These could be memorized, but they become science only when they have been integrated into a comprehensible fabric. Before this can happen a clearing must be made in the jungle of fact. This is the process of selection, which at first sight seems so scientifically immoral. The justification is simple. Nature is a complete series of cross-connections, with every phenomenon existing in the environment created by the others. A full description of any phenomenon would therefore be enormously, even infinitely, long. It is the recognition of the omnipresence of interconnections that has abolished the simple truth of our forefathers. Of necessity therefore we set up a canon of relevant facts, and the skill with which that is done controls the progress of science.

Science is not a mechanically produced and packaged commodity, guaranteed untouched by human head. Both in method and direction it depends on the personal idiosyncratic choice of scientists, who select their facts and themes, consciously or unconsciously, in accordance with their environment and with the end they have in view.

Research workers and practical men produce all the facts and most of the ideas. Science therefore springs from the activities of empirics and not philosophers. It would be a tidier structure if this were not so, but one of the facts is that science has developed in spite of and not because of the philosophers. In any discussion like this it is essential to keep in mind the unruly rabble of empirics and to attempt the kind of systematization that they could read and accept. There are already sufficient treatises on Induction, Deduction, and the Scientific Method. They are tidy and coherent exercises, but they are read mainly by those producing rival tidy and coherent exercises. Scientists are only to a very limited extent scientific; they use admirable critical judgment on the substance of their experiments while being naively uncritical about the context into which these experiments fit.

But what precisely are these facts that we struggle to co-ordinate? Eddington, intending to be scornful, called them "pointer readings." Blake said, "I question not my Corporeal or Vegetative Eye any more than I would question a Window concerning a Sight. I look thro' it and not with it." The two attitudes have this much in common that they presuppose an underlying reality either in the external world, or in the head, or in both, about which the facts give some information. Our picture of Nature has to be compatible with the facts. That is, they operate negatively to restrict the range of choice; but when we try to project ideas forward they give hints rather than evidence. If we disparage facts thus we may be less disturbed by the necessity for neglecting many of them. For the present purpose a fact is simply a description of Nature from which reasonable efforts have been made to exclude interpretations. Little more can be said because interpretations—many of them misleading, as optical illusions and Aristotle's parlor trick of rubbing the nose with crossed fingers show—are part of the innate or early acquired fabric of sense impressions. It is a pity that the fundamental stuff of science is so ill-defined, but it remains so in spite of a vast literature aimed at more precise definition.

The first reason justifying the neglect of a fact may be quantitative. Francis Thompson set out a sound piece of Newtonian physics in the proposition

> . . . . . thou canst not stir a flower
> Without troubling a star.

But the *Nautical Almanac* has not yet found it necessary to record the date of the Chelsea Flower Show. It is only in well-explored fields that this reason is valid, and even in them mistakes can easily be made about the scale of the influences that may alter the course of an action. With increased knowledge of the effects of catalysts in chemistry, and of servomechanisms, people make less confident judgments about which aspects of a process they can neglect.

There is less experience in biology justifying us in brushing certain facts aside. Thus a biologist could not approach Eddington's well-known problem* about the elephant sliding down a grassy hillside by putting $W=2$ tons for the elephant and $\theta=50°$ for the hillside. On the contrary, the first move might well complicate matters further by setting down the sex of the elephant and the predominant species of grass on the slope. Only experiment would show whether these were relevant to the biologist's interest.

So long as facts are selected and neglected deliberately and explicitly the process need do little permanent harm. Unquestionably it increases the comprehensibility of Nature and, within limits, need not falsify it too much; we would only confuse the picture if we tried to discuss at once all the facts that are known. But when too much is neglected almost any result can be

---

*Sir Arthur Eddington, in *The Nature of the Physical World* (N. Y.: Macmillan, 1928), explains the kind of knowledge with which exact science is concerned. An examination paper in physics might begin "An elephant slides down a grassy hillside . . . " but "the experienced candidate knows that he need not pay attention to this; it is only put in to give an impression of realism. He reads on: 'The mass of the elephant is two tons.' Now we are getting down to business. The elephant fades out of the problem and a mass of two tons takes its place. . . . The poetry fades out of the problem, and by the time the serious application of the exact science begins we are left with only pointer readings" (pp. 252–53). (AB)

achieved when there are many facts to choose from; the work of a scientist then begins to resemble that of a sculptor. In a sense, the statue the latter creates existed all along within the block of stone and all he had to do was chip away the irrelevant pieces that were obscuring our view of it. But different sculptors can, within broad dimensional limits, make quite different statues from the same block. So also with scientists confronted with the same facts if they discard too many of them.

The same danger arises in other fields of activity. Historians generally start a controversy with the accusation that their opponents are selecting their facts. This selection is also responsible for the odium attaching to Plato's system of government and to the practices attributed to totalitarian States. Nevertheless, here also it may be unavoidable. As sound a humanist as Anatole France saw this and said: "But what is an event? Is it any fact whatsoever? No. It is a notable fact. How does the historian judge whether a fact is notable or not? He judges arbitrarily according to his own tastes and caprices." That is to say, he judges according to whether the fact aids comprehension and clarifies the picture or confuses both.

The neglect of fact is the price paid for achieving comprehensibility now, and the important issue is not whether people do it but whether they do it well. The facts neglected as irrelevant and unassimilable by this generation are likely to be the significant and indicative facts of the next. It is for this reason that scientists are so often said to be lucky. They realize that experiments do not "go wrong" and that the irregular or unexpected result is due to a factor that someone will sometime control. The fact that differences appear, when circumstances are supposed to be the same, is evidence either of error or of failure to control a relevant factor. It would generally be well to stop the one or study the other. Bearing in mind the particular object that the experimenter had in mind in his work, it is clear that it may not always be worth while to try to control these factors and it may be better to use statistical methods for compensating for the variation. This involves neglecting much of the observed fact. Statistical methods are of immense value in designing experiments and in getting scientific information by the analysis of what has happened in an uncontrollable population, in an experiment designed for some other purpose, or in the course of routine or commercial operations. But in foolish hands Statistics can become a means of covering up experimental deficiencies. The refusal to accept accident as the cause of a phenomenon is one of the more effective stimulants for the uncovering of new categories of fact.

Traditionally, assumptions are dealt with according to the principle attributed to Occam, *Entia non sunt multiplicanda praeter necessitatem.* That covers the details. More difficulty arises with the broad general assumptions that unknowables exist and that there are unifying principles lying beyond science. Many philosophers and experimenters from Canada through Lucretius and Laplace and on to our contemporaries have been emphatic that they needed no such unifying hypothesis, but the idea is still with us. It may there-

fore be worth while to argue that each type of assumption is both objection-
able in principle and obstructive in practice.

The Principle of Parsimony is much older than Occam, and the cele-
brated phrase does not occur in his known writings. His master, Duns Scotus,
had written: *Generale enim principium est, quod si aliquid potest aeque bene
fieri per pauciora sicut per plura, nullo modo talis pluralitas debet poni.* And
Dante expresses the same idea: *Quod potest fieri per unum, melius est fieri
per unum quam per plura.* Much earlier, Ptolemy and even Aristotle had used
comparable phrases. But the application of the principle is more important
than its authorship. We prefer whichever interpretation of a set of observations
is the simplest, not because Nature is of necessity simple and we are subtle but
rather because interpretations are comprehensible in proportion to their simplicity. The simpler we can make a formulation that is still compatible with
the selected facts, the more fully experts will understand it, and the larger
will be the number of the inexpert who understand it partially. It is out of
this widespread understanding that the next stage of progress comes. We avoid
assumptions, as we select facts, so that science may be communicable. The
process works passably in many sciences, but in biology the more complex
and, as it were, backhanded of two interpretations has often proved the more
durable. Nothing is gained by postulating entities gratuitously, but the fact
that one interpretation involves fewer than another is not, of itself, a reason
for adopting it.

God is undoubtedly the simplest of the unifying hypotheses and the one
with the greatest tendency to remove domains of experience from experimental study. We may define God as that part of experience that can never be
made amenable to experiment. That has the merit of recognizing the possible
validity of the basic assumption without attempting, now, to define its
domain. If, for example, Galton's experiments on prayer had shown it to be
efficacious, it is unlikely that it would have led to a revival of religion but
rather that it would have stimulated research on thought transference or
some such mundane theme. The domain of experiment is itself a matter for
experiment.

The assumption that there is such an underlying unity does not lead to
testable statements. It cannot therefore be disproved; equally it cannot be
shown to be necessary. Most of experience is not amenable to experiment
because the techniques have not been learnt. Scientists are so well aware of
this that they can dismiss scornfully the usual smug restrictions couched in
such phrases as

There are more things in heaven and earth, Horatio,
Than are dreamt of in your philosophy,

or "There are Higher Truths of which you know nothing." The use of phrases
like these springs from the idea of a blinkered pedant, on the one hand, and
an inspired visionary, on the other. The assumption that the scientific method
has only a limited validity is commonly made by the religious, by artists, and

by investigators of supernormal phenomena. Criticism sometimes takes the form that the scientific method is dull and plodding; from some quarters this criticism could be accepted, but a competent scientist who has just observed something knows more about joy and reverence than the whole bench of bishops.

Even faith is not the prerogative of the religious, for we cannot always be scientific, and even the most sceptical scientist takes some things on trust. Thus biologists generally do not inquire deeply into the electrical equipment that they use and accept gadgets that simply say what sequence to press the knobs in. We do this because someone understands the mechanism and can repair it if it goes wrong. It would be better if we had mastered the machine ourselves, but there are conflicting demands on time and attention. The "take it on trust" attitude is only permissible when there is a demonstrated basis for the trust, and this exists over instrument design. On the broader issues there is no justification for trust and we may be excused for thinking that the religious understand Nature less well than we do and are even less likely to produce trustworthy systematizations.

Science is in its infancy, and there are vistas of experience not yet co-ordinated, but other modes of thought have not co-ordinated them either. For as long as the critics confine themselves to criticism they are on firm ground. Most of the deficiencies that they see in science exist; we see them too. Much is made of the disagreements, both within and between the different sciences, which so often enliven the scientific scene. Religious and artistic disagreements are also known, and would probably be commoner if the conclusions come to by these methods were sufficiently precisely formulated. We make an unnecessary and limiting assumption unless we conclude that the scientific or experimental method is potentially applicable everywhere. Science is not the antithesis of the religious or poetic approach, but historically it is a later mode of approach to fields in which the pioneer work has been done by the artists and the religious. At each time there are fields of experience in which these pioneer methods are the only ones suitable because too few facts have been marshalled. Thus, much of what is now Astronomy, Agriculture, and Medicine has only recently moved out of the poetic and religious domain, and those who maintained that these subjects were amenable to logic and experiment were at one time ridiculed.

Conceived in this way, there is no hostility between science and religion or the arts, for they should hardly overlap. Hostility only develops when an attempt is made to preserve, as suitable for intuitional or non-objective statements, fields into which experiment has moved or is moving. This advance of science is often deplored. It is hard to see why, for the phenomena remain and a comprehension of the processes underlying them should increase artistic appreciation. But some artists prefer knowledge, like buildings, to be mellow. The practical antithesis is between the logical and experimental and the dogmatic and intuitional approach to experience. It is a moving antithesis and, odd as it may seem at first sight, the advance of science is opening up new fields for being dogmatic and intuitional in; but the non-scientists are not colonizing them. . . .

Turning now to assumptions with less universal application; it is convenient to separate assumptions that are made, although the state of affairs in which the opposite is true would not conflict with any well-established observations, and those that are made, though they may not be rigidly enough formulated, because the opposite is incompatible with observation. The second category need not delay us long; there are many that all will accept as necessary and a few that it is disconcerting to find being doubted. Thus the assumption that time moves steadily one way underlies most of our science, law, business, and games, but it is apparently contradicted by some experiments in thought transference. Most of us are reluctant to accept them because of the scale of the revolution that would be called for if we ever had to agree that an effect could precede its cause. While admitting the remote possibility that it may prove invalid, we are likely to cling to this assumption.

Of the assumptions that are made gratuitously, those that limit the range of possibilities are the most obstructive in practice. This is a type of assumption to which materialists are especially prone, for they often have limited imaginations and tend to look on particular regions of science as finished, except for some details. Flatfooted materialism characterizes poor scientists, but it is often wrongly attributed to great ones. For example:

> Nature and Nature's laws lay hid in night:
> God said, Let Newton be! and all was light.

All? Newton claimed the precise opposite, as his well-known comparison of himself to a child playing on the sea-shore shows. We see now how right he was. He did not, for example, reckon with electricity as a serious force.

Many of Newton's contemporaries probably thought that the main outline of Nature was complete. The same arrogant attitude was again taken up at the end of the nineteenth century, and traces of it seem even now to lurk in the phrase "fundamental particles." The particles referred to are clearly fundamental if Nature is probed in a certain way. So also the atom could not be cut with the sort of knives that Democritus and Dalton had in mind. But a new tool for probing could alter the whole picture and, incidentally, introduce causality into subatomic phenomena. It is amusing to speculate on the effects of this, if it should happen, on religious pronouncements. In the nineteenth century the "fortuitous concourse of atoms" was distasteful to theologians, but the apparently even more fortuitous behavior of electrons was, in the twentieth century, hailed as a justification for the doctrine of free will. But some scientists have retained a liking for causality, and there is good historical precedent for their attitude. Einstein put it flippantly: *Der liebe Gott würfelt nicht.** Just as the uncuttable atom satisfied the observations

*God doesn't play at dice.

of the eighteenth but not the twentieth century, so the ultimate quantum satisfies those of the twentieth but may not satisfy those of the twenty-first. Ultimates have never tended to stay ultimate for long, and there is no reason to think that ultimate particles are in a privileged position.

So too at the other extreme. *Cogito ergo sum* could perhaps be reversed. I exist therefore I think. Processes comparable to thought may be inseparable from the operation of systems of a certain size and degree of complexity: the convective systems inside a body like the earth or the radiative systems in a star or galaxy come to mind. The possibilities of apprehending such "thought" are remote. But we only apprehend thought in other people by means of the indirect and inadequate vehicles of behavior and speech. A few centuries after we have managed to communicate regularly with one another by some direct method we may begin to get a glimpse of "thought" elsewhere.

Suggestions like these are necessarily woolly and vague because the imagination is feeble. There must, however, be complete new domains of science waiting to be entered sometime. Fundamental research now is largely concerned with problems that were not even imagined a hundred years ago; it is absurdly arrogant to assume that this will not happen again, and it is by keeping such suggestions, coming from various directions, partly in mind that the first glimmerings of a relevant observation are most likely to be recognized and cherished. The developments will not be in the expected directions; as in *Alcestis*

> And the end men looked for cometh not,
> And a path is there where no man thought,
> So hath it fallen here.

But unless we assume that the totally unexpected will happen, it is hard to see what the scientists of the twenty-first century will busy themselves with.

There are also dangerous assumptions about the scientific method. One is that a theoretical approach to an observational subject can be useful. In mathematics conclusions may be of interest and value whether or not they have any counterpart in the observable world. A coherent set of relations is an end in itself. But when we start with observations, theoretical conclusions have to be compatible with further observations, and there may be a delay between the formulation of the conclusions and the next experimental steps. During this time it is important not to criticize the details but to remain sceptical of the whole mode of the approach. Any other reaction amounts to an admission of its validity. Thus the comment should take the form: "You convince me that the details of your picture are probably correct if you have the broad outline correct, but I am not convinced that you have even been facing in the right direction."

There are many examples of theoretically impeccable deductions shown later by experiment to be false. This might have been enough to demolish the theoretical mode of approach were it not that purely theoretical conclusions are sometimes confirmed empirically later. This is galling for the empiric, and he is apt to fall back on suggesting Cowper's couplet to the theoretician as a motto:

'Tis hard if all is false that I advance—
A fool must now and then be right by chance.

The empiric maintains that it is not sufficient merely to be right; a statement is not useful unless it is right for the right reasons. Otherwise it is not sufficiently firmly based to allow it to be used as a base for further development. Thus Medicus distilled from his inner consciousness a structure for uric acid that was later established by Fischer's rigorous experimental methods. Only Fischer's formulation was of any use in the further development of the subject. Nature is only retrospectively logical. There are always many routes that could be followed, in apparent logic, forward from any empirical position, and only further facts can show which route is correct. When this route is agreed it is easy to mistake an empirical advance for a deduction. Restrained induction is this process of thinking of several possibilities and then waiting for the facts to select one. In a similar way we sometimes seem to be remembering a road we have travelled only once or twice before when in fact we cannot say what will be round the next bend. But when we see the new scene we recognize forgotten points and if, after a time, we are no longer recognizing scenes, we conclude that a wrong turning has been taken and go back. The identification fills a role for which logic and memory were inadequate.

Empiricism need not be restricted to the subject matter of science; it can usefully be extended to the technique also. Thus experience shows that it is seldom sufficient to oppose a baseless conclusion by the bald assertion that it is baseless, and therefore not to be preferred to many of the alternatives. It is more effective to propose a rival though equally baseless conclusion. A wrangle then starts, and in the course of it the correct impression is conveyed that, in the field under discussion, fact and logic are not well founded. Until such a wrangle starts people do not think about fundamentals; they think, and want to go on thinking, that the foundations are sound. In practice, most of us cannot bring ourselves to use the technique of counter-nonsense as a means of getting rid of baseless assumptions or conclusions. In the same way some psychologists believe that childhood frustrations are the cause of much that is useful and productive in a personality and yet may hesitate deliberately to frustrate their children. But we generally lack neither baseless conclusions nor frustrations for long. Thus the most effective agent in forcing general recognition of many points of weakness in the genetical systematizations of Weissman and Morgan was Lysenko's equally unsatisfactory alternative.

But, pursuing the unnecessary assumption further, we may consider the assumption just made that a baseless conclusion is to be avoided. It is necessary to avoid being metaphysical in opposition to metaphysics. Before damning a scientist for his metaphysical outlook it is as well to be sure that it is interfering with the discovery of new phenomena. In spite of etymology, the fundamentals of a subject are often the least secure part of it. We cannot, however, indefinitely discuss them. A few axioms and assumptions are necessary if we are to advance a science and, as long as their status is recognized, they do little harm. Some scientists are so obsessed with the difficulties and uncertainties and the impossibility of ever getting an absolute statement that they relapse into critical, sceptical, unproductivity. Here as elsewhere faith is not a substitute for works, and it is better to have a productive scientist with a silly philosophy than an unproductive one whose philosophy is impeccable.

The health of a science depends on a just proportion between crude observation and the integrated body of logic and assumption; the ratio varies with the state of development of the science. Eddington remarked wisely that "Progress is marked not so much by the problems we are able to solve as by the questions we are enabled to ask." Clearly the process of formulating a question has a great psychological effect on the questioner; it focuses his attention on what he thinks he wants to know. Hence the adage "a question posed is already half solved." Precise formulation may have less effect on Nature. The elaborate theoretical planning advocated by Bacon and more recent advocates of the idea of "Solomon's House" may be useful in some sciences, but often the answer to the question may be as equivocal as those of the Delphic oracle. A "fool experiment" is a question based on unsystematized experience, and it may produce as much information as one more carefully posed. To use an analogy: If Nature were in fact one of these ample symbolic women that loll around the plinths of statues of the eminent, and if our job were to find out as much as possible about her, we could do it by asking a series of carefully framed questions or by sticking a pin into one of the inviting curves. Both the Delphic answer and the yelp need careful analysis Each is the response to a "spanner dropped into the works," and the responses have more in common than our theoreticians like to think. Perhaps Bacon realized this too when he wrote: "The secrets of Nature betray themselves more readily when tormented by art than when left to their own courses." Tormenting, whatever form it takes, produces a set of new facts, and out of this medley we pick the ones we think can be co-ordinated within the framework of the assumptions we have arbitrarily decided to accept. The conclusion, therefore, is that we regretfully have to disregard facts for the sake of achieving comprehensibility, but in doing so must make an intuitive or aesthetic judgment about whether the disregarded fact could conceivably invalidate the whole position. Equally regretfully we must admit assumptions while remaining unconvinced of their validity. The only justification possible of such illogical conduct is that it works. Though we may disagree with Bacon's methodology, this pragmatic justification may be sufficient if we accept his opinion that the object of science is to be useful.

R. G. COLLINGWOOD
from *The Idea of History*

. . . Since the time of Descartes, and even since the time of Kant, mankind has acquired a new habit of thinking historically. I do not mean that there were no historians worthy of the name until a century and a half ago; that would be untrue: I do not even mean that since then the bulk of historical knowledge and the output of historical books have enormously increased; that would be true but relatively unimportant. What I mean is that during this time historical thought has worked out a technique of its own, no less definite in its character and certain in its results than its elder sister, the technique of natural science; and that, in thus entering upon the *sichere Gang einer Wissenschaft*,* it has taken a place in human life from which its influence has permeated and to some extent transformed every department of thought and action.

Among others, it has profoundly influenced philosophy; but on the whole the attitude of philosophy towards this influence has been more passive than active. Some philosophers are inclined to welcome it; others resent it; comparatively few have thought philosophically about it. Attempts have been made, chiefly in Germany and Italy, to answer the questions: What is historical thinking? and What light does it throw on the traditional problems of philosophy? and by answering these questions to do for the historical consciousness of today what Kant's transcendental analytic did for the scientific consciousness of the eighteenth century. But for the most part, and especially in this country, it has been usual to ignore all such questions, and to discuss the problems of knowledge in seeming unawareness that there is such a thing as history. This custom can of course be defended. It may be argued that history is not knowledge at all, but only opinion, and unworthy of philosophical study. Or it may be argued that, so far as it is knowledge, its problems are those of knowledge in general, and call for no special treatment. For myself, I cannot accept either defense. If history is opinion, why should philosophy on that account ignore it? If it is knowledge, why should philosophers not study its methods with the same attention that they give to the very different methods of science? And when I read the works of even the greatest contemporary and recent English philosophers, admiring them deeply and learning from them more than I can hope to acknowledge, I find myself constantly haunted by the thought that their accounts of knowledge, based as they seem to be primarily on the study of perception and of scientific

---

*sure path of a scientific study

thinking, not only ignore historical thinking but are actually inconsistent with there being such a thing.

No doubt, historical thought is in one way like perception. Each has for its proper object something individual. What I perceive is this room, this table, this paper. What the historian thinks about is Elizabeth or Marlborough, the Peloponnesian War or the policy of Ferdinand and Isabella. But what we perceive is always like this, the here, the now. Even when we hear a distant explosion or see a stellar conflagration long after it has happened, there is still a moment at which it is here and now perceptible, when it is this explosion, this new star. Historical thought is of something which can never be a this, because it is never a here and now. Its objects are events which have finished happening, and conditions no longer in existence. Only when they are no longer perceptible do they become objects for historical thought. Hence all theories of knowledge that conceive it as a transaction or relation between a subject and an object both actually existing, and confronting or compresent to one another, theories that take acquaintance as the essence of knowledge, make history impossible.

In another way history resembles science: for in each of them knowledge is inferential or reasoned. But whereas science lives in a world of abstract universals, which are in one sense everywhere and in another nowhere, in one sense at all times and in another at no time, the things about which the historian reasons are not abstract but concrete, not universal but individual, not indifferent to space and time but having a where and a when of their own, though the where need not be here and the when cannot be now. History, therefore, cannot be made to square with theories according to which the object of knowledge is abstract and changeless, a logical entity towards which the mind may take up various attitudes.

Nor is it possible to give an account of knowledge by combining theories of these two types. Current philosophy is full of such combinations. Knowledge by acquaintance and knowledge by description; eternal objects and the transient situations into which they are ingredient; realm of essence and realm of matter; in these and other such dichotomies, as in the older dichotomies of matters of fact and relations between ideas, or truths of fact and truths of reason, provision is made for the peculiarities both of a perception which grasps the here and now, and of the abstract thought that apprehends the everywhere and always: the αἴσθησις and νόησις of philosophical tradition. But just as history is neither αἴσθησις nor νόησις, so it is not a combination of the two. It is a third thing, having some of the characteristics of each, but combining them in a way impossible to either. It is not partly acquaintance with transient situations and partly reasoned knowledge of abstract entities. It is wholly a reasoned knowledge of what is transient and concrete.

My purpose here is to offer a brief account of this third thing which is history; and I will begin by stating what may be called the common-sense theory of it, the theory which most people believe, or imagine themselves to believe, when first they reflect on the matter.

According to this theory, the essential things in history are memory and authority. If an event or a state of things is to be historically known, first of all some one must be acquainted with it; then he must remember it; then he must state his recollection of it in terms intelligible to another; and finally that other must accept the statement as true. History is thus the believing some one else when he says that he remembers something. The believer is the historian; the person believed is called his authority.

This doctrine implies that historical truth, so far as it is at all accessible to the historian, is accessible to him only because it exists ready made in the ready-made statements of his authorities. These statements are to him a sacred text, whose value depends wholly on the unbrokenness of the tradition they represent. He must therefore on no account tamper with them. He must not mutilate them; he must not add to them; and, above all, he must not contradict them. For if he takes it upon himself to pick and choose, to decide that some of his authority's statements are important and others not, he is going behind his authority's back and appealing to some other criterion; and this, on the theory, is exactly what he cannot do. If he adds to them, interpolating in them constructions of his own devising, and accepting these constructions as additions to his knowledge, he is believing something for a reason other than the fact that his authority has said it; and this again he has no right to do. Worst of all, if he contradicts them, presuming to decide that his authority has misrepresented the facts, and rejecting his statements as incredible, he is believing the opposite of what he has been told, and committing the worst possible offense against the rules of his craft. The authority may be garrulous, discursive, a gossip and a scandal-monger; he may have overlooked or forgotten or omitted facts; he may have ignorantly or wilfully mis-stated them; but against these defects the historian has no remedy. For him, on the theory, what his authorities tell him is the truth, the whole accessible truth, and nothing but the truth.

These consequences of the common-sense theory have only to be stated in order to be repudiated. Every historian is aware that on occasion he does tamper in all these three ways with what he finds in his authorities. He selects from them what he thinks important, and omits the rest; he interpolates in them things which they do not explicitly say; and he criticizes them by rejecting or amending what he regards as due to misinformation or mendacity. But I am not sure whether we historians always realize the consequences of what we are doing. In general, when we reflect on our own work, we seem to accept what I have called the common-sense theory, while claiming our own rights of selection, construction, and criticism. No doubt these rights are inconsistent with the theory; but we attempt to soften the contradiction by minimizing the extent to which they are exercised, thinking of them as emergency measures, a kind of revolt into which the historian may be driven at times by the exceptional incompetence of his authorities, but which does not fundamentally disturb the normal peaceful regime in which he placidly believes what he is told because he is told to believe it. Yet these things, however seldom they are done, are either historical crimes or facts fatal to the theory: for on the theory they ought to be done, not rarely, but never. And in fact they are neither criminal nor exceptional. Throughout the course of his work the historian is selecting, constructing, and criticizing; it is only by doing these things that he maintains his thought upon the *sichere Gang einer Wissenschaft*. By explicitly recognizing this fact it is possible to effect what, again borrowing a Kantian phrase, one might call a Copernican revolution in the theory of history: the discovery that, so far from relying on an authority other than himself, to whose statements his thought must conform, the historian is his own authority and his thought autonomous, self-authorizing, possessed of a criterion to which his so-called authorities must conform and by reference to which they are criticized.

The autonomy of historical thought is seen at its simplest in the work of selection. The historian who tries to work on the common-sense theory, and accurately reproduce what he finds in his authorities, resembles a landscape painter who tries to work on that theory of art which bids the artist copy nature. He may fancy that he is reproducing in his own medium the actual shapes and colors of natural things; but however hard he tries to do this he is always selecting, simplifying, schematizing, leaving out what he thinks unimportant and putting in what he regards as essential. It is the artist, and not nature, that is responsible for what goes into the picture. In the same way, no historian, not even the worst, merely copies out his authorities; even if he puts in nothing of his own (which is never really possible), he is always leaving out things which, for one reason or another, he decides that his own work does not need or cannot use. It is he, therefore, and not his authority, that is responsible for what goes in. On that question he is his own master: his thought is to that extent autonomous.

An even clearer exhibition of this autonomy is found in what I have called historical construction. The historian's authorities tell him of this or that phase in a process whose intermediate phases they leave undescribed; he then interpolates these phases for himself. His picture of his subject, though it may consist in part of statements directly drawn from his authorities, consists also, and increasingly with every increase in his competence as an historian, of statements reached inferentially from those according to his own criteria, his own rules of method, and his own canons of relevance. In this part of his work he is never depending on his authorities in the sense of repeating what they tell him; he is relying on his own powers and constituting himself his own authority; while his so-called authorities are now not authorities at all but only evidence.

The clearest demonstration of the historian's autonomy, however, is provided by historical criticism. As natural science finds its proper method when the scientist, in Bacon's metaphor, puts Nature to the question, tortures her by experiment in order to wring from her answers to his own questions, so history finds its proper method when the historian puts his authorities in the witness-box, and by cross-questioning extorts from them information which in their original statements they have withheld, either because they did not wish to give it or because they did not possess it. Thus, a commander's dispatches may claim a victory; the historian, reading them in a critical spirit, will ask: "If it was a victory, why was it not followed up in this or that way?" and may thus convict the writer of concealing the truth. Or, by using the same method, he may convict of ignorance a less critical predecessor who has accepted the version of the battle given him by the same dispatches.

The historian's autonomy is here manifested in its extremest form, because it is here evident that somehow, in virtue of his activity as an historian, he has it in his power to reject something explicitly told him by his authorities and to substitute something else. If that is possible, the criterion of historical truth cannot be the fact that a statement is made by an authority. It is the truthfulness and the information of the so-called authority that are in question; and this question the historian has to answer for himself, on his own authority. Even if he accepts what his authorities tell him, therefore, he accepts it not on their authority but on his own; not because they say it, but because it satisfies his criterion of historical truth.

The common-sense theory which bases history upon memory and authority needs no further refutation. Its bankruptcy is evident. For the historian there can never be authorities, because the so-called authorities abide a verdict which only he can give. Yet the common-sense theory may claim a qualified and relative truth. The historian, generally speaking, works at a subject which others have studied before him. In proportion as he is more of a novice, either in this particular subject or in history as a whole, his forerunners are, relatively to his incompetence, authoritative; and in the limiting case where his incompetence and ignorance were absolute, they could be called authorities without qualification. As he becomes more and more master of his craft and his subject, they become less and less his authorities, more and more his fellow students, to be treated with respect or contempt according to their deserts.

And as history does not depend on authority, so it does not depend upon memory. The historian can rediscover what has been completely forgotten, in the sense that no statement of it has reached him by an unbroken tradition from eyewitnesses. He can even discover what, until he discovered it, no one ever knew to have happened at all. This he does partly by the critical treatment of statements contained in his sources, partly by the use of what are called unwritten sources, which are increasingly employed as history becomes increasingly sure of its own proper methods and its own proper criterion.

I have spoken of the criterion of historical truth. What is this criterion? According to the common-sense theory, it is the agreement of the statements made by the historian with those which he finds in his authorities. This answer we now know to be false, and we must seek another. We cannot renounce the search. Some answer to the question there must be, for without a criterion there can be no criticism. One answer to this question was offered by the greatest English philosopher of our time in his pamphlet on *The Pre-suppositions of Critical History*. Bradley's essay was an early work with which in his maturity he was dissatisfied; but, unsatisfactory though it certainly is, it bears the stamp of his genius. In it Bradley faces the question how it is possible for the historian, in defiance of the common-sense theory, to turn the tables on his so-called authorities and to say "This is what our authorities record, but what really happened must have been not this but that."

His answer to this question was that our experience of the world teaches us that some kinds of things happen and others do not; this experience, then, is the criterion which the historian brings to bear on the statements of his authorities. If they tell him that things happened of a kind which, according to his experience, does not happen, he is obliged to disbelieve them; if the things which they report are of a kind which according to his experience does happen, he is free to accept their statements.

There are many obvious objections to this idea, on which I shall not insist. It is deeply tinged with the empiricist philosophy against which Bradley was soon so effectively to rebel. But apart from this there are certain special points in which the argument appears to me defective.

First, the proposed criterion is a criterion not of what did happen but of what could happen. It is in fact nothing but Aristotle's criterion of what is admissible in poetry; and hence it does not serve to discriminate history from fiction. It would no doubt be satisfied by the statements of a historian, but it would be satisfied no less adequately by those of a historical novelist. It cannot therefore be the criterion of critical history.

Secondly, because it can never tell us what did happen, we are left to rely for that on the sheer authority of our informant. We undertake, when we apply it, to believe everything our informant tells us so long as it satisfies the merely negative criterion of being possible. This is not to turn the tables on our authorities; it is blindly to accept what they tell us. The critical attitude has not been achieved.

Thirdly, the historian's experience of the world in which he lives can only help him to check, even negatively, the statements of his authorities in so far as they are concerned not with history but with nature, which has no history. The laws of nature have always been the same, and what is against nature now was against nature two thousand years ago; but the historical as distinct from the natural conditions of man's life differ so much at different times that no argument from analogy will hold. That the Greeks and Romans exposed their new-born children in order to control the numbers of their population is no less true for being unlike anything that happens in the experience of contributors to the *Cambridge Ancient History*. In point of fact Bradley's treatment of the subject grew not out of the ordinary course of historical study but out of his interest in the credibility of the New Testament narratives, and in particular their miraculous element; but a criterion which only serves in the case of miracle is of sadly little use to the weekday historian.

Bradley's essay, inconclusive though it is, remains memorable for the fact that in it the Copernican revolution in the theory of historical knowledge has been in principle accomplished. For the common-sense theory, historical truth consists in the historian's beliefs conforming to the statements of his authorities; Bradley has seen that the historian brings with him to the study of his authorities a criterion of his own by reference to which the authorities themselves are judged. What it is, Bradley failed to discover. It remains to be seen whether, sixty years later, his problem, which in the meantime I believe no English-speaking philosopher has discussed in print, can be advanced beyond the point at which he left it.

I have already remarked that, in addition to selecting from among his authorities' statements those which he regards as important, the historian must in two ways go beyond what his authorities tell him. One is the critical way, and this is what Bradley has attempted to analyze. The other is the constructive way. Of this he has said nothing, and to this I now propose to return. I described constructive history as interpolating, between the statements borrowed from our authorities, other statements implied by them. Thus our authorities tell us that on one day Caesar was in Rome and on a later day in Gaul; they tell us nothing about his journey from one place to the other, but we interpolate this with a perfectly good conscience.

This act of interpolation has two significant characteristics. First, it is in no way arbitrary or merely fanciful: it is necessary or, in Kantian language, *a priori*. If we filled up the narrative of Caesar's doings with fanciful details such as the names of the persons he met on the way, and what he said to them, the construction would be arbitrary: it would be in fact the kind of construction which is done by a historical novelist. But if our construction involves nothing that is not necessitated by the evidence, it is a legitimate historical construction of a kind without which there can be no history at all.

Secondly, what is in this way inferred is essentially something imagined. If we look out over the sea and perceive a ship, and five minutes later look again and perceive it in a different place, we find ourselves obliged to imagine it as having occupied intermediate positions when we were not looking. That is already an example of historical thinking; and it is not otherwise that we find ourselves obliged to imagine Caesar as having travelled from Rome to Gaul when we are told that he was in these different places at these successive times.

This activity, with this double character, I shall call *a priori* imagination; and, though I shall have more to say of it hereafter, for the present I shall be content to remark that, however unconscious we may be of its operation, it is this activity which, bridging the gaps between what our authorities tell us, gives the historical narrative or description its continuity. That the historian must use his imagination is a commonplace; to quote Macaulay's *Essay on History*, "a perfect historian must possess an imagination sufficiently powerful to make his narrative affecting and picturesque"; but this is to underestimate the part played by the historical imagination, which is properly not

ornamental but structural. Without it the historian would have no narrative
to adorn. The imagination, that "blind but indispensable faculty" without
which, as Kant has shown, we could never perceive the world around us, is
indispensable in the same way to history: it is this which, operating not
capriciously as fancy but in its *a priori* form, does the entire work of historical construction.

Two misunderstandings may here be forestalled. First, it may be thought
that by imagining we can present to ourselves only what is imaginary in the
sense of being fictitious or unreal. This prejudice need only be mentioned in
order to be dispelled. If I imagine the friend who lately left my house now
entering his own, the fact that I imagine this event gives me no reason to
believe it unreal. The imaginary, simply as such, is neither unreal nor real.

Secondly, to speak of *a priori* imagination may seem a paradox, for it
may be thought that imagination is essentially capricious, arbitrary, merely
fanciful. But in addition to its historical function there are two other functions of *a priori* imagination which are, or ought to be, familiar to all. One is
the pure or free, but by no means arbitrary, imagination of the artist. A man
writing a novel composes a story where parts are played by various characters.
Characters and incidents are all alike imaginary; yet the whole aim of the
novelist is to show the characters acting and the incidents developing in a
manner determined by a necessity internal to themselves. The story, if it is a
good story, cannot develop otherwise than as it does; the novelist in imagining
it cannot imagine it developing except as it does develop. Here, and equally
in all other kinds of art, the *a priori* imagination is at work. Its other familiar
function is what may be called the perceptual imagination, supplementing
and consolidating the data of perception in the way so well analyzed by Kant,
by presenting to us objects of possible perception which are not actually perceived: the under side of this table, the inside of an unopened egg, the back
of the moon. Here again the imagination is *a priori*: we cannot but imagine
what cannot but be there. The historical imagination differs from these not
in being *a priori*, but in having as its special task to imagine the past: not an
object of possible perception, since it does not now exist, but able through
this activity to become an object of our thought.

The historian's picture of his subject, whether that subject be a sequence
of events or a past state of things, thus appears as a web of imaginative construction stretched between certain fixed points provided by the statements
of his authorities; and if these points are frequent enough and the threads
spun from each to the next are constructed with due care, always by the
a priori imagination and never by merely arbitrary fancy, the whole picture
is constantly verified by appeal to these data, and runs little risk of losing
touch with the reality which it represents.

Actually, this is very much how we do think of historical work, when
the common-sense theory has ceased to satisfy us, and we have become aware
of the part played in it by the constructive imagination. But such a conception
is in one way seriously at fault: it overlooks the no less important part played

by criticism. We think of our web of construction as pegged down, so to speak, to the facts by the statements of authorities, which we regard as data or fixed points for the work of construction. But in so thinking we have slipped back into the theory, which we now know to be false, that truth is given us ready made in these statements. We know that truth is to be had, not by swallowing what our authorities tell us, but by criticizing it; and thus the supposedly fixed points between which the historical imagination spins its web are not given to us ready made; they must be achieved by critical thinking.

There is nothing other than historical thought itself, by appeal to which its conclusions may be verified. The hero of a detective novel is thinking exactly like an historian when, from indications of the most varied kinds, he constructs an imaginary picture of how a crime was committed, and by whom. At first, this is a mere theory, awaiting verification, which must come to it from without. Happily for the detective, the conventions of that literary form dictate that when his construction is complete it shall be neatly pegged down by a confession from the criminal, given in such circumstances that its genuineness is beyond question. The historian is less fortunate. If, after convincing himself by a study of the evidence already available that Bacon wrote the plays of Shakespeare or that Henry VII murdered the Princes in the Tower, he were to find an autograph document confessing the fact, he would by no means have verified his conclusions; the new document, so far from closing the inquiry, would only have complicated it by raising a new problem, the problem of its own authenticity.

I began by considering a theory according to which everything is given: according to which all truth, so far as any truth is accessible to the historian, is provided for him ready made in the ready-made statements of his authorities. I then saw that much of what he takes for true is not given in this way but constructed by his *a priori* imagination; but I still fancied that this imagination worked inferentially from fixed points given in the same sense. I am now driven to confess that there are for historical thought no fixed points thus given: in other words, that in history, just as there are properly speaking no authorities, so there are properly speaking no data.

Historians certainly think of themselves as working from data; where by data they mean historical facts possessed by them ready made at the beginning of a certain piece of historical research. Such a datum, if the research concerns the Peloponnesian War, would be, for example, a certain statement of Thucydides, accepted as substantially true. But when we ask what gives historical thought this datum, the answer is obvious: historical thought gives it to itself, and therefore in relation to historical thought at large it is not a datum but a result or achievement. It is only our historical knowledge which tells us that these curious marks on paper are Greek letters; that the words which they form have certain meanings in the Attic dialect; that the passage is authentic Thucydides, not an interpolation or corruption; and that on this occasion Thucydides knew what he was talking about and was trying to tell the truth. Apart from all this, the passage is merely a pattern of black marks on white paper: not any historical fact at all, but something existing here and now, and perceived by the historian. All that the historian means, when he describes certain historical facts as his data, is that for the purposes of a particular piece of work there are certain historical problems relevant to that work which for the present he proposes to treat as settled; though, if they are settled, it is only because historical thinking has settled them in the past, and they remain settled only until he or some one else decides to reopen them.

His web of imaginative construction, therefore, cannot derive its validity from being pegged down, as at first I described it, to certain given facts. That description represented an attempt to relieve him of the responsibility for the nodal points of his fabric, while admitting his responsibility for what he constructs between them. In point of fact, he is just as responsible for the one as for the other. Whether he accepts or rejects or modifies or reinterprets what his so-called authorities tell him, it is he that is responsible for the statement which, after duly criticizing them, he makes. The criterion that justifies him in making it can never be the fact that it has been given him by an authority.

This brings me back to the question what this criterion is. And at this point a partial and provisional answer can be given. The web of imaginative construction is something far more solid and powerful than we have hitherto realized. So far from relying for its validity upon the support of given facts, it actually serves as the touchstone by which we decide whether alleged facts are genuine. Suetonius tells me that Nero at one time intended to evacuate Britain. I reject his statement, not because any better authority flatly contradicts it, for of course none does; but because my reconstruction of Nero's policy based on Tacitus will not allow me to think that Suetonius is right. And if I am told that this is merely to say I prefer Tacitus to Suetonius, I confess that I do: but I do so just because I find myself able to incorporate what Tacitus tells me into a coherent and continuous picture of my own, and cannot do this for Suetonius.

It is thus the historian's picture of the past, the product of his own *a priori* imagination, that has to justify the sources used in its construction. These sources are sources, that is to say, credence is given to them, only because they are in this way justified. For any source may be tainted: this writer prejudiced, that misinformed; this inscription misread by a bad epigraphist, that blundered by a careless stonemason; this potsherd placed out of its context by an incompetent excavator, that by a blameless rabbit. The critical historian has to discover and correct all these and many other kinds of falsification. He does it, and can only do it, by considering whether the picture of the past to which the evidence leads him is a coherent and continuous picture, one which makes sense. The *a priori* imagination which does the work of historical construction supplies the means of historical criticism as well.

Freed from its dependence on fixed points supplied from without, the historian's picture of the past is thus in every detail an imaginary picture, and

its necessity is at every point the necessity of the *a priori* imagination. Whatever goes into it, goes into it not because his imagination passively accepts it,
but because it actively demands it.

The resemblance between the historian and the novelist, to which I have
already referred, here reaches its culmination. Each of them makes it his business to construct a picture which is partly a narrative of events, partly a description of situations, exhibition of motives, analysis of characters. Each aims
at making his picture a coherent whole, where every character and every situation is so bound up with the rest that this character in this situation cannot
but act in this way, and we cannot imagine him as acting otherwise. The
novel and the history must both of them make sense; nothing is admissible
in either except what is necessary, and the judge of this necessity is in both
cases the imagination. Both the novel and the history are self-explanatory,
self-justifying, the product of an autonomous or self-authorizing activity; and
in both cases this activity is the *a priori* imagination.

As works of imagination, the historian's work and the novelist's do not
differ. Where they do differ is that the historian's picture is meant to be true.
The novelist has a single task only: to construct a coherent picture, one that
makes sense. The historian has a double task: he has both to do this, and to
construct a picture of things as they really were and of events as they really
happened. This further necessity imposes upon him obedience to three rules
of method, from which the novelist or artist in general is free.

First, his picture must be localized in space and time. The artist's need
not; essentially, the things that he imagines are imagined as happening at no
place and at no date. Of *Wuthering Heights* it has been well said that the
scene is laid in Hell, though the place-names are English; and it was a sure
instinct that led another great novelist to replace Oxford by Christminster,
Wantage by Alfredston, and Fawley by Marychurch, recoiling against the
discord of topographical fact in what should be a purely imaginary world.

Secondly, all history must be consistent with itself. Purely imaginary
worlds cannot clash and need not agree; each is a world to itself. But there
is only one historical world, and everything in it must stand in some relation
to everything else, even if that relation is only topographical and chronological.

Thirdly, and most important, the historian's picture stands in a peculiar
relation to something called evidence. The only way in which the historian or
any one else can judge, even tentatively, of its truth is by considering this
relation; and, in practice, what we mean by asking whether an historical
statement is true is whether it can be justified by an appeal to the evidence:
for a truth unable to be so justified is to the historian a thing of no interest.
What is this thing called evidence, and what is its relation to the finished
historical work?

We already know what evidence is not. It is not ready-made historical
knowledge, to be swallowed and regurgitated by the historian's mind. Everything is evidence which the historian can use as evidence. But what can he so
use? It must be something here and now perceptible to him: this written page,

this spoken utterance, this building, this finger-print. And of all the things perceptible to him there is not one which he might not conceivably use as evidence on some question, if he came to it with the right question in mind. The enlargement of historical knowledge comes about mainly through finding how to use as evidence this or that kind of perceived fact which historians have hitherto thought useless to them.

The whole perceptible world, then, is potentially and in principle evidence to the historian. It becomes actual evidence in so far as he can use it. And he cannot use it unless he comes to it with the right kind of historical knowledge. The more historical knowledge we have, the more we can learn from any given piece of evidence; if we had none, we could learn nothing. Evidence is evidence only when some one contemplates it historically. Otherwise it is merely perceived fact, historically dumb. It follows that historical knowledge can only grow out of historical knowledge; in other words, that historical thinking is an original and fundamental activity of the human mind, or, as Descartes might have said, that the idea of the past is an "innate" idea.

Historical thinking is that activity of the imagination by which we endeavor to provide this innate idea with detailed content. And this we do by using the present as evidence for its own past. Every present has a past of its own, and any imaginative reconstruction of the past aims at reconstructing the past of this present, the present in which the act of imagination is going on, as here and now perceived. In principle the aim of any such act is to use the entire perceptible here-and-now as evidence for the entire past through whose process it has come into being. In practice, this aim can never be achieved. The perceptible here-and-now can never be perceived, still less interpreted, in its entirety; and the infinite process of past time can never be envisaged as a whole. But this separation between what is attempted in principle and what is achieved in practice is the lot of mankind, not a peculiarity of historical thinking. The fact that it is found there only shows that herein history is like art, science, philosophy, the pursuit of virtue, and the search for happiness.

It is for the same reason that in history, as in all serious matters, no achievement is final. The evidence available for solving any given problem changes with every change of historical method and with every variation in the competence of historians. The principles by which this evidence is interpreted change too; since the interpreting of evidence is a task to which a man must bring everything he knows: historical knowledge, knowledge of nature and man, mathematical knowledge, philosophical knowledge; and not knowledge only, but mental habits and possessions of every kind: and none of these is unchanging. Because of these changes, which never cease, however slow they may appear to observers who take a short view, every new generation must rewrite history in its own way; every new historian, not content with giving new answers to old questions, must revise the questions themselves; and—since historical thought is a river into which none can step twice —even a single historian, working at a single subject for a certain length of time, finds when he tries to reopen an old question that the question has changed.

This is not an argument for historical scepticism. It is only the discovery of a second dimension of historical thought, the history of history: the discovery that the historian himself, together with the here-and-now which forms the total body of evidence available to him, is a part of the process he is studying, has his own place in that process, and can see it only from the point of view which at this present moment he occupies within it.

But neither the raw material of historical knowledge, the detail of the here-and-now as given him in perception, nor the various endowments that serve him as aids to interpreting this evidence, can give the historian his criterion of historical truth. The criterion is the idea of history itself: the idea of an imaginary picture of the past. That idea is, in Cartesian language, innate; in Kantian language, *a priori*. It is not a chance product of psychological causes; it is an idea which every man possesses as part of the furniture of his mind, and discovers himself to possess in so far as he becomes conscious of what it is to have a mind. Like other ideas of the same sort, it is one to which no fact of experience exactly corresponds. The historian, however long and faithfully he works, can never say that his work, even in crudest outline or in this or that smallest detail, is done once for all. He can never say that his picture of the past is at any point adequate to his idea of what it ought to be. But, however fragmentary and faulty the results of his work may be, the idea which governed its course is clear, rational, and universal. It is the idea of the historical imagination as a self-dependent, self-determining, and self-justifying form of thought.

Perspective and Context

C. S. Peirce thought of his *semeiotics* as the primary science of man because man is defined by his use of signs; indeed, Peirce argued in one virtuoso lecture that man is himself a sign. Semiotics could come to play in the modern university the role once assumed by Lady Grammar in late medieval settings; in any case, the friendly relationship of semiotics and anthropology, familiar in Lévi-Strauss' use of Saussure and, long before, Ogden and Richards' use of Malinowski, is a model of the cross-fertilization all interdisciplinary efforts should encourage.

Clifford Geertz, who describes himself as "a meanings and symbols ethnographer," has a very subtle grasp of how interpretation functions in "the act of knowing," which Walker Percy notes is left out of account in semiotics of the positivist variety. Borrowing from Gilbert Ryle the curious phrase "thick description," Geertz shows us how the anthropologist must develop contexts, comparison fields, in which particular examples can be seen as representative of one or another concept and interpreted so that they can in turn serve as speculative instruments. ("Thick description" is an invaluable technique for the sociolinguist and for teachers learning to document what's happening in their classrooms. See Part III, 232–235.) I know of no clearer demonstration of the activities of mind which Vygotsky specifies as essential to the dynamics of concept formation than this essay provides. A match for Collingwood's, Geertz's essay could well be entitled "The Anthropological Imagination."

Jane Addams was neither semiotician, psychologist, anthropologist, nor journalist, but neither was she simply a social reformer and an educational innovator. I think of her as a philosopher and teacher who has much to tell us about the moral dimension of our work in teaching reading and writing. In this early essay, she shows us something of what Whitehead means when he says that "language is expression from one's past into one's present." Nothing in this entire collection better illustrates the power of imagination than Jane Addams' account of her insight into the meaning of the Egyptian tombs she visited in 1908.

C. S. PEIRCE
(on interpretation)

7.536   All flow of time involves learning; and all learning involves the flow of time. . . . All learning is virtually reasoning. . . . Mere experience of a sense-reaction is not learning. That is only something from which something can be learned, by interpreting it. The interpretation is the learning. . . . Every reasoning involves another reasoning which in its turn involves another, and so on ad infinitum. Every reasoning connects something already acquired so that we thereby learn what has been unknown. It is thus that the present is so welded to what is just past as to render what is just coming about inevitable. The consciousness of the present, as the boundary between past and future, involves them both. Reasoning is a new experience which involves something old and something hitherto unknown. The past . . . is the *ego*. My recent past is my uppermost *ego*; my distant past is my more generalized *ego*. The past of the community is *our ego*. In attributing a flow of time to unknown events we impute a quasi-*ego* to the universe. The present is the immediate representation we are just learning that brings the future, or non-ego, to be assimilated into the ego. It is thus seen that learning or representation is the third Kainopythagorean category.*

CLIFFORD GEERTZ
"Thick Description: Toward an Interpretive
Theory of Culture"

I

In her book, *Philosophy in a New Key,* Susanne Langer remarks that certain ideas burst upon the intellectual landscape with a tremendous force. They resolve so many fundamental problems at once that they seem also to promise that they will resolve all fundamental problems, clarify all obscure issues. Everyone snaps them up as the open sesame of some new positive science, the conceptual center-point around which a comprehensive system of analysis

---

*These categories are the psychological analogues of the logical categories of First-ness, Secondness, and Thirdness. (AB)

can be built. The sudden vogue of such a *grande idée*, crowding out almost everything else for a while, is due, she says, "to the fact that all sensitive and active minds turn at once to exploiting it. We try it in every connection, for every purpose, experiment with possible stretches of its strict meaning, with generalizations and derivatives."

After we have become familiar with the new idea, however, after it has become part of our general stock of theoretical concepts, our expectations are brought more into balance with its actual uses, and its excessive popularity is ended. A few zealots persist in the old key-to-the-universe view of it; but less driven thinkers settle down after a while to the problems the idea has really generated. They try to apply it and extend it where it applies and where it is capable of extension; and they desist where it does not apply or cannot be extended. It becomes, if it was, in truth, a seminal idea in the first place, a permanent and enduring part of our intellectual armory. But it no longer has the grandiose, all-promising scope, the infinite versatility of apparent application, it once had. The second law of thermodynamics, or the principle of natural selection, or the notion of unconscious motivation, or the organization of the means of production does not explain everything, not even everything human, but it still explains something; and our attention shifts to isolating just what that something is, to disentangling ourselves from a lot of pseudoscience to which, in the first flush of its celebrity, it has also given rise.

Whether or not this is, in fact, the way all centrally important scientific concepts develop, I don't know. But certainly this pattern fits the concept of culture, around which the whole discipline of anthropology arose, and whose domination that discipline has been increasingly concerned to limit, specify, focus, and contain. It is to this cutting of the culture concept down to size, therefore actually insuring its continued importance rather than undermining it, that the essays below are all, in their several ways and from their several directions, dedicated. They all argue, sometimes explicitly, more often merely through the particular analysis they develop, for a narrowed, specialized, and, so I imagine, theoretically more powerful concept of culture to replace E. B. Tylor's famous "most complex whole," which, its originative power not denied, seems to me to have reached the point where it obscures a good deal more than it reveals.

The conceptual morass into which the Tylorean kind of *pot-au-feu* theorizing about culture can lead, is evident in what is still one of the better general introductions to anthropology, Clyde Kluckhohn's *Mirror for Man*. In some twenty-seven pages of his chapter on the concept, Kluckhohn managed to define culture in turn as: (1) "the total way of life of a people"; (2) "the social legacy the individual acquires from his group"; (3) "a way of thinking, feeling, and believing"; (4) "an abstraction from behavior"; (5) a theory on the part of the anthropologist about the way in which a group of people in fact behave; (6) a "storehouse of pooled learning"; (7) "a set of standardized orientations to recurrent problems"; (8) "learned behavior";

(9) a mechanism for the normative regulation of behavior; (10) "a set of techniques for adjusting both to the external environment and to other men"; (11) "a precipitate of history"; and turning, perhaps in desperation, to similes, as a map, as a seive, and as a matrix. In the face of this sort of theoretical diffusion, even a somewhat constricted and not entirely standard concept of culture, which is at least internally coherent and, more important, which has a definable argument to make is (as, to be fair, Kluckhohn himself keenly realized) an improvement. Eclecticism is self-defeating not because there is only one direction in which it is useful to move, but because there are so many: it is necessary to choose.

The concept of culture I espouse, and whose utility the essays below attempt to demonstrate, is essentially a semiotic one. Believing, with Max Weber, that man is an animal suspended in webs of significance he himself has spun, I take culture to be those webs, and the analysis of it to be therefore not an experimental science in search of law but an interpretive one in search of meaning. It is explication I am after, construing social expressions on their surface enigmatical. But this pronouncement, a doctrine in a clause, demands itself some explication.

II

Operationalism as a methodological dogma never made much sense so far as the social sciences are concerned, and except for a few rather too well-swept corners—Skinnerian behaviorism, intelligence testing, and so on—it is largely dead now. But it had, for all that, an important point to make, which, however we may feel about trying to define charisma or alienation in terms of operations, retains a certain force: if you want to understand what a science is, you should look in the first instance not at its theories or its findings, and certainly not at what its apologists say about it; you should look at what the practitioners of it do.

In anthropology, or anyway social anthropology, what the practitioners do is ethnography. And it is in understanding what ethnography is, or more exactly *what doing ethnography is,* that a start can be made toward grasping what anthropological analysis amounts to as a form of knowledge. This, it must immediately be said, is not a matter of methods. From one point of view, that of the textbook, doing ethnography is establishing rapport, selecting informants, transcribing texts, taking genealogies, mapping fields, keeping a diary, and so on. But it is not these things, techniques and received procedures, that define the enterprise. What defines it is the kind of intellectual effort it is: an elaborate venture in, to borrow a notion from Gilbert Ryle, "thick description."

Ryle's discussion of "thick description" appears in two recent essays of his (now reprinted in the second volume of his *Collected Papers*) addressed to the general question of what, as he puts it, *"Le Penseur"* is doing: "Thinking and Reflecting" and "The Thinking of Thoughts." Consider, he says, two boys rapidly contracting the eyelids of their right eyes. In one, this is an

involuntary twitch; in the other, a conspiratorial signal to a friend. The two
movements are, as movements, identical; from an I-am-a-camera, "phenom-
enalistic" observation of them alone, one could not tell which was twitch and
which was wink, or indeed whether both or either was twitch or wink. Yet the
difference, however unphotographable, between a twitch and a wink is vast;
as anyone unfortunate enough to have had the first taken for the second
knows. The winker is communicating, and indeed communicating in a quite
precise and special way: (1) deliberately, (2) to someone in particular, (3) to
impart a particular message, (4) according to a socially established code, and
(5) without cognizance of the rest of the company. As Ryle points out, the
winker has not done *two* things, contracted his eyelids and winked, while
the twitcher has done only *one*, contracted his eyelids: Contracting your
eyelids on purpose when there exists a public code in which so doing counts
as a conspiratorial signal *is* winking. That's all there is to it: a speck of behavior, a fleck of culture, and—*voilà!*—a gesture.

That, however, is just the beginning. Suppose, he continues, there is a
third boy, who, "to give malicious amusement to his cronies," parodies the
first boy's wink, as amateurish, clumsy, obvious, and so on. He, of course,
does this in the same way the second boy winked and the first twitched:
by contracting his right eyelids. Only this boy is neither winking nor twitching, he is parodying someone else's, as he takes it, laughable, attempt at
winking. Here, too, a socially established code exists (he will "wink" laboriously, overobviously, perhaps adding a grimace—the usual artifices of the
clown); and so also does a message. Only now it is not conspiracy but ridicule
that is in the air. If the others think he is actually winking, his whole project
misfires as completely, though with somewhat different results, as if they
think he is twitching. One can go further: uncertain of his mimicking abilities,
the would-be satirist may practice at home before the mirror, in which case
he is not twitching, winking, or parodying, but rehearsing; though so far as
what a camera, a radical behaviorist, or a believer in protocol sentences would
record he is just rapidly contracting his right eyelids like all the others. Complexities are possible, if not practically without end, at least logically so. The
original winker might, for example, actually have been fake-winking, say, to
mislead outsiders into imagining there was a conspiracy afoot when there in
fact was not, in which case our descriptions of what the parodist is parodying
and the rehearser rehearsing of course shift accordingly. But the point is that
between what Ryle calls the "thin description" of what the rehearser (parodist, winker, twitcher . . .) is doing ("rapidly contracting his right eyelids")
and the "thick description" of what he is doing ("practicing a burlesque of a
friend faking a wink to deceive an innocent into thinking a conspiracy is in
motion") lies the object of ethnography: a stratified hierarchy of meaningful
structures in terms of which twitches, winks, fake-winks, parodies, rehearsals
of parodies are produced, perceived, and interpreted, and without which they
would not (not even the zero-form twitches, which, *as a cultural category,*
are as much nonwinks as winks are nontwitches) in fact exist, no matter what
anyone did or didn't do with his eyelids.

Like so many of the stories Oxford philosophers like to make up for themselves, all this winking, fake-winking, burlesque-fake-winking, rehearsed-burlesque-fake-winking, may seem a bit artificial. In way of adding a more empirical note, let me give, deliberately unpreceded by any prior explanatory comment at all, a not untypical excerpt from my own field journal to demonstrate that, however evened off for didactic purposes, Ryle's example presents an image only too exact of the sort of piled-up structures of inference and implication through which an ethnographer is continually trying to pick his way:

> The French [the informant said] had only just arrived. They set up twenty or so small forts between here, the town, and the Marmusha area up in the middle of the mountains, placing them on promontories so they could survey the countryside. But for all this they couldn't guarantee safety, especially at night, so although the *mezrag*, trade-pact, system was supposed to be legally abolished it in fact continued as before.
>
> One night, when Cohen (who speaks fluent Berber), was up there, at Marmusha, two other Jews who were traders to a neighboring tribe came by to purchase some goods from him. Some Berbers, from yet another neighboring tribe, tried to break into Cohen's place, but he fired his rifle in the air. (Traditionally, Jews were not allowed to carry weapons; but at this period things were so unsettled many did so anyway.) This attracted the attention of the French and the marauders fled.
>
> The next night, however, they came back, one of them disguised as a woman who knocked on the door with some sort of a story. Cohen was suspicious and didn't want to let "her" in, but the other Jews said, "oh, it's all right, it's only a woman." So they opened the door and the whole lot came pouring in. They killed the two visiting Jews, but Cohen managed to barricade himself in an adjoining room. He heard the robbers planning to burn him alive in the shop after they removed his goods, and so he opened the door and, laying about him wildly with a club, managed to escape through a window.
>
> He went up to the fort, then, to have his wounds dressed, and complained to the local commandant, one Captain Dumari, saying he wanted his *'ar*—i.e., four or five times the value of the merchandise stolen from him. The robbers were from a tribe which had not yet submitted to French authority and were in open rebellion against it, and he wanted authorization to go with his *mezrag*-holder, the Marmusha tribal *sheikh*, to collect the indemnity that, under traditional rules, he had coming to him. Captain Dumari couldn't officially give him permission to do this, because of the French prohibition of the *mezrag* relationship, but he gave him verbal authorization, saying, "If you get killed, it's your problem."
>
> So the *sheikh*, the Jew, and a small company of armed Marmushans went off ten or fifteen kilometers up into the rebellious area, where there

were of course no French, and, sneaking up, captured the thief-tribe's
shepherd and stole its herds. The other tribe soon came riding out on
horses after them, armed with rifles and ready to attack. But when they
saw who the "sheep thieves" were, they thought better of it and said,
"all right, we'll talk." They couldn't really deny what had happened—
that some of their men had robbed Cohen and killed the two visitors—
and they weren't prepared to start the serious feud with the Marmusha
a scuffle with the invading party would bring on. So the two groups
talked, and talked, and talked, there on the plain amid the thousands of
sheep, and decided finally on five-hundred-sheep damages. The two
armed Berber groups then lined up on their horses at opposite ends of
the plain, with the sheep herded between them, and Cohen, in his black
gown, pillbox hat, and flapping slippers, went out alone among the
sheep, picking out, one by one and at his own good speed, the best ones
for his payment.

So Cohen got his sheep and drove them back to Marmusha. The
French, up in their fort, heard them coming from some distance ("Ba,
ba, ba" said Cohen, happily, recalling the image) and said, "What the
hell is that?" And Cohen said, "That is my 'ar.'" The French couldn't
believe he had actually done what he said he had done, and accused him
of being a spy for the rebellious Berbers, put him in prison, and took his
sheep. In the town, his family, not having heard from him in so long a
time, thought he was dead. But after a while the French released him
and he came back home, but without his sheep. He then went to the
Colonel in the town, the Frenchman in charge of the whole region, to
complain. But the Colonel said, "I can't do anything about the matter.
It's not my problem."

Quoted raw, a note in a bottle, this passage conveys, as any similar one
similarly presented would do, a fair sense of how much goes into ethnographic
description of even the most elemental sort—how extraordinarily "thick" it is.
In finished anthropological writings, including those collected here, this fact
—that what we call our data are really our own constructions of other people's
constructions of what they and their compatriots are up to—is obscured because most of what we need to comprehend a particular event, ritual, custom,
idea, or whatever is insinuated as background information before the thing
itself is directly examined. (Even to reveal that this little drama took place
in the highlands of central Morocco in 1912—and was recounted there in
1968—is to determine much of our understanding of it.) There is nothing particularly wrong with this, and it is in any case inevitable. But it does lead to
a view of anthropological research as rather more of an observational and
rather less of an interpretive activity than it really is. Right down at the
factual base, the hard rock, insofar as there is any, of the whole enterprise,
we are already explicating: and worse, explicating explications. Winks upon
winks upon winks.

Analysis, then, is sorting out the structures of signification—what Ryle called established codes, a somewhat misleading expression, for it makes the enterprise sound too much like that of the cipher clerk when it is much more like that of the literary critic—and determining their social ground and import. Here, in our text, such sorting would begin with distinguishing the three unlike frames of interpretation ingredient in the situation, Jewish, Berber, and French, and would then move on to show how (and why) at that time, in that place, their copresence produced a situation in which systematic misunderstanding reduced traditional form to social farce. What tripped Cohen up, and with him the whole, ancient pattern of social and economic relationships within which he functioned, was a confusion of tongues.

I shall come back to this too-compacted aphorism later, as well as to the details of the text itself. The point for now is only that ethnography is thick description. What the ethnographer is in fact faced with—except when (as, of course, he must do) he is pursuing the more automatized routines of data collection—is a multiplicity of complex conceptual structures, many of them superimposed upon or knotted into one another, which are at once strange, irregular, and inexplicit, and which he must contrive somehow first to grasp and then to render. And this is true at the most down-to-earth, jungle field work levels of his activity: interviewing informants, observing rituals, eliciting kin terms, tracing property lines, censusing households . . . writing his journal. Doing ethnography is like trying to read (in the sense of "construct a reading of") a manuscript—foreign, faded, full of ellipses, incoherencies, suspicious emendations, and tendentious commentaries, but written not in conventionalized graphs of sound but in transient examples of shaped behavior.

III

Culture, this acted document, thus is public, like a burlesqued wink or a mock sheep raid. Though ideational, it does not exist in someone's head; though unphysical, it is not an occult entity. The interminable, because unterminable, debate within anthropology as to whether culture is "subjective" or "objective," together with the mutual exchange of intellectual insults ("idealist!"—"materialist!"; "mentalist!"—"behaviorist!"; "impressionist!"—"positivist!") which accompanies it, is wholly misconceived. Once human behavior is seen as (most of the time; there *are* true twitches) symbolic action—action which, like phonation in speech, pigment in painting, line in writing, or sonance in music, signifies—the question as to whether culture is patterned conduct or a frame of mind, or even the two somehow mixed together, loses sense. The thing to ask about a burlesqued wink or a mock sheep raid is not what their ontological status is. It is the same as that of rocks on one hand and dreams on the other—they are things of this world. The thing to ask is what their import is: what it is, ridicule or challenge, irony or anger, snobbery or pride, that, in their occurrence and through their agency, is getting said.

This may seem like an obvious truth, but there are a number of ways to obscure it. One is to imagine that culture is a self-contained "super-organic" reality with forces and purposes of its own; that is, to reify it. Another is to claim that it consists in the brute pattern of behavioral events we observe in fact to occur in some identifiable community or other; that is, to reduce it. But though both these confusions still exist, and doubtless will be always with us, the main source of theoretical muddlement in contemporary anthropology is a view which developed in reaction to them and is right now very widely held—namely, that, to quote Ward Goodenough, perhaps its leading proponent, "culture [is located] in the minds and hearts of men."

Variously called ethnoscience, componential analysis, or cognitive anthropology (a terminological wavering which reflects a deeper uncertainty), this school of thought holds that culture is composed of psychological structures by means of which individuals or groups of individuals guide their behavior. "A society's culture," to quote Goodenough again, this time in a passage which has become the *locus classicus* of the whole movement, "consists of whatever it is one has to know or believe in order to operate in a manner acceptable to its members." And from this view of what culture is follows a view, equally assured, of what describing it is—the writing out of systematic rules, an ethnographic algorithm, which, if followed, would make it possible so to operate, to pass (physical appearance aside) for a native. In such a way, extreme subjectivism is married to extreme formalism, with the expected result: an explosion of debate as to whether particular analyses (which come in the form of taxonomies, paradigms, tables, trees, and other ingenuities) reflect what the natives "really" think or are merely clever simulations, logically equivalent but substantively different, of what they think.

As, on first glance, this approach may look close enough to the one being developed here to be mistaken for it, it is useful to be explicit as to what divides them. If, leaving our winks and sheep behind for the moment, we take, say, a Beethoven quartet as an, admittedly rather special but, for these purposes, nicely illustrative, sample of culture, no one would, I think, identify it with its score, with the skills and knowledge needed to play it, with the understanding of it possessed by its performers or auditors, nor, to take care, *en passant,* of the reductionists and reifiers, with a particular performance of it or with some mysterious entity transcending material existence. The "no one" is perhaps too strong here, for there are always incorrigibles. But that a Beethoven quartet is a temporally developed tonal structure, a coherent sequence of modeled sound—in a word, music—and not anybody's knowledge of or belief about anything, including how to play it, is a proposition to which most people are, upon reflection, likely to assent.

To play the violin it is necessary to possess certain habits, skills, knowledge, and talents, to be in the mood to play, and (as the old joke goes) to have a violin. But violin playing is neither the habits, skills, knowledge, and so on, nor the mood, nor (the notion believers in "material culture" apparently embrace) the violin. To make a trade pact in Morocco, you have to do certain things in certain ways (among others, cut, while chanting Quranic Arabic, the throat of a lamb before the assembled, undeformed, adult male members of your tribe) and to be possessed of certain psychological characteristics (among others, a desire for distant things). But a trade pact is neither the throat cutting nor the desire, though it is real enough, as seven kinsmen of our Marmusha sheikh discovered when, on an earlier occasion, they were executed by him following the theft of one mangy, essentially valueless sheepskin from Cohen.

Culture is public because meaning is. You can't wink (or burlesque one) without knowing what counts as winking or how, physically, to contract your eyelids, and you can't conduct a sheep raid (or mimic one) without knowing what it is to steal a sheep and how practically to go about it. But to draw from such truths the conclusion that knowing how to wink is winking and knowing how to steal a sheep is sheep raiding is to betray as deep a confusion as, taking thin descriptions for thick, to identify winking with eyelid contractions or sheep raiding with chasing woolly animals out of pastures. The cognitivist fallacy—that culture consists (to quote another spokesman for the movement, Stephen Tyler) of "mental phenomena which can [he means "should"] be analyzed by formal methods similar to those of mathematics and logic"—is as destructive of an effective use of the concept as are the behaviorist and idealist fallacies to which it is a misdrawn correction. Perhaps, as its errors are more sophisticated and its distortions subtler, it is even more so.

The generalized attack on privacy theories of meaning is, since early Husserl and late Wittgenstein, so much a part of modern thought that it need not be developed once more here. What is necessary is to see to it that the news of it reaches anthropology; and in particular that it is made clear that to say that culture consists of socially established structures of meaning in terms of which people do such things as signal conspiracies and join them or perceive insults and answer them, is no more to say that it is a psychological phenomenon, a characteristic of someone's mind, personality, cognitive structure, or whatever, than to say that Tantrism, genetics, the progressive form of the verb, the classification of wines, the Common Law, or the notion of "a conditional curse" (as Westermarck defined the concept of 'ar in terms of which Cohen pressed his claim to damages) is. What, in a place like Morocco, most prevents those of us who grew up winking other winks or attending other sheep from grasping what people are up to is not ignorance as to how cognition works (though, especially as, one assumes, it works the same among them as it does among us, it would greatly help to have less of that too) as a lack of familiarity with the imaginative universe within which their acts are signs. As Wittgenstein has been invoked, he may as well be quoted:

> We . . . say of some people that they are transparent to us. It is, however, important as regards this observation that one human being can be a

complete enigma to another. We learn this when we come into a strange country with entirely strange traditions; and, what is more, even given a mastery of the country's language. We do not *understand* the people. (And not because of not knowing what they are saying to themselves.) We cannot find our feet with them.

IV

Finding our feet, an unnerving business which never more than distantly succeeds, is what ethnographic research consists of as a personal experience; trying to formulate the basis on which one imagines, always excessively, one has found them is what anthropological writing consists of as a scientific endeavor. We are not, or at least I am not, seeking either to become natives (a compromised word in any case) or to mimic them. Only romantics or spies would seem to find point in that. We are seeking, in the widened sense of the term in which it encompasses very much more than talk, to converse with them, a matter a great deal more difficult, and not only with strangers, than is commonly recognized. "If speaking *for* someone else seems to be a mysterious process," Stanley Cavell has remarked, "that may be because speaking *to* someone does not seem mysterious enough."

Looked at in this way, the aim of anthropology is the enlargement of the universe of human discourse. That is not, of course, its only aim—instruction, amusement, practical counsel, moral advance, and the discovery of natural order in human behavior are others; nor is anthropology the only discipline which pursues it. But it is an aim to which a semiotic concept of culture is peculiarly well adapted. As interworked systems of construable signs (what, ignoring provincial usages, I would call symbols), culture is not a power, something to which social events, behaviors, institutions, or processes can be causally attributed; it is a context, something within which they can be intelligibly—that is, thickly—described.

The famous anthropological absorption with the (to us) exotic—Berber horsemen, Jewish peddlers, French Legionnaires—is, thus, essentially a device for displacing the dulling sense of familiarity with which the mysteriousness of our own ability to relate perceptively to one another is concealed from us. Looking at the ordinary in places where it takes unaccustomed forms brings out not, as has so often been claimed, the arbitrariness of human behavior (there is nothing especially arbitrary about taking sheep theft for insolence in Morocco), but the degree to which its meaning varies according to the pattern of life by which it is informed. Understanding a people's culture exposes their normalness without reducing their particularity. (The more I manage to follow what the Moroccans are up to, the more logical, and the more singular, they seem.) It renders them accessible: setting them in the frame of their own banalities, it dissolves their opacity.

It is this maneuver, usually too casually referred to as "seeing things from the actor's point of view," too bookishly as "the *verstehen* approach," or too technically as "emic analysis," that so often leads to the notion that

anthropology is a variety of either long-distance mind reading or cannibal-isle
fantasizing, and which, for someone anxious to navigate past the wrecks of a
dozen sunken philosophies, must therefore be executed with a great deal of
care. Nothing is more necessary to comprehending what anthropological
interpretation is, and the degree to which it *is* interpretation, than an exact
understanding of what it means—and what it does not mean—to say that our
formulations of other people's symbol systems must be actor-oriented.[1]

What it means is that descriptions of Berber, Jewish, or French culture
must be cast in terms of the constructions we imagine Berbers, Jews, or
Frenchmen to place upon what they live through, the formulae they use to
define what happens to them. What it does not mean is that such descriptions
are themselves Berber, Jewish, or French—that is, part of the reality they are
ostensibly describing; they are anthropological—that is, part of a developing
system of scientific analysis. They must be cast in terms of the interpretations
to which persons of a particular denomination subject their experience, because that is what they profess to be descriptions of; they are anthropological
because it is, in fact, anthropologists who profess them. Normally, it is not
necessary to point out quite so laboriously that the object of study is one
thing and the study of it another. It is clear enough that the physical world
is not physics and *A Skeleton Key to Finnegan's Wake* not *Finnegan's Wake.*
But, as, in the study of culture, analysis penetrates into the very body of the
object—that is, *we begin with our own interpretations of what our informants
are up to, or think they are up to, and then systematize those*—the line between (Moroccan) culture as a natural fact and (Moroccan) culture as a theoretical entity tends to get blurred. All the more so, as the latter is presented
in the form of an actor's-eye description of (Moroccan) conceptions of everything from violence, honor, divinity, and justice, to tribe, property, patronage,
and chiefship.

In short, anthropological writings are themselves interpretations, and
second and third order ones to boot. (By definition, only a "native" makes
first order ones: it's *his* culture.)[2] They are, thus, fictions; fictions, in the
sense that they are "something made," "something fashioned"—the original
meaning of *fictiō*—not that they are false, unfactual, or merely "as if"
thought experiments. To construct actor-oriented descriptions of the involvements of a Berber chieftain, a Jewish merchant, and a French soldier with

---

[1] Not only other peoples': anthropology *can* be trained on the culture of which it is
itself a part, and it increasingly is; a fact of profound importance, but which, as it raises a
few tricky and rather special second order problems, I shall put to the side for the moment.

[2] The order problem is, again, complex. Anthropological works based on other
anthropological works (Lévi-Strauss', for example) may, of course, be fourth order or
higher, and informants frequently, even habitually, make second order interpretations—
what have come to be known as "native models." In literate cultures, where "native"
interpretation can proceed to higher levels—in connection with the Maghreb, one has only
to think of Ibn Khaldun; with the United States, Margaret Mead—these matters become
intricate indeed.

one another in 1912 Morocco is clearly an imaginative act, not all that different from constructing similar descriptions of, say, the involvements with one another of a provincial French doctor, his silly, adulterous wife, and her feckless lover in nineteenth century France. In the latter case, the actors are represented as not having existed and the events as not having happened, while in the former they are represented as actual, or as having been so. This is a difference of no mean importance; indeed, precisely the one Madame Bovary had difficulty grasping. But the importance does not lie in the fact that her story was created while Cohen's was only noted. The conditions of their creation, and the point of it (to say nothing of the manner and the quality) differ. But the one is as much a *fictiō*—"a making"—as the other.

Anthropologists have not always been as aware as they might be of this fact: that although culture exists in the trading post, the hill fort, or the sheep run, anthropology exists in the book, the article, the lecture, the museum display, or, sometimes nowadays, the film. To become aware of it is to realize that the line between mode of representation and substantive content is as undrawable in cultural analysis as it is in painting; and that fact in turn seems to threaten the objective status of anthropological knowledge by suggesting that its source is not social reality but scholarly artifice.

It does threaten it, but the threat is hollow. The claim to attention of an ethnographic account does not rest on its author's ability to capture primitive facts in faraway places and carry them home like a mask or a carving, but on the degree to which he is able to clarify what goes on in such places, to reduce the puzzlement—what manner of men are these?—to which unfamiliar acts emerging out of unknown backgrounds naturally give rise. This raises some serious problems of verification, all right—or, if "verification" is too strong a word for so soft a science (I, myself, would prefer "appraisal"), of how you can tell a better account from a worse one. But that is precisely the virtue of it. If ethnography is thick description and ethnographers those who are doing the describing, then the determining question for any given example of it, whether a field journal squib or a Malinowski-sized monograph, is whether it sorts winks from twitches and real winks from mimicked ones. It is not against a body of uninterpreted data, radically thinned descriptions, that we must measure the cogency of our explications, but against the power of the scientific imagination to bring us into touch with the lives of strangers. It is not worth it, as Thoreau said, to go round the world to count the cats in Zanzibar.

V

Now, this proposition, that it is not in our interest to bleach human behavior of the very properties that interest us before we begin to examine it, has sometimes been escalated into a larger claim: namely, that as it is only those properties that interest us, we need not attend, save cursorily, to behavior at all. Culture is most effectively treated, the argument goes, purely as a symbolic system (the catch phrase is, "in its own terms"), by isolating its elements, specifying the internal relationships among those elements, and then characterizing the whole system in some general way—according to the core symbols around which it is organized, the underlying structures of which it is a surface expression, or the ideological principles upon which it is based. Though a distinct improvement over "learned behavior" and "mental phenomena" notions of what culture is, and the source of some of the most powerful theoretical ideas in contemporary anthropology, this hermetical approach to things seems to me to run the danger (and increasingly to have been overtaken by it) of locking cultural analysis away from its proper object, the informal logic of actual life. There is little profit in extricating a concept from the defects of psychologism only to plunge it immediately into those of schematicism.

Behavior must be attended to, and with some exactness, because it is through the flow of behavior—or, more precisely, social action—that cultural forms find articulation. They find it as well, of course, in various sorts of artifacts, and various states of consciousness; but these draw their meaning from the role they play (Wittgenstein would say their "use") in an ongoing pattern of life, not from any intrinsic relationships they bear to one another. It is what Cohen, the sheikh, and "Captain Dumari" were doing when they tripped over one another's purposes—pursuing trade, defending honor, establishing dominance—that created our pastoral drama, and that is what the drama is, therefore, "about." Whatever, or wherever, symbol systems "in their own terms" may be, we gain empirical access to them by inspecting events, not by arranging abstracted entities into unified patterns.

A further implication of this is that coherence cannot be the major test of validity for a cultural description. Cultural systems must have a minimal degree of coherence, else we would not call them systems; and, by observation, they normally have a great deal more. But there is nothing so coherent as a paranoid's delusion or a swindler's story. The force of our interpretations cannot rest, as they are now so often made to do, on the tightness with which they hold together, or the assurance with which they are argued. Nothing has done more, I think, to discredit cultural analysis than the construction of impeccable depictions of formal order in whose actual existence nobody can quite believe.

If anthropological interpretation is constructing a reading of what happens, then to divorce it from what happens—from what, in this time or that place, specific people say, what they do, what is done to them, from the whole vast business of the world—is to divorce it from its applications and render it vacant. A good interpretation of anything—a poem, a person, a history, a ritual, an institution, a society—takes us into the heart of that of which it is the interpretation. When it does not do that, but leads us instead somewhere else—into an admiration of its own elegance, of its author's cleverness, or of the beauties of Euclidean order—it may have its intrinsic charms; but it is something else than what the task at hand—figuring out what all that rigamarole with the sheep is about—calls for.

The rigamarole with the sheep—the sham theft of them, the reparative transfer of them, the political confiscation of them—is (or was) essentially a social discourse, even if, as I suggested earlier, one conducted in multiple tongues and as much in action as in words.

Claiming his 'ar, Cohen invoked the trade pact; recognizing the claim, the sheikh challenged the offenders' tribe; accepting responsibility, the offenders' tribe paid the indemnity; anxious to make clear to sheikhs and peddlers alike who was now in charge here, the French showed the imperial hand. As in any discourse, code does not determine conduct, and what was actually said need not have been. Cohen might not have, given its illegitimacy in Protectorate eyes, chosen to press his claim. The sheikh might, for similar reasons, have rejected it. The offenders' tribe, still resisting French authority, might have decided to regard the raid as "real" and fight rather than negotiate. The French, were they more *habile* and less *dur* (as, under Mareschal Lyautey's seigniorial tutelage, they later in fact became), might have permitted Cohen to keep his sheep, winking—as we say—at the continuance of the trade pattern and its limitation to their authority. And there are other possibilities: the Marmushans might have regarded the French action as too great an insult to bear and gone into dissidence themselves; the French might have attempted not just to clamp down on Cohen but to bring the sheikh himself more closely to heel; and Cohen might have concluded that between renegade Berbers and Beau Geste soldiers, driving trade in the Atlas highlands was no longer worth the candle and retired to the better-governed confines of the town. This, indeed, is more or less what happened, somewhat further along, as the Protectorate moved toward genuine sovereignty. But the point here is not to describe what did or did not take place in Morocco. (From this simple incident one can widen out into enormous complexities of social experience.) It is to demonstrate what a piece of anthropological interpretation consists in: tracing the curve of a social discourse; fixing it into an inspectable form.

The ethnographer "inscribes" social discourse; *he writes it down*. In so doing, he turns it from a passing event, which exists only in its own moment of occurrence, into an account, which exists in its inscriptions and can be reconsulted. The sheikh is long dead, killed in the process of being, as the French called it, "pacified"; "Captain Dumari," his pacifier, lives, retired to his souvenirs, in the south of France; and Cohen went last year, part refugee, part pilgrim, part dying patriarch, "home" to Israel. But what they, in my extended sense, "said" to one another on an Atlas plateau sixty years ago is —very far from perfectly—preserved for study. "What," Paul Ricoeur, from whom this whole idea of the inscription of action is borrowed and somewhat twisted, asks, "what does writing fix?"

Not the event of speaking, but the "said" of speaking, where we understand by the "said" of speaking that intentional exteriorization constitutive of the aim of discourse thanks to which the *sagen*—the saying— wants to become *Aus-sage*—the enunciation, the enunciated. In short, what we write is the *noema* ["thought," "content," "gist"] of the speaking. It is the meaning of the speech event, not the event as event.

This is not itself so very "said"—if Oxford philosophers run to little stories, phenomenological ones run to large sentences; but it brings us anyway to a more precise answer to our generative question, "What does the ethnographer do?"—he writes.[3] This, too, may seem a less than startling discovery, and to someone familiar with the current "literature," an implausible one. But as the standard answer to our question has been, "He observes, he records, he analyzes"—a kind of *veni, vidi, vici* conception of the matter—it may have more deep-going consequences than are at first apparent, not the least of which is that distinguishing these three phases of knowledge-seeking may not, as a matter of fact, normally be possible; and, indeed, as autonomous "operations" they may not in fact exist.

The situation is even more delicate, because, as already noted, what we inscribe (or try to) is not raw social discourse, to which, because, save very marginally or very specially, we are not actors, we do not have direct access, but only that small part of it which our informants can lead us into understanding.[4] This is not as fatal as it sounds, for, in fact, not all Cretans are liars, and it is not necessary to know everything in order to understand something. But it does make the view of anthropological analysis as the conceptual manipulation of discovered facts, a logical reconstruction of a mere reality, seem rather lame. To set forth symmetrical crystals of significance, purified of the material complexity in which they were located, and then attribute their existence to autogenous principles of order, universal properties of the human mind, or vast, a priori *weltanschauungen,* is to pretend a science that does not exist and imagine a reality that cannot be found. Cultural analysis is (or should be) guessing at meanings, assessing the guesses, and drawing explanatory conclusions from the better guesses, not discovering the Continent of Meaning and mapping out its bodiless landscape.

VI

So, there are three characteristics of ethnographic description: it is interpretive; what it is interpretive of is the flow of social discourse; and the interpreting involved consists in trying to rescue the "said" of such discourse

---

[3] Or, again, more exactly, "inscribes." Most ethnography is in fact to be found in books and articles, rather than in films, records, museum displays, or whatever; but even in them there are, of course, photographs, drawings, diagrams, tables, and so on. Self-consciousness about modes of representation (not to speak of experiments with them) has been very lacking in anthropology.

[4] So far as it has reinforced the anthropologist's impulse to engage himself with his informants as persons rather than as objects, the notion of "participant observation" has been a valuable one. But, to the degree it has led the anthropologist to block from his view the very special, culturally bracketed nature of his own role and to imagine himself something more than an interested (in both senses of that word) sojourner, it has been our most powerful source of bad faith.

from its perishing occasions and fix it in perusable terms. The *kula* is gone or altered; but, for better or worse, *The Argonauts of the Western Pacific* remains. But there is, in addition, a fourth characteristic of such description, at least as I practice it: it is microscopic.

This is not to say that there are no large-scale anthropological interpretations of whole societies, civilizations, world events, and so on. Indeed, it is such extension of our analyses to wider contexts that, along with their theoretical implications, recommends them to general attention and justifies our constructing them. No one really cares anymore, not even Cohen (well . . . maybe, Cohen), about those sheep as such. History may have its unobtrusive turning points, "great noises in a little room"; but this little go-round was surely not one of them.

It is merely to say that the anthropologist characteristically approaches such broader interpretations and more abstract analyses from the direction of exceedingly extended acquaintances with extremely small matters. He confronts the same grand realities that others—historians, economists, political scientists, sociologists—confront in more fateful settings: Power, Change, Faith, Oppression, Work, Passion, Authority, Beauty, Violence, Love, Prestige; but he confronts them in contexts obscure enough—places like Marmusha and lives like Cohen's—to take the capital letters off them. These all-too-human constancies, "those big words that make us all afraid," take a homely form in such homely contexts. But that is exactly the advantage. There are enough profundities in the world already.

Yet, the problem of how to get from a collection of ethnographic miniatures on the order of our sheep story—an assortment of remarks and anecdotes —to wall-sized culturescapes of the nation, the epoch, the continent, or the civilization is not so easily passed over with vague allusions to the virtues of concreteness and the down-to-earth mind. For a science born in Indian tribes, Pacific islands, and African lineages and subsequently seized with grander ambitions, this has come to be a major methodological problem, and for the most part a badly handled one. The models that anthropologists have themselves worked out to justify their moving from local truths to general visions have been, in fact, as responsible for undermining the effort as anything their critics—sociologists obsessed with sample sizes, psychologists with measures, or economists with aggregates—have been able to devise against them.

Of these, the two main ones have been: the Jonesville-is-the-USA "microcosmic" model; and the Easter-Island-is-a-testing-case "natural experiment" model. Either heaven in a grain of sand, or the farther shores of possibility.

The Jonesville-is-America writ small (or America-is-Jonesville writ large) fallacy is so obviously one that the only thing that needs explanation is how people have managed to believe it and expected others to believe it. The notion that one can find the essence of national societies, civilizations, great religions, or whatever summed up and simplified in so-called "typical" small towns and villages is palpable nonsense. What one finds in small towns and villages is (alas) small-town or village life. If localized, microscopic studies were really dependent for their greater relevance upon such a premise—that they captured the great world in the little—they wouldn't have any relevance.

But, of course, they are not. The locus of study is not the object of study. Anthropologists don't study villages (tribes, towns, neighborhoods . . .); they study *in* villages. You can study different things in different places, and some things—for example, what colonial domination does to established frames of moral expectation—you can best study in confined localities. But that doesn't make the place what it is you are studying. In the remoter provinces of Morocco and Indonesia I have wrestled with the same questions other social scientists have wrestled with in more central locations—for example, how comes it that men's most importunate claims to humanity are cast in the accents of group pride?—and with about the same conclusiveness. One can add a dimension—one much needed in the present climate of size-up-and-solve social science; but that is all. There is a certain value, if you are going to run on about the exploitation of the masses, in having seen a Javanese sharecropper turning earth in a tropical downpour or a Moroccan tailor embroidering kaftans by the light of a twenty-watt bulb. But the notion that this gives you the thing entire (and elevates you to some moral vantage ground from which you can look down upon the ethically less privileged) is an idea which only someone too long in the bush could possibly entertain.

The "natural laboratory" notion has been equally pernicious, not only because the analogy is false—what kind of a laboratory is it where *none* of the parameters are manipulable?—but because it leads to a notion that the data derived from ethnographic studies are purer, or more fundamental, or more solid, or less conditioned (the most favored word is "elementary") than those derived from other sorts of social inquiry. The great natural variation of cultural forms is, of course, not only anthropology's great (and wasting) resource, but the ground of its deepest theoretical dilemma: how is such variation to be squared with the biological unity of the human species? But it is not, even metaphorically, experimental variation, because the context in which it occurs varies along with it, and it is not possible (though there are those who try) to isolate the y's from x's to write a proper function.

The famous studies purporting to show that the Oedipus complex was backwards in the Trobriands, sex roles were upside down in Tchambuli, and the Pueblo Indians lacked aggression (it is characteristic that they were all negative—"but not in the South") are, whatever their empirical validity may or may not be, not "scientifically tested and approved" hypotheses. They are interpretations, or misinterpretations, like any others, arrived at in the same way as any others, and as inherently inconclusive as any others, and the attempt to invest them with the authority of physical experimentation is but methodological sleight of hand. Ethnographic findings are not privileged, just particular: another country heard from. To regard them as anything more (*or anything less*) than that distorts both them and their implications, which are far profounder than mere primitivity, for social theory.

Another country heard from: the reason that protracted descriptions of distant sheep raids (and a really good ethnographer would have gone into what kind of sheep they were) have general relevance is that they present the sociological mind with bodied stuff on which to feed. The important thing about the anthropologist's findings is their complex specificness, their circumstantiality. It is with the kind of material produced by long-term, mainly (though not exclusively) qualitative, highly participative, and almost obsessively fine-comb field study in confined contexts that the mega-concepts with which contemporary social science is afflicted—legitimacy, modernization, integration, conflict, charisma, structure, . . . meaning—can be given the sort of sensible actuality that makes it possible to think not only realistically and concretely *about* them, but, what is more important, creatively and imaginatively *with* them.

The methodological problem which the microscopic nature of ethnography presents is both real and critical. But it is not to be resolved by regarding a remote locality as the world in a teacup or as the sociological equivalent of a cloud chamber. It is to be resolved—or, anyway, decently kept at bay— by realizing that social actions are comments on more than themselves; that where an interpretation comes from does not determine where it can be impelled to go. Small facts speak to large issues, winks to epistemology, or sheep raids to revolution, because they are made to.

VII

Which brings us, finally, to theory. The besetting sin of interpretive approaches to anything—literature, dreams, symptoms, culture—is that they tend to resist, or to be permitted to resist, conceptual articulation and thus to escape systematic modes of assessment. You either grasp an interpretation or you do not, see the point of it or you do not, accept it or you do not. Imprisoned in the immediacy of its own detail, it is presented as self-validating, or, worse, as validated by the supposedly developed sensitivities of the person who presents it; any attempt to cast what it says in terms other than its own is regarded as a travesty—as, the anthropologist's severst term of moral abuse, ethnocentric.

For a field of study which, however timidly (though I, myself, am not timid about the matter at all), asserts itself to be a science, this just will not do. There is no reason why the conceptual structure of a cultural interpretation should be any less formulable, and thus less susceptible to explicit canons of appraisal, than that of, say, a biological observation or a physical experiment—no reason except that the terms in which such formulations can be cast are, if not wholly nonexistent, very nearly so. We are reduced to insinuating theories because we lack the power to state them.

At the same time, it must be admitted that there are a number of characteristics of cultural interpretation which make the theoretical development of it more than usually difficult. The first is the need for theory to stay rather closer to the ground than tends to be the case in sciences more able to give themselves over to imaginative abstraction. Only short flights of ratiocination tend to be effective in anthropology; longer ones tend to drift off into logical

dreams, academic bemusements with formal symmetry. The whole point of
a semiotic approach to culture is, as I have said, to aid us in gaining access to
the conceptual world in which our subjects live so that we can, in some extended sense of the term, converse with them. The tension between the pull
of this need to penetrate an unfamiliar universe of symbolic action and the
requirements of technical advance in the theory of culture, between the need
to grasp and the need to analyze, is, as a result, both necessarily great and
essentially irremovable. Indeed, the further theoretical development goes,
the deeper the tension gets. This is the first condition for cultural theory:
it is not its own master. As it is unseverable from the immediacies thick
description presents, its freedom to shape itself in terms of its internal logic
is rather limited. What generality it contrives to achieve grows out of the
delicacy of its distinctions, not the sweep of its abstractions.

And from this follows a peculiarity in the way, as a simple matter of
empirical fact, our knowledge of culture . . . cultures . . . a culture . . . grows:
in spurts. Rather than following a rising curve of cumulative findings, cultural
analysis breaks up into a disconnected yet coherent sequence of bolder and
bolder sorties. Studies do build on other studies, not in the sense that they
take up where the others leave off, but in the sense that, better informed and
better conceptualized, they plunge more deeply into the same things. Every
serious cultural analysis starts from a sheer beginning and ends where it manages to get before exhausting its intellectual impulse. Previously discovered
facts are mobilized, previously developed concepts used, previously formulated hypotheses tried out; but the movement is not from already proven
theorems to newly proven ones, it is from an awkward fumbling for the most
elementary understanding to a supported claim that one has achieved that
and surpassed it. A study is an advnace if it is more incisive—whatever that
may mean—than those that preceded it; but it less stands on their shoulders
than, challenged and challenging, runs by their side.

It is for this reason, among others, that the essay, whether of thirty
pages or three hundred, has seemed the natural genre in which to present
cultural interpretations and the theories sustaining them, and why, if one
looks for systematic treatises in the field, one is so soon disappointed, the
more so if one finds any. Even inventory articles are rare here, and anyway
of hardly more than bibliographical interest. The major theoretical contributions not only lie in specific studies—that is true in almost any field—but
they are very difficult to abstract from such studies and integrate into anything one might call "culture theory" as such. Theoretical formulations hover
so low over the interpretations they govern that they don't make much sense
or hold much interest apart from them. This is so, not because they are not
general (if they are not general, they are not theoretical), but because, stated
independently of their applications, they seem either commonplace or vacant.
One can, and this in fact is how the field progresses conceptually, take a line
of theoretical attack developed in connection with one exercise in ethnographic interpretation and employ it in another, pushing it forward to greater

precision and broader relevance; but one cannot write a "General Theory of Cultural Interpretation." Or, rather, one can, but there appears to be little profit in it, because the essential task of theory building here is not to codify abstract regularities but to make thick description possible, not to generalize across cases but to generalize within them.

To generalize within cases is usually called, at least in medicine and depth psychology, clinical inference. Rather than beginning with a set of observations and attempting to subsume them under a governing law, such inference begins with a set of (presumptive) signifiers and attempts to place them within an intelligible frame. Measures are matched to theoretical predictions, but symptoms (even when they are measured) are scanned for theoretical peculiarities—that is, they are diagnosed. In the study of culture the signifiers are not symptoms or clusters of symptoms, but symbolic acts or clusters of symbolic acts, and the aim is not therapy but the analysis of social discourse. But the way in which theory is used—to ferret out the unapparent import of things—is the same.

Thus we are lead to the second condition of cultural theory: it is not, at least in the strict meaning of the term, predictive. The diagnostician doesn't predict measles; he decides that someone has them, or at the very most *anticipates* that someone is rather likely shortly to get them. But this limitation, which is real enough, has commonly been both misunderstood and exaggerated, because it has been taken to mean that cultural interpretation is merely post facto: that, like the peasant in the old story, we first shoot the holes in the fence and then paint the bull's-eyes around them. It is hardly to be denied that there is a good deal of that sort of thing around, some of it in prominent places. It is to be denied, however, that it is the inevitable outcome of a clinical approach to the use of theory.

It is true that in the clinical style of theoretical formulation, conceptualization is directed toward the task of generating interpretations of matters already in hand, not toward projecting outcomes of experimental manipulations or deducing future states of a determined system. But that does not mean that theory has only to fit (or, more carefully, to generate cogent interpretations of) realities past; it has also to survive—intellectually survive—realities to come. Although we formulate our interpretation of an outburst of winking or an instance of sheep-raiding after its occurrence, sometimes long after, the theoretical framework in terms of which such an interpretation is made must be capable of continuing to yield defensible interpretations as new social phenomena swim into view. Although one starts any effort at thick description, beyond the obvious and superficial, from a state of general bewilderment as to what the devil is going on—trying to find one's feet—one does not start (or ought not) intellectually empty-handed. Theoretical ideas are not created wholly anew in each study; as I have said, they are adopted from other, related studies, and, refined in the process, applied to new interpretive problems. If they cease being useful with respect to such problems, they tend to stop being used and are more or less abandoned. If they continue being useful, throwing up new understandings, they are further elaborated and go on being used.[5]

Such a view of how theory functions in an interpretive science suggests that the distinction, relative in any case, that appears in the experimental or observational sciences between "description" and "explanation" appears here as one, even more relative, between "inscription" ("thick description") and "specification" ("diagnosis")—between setting down the meaning particular social actions have for the actors whose actions they are, and stating, as explicitly as we can manage, what the knowledge thus attained demonstrates about the society in which it is found and, beyond that, about social life as such. Our double task is to uncover the conceptual structures that inform our subjects' acts, the "said" of social discourse, and to construct a system of analysis in whose terms what is generic to those structures, what belongs to them because they are what they are, will stand out against the other determinants of human behavior. In ethnography, the office of theory is to provide a vocabulary in which what symbolic action has to say about itself— that is, about the role of culture in human life—can be expressed.

Aside from a couple of orienting pieces concerned with more foundational matters, it is in such a manner that theory operates in the essays collected here. A repertoire of very general, made-in-the-academy concepts and systems of concepts—"integration," "rationalization," "symbol," "ideology," "ethos," "revolution," "identity," "metaphor," "structure," "ritual," "world view," "actor," "function," "sacred," and, of course, "culture" itself—is woven into the body of thick-description ethnography in the hope of rendering mere occurrences scientifically eloquent.[6] The aim is to draw large conclusions from small, but very densely textured facts; to support broad assertions about the role of culture in the construction of collective life by engaging them exactly with complex specifics.

[5] Admittedly, this is something of an idealization. Because theories are seldom if ever decisively disproved in clinical use but merely grow increasingly awkward, unproductive, strained, or vacuous, they often persist long after all but a handful of people (though *they* are often most passionate) have lost much interest in them. Indeed, so far as anthropology is concerned, it is almost more of a problem to get exhausted ideas out of the literature than it is to get productive ones in, and so a great deal more of theoretical discussion than one would prefer is critical rather than constructive, and whole careers have been devoted to hastening the demise of moribund notions. As the field advances one would hope that this sort of intellectual weed control would become a less prominent part of our activities. But, for the moment, it remains true that old theories tend less to die than to go into second editions.

[6] The overwhelming bulk of the following chapters concern Indonesia rather than Morocco, for I have just begun to face up to the demands of my North African material which, for the most part, was gathered more recently. Field work in Indonesia was carried out in 1952–1954, 1957–1958, and 1971; in Morocco in 1964, 1965–1966, 1968–1969, and 1972.

Thus it is not only interpretation that goes all the way down to the most immediate observational level: the theory upon which such interpretation conceptually depends does so also. My interest in Cohen's story, like Ryle's in winks, grew out of some very general notions indeed. The "confusion of tongues" model—the view that social conflict is not something that happens when, out of weakness, indefiniteness, obsolescence, or neglect, cultural forms cease to operate, but rather something which happens when, like burlesqued winks, such forms are pressed by unusual situations or unusual intentions to operate in unusual ways—is not an idea I got from Cohen's story. It is one, instructed by colleagues, students, and predecessors, I brought to it.

Our innocent-looking "note in a bottle" is more than a portrayal of the frames of meaning of Jewish peddlers, Berber warriors, and French proconsuls, or even of their mutual interference. It is an argument that to rework the pattern of social relationships is to rearrange the coordinates of the experienced world. Society's forms are culture's substance.

VIII

There is an Indian story—at least I heard it as an Indian story—about an Englishman who, having been told that the world rested on a platform which rested on the back of an elephant which rested in turn on the back of a turtle, asked (perhaps he was an ethnographer; it is the way they behave), what did the turtle rest on? Another turtle. And that turtle? "Ah, Sahib, after that it is turtles all the way down."

Such, indeed, is the condition of things. I do not know how long it would be profitable to meditate on the encounter of Cohen, the sheikh, and "Dumari" (the period has perhaps already been exceeded); but I do know that however long I did so I would not get anywhere near to the bottom of it. Nor have I ever gotten anywhere near to the bottom of anything I have ever written about, either in the essays below or elsewhere. Cultural analysis is intrinsically incomplete. And, worse than that, the more deeply it goes the less complete it is. It is a strange science whose most telling assertions are its most tremulously based, in which to get somewhere with the matter at hand is to intensify the suspicion, both your own and that of others, that you are not quite getting it right. But that, along with plaguing subtle people with obtuse questions, is what being an ethnographer is like.

There are a number of ways to escape this—turning culture into folklore and collecting it, turning it into traits and counting it, turning it into institutions and classifying it, turning it into structures and toying with it. But they *are* escapes. The fact is that to commit oneself to a semiotic concept of culture and an interpretive approach to the study of it is to commit oneself to a view of ethnographic assertion as, to borrow W. B. Gallie's by now famous phrase, "essentially contestable." Anthropology, or at least interpretive anthropology, is a science whose progress is marked less by a perfection of consensus than by a refinement of debate. What gets better is the precision with which we vex each other.

This is very difficult to see when one's attention is being monopolized by a single party to the argument. Monologues are of little value here, because there are no conclusions to be reported; there is merely a discussion to be sustained. Insofar as the essays here collected have any importance, it is less in what they say than what they are witness to: an enormous increase in interest, not only in anthropology, but in social studies generally, in the role of symbolic forms in human life. Meaning, that elusive and ill-defined pseudoentity we were once more than content to leave philosophers and literary critics to fumble with, has now come back into the heart of our discipline. Even Marxists are quoting Cassirer; even positivists, Kenneth Burke.

My own position in the midst of all this has been to try to resist subjectivism on the one hand and cabbalism on the other, to try to keep the analysis of symbolic forms as closely tied as I could to concrete social events and occasions, the public world of common life, and to organize it in such a way that the connections between theoretical formulations and descriptive interpretations were unobscured by appeals to dark sciences. I have never been impressed by the argument that, as complete objectivity is impossible in these matters (as, of course, it is), one might as well let one's sentiments run loose. As Robert Solow has remarked, that is like saying that as a perfectly aseptic environment is impossible, one might as well conduct surgery in a sewer. Nor, on the other hand, have I been impressed with claims that structural linguistics, computer engineering, or some other advanced form of thought is going to enable us to understand men without knowing them. Nothing will discredit a semiotic approach to culture more quickly than allowing it to drift into a combination of intuitionism and alchemy, no matter how elegantly the intuitions are expressed or how modern the alchemy is made to look.

The danger that cultural analysis, in search of all-too-deep-lying turtles, will lose touch with the hard surfaces of life—with the political, economic, stratificatory realities within which men are everywhere contained—and with the biological and physical necessities on which those surfaces rest, is an ever-present one. The only defense against it, and against, thus, turning cultural analysis into a kind of sociological aestheticism, is to train such analysis on such realities and such necessities in the first place. It is thus that I have written about nationalism, about violence, about identity, about human nature, about legitimacy, about revolution, about ethnicity, about urbanization, about status, about death, about time, and most of all about particular attempts by particular peoples to place these things in some sort of comprehensible meaningful frame.

To look at the symbolic dimensions of social action—art, religion, ideology, science, law, morality, common sense—is not to turn away from the existential dilemmas of life for some empyrean realm of de-emotionalized forms; it is to plunge into the midst of them. The essential vocation of interpretive anthropology is not to answer our deepest questions, but to make available to us answers that others, guarding other sheep in other valleys, have given, and thus to include them in the consultable record of what man has said.

JANE ADDAMS
"A Personal Experience in Interpretative Memory"

Several years ago, during a winter spent in Egypt, I found within myself an unexpected tendency to interpret racial and historic experiences through personal reminiscences. I am therefore venturing to record in this closing chapter my inevitable conclusion that a sincere portrayal of a widespread and basic emotional experience, however remote in point of time it may be, has the power overwhelmingly to evoke memories of like moods in the individual.

The unexpected revival in my memory of long-forgotten experiences may have been due partly to the fact that we have so long been taught that the temples and tombs of ancient Egypt are the very earliest of the surviving records of ideas and men, that we approach them with a certain sense of familiarity, quite ready to claim a share in these "family papers and title deeds of the race."

We also consider it probable that these primitive human records will stir within us certain early states of consciousness, having learned, with the readiness which so quickly attaches itself to the pseudo-scientific phrase, that every child repeats in himself the history of the race. Nevertheless, what I, at least, was totally unprepared to encounter, was the constant revival of primitive and overpowering emotions which I had experienced so long ago that they had become absolutely detached from myself and seemed to belong to someone else—to a small person with whom I was no longer intimate, and who was certainly not in the least responsible for my present convictions and reflections. It gradually became obvious that the ancient Egyptians had known this small person quite intimately and had most seriously and naively set down upon the walls of their temples and tombs her earliest reactions in the presence of death.

At moments my adult intelligence would be unexpectedly submerged by the emotional message which was written there. Rising to the surface like a flood, this primitive emotion would sweep away both the historic record and the adult consciousness interested in it, leaving only a child's mind struggling through an experience which it found overwhelming.

It may have been because these records of the early Egyptians are so endlessly preoccupied with death, portraying man's earliest efforts to defeat it, his eager desire to survive, to enter by force or by guile into the heavens of the western sky, that the mind is pushed back into that earliest childhood when the existence of the soul, its exact place of residence in the body, its experiences immediately after death, its journeyings upward, its relation to its guardian angel, so often afforded material for the crudest speculation. In the obscure renewal of these childish fancies, there is nothing that is definite enough to be called memory; it is rather that Egypt reproduces a state of consciousness which has so absolutely passed into oblivion that only the most powerful stimuli could revive it.

This revival doubtless occurs more easily because these early records in relief and color not only suggest in their subject-matter that a child has been endowed with sufficient self-consciousness to wish to write down his own state of mind upon a wall, but also because the very primitive style of drawing to which the Egyptians adhered long after thay had acquired a high degree of artistic freedom, is the most natural technique through which to convey so simple and archaic a message. The square shoulders of the men, the stairways done in profile, and a hundred other details, constantly remind one of a child's drawings. It is as if the Egyptians had painstakingly portrayed everything that a child has felt in regard to death, and having, during the process, gradually discovered the style of drawing naturally employed by a child, had deliberately stiffened it into an unchanging convention. The result is that the traveller, reading in these drawings which stretch the length of three thousand years, the long endeavor to overcome death, finds that the experience of the two—the child and the primitive people—often become confused, or rather that they are curiously interrelated.

This begins from the moment the traveller discovers that the earliest tombs surviving in Egypt, the mastabas—which resemble the natural results of a child's first effort to place one stone upon another—are concerned only with size, as if that early crude belief in the power of physical bulk to protect the terrified human being against all shadowy evils were absolutely instinctive and universal. The mastabas gradually develop into the pyramids, of which Breasted says that "they are not only the earliest emergence of organized men and the triumph of concerted effort, they are likewise a silent, but eloquent, expression of the supreme endeavor to achieve immortality by sheer physical force." Both the mastabas at Sahkara and the pyramids at Gizeh, in the sense of Tolstoy's definition of art as that which reproduces in the spectator the state of consciousness of the artist, at once appeal to the child surviving in every adult, who insists irrationally, after the manner of children, upon sympathizing with the attempt to shut out death by strong walls.

Certainly we can all vaguely remember, when death itself, or stories of ghosts, had come to our intimate child's circle, that we went about saying to ourselves that we were "not afraid," that it "could not come here," that "the door was locked, the windows tight shut," that "this was a big house," and a great deal more talk of a similar sort.

In the presence of these primitive attempts to defeat death, and without the conscious aid of memory, I found myself living over the emotions of a child six years old, saying some such words as I sat on the middle of the stairway in my own home, which yet seemed alien because all the members of the family had gone to the funeral of a relative and would not be back until evening, "long after you are in bed," they had said. In this moment of

loneliness and horror, I depended absolutely upon the brick walls of the
house to keep out the prowling terror, and neither the talk of kindly Polly,
who awkwardly and unsuccessfully reduced an unwieldy theology to child-
language, nor the strings of paper dolls cut by a visitor, gave me the slightest
comfort. Only the blank wall of the stairway seemed to afford protection in
this bleak moment against the formless peril.

Doubtless these huge tombs were built to preserve from destruction the
royal bodies which were hidden within them at the end of tortuous and carefully concealed passages; but both the gigantic structures in the vicinity of
Memphis, and the everlasting hills, which were later utilized at Thebes, inevitably give the impression that death is defied and shut out by massive defenses.

Even when the traveller sees that the Egyptians defeated their object by
the very success of the Gizeh pyramids—for when their overwhelming bulk
could not be enlarged and their bewildering labyrinths could not be multi-
plied, effort along that line perforce ceased—there is something in the next
attempt of the Egyptians to overcome death which the child within us again
recognizes as an old experience. One who takes pains to inquire concerning
the meaning of the texts which were inscribed on the inner walls of the pyramids and the early tombs finds that the familiar terror of death is still there
although expressed somewhat more subtly; that the Egyptians are trying to
outwit death by magic tricks.

These texts are designed to teach the rites that redeem a man from
death and insure his continuance of life, not only beyond the grave but in
the grave itself. "He who sayeth this chapter and who has been justified in
the waters of Natron, he shall come forth the day after his burial." Because
to recite them was to fight successfully against the enemies of the dead, these
texts came to be inscribed on tombs, on coffins, and on the papyrus hung
around the neck of a mummy. But woe to the man who was buried without
the texts: "He who knoweth not this chapter cannot come forth by day."
Access to Paradise and all its joys was granted to any one, good or bad, who
knew the formulae, for in the first stages of Egyptian development, as in all
other civilizations, the gods did not concern themselves with the conduct of
a man toward other men, but solely with his duty to the gods themselves.

The magic formulae alone afforded protection against the shadowy dangers awaiting the dead man when first he entered the next world and enabled
him to overcome the difficulties of his journey. The texts taught him how to
impersonate particular gods and by this subterfuge to overcome the various
foes he must encounter, because these foes, having at one time been overcome
by the gods, were easily terrified by such pretense.

When I found myself curiously sympathetic with this desire "to pretend,"
and with the eager emphasis attached by the Egyptians to their magic formulae, I was inclined to put it down to that secret sympathy with magic by means
of which all children, in moments of rebellion against a humdrum world, hope
to wrest something startling and thrilling out of the environing realm of the
supernatural; but beyond a kinship with this desire to placate the evil one, to

overcome him by mysterious words, I found it baffling to trace my sympathy to a definite experi:nce. Gradually, however, it emerged, blurred in certain details, surprisingly live in others, but all of it suffused with the selfsame emotions which impelled the Egyptian to write his Book of the Dead.

To describe it as a spiritual struggle is to use much too dignified and definite a term; it was the prolonged emotional stress throughout one cold winter when revival services—protracted meetings, they were then called— were held in the village church night after night. I was, of course, not permitted to attend them, but I heard them talked about a great deal by simple adults and children, who told of those who shouted aloud for joy, or lay on the floor "stiff with power" because they were saved; and of others—it was for those others that my heart was wrung—who, although they wrestled with the spirit until midnight and cried out that they felt the hot breath of hell upon their cheeks, could not find salvation. Would it do to pretend? I anxiously asked myself, why didn't they say the right words so that they could get up from the mourners' bench and sit with the other people, who must feel so sorry for them that they would let them pretend? What were these words that made such a difference that to say them was an assurance of heavenly bliss, but if you failed to say them you burned in hell forever and ever? Was the preacher the only one who knew them for sure? Was it possible to find them without first kneeling at the mourners' bench and groaning? These words must certainly be in the Bible somewhere, and if one read it out loud all through, every word, one must surely say the right words in time; but if one died before one was grown up enough to read the Bible through— tonight, for instance—what would happen then? Surely nothing else could be so important as these words of salvation. While I did not exactly scheme to secure them, I was certainly restrained only by my impotence, and I anxiously inquired from everyone what these magic words might be; and only gradually did this childish search for magic protection from the terrors after death imperceptibly merge into a concern for the fate of the soul.

Perhaps, because it is so impossible to classify one's own childish experiences or to put them into chronological order, the traveller at no time feels a lack of consistency in the complicated attitude toward death which is portrayed on the walls of the Egyptian temples and tombs. Much of it seems curiously familiar; from the earliest times, the Egyptians held the belief that there is in man a permanent element which survives—it is the double, the Ka, the natural soul in contradistinction to the spiritual soul, which fits exactly into the shape of the body but is not blended with it. In order to save this double from destruction, the body must be preserved in a recognizable form.

This insistence upon the preservation of the body among the Egyptians, antedating their faith in magic formulae, clearly had its origin, as in the case of the child, in a desperate revolt against the destruction of the visible man.

Owing to this continued insistence upon corporeal survival, the Egyptians at length carried the art of embalming to such a state of perfection that mummies of royal personages are easily recognized from their likenesses to portrait statues. Such confidence did they have in their own increasing ability to withhold the human frame from destruction that many of the texts inscribed on the walls of the tombs assure the dead man himself that he is not dead, and endeavor to convince his survivors against the testimony of their own senses; or rather, they attempt to deceive the senses. The texts endlessly repeat the same assertion, "Thou comest not dead to thy sepulchre, thou comest living"; and yet the very reiteration, as well as the decorations upon the walls of every tomb, protray a primitive terror lest after all the body be destroyed and the element of life be lost forever. One's throat goes dry over this old fear of death expressed by men who have been so long dead that there is no record of them but this, no surviving document of their once keen reactions to life.

Doubtless the Egyptians in time overcame this primitive fear concerning the disappearance of the body, as we all do, although each individual is destined to the same devastating experience. The memory of mine came back to me vividly as I stood in an Egyptian tomb: I was a tiny child making pothooks in the village school, when one day—it must have been in the full flush of Spring, for I remember the crab-apple blossoms—during the afternoon session, the A B C class was told that its members would march all together to the burial of the mother of one of the littlest girls. Of course, I had been properly taught that people went to heaven when they died and that their bodies were buried in the cemetery, but I was not at all clear about it, and I was certainly totally unprepared to see what appeared to be the person herself put deep down into the ground. The knowledge came to me so suddenly and brutally that for weeks afterward the days were heavy with a nameless oppression and the nights were filled with horror.

The cemetery was hard by the schoolhouse, placed there, it had always been whispered among us, to make the bad boys afraid. Thither the A B C class, in awestruck procession, each child carefully holding the hand of another, was led by the teacher to the edge of the open grave and bidden to look on the still face of the little girl's mother.

Our poor knees quaked and quavered as we stood shelterless and unattended by family protection or even by friendly grownups; for the one tall teacher, while clearly visible, seemed inexpressively far away as we kept an uncertain footing on the freshly spaded earth, hearing the preacher's voice, the sobs of the motherless children, and, crowning horror of all, the hollow sound of three clods of earth dropped impressively upon the coffin lid.

After endless ages the service was over and we were allowed to go down the long hill into the familiar life of the village. But a new terror awaited me even there, for our house stood at the extreme end of the street and the last of the way home was therefore solitary. I remember a breathless run from the blacksmith shop, past the length of our lonely orchard until the carriage-house came in sight, through whose wide-open doors I could see a man moving about. One last panting effort brought me there, and after my spirit had been slightly reassured by conversation, I took a circuitous route to the house that

I might secure as much companionship as possible on the way. I stopped at the stable to pat an old horse who stood munching in his stall, and again to throw a handful of corn into the poultry yard. The big turkey gobbler who came greedily forward gave me great comfort because he was so absurd and awkward that no one could possibly associate him with anything so solemn as death. I went into the kitchen where the presiding genius allowed me to come without protest although the family dog was at my heels. I felt constrained to keep my arms about his shaggy neck while trying to talk of familiar things—would the cake she was making be baked in the little round tins or in the big square one? But although these idle words were on my lips, I wanted to cry out, "Their mother is dead; whatever, whatever will the children do?" These words, which I had overheard as we came away from the graveyard, referred doubtless to the immediate future of the little family, but in my mind were translated into a demand for definite action on the part of the children against this horrible thing which had befallen their mother.

It was with no sense of surprise that I found this long-forgotten experience spread before my eyes on the walls of a tomb built four thousand years ago into a sandy hill above the Nile, at Assuan. The man so long dead, who had prepared the tomb for himself, had carefully ignored the grimness of death. He is portrayed as going about his affairs surrounded by his family, his friends, and his servants; grain is being measured before him into his warehouse, while a scribe by his side registers the amount; the herdsmen lead forth cattle for his inspection; two of them, enraged bulls, paying no attention to the somber implication of tomb decoration, lower their huge heads, threatening each other as if there were no such thing as death in the world. Indeed, the builder of the tomb seems to have liked the company of animals, perhaps because they were so incurious concerning death. His dogs are around him, he stands erect in a boat from which he spears fish, and so on from one marvelous relief to another, but all the time your heart contracts for him, and you know that in the midst of this elaborately prepared nonchalance he is miserably terrified by the fate which may be in store for him, and is trying to make himself believe that he need not leave all this wonted and homely activity; that if his body is but properly preserved he will be able to enjoy it forever.

Although the Egyptians, in their natural desire to cling to the familiar during the strange experience of death, portrayed upon the walls of their tombs many domestic and social habits whose likeness to our own household life gives us the quick satisfaction with which the traveller encounters the familiar and wonted in a strange land, such a momentary thrill is quite unlike the abiding sense of kinship which is founded upon the unexpected similarity of ideas, and it is the latter which are encountered in the tombs of the eighteenth century dynasty. The paintings portray a great hall, at the end of which sits Osiris, the god who had suffered death on earth, awaiting those who come before him for judgment. In the center of the hall stands a huge balance in which the hearts of men are weighed, once more reminiscent of a childish conception, making clear that as the Egyptians became more anxious and scrupulous they gradually made the destiny of man dependent upon morality, and finally directed the souls of men to heaven or hell according to their merits.

There is a theory that the tremendous results of good and evil, in the earliest awakening to them, were first placed in the next world by a primitive people sore perplexed as to the partialities and injustices of mortal life. This simple view is doubtless the one the child naturally takes. In Egypt I was so vividly recalled to my first apprehension of it that the contention that the very belief in immortality is but the postulate of the idea of reward and retribution seemed to me at the moment a perfectly reasonable one.

The incident of my childhood around which it had formulated itself was very simple. I had been sent with a message—an important commission it seemed to me—to the leader of the church choir that the hymn selected for the doctor's funeral was "How blest the righteous when he dies." The village street was so strangely quiet under the summer sun that even the little particles of dust beating in the hot air were more noiseless than ever before. Frightened by the noonday stillness and instinctively seeking companionship, I hurried toward two women who were standing at a gate talking in low tones. In their absorption they paid no attention to my somewhat wistful greeting, but I heard one of them say with a dubious shake of the head that "he had never openly professed nor joined the church," and in a moment I understood that she thought the doctor would not go to heaven. What else did it mean, that half-threatening tone? Of course the doctor was good, as good as any one could be. Only a few weeks before he had given me a new penny when he had pulled my tooth, and once I heard him drive by in the middle of the night when he took a beautiful baby to the miller's house; he went to the farms miles and miles away when people were sick, and everybody sent for him the minute they were in trouble. How could any one be better than that?

In defiant constrast to the whispering women, there arose in my mind, composed doubtless of various Bible illustrations, the picture of an imposing white-robed judge seated upon a golden throne, who listened gravely to all those good deeds as they were read by the recording angel from his great book, and then sent the doctor straight to heaven.

I dimly felt the challenge of the fine old hymn in its claim of blessings for the righteous, and was defiantly ready at the moment to combat the theology of the entire community. Of my own claim to heaven I was most dubious, and I simply could not bring myself to contemplate the day when my black sins should be read aloud from the big book; but when the claim of reward in the next world for well-doing in this came to me in regard to one whose righteousness was undoubted, I was eager to champion him before all mankind and even before the judges in the shadowy world to come.

This state of mind, this mood of truculent discussion, was recalled by the wall paintings in the tomb of a nobleman in the Theban hills. In an agonized posture he awaits the outcome of his trial before Osiris. Thoth, the true scribe, records on the wall the just balance between the heart of the nobleman, which is in one pan of the scale, and the feather of truth which is in the other. The noble appeals to his heart, which has thus been separated from him, to stand by him during the weighing and not to bear testimony against him. "Oh, heart of my existence, rise not up against me; be not an enemy against me before the divine powers; thou art my Ka that is in my body, the heart that came to me from my mother." The noble even tries a bribe by reminding the Ka that his own chance of survival is dependent on his testimony at this moment. The entire effort on the part of the man being tried is to still the voice of his own conscience, to maintain stoutly his innocence even to himself.

The attitude of the self-justifying noble might easily have suggested those later childish struggles in which a sense of hidden guilt, of repeated failure in "being good," plays so large a part, and humbles a child to the very dust. That the definite reminiscence evoked by the tomb belonged to an earlier period of rebellion may indicate that the Egyptian had not yet learned to commune with his gods for spiritual refreshment.

Whether it is that the long days and magical nights on the Nile lend themselves to a revival of former states of consciousness, or that I had come to expect landmarks of individual development in Egypt, or, more likely still, that I had fallen into a profoundly reminiscent mood, I am unable to state; but certainly, as the Nile boat approached nearer to him "who sleeps in Philae," something of the Egyptian feeling for Osiris, the god to whom was attributed the romance of a hero and the character of a benefactor and redeemer, came to me through long-forgotten sensations. Typifying the annual "great affliction," Osiris, who had submitted himself to death, mutilation, and burial in the earth, returned each Spring when the wheat and barley sprouted, bringing not only a promise of bread for the body but healing and comfort for the torn mind; an intimation that death itself is beneficent and may be calmly accepted as a necessary part of an ordered universe.

Day after day, seeing the rebirth of the newly planted fields on the banks of the Nile, and touched by a fresh sense of the enduring miracle of Spring with its inevitable analogy to the vicissitudes of human experience, one dimly comprehends how the pathetic legends of Osiris, by providing the Egyptian with an example for his own destiny, not only opened the way for a new meaning in life, but also gradually vanquished the terrors of death.

Again there came a faint memory of a child's first apprehension that there may be poetry out-of-doors, of the discovery that myths have a foundation in natural phenomena, and at last a more definite reminiscence.

I saw myself a child of twelve standing stock-still on the bank of a broad-flowing river, with a little red house surrounded by low-growing willows on its opposite bank, striving to account to myself for a curious sense of familiarity, for a conviction that I had long ago known it all most intimately, although I had certainly never seen the Mississippi River before. I remember that, much puzzled and mystified, at last I gravely concluded that it was one of those intimations of immortality that Wordsworth had written about, and I went back to my cousin's camp in so exalted a frame of mind that the memory of the evening light shining through the blades of young corn growing in a field passed on the way has remained with me for more than forty years.

Was that fugitive sense of having lived before nearer to the fresher imaginations of the Egyptians, as it is nearer to the mind of a child? and did the myth of Osiris make them more willing to die because the myth came to embody a confidence in this transitory sensation of continuous life?

Such ghosts of reminiscence, coming to the individual as he visits one after another of the marvelous human documents on the banks of the Nile, may be merely manifestations of that new humanism which is perhaps the most precious possession of this generation, the belief that no altar at which living men have once devoutly worshipped, no oracle to whom a nation long ago appealed in its moments of dire confusion, no gentle myth in which former generations have found solace, can lose all significance for us, the survivors.

Is it due to this same humanism that, in spite of the overweight of the tomb, Egypt never appears to the traveller as world-weary, or as a land of the dead? Although the slender fellaheen, whom he sees all day pouring the water of the Nile on their parched fields, use the primitive shaduf of their remote ancestors, and the stately women bear upon their heads water-jars of a shape unchanged for three thousand years, modern Egypt refuses to belong to the past and continually makes the passionate living appeal for those hard-pressed in the struggle for bread.

Under the smoking roofs of the primitive clay houses lifted high above the level of the fields, because resting on the ruins of villages which have crumbled there from time immemorial, mothers feed their children, clutched by the old fear that there is not enough for each to have his portion; and the traveller comes to realize with a pang that the villages are built upon the bleak, barren places quite as the dead are always buried in the desert because no black earth can be spared, and that each new harvest, cut with sickles of a curve already ancient when Moses was born, in spite of its quick ripening, is garnered barely in time to save the laborer from actual starvation.

Certain it is that through these our living brothers, or through the unexpected reactions of memory to racial records, the individual detects the growth within of an almost mystical sense of the life common to all the centuries, and of the unceasing human endeavor to penetrate into the unseen world. These records also afford glimpses into a past so vast that the present generation seems to float upon its surface as thin as a sheet of light which momentarily covers the ocean and moves in response to the black waters beneath it.

Part Four

A poet is a man willing to come under the bondage of limitations, if he can find them.

Allen Tate

In all cultural matters it is the form of growth that enables us to understand the form of the existing product.

Ernst Cassirer

Order seems to come from searching for disorder, and awkwardness from searching for harmony or likeness, or the following of a system. The truest order is what you already find there, or that will be given if you don't try for it. When you arrange, you fail.

Fairfield Porter

Art does not render the visible but renders visible.

Paul Klee

Artists at Work

Artists at work have a lot to teach us about the composing process. I think there is probably more to be learned by teachers of writing from time spent backstage and in practice rooms and studios than from time spent at conferences or in the study of rhetorical theory. We need to see the imagination in action in order to understand it as the forming power. Performers are faced with different challenges and constraints from those faced by the creative artist, but as we watch and listen to them practice, we are witnessing that *recreation* which art always requires, whether from audience or performer. Letting our students in on the processes by which works of art are created and recreated can help them discover that composing and interpreting are ways of knowing, that art is a form of knowledge.

The best course I ever took was one called "Related Arts" and referred to affectionately as "Related Everything." It was taught by a painter, a singer and music historian, and poet-folklorist, and its aim was not so much to relate the arts to one another as to relate us to the arts, by training our powers of observation, educating a sense of formal pattern, and, incidentally, improving our taste. We listened to Pachelbel and Meade "Lux" Lewis to learn to hear the form of a *passacaglia.* We then tried to identify elements comparable to the *basso continuo* in various poems. We defined *stretto* as exemplified in several organ fugues of J. S. Bach and then tried to establish an analogue in the overlapping contours of mountains in Chinese paintings. We read passages from Aquinas and studied slides of facades and groined vaults. We read some aesthetics and quite a lot about the history of styles. The final assignment was to choose works which we detested from each of the Fine Arts, as well as ones we appreciated, and to see what would happen to our attitudes as we studied the works in various contexts. I remember to my shame that two of my Detesteds were Frank Lloyd Wright and Joan Miro; I learned to enjoy both. El Greco, one of the Favorites, lost much of his appeal, but by semester's end, I loved Brahms more than ever. Years later when I read C. S. Lewis's *An Experiment in Criticism,* I found there further analysis of some of the distinctions that course had taught me to make. It is a tremendous advance to ask not "What is the author/dancer/painter trying to say?" but "What has the artist made?" It leads to an understanding of the interdependence of *logos* (something said) and *poiema* (something made) which Lewis decides is essential to critical appreciation.

What the student of composition can learn from a study of the arts is of the greatest importance: the uses of chaos; the foolishness of depending on inspiration; the wisdom of depending on inspiration; the role of practice; the ambiguities of "the audience"; the dialectic of creativity and criticism. And patience.

The artist, whose power of imagination has so often been seen as an imitation of sacred power, does not create from nothing. From the chaos of experience, including the experience of his training in one or another tradition, the artist continually produces forms, bringing them into being by seeing one thing in terms of another, letting the emergent form lead him to further forming. This forming can happen only if he patiently lets it happen: learning the uses of chaos is contingent on developing a tolerance of ambiguity. But it is an active patience, what Keats called "negative capability": "that is, when a man is capable of being in uncertainties, mysteries, doubts, without any irritable reaching after fact and reason . . .". Inspiration does not just happen; feeling is powerless to realize itself. But if knowing how to proceed is a *sine qua non,* it must nevertheless not move to the front; unless technique is subordinate, it will kill spirit. Artists find ways of saying this as they rediscover their relationship to the materials with which they work—both the medium and the subject. The emphasis is often on earning the right to ignore technique, a possibility only when, in modern jargon, it is "internalized." If, just as Aristotle declared, it is the end of philosophy to be able to dispense with philosophy, so artists admonish themselves and their disciples not to think they can take short cuts in order to avoid discipline.

No artist lives or works outside a tradition, the presuppositions and procedures handed down to him from his predecessors. He may reject tradition or set it aside, turn it upside down, transform it utterly, but he must make it his own in order to do so. He must earn his heritage, which is to say that what Paul Klee calls the artist's "sense of direction" is developed as he makes himself familiar with his art so that he can *transmit.* Artists from all times and places attest to the experience of feeling themselves the means by which reality can be known.

The ambivalent attitude towards technique—it is essential but must not be apparent—is represented in the paradoxical metaphors, the radically ambiguous maxims, the contradictory advice master artists offer those who seek instruction. The Chinese painters whose advice is gathered in the seventeenth century manual known as *The Mustard Seed Garden* list The Six Canons, The Six Qualities, The Three Faults, The Twelve Things to Avoid, but just as it looks as if it's all a matter of dogma, they will recapitulate with a rule like "Splash ink, spare ink." Furthermore, practice and exercise, necessary as they are, do not come "first": they must somehow be seen as the means to the means of making meaning. As *The Mustard Seed Garden* has it, "Drawing must be linked with idea (*i*), for without meaning (*i*), the brush cannot function properly."

Just when, and under what circumstances, the apprentice is to turn to principles or to masters to be imitated is, generally, a matter not of protocol but of judgment. Just what one is to make of Nature is determined by tradition, but all artists find there, in Creation, the model and/or metaphor of that other creation of art. (Leonardo carefully differentiates the two by using *create* of Nature and *generate* of the Artist.) When Cézanne speaks of *realisation,* he means finding forms to represent the sense one has of Nature's forms. Around 1900 when he was writing the letters printed here, the French Academy warned that *réaliser* was being corrupted by the influence of the English *realize,* meaning *to understand* or *to render precisely.** Cézanne surely held to the French sense of the word as an activity by which the artist seeks to embody spirit, to bring into being in one form what he finds manifest in another.

The search for sameness among differences—singling out, identifying salient features, remembering and recognizing them—is highlighted when the artist works within a tradition in which there is a lively metaphysics to define that dialectic. When Gerard Manley Hopkins looks hard to find the inscape of oakleaves, he is looking for *thisness* (haecceitas), the signature of the Creator. Such a passage as the one included here dramatizes the fact that the apprehension of form is abstraction. In the passage from his notebooks, the abstraction is accomplished discursively; in one poem after another, abstraction is achieved in the mode of what Mrs. Langer calls "direct, intensive insight," by means of images which represent all those acts of mind whereby the form of a trout or a mud puddle has been apprehended.

And of course a writer's record of his mind's activity can show us how observation is never simply a matter of "making it specific," "getting the details," "showing, not telling." Authentic observation—in the laboratory, in the studio, in the pasture or the cradle—is always conceptual, always abstract, always a process of making meaning. Scientists know this as well as poets do, but the testimony of poets is more abundant and better known. (And more readily available, which is why I have included only one such passage.) Investigating what poets and other writers have to say, especially in notebooks, journals, and letters (interviews might be less candid) is instructive for us all. Writers puzzle over how to get started and what to do next, questioning purposes and procedures and occasionally in the course of such self-interrogation they formulate views of art and life. But what we chiefly gather, listening in on these inner dialogues ("internal colloquies," as I. A. Richards called them) is not aesthetics or morality but an understanding of habits of mind and work, about the time composing takes and how it can be worth it. Poets, like painters, can teach us the value (and delight) of looking —and looking again.

*Warren Herendeen made this point in the course of our discussion of Cézanne's letters in the NEH Summer Seminar I directed at the University of Massachusetts/Boston in 1980.

SAMUEL TAYLOR COLERIDGE
from *Biographia Literaria*

The poet, described in ideal perfection, brings the whole soul of man into activity, with the subordination of its faculties to each other according to their relative worth and dignity. He diffuses a tone and spirit of unity, that blends, and (as it were) *fuses,* each into each by that synthetic and magical power, to which I would exclusively appropriate the name of Imagination. This power, first put in action by the will and understanding, and retained under their irremissive, though gentle and unnoticed, control, *laxis effertur habenis* [swept along, unreined] , reveals itself in the balance or reconcilement of opposite or discordant qualities: of sameness with difference; of the general with the concrete; the idea with the image; the individual with the representative; the sense of novelty and freshness with old and familiar objects; a more than usual state of emotion with more than usual order; judgment ever awake and steady self-possession with enthusiasm and feeling profound or vehement; and while it blends and harmonizes the natural and the artificial, still subordinates art to nature; the manner to the matter; and our admiration of the poet to our sympathy with the poetry.

PAUL KLEE
from *The Thinking Eye*

I begin with chaos, that is the most natural. And I am at ease, because at the start I may myself be chaos. Chaos is an unordered state of things, a confusion. "Cosmogenetically" speaking, it is a mythical primordial state of the world, from which the ordered chaos develops step by step or suddenly, on its own or at the hand of a creator. Natural movement from white to black is not unregulated, but unarticulated. It is regulated by comparison with chaos, in which light and darkness are still undivided. It has the natural order of an unbroken flow from one pole to the other. This movement or distribution of tension is infinitely subtle. The minute particles can scarcely be distinguished. A definite orientation is not possible. Position cannot be sharply fixed, because the flux, the subtle flow, takes certainty, gently but surely, away with it.

PAUL KLEE
from "On Modern Art"

May I use a simile, a simile of the tree? The artist has studied this world of variety and has, we may suppose, unobtrusively found his way in it. His sense of direction in nature and life, this branching and spreading array, I shall compare with the root of the tree. From the root the sap flows to the artist, flows through him, flows to his eye. Thus he stands as the trunk of the tree. Battered and stirred by the strength of the flow, he moulds his vision into his work. As, in full view of the world, the crown of the tree unfolds and spreads in time and in space, so with his work. Nobody would affirm that the tree grows its crown in the image of its root. Between above and below can be no mirrored reflection. It is obvious that different functions expanding in different elements produce vital divergences. But it is just the artist who at times is denied those departures from nature which his art demands. He has even been charged with incompetence and deliberate distortion. And yet, standing at his appointed place, the trunk of the tree, he does nothing other than gather and pass on what comes to him from its depths. He neither serves nor rules—he transmits. His position is humble. And the beauty at the crown is not his own. He is merely a channel.

PAUL CÉZANNE
from *Letters*

1. Treat Nature in terms of the cylinder, the sphere, the cone, with everything set in perspective so that each side of an object or a plane is directed towards a central point. The lines parallel to the horizon establish breadth, that is, a section of Nature—or, if you prefer, the spectacle which the Pater Omnipotens Aeterne Deus spreads before our eyes. The lines running perpendicular to that horizon establish depth. Now, Nature for us mortals exists more in depth than in surface; hence the necessity for introducing enough blue tones into the reds and yellows, by which we represent the vibration of light, to make the atmosphere perceptible.

2. To achieve progress towards realization, only Nature counts and the eye learns by contact with it. The eye becomes concentric through looking

*To a young friend, Emile Bernard, April 15, July 25, December 23 in 1904; undated, 1905; and to his son, Paul Cézanne, September 8, 1906. My translation. (AB)

and working. I mean to say that in an orange, an apple, a ball, a head, there is a focal point and this point is always the one nearest our eye, regardless of the effects of light and shade and coloration. The edges of the objects recede towards a center located on our horizon. With just a little temperament, one can be quite a painter. One can do very fine work without being a great harmonist or colorist. It is enough to have a sense of art—and no doubt it is that feeling which scandalizes the bourgeois. Thus institutes, pensions, and honors are intended only for idiots, fools, and knaves. Don't go in for the criticism of art; keep up the painting: that's what'll save us.

3. Yes, I share your admiration for the greatest of the Venetians: we both pay homage to Tintoretto. Your need to find a moral and intellectual point of support in works that will never be surpassed surely keeps you on the *qui vive* searching incessantly for the way which will provide your own means of expression, when you confront Nature. And when you are there, rest assured that you will quite naturally and without effort discover the very methods employed by the four or five masters of Venice. I'm quite dogmatic about this. [While we painters are learning to understand the relationship of light and color] , we flounder. During this period, we go to the great masterpieces the ages have handed down to us, and we find in them solace and a support, like a plank held out to a swimmer.

4. The Louvre is the book in which we learn to read. But we must not be content to memorize the beautiful formulas of our illustrious predecessors. Let us get out and study beautiful Nature; let us try to discover her spirit; let us express ourselves according to our own temperaments. Time and reflection tend to modify our vision little by little and finally comprehension comes to us. In this rainy weather, it is impossible to put these theories to the test out of doors, however sound they might be. But perserverance teaches us to understand interiors, just as we do Nature. Complacency alone obstructs our intelligence, which needs a good whipping.*

5. I will tell you [his son Paul] that, as a painter, I am becoming more clear-sighted in front of Nature, but that for me the realization of my sensations is always very painful. I cannot attain the intensity which overtakes my senses—I have not the magnificent richness of color that animates nature. Here, on the banks of the river, the motifs are plentiful. The same subject seen from a different angle suggests a study of the greatest interest and so varied that I think I could occupy myself for months without changing my place, simply leaning a bit now to the right, a bit to the left.

---

*What Cézanne writes is close to "We should get off our duff." (Les vieux culots seuls obstruent notre intelligence, qui a besoin d'etre fouettée.)

GERARD MANLEY HOPKINS
from *Notebooks*

July 11 (1867). . . . Oaks: the organization of this tree is difficult.
Speaking generally no doubt the determining planes are concentric, a system
of brief contiguous and continuous tangents, whereas those of the cedar wd.
roughly be called horizontals and those of the beech radiating but modified
by droop and by a screw-set towards jutting points. But beyond this since
the normal growth of the boughs is radiating and the leaves grow some way
in there is of course a system of spoke-wise clubs of green—sleeve-pieces. And
since the end shoots curl and carry young and scanty leaf-stars these clubs
are tapered, and I have seen also the pieces in profile with chiselled outlines,
the blocks thus made detached and lessening towards the end. However the
star knot is the chief thing: it is whorled, worked around a little and this is
what keeps up the illusion of the tree: the leaves are rounded inwards and
figure out ball-knots. Oaks differ much, and much turns on the broadness of
the leaf, the narrower giving the crisped and starry and catherine-wheel forms,
the broader the flat-pieced mailed or shard-covered one, in wh. it is possible
to see composition in dips etc., on wider bases than the single knot or cluster.
But I shall study them further. See the 19th.

July 19. . . . Alone in the woods and in Mr. Nelthorpe's park, whence
one gets such a beautiful view southwards over the country. I have now found
the law of the oak leaves. It is of platter-shaped stars altogether; the leaves lie
close like pages, packed in and as if drawn tightly to. But these old packs, wh.
lie at the end of their twigs, throw out now young shoots alternately and
slimly leaved, looking like bright keys. All the sprays but markedly these ones
shape out and as it were embrace greater circles and the dip and toss of these
makes the wider and less organic articulations of the tree.

The Mustard Seed Garden Manual of Painting
(selections)

Lu Ch'ai says:

Among those who study painting, some strive for an elaborate effect and others prefer the simple. Neither complexity in itself nor simplicity is enough.

Some aim to be deft, others to be laboriously careful. Neither dexterity nor conscientiousness is enough.

Some set great value on method, while others pride themselves on dispensing with method. To be without method is deplorable, but to depend entirely on method is worse.

You must learn first to observe the rules faithfully; afterwards modify them according to your intelligence and capacity. The end of all method is to seem to have no method.

Among the masters, it was a different matter. Ku (K'ai-chih) Ch'ang-k'ang applied his colors sprinkling and splashing, and the grass and flowers seemed to grow at the movement of his hand. Han Kan, whose picture *The Yellow Horse* was unique, used to pray[1] before he painted, and his brush was inspired. At a later stage, therefore, one may choose either to proceed methodically or to paint seemingly without method.

First, however, you must work hard. Bury the brush again and again in the ink and grind the inkstone to dust. Take ten days to paint a stream and five to paint a rock. Then, later, you may try to paint the landscape at Chialing. Li Ssŭ-hsün took months to paint it; Wu Tao-tzŭ did it in one evening. Thus, at a later stage, one may proceed slowly and carefully or one may rely on dexterity.

---

[1] The character *ch'ing* (to pray) is composed of *yen* (to speak), a drawing of words issuing from the mouth, and *ch'ing* (green), made up of *shêng* (to produce, to grow, life) over *tan* (red), forming a vivid pictographic description of the process of growing as "burning with life." Thus "to pray" might be rendered as "asking for the fire of life"; among Taoists and Zen Buddhists, it is the emptying of the mind and heart in the practice of meditation in order to be filled with and to reflect the *Tao*, moreover to become identified with the *Tao* in the object painted.

First, however, learn to hold in your thoughts the Five Peaks. Do not concentrate on the whole ox.[2] Study ten thousand volumes and walk ten thousand miles. Clear the barriers set by Tung and Chü, and pass straightway into the mansions of Ku and Cheng. Follow Ni Yun-lin painting in the style of Yu Ch'êng: when he painted, mountains soared and springs flowed, waters ran clear and forests spread vast and lonely. Be like Kuo Shu-hsien, who with one stroke of the brush released a kite on a hundred-foot string, who painted with equal facility the large and the small—towers and many-storied buildings as easily as the hair of oxen and the thread of a silkworm. Thus, at a later stage, an elaborate effect is acceptable and a simple one is equally acceptable.

If you aim to dispense with method, learn method. If you aim at facility, work hard. If you aim for simplicity, master complexity.

Finally, there are the Six Canons, the Six Essentials, the Six Qualities, the Three Faults, and the Twelve Things To Avoid. How can one disregard them?

* * *

The Six Canons (*Lu Fa*)

In the Southern Ch'i period (479–501), Hsieh Ho said:

> Circulation of the *Ch'i* (Breath, Spirit, Vital Force of Heaven) produces movement of life.
>
> Brush creates structure.
>
> According to the object draw its form.
>
> According to the nature of the object apply color.
>
> Organize composition with the elements in their proper places.
>
> In copying, seek to pass on the essence of the master's brush and methods.

[2] "The whole ox" alludes to the story in the *Chuang Tzŭ* about Prince Hui's cook, who, because he had devoted himself to the *Tao*, developed his skill as a butcher into an art; when he first started cutting up bullocks, he saw "the whole ox," but he learned through *Tao* to use his mind properly and to work according to his knowledge of the construction of the animal, therefore he achieved results in perfect harmony. (Giles, *Chuang Tzŭ*, pp. 33 ff.) These first two references pertain to the spirit and inner resources, which Lu Ch'ai follows up with a much-quoted phrase about the necessity for a painter to broaden his horizons by study and experience, including wide and keen observation, eventually to find in enrichment of spirit the secret of the rhythm of nature. (The dictum not to concentrate on "the whole ox" is confusing at first since that would seem to be the best way to discover "the rhythm of nature." From the context it is clear that the phrase means something like "the details of the organized whole" or "the object without the process." Here is Leonardo da Vinci making a comparable point about procedures: "Now have you never thought about how poets compose their verses? They do not trouble to trace beautiful letters nor do they mind crossing out several lines so as to make them better. So, painter, rough out the arrangement of the limbs of your figures and first attend to the movements appropriate to the mental state of the creatures that make up your picture rather than to the beauty and perfection of their parts." [AB])

(Lu Ch'ai, citing one school of thought adds:)

All but the First Canon can be learned and practiced to the point of true accomplishment. (As for the ability to make manifest aspects of the) *Ch'i* in its constant revolving and mutation, one has to be born with that gift.

The Six Essentials (*Lu Yao*) and the Six Qualities (*Lu Ch'ang*)

In the Sung period, Liu Tao-ch'un said:

First Essential: Action of the *Ch'i* and powerful brushwork go together.

Second Essential: Basic design should be according to tradition.

Third Essential: Originality should not disregard the *li* (the principles or essence) of things.

Fourth Essential: Color (if used) should enrich.

Fifth Essential: The brush should be handled with *tzǔ jan* (spontaneity).

Sixth Essential: Learn from the masters but avoid their faults.

First Quality: To display brushstroke power with good brushwork control.

Second Quality: To possess sturdy simplicity with refinement of true talent.

Third Quality: To possess delicacy of skill with vigor of execution.

Fourth Quality: To exhibit originality, even to the point of eccentricity, without violating the *li* of things.

Fifth Quality: In rendering space by leaving the silk or paper untouched, to be able nevertheless to convey nuances of tone.

Sixth Quality: On the flatness of the picture plane, to achieve depth and space.

The Three Faults (*San Ping*)

In the Sung period, Kuo Jo-hsü said:

The Three Faults all are connected with the handling of the brush.

The first is described as "boardlike" (*p'an*), referring to the stiffness of a weak wrist and a sluggish brush. Shapes of objects become flat and thin, lacking in solidity.

The second is described as "carving" (*k'o*), referring to the labored movement of the brush caused by hesitation. Heart and hand are not in accord. In drawing, the brush is awkward.

The third is described as "knotted" (*chieh*), referring to the knotted effect when the brush seems to be tied, or in some way hindered from moving freely, and lacks pliancy.

The Twelve Things To Avoid (*Shih Erh Chi*)

In the Yuan period, Jao Tzŭ-jan said:

The first thing to avoid is a crowded, ill-arranged composition.

The second, far and near not clearly distinguished.

The third, mountains without *Ch'i*, the pulse of life.[3]

The fourth, water with no indication of its source.

The fifth, scenes lacking any places made inaccessible by nature.[4]

The sixth, paths with no indication of beginning and end.

The seventh, stones and rocks with one face.[5]

The eighth, trees with less than four main branches.

The ninth, figures unnaturally distorted.

The tenth, buildings and pavilions inappropriately placed.

The eleventh, atmospheric effects of mist and clearness neglected.[6]

The twelfth, color applied without method.

[3] Lit., "mountains lacking *ch'i* in their veins and arteries," referring not only to the need for pictorial vitality created by composition and drawing but to the idea of infusing the mountains with a quality of spirit, particularly since mountains were symbols of life, of the *Yang* (of Heaven and the Spirit). This Third Thing To Avoid pairs with the Fourth, about water, the element regarded as a source of life and associated with the *Yin*. Mountains and water are not only the main structural elements in a landscape painting, but as symbols of the *Yin* and *Yang* they are structural ideas, hence the significance of the term *shan shui* (mountain-water) for landscape pictures. The First and Second Things To Avoid are concerned with composition. They imply attention to an inner rhythm perceptible through a well-composed painting; this is a concept of rhythm that heightens the tensions of the design, of the far and near, of what pertains to background and foreground and to the higher and lower parts of the picture, and the corresponding tensions in such details as the direction of tree branches and of footpaths; each by analogy is related to the idea of the movement and rhythm of the *Tao* and the eternal complementary action of the *Yin* and *Yang*.

[4] The Fifth and Sixth Things are concerned with the natural and logical: landscapes where no human being has wandered naturally have places inaccessible and, in some instances, dangerous; on the other hand, where man has ventured, paths are a sign of his presence and should naturally lead somewhere.

[5] At the beginning of the *Book of Trees*, Lu Ch'ai mentions the principle applied to rocks and also to trees: A rock has three faces, referring to the third dimension and technical skill in rendering it and, symbolically, to the One (the rock, mountain, Heaven, *Yang*, or the *Tao*, depending on the angle of interpretation) manifest through the Three. A tree has four main branches and is represented as having solidity, roundness, and unity; it is also a universal symbol of the One—the Tree of Life, its roots deep in Earth, its crown reaching to Heaven, its branches and leaves extending in all four directions.

[6] Literally, "lack of harmony among the waves of clouds and waves of water."

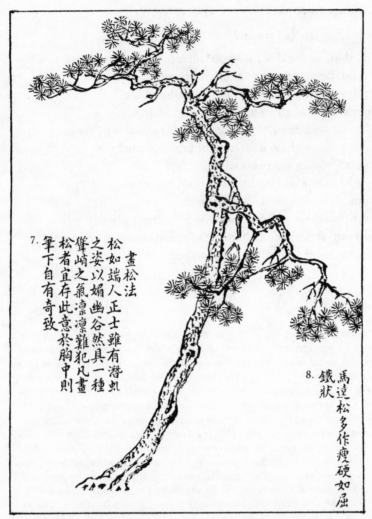

7. 畫松法
松如端人正士雖有潛虬
之姿以媚幽谷然具一種
嶝崎之氣凜凜難犯凡畫
松者宜存此意於胸中則
筆下自有奇致

8. 馬遠松多作瘦硬如屈
鐵狀

[7]This paragraph illustrates three levels of meaning. The pine is a decorative subject loved for its sinuous grace, ruggedness, and venerable age. The pine trunk and branches are like the body of a young dragon, symbolic of earthly and imperial power, and also of the *Yang*. And, finally, a pine stands for the inner spiritual power and potential in individuals, the young dragon hidden (*ch'ien*, "to secrete": a pictograph of "water murmuring" that might be interpreted as the source or unconscious) and about to uncoil and rise from the deep gorge (*yu*, "deep," is the same character as in *yu ming,* the Underworld). *Sung chiao,* here rendered "ready to spring forth," is literally "to excite or to soar." *Sung* is composed of "ear" and "to obey," which suggest listening or tuning in with the *Tao.* The description of the young dragon hidden and about to uncoil implies a state of stillness and waiting to comply. *Chiao* (steep, harsh, vigorous) is composed of *shan* (mountain) and *hsiao* (to be like one's father—not degenerate), which might be summed up as "moral."

[8]Translated: "Pines painted by Ma Yüan were lean and strong as iron."

持竿舉楫不必盡
露全身於蘆中柳
下一舸熟綴自有
神龍見首不見尾
之妙然亦須看所
畫之地方地方若
促全然橫畫一舟
上下塞滿有何妙
處故只宜露首露尾
有餘不盡之為妙也

[9] In drawing a figure who is rowing, it is not necessary to show the whole boat. Boats drawn among reeds and under willows are primarily for decoration. As in drawing the divine dragon with the head but not the tail, it is the placing that is important. If the site is small and an entire boat is drawn, the boat will seem to fill the whole space, crowding the composition. What skill is there in this? Under such circumstances one end of the boat should be shown, not the whole craft. That takes skill.

INGMAR BERGMAN

(from an interview)

Slowly, slowly, over the years, I have arrived at a technique for collaborating with my actors. I sit quietly at home, make all my preparations in detail, plan the sets and draw them in detail, until I have it all in my head. But as soon as I get into the studio with the camera and the actors, it can happen in the course of the first run-through that a tone of voice, a gesture, or some independent expression on the part of the actors makes me change the whole thing. Even though nothing's been said explicitly between us, I feel it will be better that way. Such an awful lot of things go on between me and the actors, on a level which defies analysis. . . .

Everyone went on saying I was an idiot, until, ruthlessly, step by step, I had taught myself everything to do with my profession. No one can rap me over the knuckles in technical matters today. And this means that nowadays I can behave much more like an orchestral conductor. Imagine a conductor who doesn't know how to play the various instruments, who can't show his musicians what they've got to do at various places, where the fellow who's playing the bassoon is to breathe, whether a note should be an upstroke or a downstroke, whether the tympanist is to use his arms or his wrists. A conductor who says to his musicians, "Remember, this is a microcosm reflected in a macrocosm" or something of that sort, is finished. But if he says, "Breathe here. Squeeze your lips together like this. Take an upstroke here. Stress this bit of syncopation," then they know what it's all about. It's precisely the same with actors and technicians. In the first place, always give them purely technical instructions. . . . One of my strongest cards . . . is that I never argue with my own intuition. Over the years I've learned that so long as I'm not emotionally involved—which always clouds one's ability to decide matters intuitively—I can follow it with a fair degree of confidence. But then, after one has decided something intuitively, it's necessary to follow it up intellectually. Intuition reaches out far into the dark. Afterwards one must try to go on foot to the spot where intuition's javelin has landed, using one's common sense. In principle I can say that in me, everything to do with actors takes place on the intuitive level. . . .

Behind each improvisation there must be preparation. . . .

The rehearsals are the creative period. Performances are a recreation. . . .

I never edit while shooting. I'd find it too depressing. Besides, editing, for me, is a sort of erotic pleasure. I'd like to save it up.

BARBARA HEPWORTH
from *Barbara Hepworth: A Pictorial Autobiography*

All of my early memories are of forms and shapes and textures. Moving through and over the West Riding landscape with my father in his car, the hills were sculptures; the roads defined forms. Above all, there was the sensation of moving physically over the contours of fulnesses and concavities, through hollows and over peaks—feeling, touching, seeing, through mind and hand and eye. This sensation has never left me. I, the sculptor, AM the landscape. I am the form and I am the hollow, the thrust and the contour.

There is an inside and an outside to every form. When they are in special accord, as for instance a nut in its shell or a child in the womb, or in the structure of shells or crystals, or when one senses the architecture of bones in the human figure, then I am most drawn to the effect of light. Every shadow cast by the sun from an ever-varying angle reveals the harmony of the inside and outside. Light gives full play to our tactile perceptions through the experience of our eyes, and the vitality of forms is revealed by the interplay between space and volume.

I do not want to make a stone horse that is trying to and cannot smell the air. How lovely is the horse's sensitive nose, the dog's moving ears and deep eyes; but to me these are not stone forms and the love of them and the emotion and the love of them can only be expressed in more abstract terms. I do not want to make a machine that cannot fulfill its essential purpose; but to make exactly the right relation of masses, a living thing in stone, to express my awareness and thought of these things. . . . The predisposition to carve is not enough, there must be a positive living and moving towards an ideal. The understanding of form and color in the abstract is an essential of carving or painting; but it is not simply the desire to avoid naturalism in the carving that leads to an abstract work. I feel that the conception itself, the quality of thought that is embodied, must be abstract—an impersonal vision individualized in the particular medium. In the contemplation of Nature we are perpetually renewed, our sense of mystery and our imagination is kept alive, and rightly understood, it gives us the power to project into a plastic medium some universal or abstract vision of beauty.

A constructive work [in the sense of "constructivist"] is an embodiment of freedom itself and is unconsciously perceived even by those who are consciously against it. The desire to live is the strongest human emotion, it springs from the depths of our unconscious sensibility—and the desire to give life is our most potent, constructive, conscious expression of this intuition. (1937, *Circle*)

Color and form go hand in hand—brown fields & green hills cannot be divorced from the earth's shape—a square becomes a triangle, a triangle a circle, a circle an oval by the continuous curve of folding, and we return, always, to the essential human form—the human form in landscape.

A particularly beautiful example of the difference between physical and spiritual animation can be observed in a delicate operation on the human hand. There you have the inanimate hand asleep and the active, conscious hand: the relation of these two was so beautiful it made me look in a new light at human faces, hands when people are talking, at the way a tree grows, and a flower. (1948; after visiting a hospital.)

Working realistically replenishes one's love for life, humanity, and the earth. Working abstractly seems to release one's personality and sharpen the perceptions, so that in the observation of life it is the wholeness or inner intention which moves one so profoundly: the components fall into place, the detail is significant of unity.

My left hand is my thinking hand. The right is only a motor hand. This holds the hammer. The left hand, the thinking hand, must be relaxed, sensitive. The rhythms of thought pass through the fingers and grip of this hand into the stone. It is also a listening hand. It listens for basic weaknesses or flaws in the stone; for the possibility or imminence of fractures.

All landscape needs a figure—and when a sculptor is the spectator he is aware that every landscape evokes a special image. In creating this image the artist tries to find a synthesis of his human experience and the quality of the landscape. The forms and piercings, the weight and poise of the concrete image also become evocative—a fusion of experience and myth. Working in the abstract way seems to release one's personality and sharpen the perceptions so that in the observation of humanity or landscape it is the wholeness of inner intention which moves one so profoundly. The components fall into place and one is no longer aware of the detail except as the necessary significance of wholeness and unity . . . a rhythm of form which has its roots in earth but reaches outwards towards the unknown experiences of the future. The thought underlying this form is, for me, the delicate balance the spirit of man maintains between his knowledge and the laws of the universe.

* * *

In sculpture there must be a complete realization of the structure and quality of the stone or wood which is being carved. But I do not think that this alone supplies the life and vitality of sculpture. I believe that the understanding of the material and the meaning of the form being carved must be in perfect equilibrium. There are fundamental shapes which speak at all times and periods in the language of sculpture.

It is difficult to describe in words the meaning of forms because it is precisely this emotion which is conveyed by scultpure alone. Our sense of touch is a fundamental sensibility which comes into action at birth—our stereognostic sense—the ability to feel weight and form and assess its significance. The forms which have had special meaning for me since childhood have been the standing form (which is the translation of my feeling towards the human being standing in landscape); the two forms (which is the tender relationship of one living thing beside another); and the closed form, such as the oval, spherical or pierced form (sometimes incorporating color) which translates for me the association and meaning of gesture in landscape; in the repose of say a mother and child, or the feeling of the embrace of living things, either in nature or in the human spirit. In all these shapes the translation of what one feels about man and nature must be conveyed by the sculptor in terms of mass, inner tension and rhythm, scale in relation to our human size and the quality of surface which speaks through our hands and eyes.

I think that the necessary equilibrium between the material I carve and the form I want to make will always dictate an abstract interpretation in my sculpture—for there are essential stone shapes and essential wood shapes which are impossible for me to disregard. All my feeling has to be translated into this basic framework, for sculpture is the reaction of a *real object* which relates to our human body and spirit as well as to our visual appreciation of form and color content.

* * *

For twenty-five years, walking through these streets, I have felt through my feet the geological shape of the place. The aerial view proved to me my point; it is through our senses that form, colour and meaning are given to everything we make and do. I wrote about St Ives many years ago: "The sea, a flat diminishing plane, held within itself the capacity to radiate an infinitude of blues, greys, greens and even pinks of strange hues, the lighthouse and its strange rocky island was the eye: the Island of St Ives an arm, a hand, a face. The rock formation of the great bay had a withinness of form that led my imagination straight to the country of West Penwith behind me—although the visual thrust was straight out to sea. The incoming and receding tides made strange and wonderful calligraphy on the pale granite sand that sparkled with felspar and mica. The rich mineral deposits of Cornwall were apparent on the very surface of things; geology and prehistory—a thousand facts induced a thousand fantasies of form and purpose, structure and life which had gone into the making of what I saw and what I was."

It is very difficult in cities to be aware of these marvelous happenings, which become very potent if one really begins living and putting down roots, and I am so fortunate here to have a garden and space and buildings where I can make such a mess and be tolerated. And so one isn't an oddity, but just another chap rushing out in overalls to buy some more files at the nearest shop. St Ives has absolutely enraptured me, not merely for its beauty, but the naturalness of life—I love the way people will just stand in the way talking and laughing, they won't move. The sense of community is, I think, a very important factor in an artist's life.

* * *

The sculptor must search with passionate intensity for the underlying principle of the organization of mass and tension—the meaning of gesture and the structure of rhythm.

In my search for these values I like to work both realistically and abstractly. In my drawing and painting I turn from one to the other as a necessity or impulse and not because of a preconceived design of action. When drawing what I see I am usually most conscious of the underlying principle of abstract form in human beings and their relationship one to the other. In making my abstract drawings I am most often aware of those human values which dominate the structure and meaning of abstract forms.

Sculpture is the fusion of these two attitudes and I like to be free as to the degree of abstraction and realism in carving.

The dominant feeling will always be the love of humanity and nature; and the love of sculpture for itself.

DORIS HUMPHREY
from *The Art of Making Dances*

There are elements in literature which cannot be translated into dance. Language can give us facts, situations, relationships, and states of being which are very difficult for the art of movement alone to tell. You cannot say in dance, "This is my mother-in-law," unless there is a careful sequence leading to such a statement. It would have to be established in three relationships: mother-girl, husband-girl, mother-in-law-husband. But words have said it all in two seconds. Conversely, a character and behavior delineation which would take the author pages to complete might be done in seconds by the dancer. These time differences represent pitfalls in resorting to literary themes, especially in poetry. And there are others. Some key ideas—assuming that they are important—cannot be stated at all. For example, suppose we are going to make a dance-drama out of the story of Jephthah's daughter. The tragedy lies in J's vow to kill the first creature who meets him on his return if God will help him to defeat the enemy. One could not depend on more than ten per cent of an audience remembering the story, or dutifully looking at a program note. So, left to movement alone, we would see J praying earnestly in one scene, and meeting his daughter with a sword in the next. Even if there were a full battle scene, showing J victorious, this would be confusing. Dilemmas of this kind have been solved by using a narrator, but this is not a favorite device, and is very difficult to deal with, besides.

JOYCE MEKEEL

(a conversation with Ann Berthoff about music notation)

JM: Music has been slow in coming to find ways of dealing with the irrational, or perhaps more accurately, in coming to terms with the fact that reason, or the rational approach, is incapable of answering all one's questions. Kant tried to show that there were inevitable limits to human reason 150 years ago; but nobody really paid any attention until things like Heisenberg's Principle of Indeterminacy and Gödel's proof began to turn up; i.e., not until scientists themselves, the great upholders of the rational, said that it was impossible to completely systematize reality, to enclose it in a logical structure, did people begin to accept the presence of the irrational, or if you want, the many-sidedness of reality, the inexplicability of much of human existence. Writers and painters began to deal with the problem—Picasso's cubism, seeing two ways at once, the Surrealists' use of dreams, and the writers' device of stream of consciousness. But somehow it was all very threatening to composers, and I think it had something to do with notation. Notating something is a process of translation into symbols and that seems to demand a "rational" state of mind, a "logical" approach. It's like a filter system through which the ineffable has to pass. I wonder if it's any coincidence that when Schumann and Wolfe went mad they stopped writing music—but Van Gogh went right on painting. Writers don't have to translate in the same way because words are everyday commodities. Anyway, composers seemed to retreat into a desperate search for order, for the rational. So you have Schönberg erecting this marvelous intellectual edifice of the twelve-tone system, and Stravinsky retreating into Neoclassicism and Bartok getting involved in all kinds of complicated mathematical ratios, the Golden Mean, the Fibonacci series, and so on. And going aleatoric, of course, is just the other side of the same coin: Let's just make everything chance.

AB: The two sides of that coin are complete, total control. . . .

JM: Or—"To hell with it! We can't make it rational anyway, so we'll make it totally irrational." In overreacting to the rational approach, one goes to the other extreme.

AB: Meanwhile, underneath all this what was happening?

JM: Composers were losing their audience, and deliberately saying: "We don't care and anyway, you wouldn't understand it. It's too intellectual; it has to do with mathematical relations." They were also losing their visceral connection to music, and that I think is what was really turning audiences off. Then some composers began asking: "How do we get the visceral back in?" The trouble was that the compositional rules had become totally negative— thou shalt not have down beats, thou shalt not write fifths, octaves, or triads, thou shalt not sound tonal, etc. Any artist who has to start out from negative premises is in serious trouble.

AB: How do you get feeling back into music?

JM: Well, that's why I think there was so much quoting going on a few years back. Composers said: "I'd better not do it so it sounds like my notes, so I'll do it as a quote. I'll quote Mozart, or Mahler, or this popular tune and then nobody can accuse me of going tonal; they're not my notes, I'm just quoting." But after quoting long enough, some of them just said "to hell with it" and went back to tonality. Some of them are even going so far as to re-create past musical languages like Beethoven's, or Mahler's—and they openly admit that they are much more comfortable with those languages. To do so (and some of the composers who are doing this turn-about are erstwhile twelve-tone composers, the most "rational" of all) is to admit the bankruptcy of an aesthetic based on negative premises. However, recreating a past language is ducking the issue. Those composers aren't really working on the problem—how to be expressive in a contemporary idiom—except perhaps in a negative way.[1] I don't think music has ever been faced with so many serious problems: language problems, notational problems, timbral problems, formal problems . . .

AB: When you set about composing, then, what's the chief problem?

JM: The central problem is the language.

AB: The *musical* language? Is that a lot like *language* language?

JM: The way you make a phrase—in language or music—is by arranging things hierarchically, in some sense. Foregrounding, backgrounding, tonic versus dominant, stable harmonies versus unstable. But the existence of those categories is based on established hierarchies, and what composers have done for much of this century is to religiously work to obliterate those hierarchies. And if you do that, you lose an important way to make a form. How to write a long piece that is formally coherent is the major problem today. Now if all pitches are equal, you have no pitch hierarchy. If you've said that you've maintained a constant level of dissonance, you've erased the hierarchy which distinguishes consonance and dissonance; there's no contrast. And one way of building a hierarchy is by contrasts.

AB: If all interpretation is MISinterpretation, then you've destroyed the concept: is that analogous?

JM: Yes. We've worked systematically for almost seventy years, destroying the pitch or harmonic hierarchies on which a musical language could be established.

---

[1] Much of this discussion, and what follows, can be summed up in Dick Higgins' excellent words: "There is an avant garde. It does not consist of those who simply are content to attack the past: these are the victims of the past. The avant garde consists of those who are sufficiently at ease with the past not to have to compete with it or duplicate it." ["Does Avant Garde Mean Anything?" *Arts in Society* (Spring–Summer 1970), 7: 27–32.] (JM)

AB: Isn't this pretty ironic? That the way of accounting for the irrational is to restore order? People have gotten off the track, aren't you saying,
by confusing formlessness and the irrational? But the irrational has its form
and it must be discovered. What's holding things up?

JM: What I see in musical composition is first of all the cult of personality. Everybody's looking over his left shoulder to see what the other guy
is doing. Everybody's trying to be different, in what turns out to be exactly
the same way. It's a real disease. What's needed is genuine introspection. You
hide yourself in the attic and look within, look for what's already there in
your own heritage.

AB: But when you look inward, you find the irrational all right, but
don't you also find the conventions?

JM: But you have to come to terms with them. A student came to me
the other day. Oh it was rather sad! He wanted me to give him a framework,
a language, so that he could know which note should come next. He'd tried
using an octatonic scale, a twelve-tone row, everything—but, he said, it still
didn't help. "When I do jazz improvisations and I write down all those jazz
things, I don't have that problem." And I said "What's that? Your composition is here and your jazz is over there?" "Yes, here I'm *composing,* and that
other is just jazz." "But you *have* a language over there!" "Yes, but that's all
just conventions and everybody knows about them." "Well, you have to start
with where you are! There's no reason that you can't work from there to
something that's you, but what *won't* work is to 'paste on' something that
feels exterior to yourself. That will never work! No wonder you're unhappy!"
He didn't really think he had something legitimate already; he didn't realize
that he already had the materials for building his own language.

* * *

AB: Can we go back to the problem of notation? Is it something like
the confusion linguists perennially fall into when they mix up signal and message? when critics mix up language and discourse, the analytic categories
appropriate to each? Code and codification. You can't analyze "Pass the salt."
as an utterance, except by considering the meaning that is being made.

JM: I suppose the closest equivalent of the code-codification problem
in music is the question of what is actually notated in a musical score. Recent
work on how children encode simple rhythms and tunes shows there is a
level of experience which is not represented in conventional notation. What
children encode, what amateur listeners grasp, and what a professional performer ultimately relies on is what Jean Bamberger refers to as the "felt
path" through the musical experience. Gross levels of change, beginnings and
endings, groupings, or, in more conventional terms, the *phrasing* is only partially indicated in a musical score.

AB: What do children do when you ask them to write down a tune or
rhythm?

JM: They draw pictures—a big circle for a long note or a low one, a small circle for a short note or a high one. Closure or grouping is indicated by a space, a hole separating one cluster of events from another. But perhaps the best way of getting at a sense of "path" through a musical experience is to watch a child construct a tune, "Frère Jacques" for example, with Montessori bells. The child lines up the bells in terms of the temporal sequence of events, and "playing the tune" is conceived of as moving linearly from one bell to the next.

The problem comes with the fourth note or event. The child wants to place a fourth bell after the third as representing the next event temporally. However, the pitch of the first note of "Frère Jacques" and the fourth are identical so when the child goes searching for the appropriate bell he can't find it because it has already been used. (There is only one bell per pitch class in the Montessori collection.) There is some confusion then between the tune's motion forward in time and the necessity of reverse physical motion back to the first note.

The fourth note is not heard as being "the same" as the first and indeed functionally it is *not* the same: the first note is a beginning and the fourth signals closure. Furthermore, it's possible to harmonize the first and fourth notes with different chords further emphasizing their different function. In fact, experience with college level ear-training classes shows that the identity of two pitches in this sort of context (same pitch with different chordal accompaniment) is very often not perceived. The formal musical symbol is identical, but the musical context, function, and felt path is not. It is the contextual, functional information that is largely ignored in conventional notation and it is precisely that information that guides the professional performer, the amateur listener, and the child.

AB: Notation with its overriding form seems to mess up the natural apprehension.

JM: Exactly. Formal notation ignores an important level of musical understanding, the way we perceive music directly, affectively, figurally . . .

AB: Physiognomically . . .

JM: A whole level of information is lost in the process of translation from sound to symbol. The way you perform, the way you perceive is in . . .

AB: little clusters, little figurations . . .

JM: diagrams and little pictures which the formal notation hasn't much to do with.

AB: It's entirely arbitrary, conventional . . . Well then, what is the bridge from the figural, children's pictures, which *do* reflect their apprehension, to the conventional forms of notation?

JM: What do you think I'm working on! It's very important to realize that what you need when you perform is what you *begin* with in perceiving figurally. This picture tells you that these four notes go together and that one that those six go together, a crucial piece of information that is not readily grasped in looking at a conventionally notated piece of music. The kids' pictures and what they do with the bells does give you that information. This is where I'd like college-level ear-training classes to start, with the figural. Freshmen know more than the teacher knows that they know, and more importantly, more than *they* know that they know. But they don't trust that knowledge, because they don't have the bridge to get themselves from what they know tacitly to the notation. And I myself don't really know how to get them to use their natural figural sense. Drawing pictures is probably out for college classes. They have been using conventional notation for so long that to ask them to do that would seem like baby stuff. I've actually tried and they don't really comprehend what it is you're after.

AB: And your colleagues probably think you're going backwards.

JM: Worse than that, there is no realization of the significance of these matters, and certainly no curiosity about them. Art education deals explicitly with visual perception, but teachers of music theory are largely unaware of the literature on music perception. They continue to argue the relative merits of various texts instead of getting down to the basic issues those texts ignore: what is a musical ear? how does it work? how does the brain process aural information? How can I persuade my colleagues to think about these things?

AB: What do you think I'm working on!

Sources

Multiple entries for a single author are listed in the order in which they appear in this collection. Whenever an edition is readily available, I have listed it rather than the collection or edition in which the essay or article first appeared.

Addams, Jane, *The Long Road of Woman's Memory* (New York: Macmillan, 1916).

Arnheim, Rudolf, *Visual Thinking* (Berkeley: University of California Press, 1969).

————, *Art and Visual Perception* (Berkeley: University of California Press, 1954).

Auden, W. H., "The True Word Twisted by Misuse and Magic." Address on occasion of receiving the national medal for literature, Washington, 1967.

Bachelard, Gaston, *The Psychoanalysis of Fire,* Tr. Alan C. M. Ross (Boston: Beacon, 1946).

Barfield, Owen, *Poetic Diction* (Middletown: Wesleyan University Press, 1973).

————, *The Rediscovery of Meaning* (Middletown: Wesleyan University Press, 1977).

Bergman on Bergman: Interviews with Ingmar Bergman, Tr. Paul Britten Austin (New York: Simon & Schuster, 1970).

Black, Max, *The Labyrinth of Language* (New York: New American Library, 1968).

Burke, Kenneth, *Counterstatement* (1931; Los Altos, CA: Hermes, 1953).

————, "De Beginnibus," *Bennington College Bulletin,* November, 1962.

————, *Permanence and Change* (1935; New York: Bobbs-Merrill, 1955).

Cassirer, Ernst, *An Essay on Man* (New Haven: Yale University Press, 1944).

————, *Language and Myth,* Tr. Susanne K. Langer (New York: Harper, 1946).

Cézanne, Paul, *Correspondance,* ed. John Rewald (1937; Paris: Grasset, 1978).

Collingwood, R. G., *The Idea of History* (London: Oxford University Press, 1946).

Fein, Sylvia, *Heidi's Horse* (Pleasant Hill, CA: Exelrod Press, 1976).

Geertz, Clifford, *The Interpretation of Cultures* (New York: Basic Books, 1973).

Gibson, James J., "Pictures, Perspective, and Perception," *Daedalus*, Winter, 1960.

Gombrich, E. H., *Art and Illusion* (New York: Bollingen Foundation, 1960).

Gregory, R. L., *The Intelligent Eye* (New York: McGraw-Hill, 1970).

Hepworth, Barbara, *Barbara Hepworth: A Pictorial Autobiography* (New York: Praeger, 1970).

Hopkins, Gerard Manley, *Notebooks,* ed. W. H. Gardner (New York: Oxford University Press, 1948).

Humphrey, Doris, *The Art of Making Dances* (New York: Grove, 1978).

Jonas, Hans, *The Phenomenon of Life* (New York: Delta, 1968).

Klee, Paul, *Notebooks* (London: Lund Humphries, 1961).

————, *On Modern Art* (London: Faber and Faber, 1948).

Langer, Susanne K., *Philosophy in a New Key* (Cambridge: Harvard University Press, 1957).

————, *Philosophical Sketches* (Baltimore: The Johns Hopkins University Press, 1962).

————, "On Cassirer's Theory of Language and Myth," in *The Philosophy of Ernst Cassirer,* ed. Paul Arthur Schilpp (Evanston: The Library of Living Philosophers, 1949).

The Mustard Seed Garden Manual of Painting, Tr. Mai-Mai Sze (Princeton: Princeton University Press, 1956).

Ogden, C. K., *Opposition* (Bloomington: Indiana University Press, 1967).

Oppenheimer, J. Robert, "Analogy in Science," *The American Psychologist,* 11 (1956).

The Collected Papers of Charles Sanders Peirce, ed. Charles Hartshorne and Paul Weiss, six volumes (Cambridge: Harvard University Press, 1931–35).

Percy, Walker, *The Message in the Bottle: How Queer Man Is, How Queer Language Is, and What One Has to Do with the Other* (New York: Farrar, Straus and Giroux, 1975).

Pirie, N. W., "Selecting Facts and Avoiding Assumptions," *The Rationalist Annual,* 8.

Richards, I. A., *The Philosophy of Rhetoric* (New York: Oxford University Press, 1936).

————, *Poetries: Their Media and Ends,* ed. Trevor Eaton (The Hague: Mouton, 1974).

————, *Speculative Instruments* (New York: Harcourt, 1955).

Schrödinger, Erwin, *Mind and Matter* (Cambridge: Cambridge University Press, 1958).

Stark, Freya, *Perseus in the Wind* (London: John Murray, 1948).

————, *The Journey's Echo* (New York: Harcourt, 1964).

Vygotsky, L. S., *Mind in Society,* ed. Michael Cole, Vera John-Steiner, Sylvia Scribner, Ellen Souberman (Cambridge: Harvard University Press, 1978).